KEY FACTS KEY CASES

Tort Law

Chris Turner

 Routledge
Taylor & Francis Group

LONDON AND NEW YORK

First published 2014
by Routledge
2 Park Square, Milton Park, Abingdon, Oxon OX14 4RN

and by Routledge
711 Third Avenue, New York, NY 10017

Routledge is an imprint of the Taylor & Francis Group, an informa business

© 2014 Chris Turner

British Library Cataloguing in Publication Data
A catalogue record for this book is available from the British Library.

Library of Congress Cataloging in Publication Data
A catalog record for this book has been requested.

ISBN: 978–0–415–83334–9 (pbk)
ISBN: 978–1–315–87117–2 (ebk)

Typeset in Helvetica
by RefineCatch Limited, Bungay, Suffolk

Contents

Chapter 11

Chapter 12

Preface

This new series of Key Facts Key Cases is built on the two well-known series, Key Facts and Key Cases. Each title in the Key Facts series now incorporates a Key Cases section at the end of most chapters which is designed to give a clear understanding of important cases. This is useful when studying a new topic and invaluable as a revision aid. Each case is broken down into fact and law. In addition many cases are extended by the use of important extracts from the judgment or by comment or by highlighting problems. In some instances students are reminded that there is a link to other cases or material. If the link case is in another part of the book, the reference will be clearly shown. Some links will be to additional cases or materials that do not feature in the book.

The basic Key Facts sections are a practical and complete revision aid that can be used by students of law courses at all levels from A Level to degree and beyond, and in professional and vocational courses.

They are designed to give a clear view of each subject. This will be useful to students when tackling new topics and is invaluable as a revision aid.

Most chapters open with an outline in diagram form of the points covered in that chapter. The points are then developed in a structured list form to make learning easier. Supporting cases are given throughout by name and for some complex areas facts are given to reinforce the point being made. The most important cases are then given in more detail.

The Key Facts Key Cases series aims to accommodate the syllabus content of most qualifications in a subject area, using many visual learning aids.

Tort Law is a core subject in all qualifying law degrees. It is also a vital subject in which to gain a good understanding since it involves events that we commonly and unfortunately experience in our own daily lives whether through road traffic accidents or unwanted contact or even intolerable neighbours.

The topics covered for Tort Law include all of the main areas of all mainstream syllabuses.

In the Key Cases sections in order to give a clear layout, symbols have been used at the start of each component of the case. The symbols are:

 Key Facts – These are the basic facts of the case.

 Key Law – This is the major principle of law in the case.

 Key Judgment – This is an actual extract from a judgment made on the case.

 Key Comment – Influential or appropriate comments made on the case.

 Key Problem – Apparent inconsistencies or difficulties in the law.

 Key Link – This indicates other cases which should be considered with this case.

The Key Link symbol alerts readers to links within the book and also to cases and other material, especially statutory provisions, that are not included.

The court abbreviations used in the key case sections of this book are shown below.

Ass	Assize Court	CA	Court of Appeal
CC	County Court	CCA	Court of Criminal Appeal
CCR	Crown Cases Reserved	CH	Court of Chancery
ChDiv	Chancery Division	CJEU	Court of Justice of the European Union
C-MAC	Court Martial Appeal Court	CP	Court of Probate
DC	Divisional Court	EAT	Employment Appeal Tribunal

ECHR	European Court of Human Rights	ECJ	European Court of Justice
ET/IT	Employment tribunal/ Industrial tribunal	Exch	Court of the Exchequer
HC	High Court	HL	House of Lords
KBD	King's Bench Division	NIRC	National Industrial Relations Court
PC	Privy Council	QBD	Queen's Bench Division
RC	Rolls Court	SC	Supreme Court

The law is as I believe it to be on 1 August 2013.

Table of Cases

1 The nature of tortious liability

▶ 1.1 General principles of tortious liability

1.1.1 The character of tort

1   The word tort comes from the French, meaning 'wrong'.

2   Tort concerns civil wrongs leading to possible compensation.

3   A common definition is: 'Tortious liability arises from the breach of a duty primarily fixed by law; such duty is towards persons generally and its breach is redressable by an action for unliquidated damages' (Winfield).

4   Character is dictated by historical background, so a better definition is: 'subject to statutory intervention, a tort is a wrong which in former times would have been remediable by one of the actions for trespass (for direct wrongs) or trespass upon the case (for indirect wrongs)' (Cooke) – so should refer to a law of torts.

5   The standard modern model is as follows: the defendant's act or omission causes damage to the claimant through the fault of the defendant, and damage is of a type which attracts liability in law.

6   However, there are complications:

   a)   strict liability torts do not require faults to be proved;

   b)   the type of damage caused may not give rise to liability (*damnum sine injuria*);

   c)   some conduct results in liability even without damage (*injuria sine damno*).

1.1.2 The aims of tort

1   There are two principal objectives in tort: deterrence and compensation.

   a)   **Deterrence** operates more on a market than an individual basis – the idea is to reduce the cost of accidents.

b) **Compensation** – the purpose of damages is to put the victim in the same position as if tort did not occur (reliance loss).

2   A key question is whether the system adequately compensates victims.

3   Points to consider:

   ● only those who can show fault can be compensated;

   ● both Pearson and Woolf reports identified delay and costs as major drawbacks;

   ● reductions in value of compensation: pressure is on the claimant to settle – usually for two-thirds to three-quarters;

   ● unpredictability;

   ● no point suing 'a man of straw' – exceptions are third party insurance under Road Traffic Acts; vicarious liability; Employer's Liability (Compulsory Insurance) Act 1969;

   ● the system discourages claims: only one in ten potential personal injury claims are pursued;

   ● the effect of the Woolf reforms on encouraging or deterring claims.

1.1.3 Alternative methods of compensation

1   These were considered as early as Royal Commission on Civil Liability and Compensation for Personal Injury (Pearson Commission) 1978.

2   The Commission was the follow-up to the Thalidomide scandal.

3   The Commission did not recommend an end to the tort system in personal injury, but did recommend a partial no-fault system.

4   New Zealand operates such a scheme: benefits up to 80 per cent of earnings; limited lump sum amounts in permanent disability – 1982 reforms found no one in favour of returning to fault system.

5   Public insurance is one alternative – Pearson showed that the cost of obtaining tort compensation is much higher than the cost of administering the Social Security system.

6   Private insurance – too expensive for many people, and not within British culture.

7   Compensation from public schemes, e.g. Criminal Injuries Compensation Scheme, Motor Insurance Bureau, if applicable.

1.1.4 The interests the law of torts protects

1   It is possible to classify torts according to type of interest.

2   These include the following.

   a) Personal security:

   - original trespass actions, e.g. battery, etc.;
   - more recently includes negligence, e.g. medical negligence;
   - and psychiatric extensions, e.g. nervous shock;
   - and now there is a developing tort of harassment under the Protection from Harassment Act 1997.

   b) Property:

   - interests in land protected by trespass, nuisance (*Rylands v Fletcher* (1868));
   - interests in chattels by trespass, conversion, statute.

   c) Reputation:

   - an extension of personal security;
   - protected by defamation, malicious falsehood, etc.

   d) Economic loss:

   - much more controversial and problematic;
   - is limited because of the difficulty of distinguishing between lawful and unlawful business activities;
   - economic torts associated with competing activities of trade unions and businesses, e.g. procuring a breach of contract;
   - the law also recognises an action for economic loss caused by a negligently made statement;
   - but not for pure economic loss caused by an action.

1.1.5 Tort and mental states

1   There are three possible states of mind relevant to liability in tort, as listed below.

2   a)   Malice:

   - improper motive, generally has no relevance in tort (*Bradford Corporation v Pickles* (1895));
   - but there are two exceptions:

    i)   where malice is an ingredient, e.g. malicious prosecution;

    ii) where malice is an unreasonable act, as in nuisance (*Christie v Davey* (1893)).

b) Intention. Three possible groups:

- torts deriving from the writ of trespass, e.g. assault;
- fraud – defendant makes statement knowing it is untrue;
- conspiracy – where claimant can show that the prime purpose of the conspirators is to harm him.

c) Negligence:

- a major tort in its own right, but also indicative of an objective standard imposed by law;
- liability results from falling below the set standard;
- the consequences of applying negligence as test of liability are that victims unable to show fault go uncompensated, and process of investigating facts needed to prove fault is costly and prohibitive.

1.1.6 Relationships with other areas of law

1 With crime.

  a) Dual liability is possible, but distinctions include:

- the parties, e.g. the state's involvement in crime;
- the outcome, e.g. liability as opposed to punishment;
- terminology and procedural differences;
- the standard of proof.

  b) But they are not always so different, e.g. the right of the court to impose sanctions in medieval trespass actions.

2 With contract.

  a) Duties in tort are imposed by law and apply generally, but contract duties are agreed by the parties and apply to them only.

  b) Statute does now impose many contractual duties irrespective of the will of the parties.

  c) There are potential overlaps, e.g. negligence and breach of implied conditions.

  d) Difficulties are created both by the exceptions to the privity rules in contract, and by the tort action for economic loss, which blur the distinctions between the two areas.

e) Sometimes a claimant has a choice in which area to sue, e.g. in contract for private medicine where there is negligence.

1.1.7 The effects of the Human Rights Act 1998

1   This can have a major impact on many areas of law, not just tort.

2   The Act gives statutory effect to, and incorporates into English law, the European Convention on Human Rights.

3   Judges therefore have a new role as watchdogs of the Convention.

4   The Act demands all primary and secondary legislation to be interpreted to be compatible with provisions of the Convention.

5   Many Convention Articles are appropriate to the law of torts:

- Article 2 – the right to life (appropriate to medical torts);
- Article 3 – freedom from torture, inhuman or degrading treatment (trespass to the person);
- Article 4 – freedom from slavery;
- Article 5 – the right to liberty apart from lawful arrest;
- Article 8 – the right to respect for private and family life, home and correspondence (defamation, trespass, nuisance);
- Article 9 – freedom of thought, conscience and religion (defamation, unlawful arrest);
- Article 10 – freedom of expression (defamation).

6   The UK has faced many claims in the European Court of Human Rights and has a worse record than many other signatories (*Z v UK* (2001)).

▶ 1.2 Fault and no-fault liability

1   Fault liability is unfair to claimants, because of difficulty of proof and evidence, and because victims of publicised events are advantaged.

2   It is unfair on defendants because there is no way of accounting for degree of culpability.

3   It is unfair on society generally because it creates classes of victims who can be compensated and classes that cannot.

4   It is also depends heavily on policy, so is arbitrary.

5   It is justified both for punishing wrongdoers and deterrent value.

6   Pearson has advocated no-fault schemes – two no-fault medical negligence bills since, but neither was accepted.

❱ 1.3 Joint and several tortfeasors

1.3.1 Joint and several liability

1   Liability is straightforward, with a single act causing loss or injury.

2   Often more than one breach of duty, or more than one act causes the damage, and liability may be independent, or joint, or several.

3   Independent liability is straightforward:

  ● two separate tortfeasors cause damage through separate torts;

  ● damage is separate, so each tortfeasor is liable for the particular damage caused.

4   Joint liability can arise in a number of different ways.

  ● All tortfeasors commit the same tortious act, often with a shared purpose (*Brooke v Bool* (1928)).

  ● If vicarious liability applies both employer and employee are jointly liable though only one would be sued – (sometimes tortfeasors are joined, e.g. in medical negligence).

  ● In non-delegable duties a person hiring an independent contractor causing the damage can be jointly liable.

  ● Where one person authorises the tort of another.

  ● Where the tort is committed by one member of a partnership each partner is jointly liable, but, since the damage comes from one tort, the claimant can only claim one lot of damages.

5   Several liability involves two separate tortfeasors causing the same damage through coincidental, independent acts:

  ● the claimant chooses who to sue – usually the one with money;

  ● since there is only one lot of damage the claimant can only recover once.

6   The practical result of the distinction between joint and several is that release of liability to a joint tortfeasor releases the others, while release to a several tortfeasor will not.

1.3.2 Contributions between tortfeasors

1   Now governed by the Civil Liability (Contribution) Act 1978.

2   The basic proposition is in s 1: 'any person liable in respect of any damage suffered by another person may recover a contribution from any other

person liable in respect of the same damage (whether jointly liable with him or otherwise)'.

3   The person seeking a contribution must be actually or hypothetically liable.

4   Applies to any type of action, and wrongdoer's liability to claimant need not be based on breach of the same obligation – s 6(1).

5   By s 2(1) the amount of contribution is that which is 'just and equitable having regard to the extent of that person's responsibility for the damage' (*Fitzgerald v Lane* (1988)).

6   By s 1(2) a settlement by one tortfeasor does not remove his right to claim a contribution from the other, whether or not he himself was actually liable to the claimant (changing the old law where D1 could only claim from D2 if he could prove D2 was liable).

7   If a claimant's action against a person from whom contribution is sought is time barred, this does not prevent recovery of a contribution unless a two-year limitation period in s 1(3) has expired.

▶ 1.4 General defences

1.4.1 Introduction

1   Defences can be both specific and general.

2   Some torts, e.g. defamation, have a range of specific defences.

3   Many defences, e.g. those in negligence, apply generally.

4   Most provide a total defence by showing the defendant is not at fault, others provide a partial defence only.

1.4.2 *Volenti non fit injuria* (consent)

1   This means no injury is done to one who voluntarily accepts a risk.

2   It does not apply where the claimant only knew of the existence of the risk rather than understanding it (*Stermer v Lawson* (1977)).

3   Nor does it apply where the claimant is forced to accept the risk (*Smith v Baker* (1891)).

4   It commonly applies in sporting situations if physical harm is likely (*Simms v Leigh RFC* (1969) and *Condon v Basi* (1985)).

5   It is important in the medical context (*Sidaway v Governors of Bethlem Royal Hospital* (1985)) where one issue is whether or not there is a requirement of informed consent.

6   It occasionally applies in certain employment situations (*Gledhill v Liverpool Abattoir Co Ltd* (1957)).

1.4.3 Inevitable accident

1   A defendant is never liable for a pure accident.

2   Pure accident means one beyond the defendant's control (*Stanley v Powell* (1891)).

1.4.4 Act of God

1   Concerns extreme weather conditions.

2   However, they must be unforeseeable conditions, not merely bad weather (*Nichols v Marsland* (1876)).

1.4.5 Self-defence

1   Everybody is entitled to defend himself.

2   But only by using reasonable force (*Lane v Holloway* (1968)).

1.4.6 Statutory authority

1   No liability if act authorised (*Vaughan v Taff Vale Railway* (1928)).

1.4.7 Illegality (*ex turpi causa non oritur actio*)

1   A defendant can avoid liability where the claimant suffers the harm while engaged in an illegal act (*Ashton v Turner* (1981)).

2   However, see more recently *Revill v Newbery* (1996).

1.4.8 Necessity

1   Applies if an act is done to avoid worse damage (*Watt v Herts CC* (1954)).

2   Saving life is an obvious example (*Leigh v Gladstone* (1909)).

1.4.9 Contributory negligence

1   Originally this was a complete defence, but now governed by the Law Reform (Contributory Negligence) Act 1945 and partial only.

2   The effect is to reduce the claimant's damages where (s)he has contributed to his/her own harm (*Sayers v Harlow DC* (1958)).

3   It is now commonplace when accepting lifts from drunk drivers (*Stinton v Stinton* (1993)) or failing to wear crash helmets while a passenger on a motorbike (*O'Connell v Jackson* (1972)), or failing to wear a seat belt (*Froom v Butcher* (1976)).

4   It is not necessary to show that the claimant owed a duty of care, merely that (s)he failed to take care in all the circumstances.

5   However, causation must always be proved – the claimant's act in fact helped cause the damage suffered (*Woods v Davidson* (1930)). This can be complex when exposure to asbestos and smoking are possible causes of lung diseases (*Badger v Ministry of Defence* (2005)).

6   There has been debate as to whether 100 per cent reduction of damages is possible – *Jayes v IMI (Kynoch) Ltd* (1985) made such an award, *Pitts v Hunt* (1990) argued this was not possible, and the possibility was raised again in *Reeves v Commissioner of Police* (1998).

Key Cases Checklist

1.1.5.2   *Bradford Corporation v Pickles* [1895] AC 587   (HL)

Key Facts

The claimant supplied water to Bradford from sources that ran through underground channels beneath the defendant's land. The claimant alleged that, in an attempt to force it to buy his land, the defendant drained water from his land, causing the claimant's reservoir to empty. The claimant sought an injunction to prevent the defendant from drawing water from his land but this was denied.

Key Law

The defendant's motive for drawing water from his land was held to be irrelevant, even if it was through malice. The defendant was legitimately exercising property rights in extracting water from his land. The claimant only had rights to the water once it reached his land and the injunction was denied.

1.1.7.6   ***Z and others v United Kingdom* [2001] 2 FLR 612; [2001] EHRR 3**   `ECHR`

Key Facts

A family of young children first came to the attention of a Social Services Department in 1987. The local authority failed to apply for a care order until 1992. In the meantime, neighbours, teachers, police, doctors and health visitors all expressed concern about the children's welfare. A psychiatrist who examined the children in 1993 reported that it was the worst case of neglect and emotional abuse that she had ever seen. The Official Solicitor brought an action for negligence against the local authority, arguing that the children had suffered long-term damage that could have been avoided if the council had acted promptly. The action failed in the House of Lords (now the Supreme Court) and was taken to the European Court of Human Rights.

Key Law

The House of Lords (now the Supreme Court) held that it would not be just or reasonable to impose a duty since it would cut across the council's other statutory duties, removing resources that could otherwise be used for child protection. The Children Act 1989 was for public benefit generally, not private rights. The European Court of Human Rights accepted that the children were subjected to inhuman and degrading treatment contrary to Art 3, denied a fair trial contrary to Art 6, and refused an effective remedy contrary to Art 13.

Key Comment

The result of this ruling is that English courts will have to rethink the apparent blanket immunity from liability that they have in the past been prepared to extend to public bodies in negligence actions.

1.4.2.3

Smith v Baker [1891] AC 325

 HL

Key Facts

A quarry worker was injured when a crane moved rocks over his head and some fell on him. He had previously complained that the practice was dangerous and the defendant argued that the fact that he continued to work meant that he had voluntarily accepted the risk of harm. The defence failed.

Key Law

The House held that, while the workman may have consented to general dangers relating to his work he could not be said to have accepted the risk of the specific harm suffered.

Key Judgment

Lord Halsbury LC explained:

'a person who relies on the maxim must shew a consent to the particular thing done . . . It appears to me that the proposition upon which the defendants must rely must be a far wider one than is involved in the maxim.'

1.4.3.2

Stanley v Powell [1891] 1 QB 86

QBD

Key Facts

During a pheasant shoot the defendant 'accidentally' shot a beater, a man whose role it was to beat the ground so that the birds would fly up out of the moorland. The defendant successfully claimed an inevitable accident because he was able to show that the injury was caused when the pellet ricocheted off trees.

Key Law

The court held that if the claimant was unable to show that the defendant acted negligently then the damage must have occurred accidentally, which therefore provided a complete defence.

1.4.4.2   *Nichols v Marsland* (1876) 2 ExD 1   CA

 Key Facts

The defendant had created artificial lakes on his land. During an exceptionally heavy rain storm described as 'the worst in living memory' the lakes burst their banks and flooded neighbouring land.

 Key Law

The court held that the defendant should not be liable if the escape occurred through reasons beyond his own fault but by Act of God.

 1.4.7.2   *Revill v Newbery* [1996] QB 567   CA

 Key Facts

An allotment holder, the defendant, fed up with trespassers on his allotment, lay in wait in his shed and then fired through a hole in the door at a trespasser, injuring him. The defendant's claim, that the illegal actions of the trespasser relieved him of all liability, failed.

Key Law

The court held that the defendant's actions were out of proportion in the circumstances and the defence would fail. One reason was that this would thwart the clear intentions of Parliament in the Occupiers' Liability Act 1984 to create a duty of care towards trespassers.

 Key Judgment

Evans LJ suggested that if the defence were to apply in such circumstances:

'it would mean that the trespasser . . . was effectively an outlaw, who was debarred by the law from recovering compensation for any injury which he might sustain'.

Key Problem

The extent to which a person is entitled to protect his property from trespassers is very contentious with the public. The Government is currently looking at the possibility of giving greater rights to the owners of land against trespassers.

1.4.9.3   *Froom v Butcher* [1976] QB 286   CA

Key Facts

A car accident was caused by the defendant's negligence but the claimant was not wearing a seat belt. He suffered head and chest injuries. His claim succeeded but damages were reduced by 20 per cent.

Key Law

The court applied an objective standard of care in determining that the claimant had worsened the injuries. A prudent person would have worn a seat belt, so damages were reduced by 20 per cent.

Key Comment

The judgment was at a time when reduction in damages was being used to persuade people to wear seat belts. The introduction of criminal charges has undoubtedly been more of a deterrent to failing to wear seat belts. Lord Denning's apportionment of blame also seems quite arbitrary.

2 Negligence: basic elements

Lord Atkin's test in *Donoghue v Stevenson*

The Neighbour Principle: take reasonable care to avoid acts or omissions that would reasonably foreseeably injure a person so closely affected that you should have them in your contemplation.

Lord Wilberforce's two-part test in *Anns v Merton LBC*

- Is there sufficient proximity between claimant and defendant to impose a duty?
- Is there any reason of policy not to impose duty?

Overruled in *Murphy v Brentwood DC* because:
- duty too general based on policy alone;
- gave judges too much power.

DUTY OF CARE

The role of policy

Many factors influence judges, eg:
- loss allocation (*Nettleship v Weston*);
- protecting professionals (*Hatcher v Black*);
- opening the floodgates.

Judges sometimes refuse to impose a duty on policy grounds, eg:
- immunity of judges (*Sirros v Moore*);
- wrongful life (*McKay v Essex AHA*).

Caparo v Dickman three-part test

- Reasonable foreseeability (*Fardon v Harcourt-Rivington*).
- Proximity (*Hill v Chief Constable of West Yorkshire*).
- Fair and reasonable to impose a duty (*Ephraim v Newham LBC*).

▶ 2.1 Duty of care

2.1.1 Negligence – origins and character

1   The modern starting point is Lord Atkin's judgment in *Donoghue v Stevenson* (1932), which established negligence as a separate tort – though its origins were in actions on the case.

2   A new approach was needed, as no other action was available.

3   The judgment contained five key elements.

● Negligence is a separate tort.

● Lack of privity of contract is irrelevant to mounting an action.

● Negligence is proved as a result of satisfying a three-part test:

   i)   there must be a duty of care owed by defendant to claimant;

   ii) the duty is breached by the defendant falling below the appropriate standard of care;

   iii) the defendant causes damage to the claimant that is not too remote a consequence of the breach.

● Lord Atkin's 'Neighbour Principle': 'You must take reasonable care to avoid acts or omissions which you can reasonably foresee would be likely to injure your neighbour. Who, then, in law, is my neighbour? Persons who are so closely and directly affected by my act that I ought reasonably to have them in my contemplation as being affected so when I am directing my mind to the acts or omissions in question'.

● A manufacturer owes a duty to consumers and users of his products not to cause them harm.

4   Thus broad principles were established to determine liability.

5   The law developed incrementally, establishing new duties.

6   Policy has always been a crucial element so the court will not only decide whether there is a duty, but whether there should be.

7   Many factors influence the judges:

● loss allocation (*Nettleship v Weston* (1971));

● moral considerations;

● practical considerations;

● protecting professionals (*Hatcher v Black* (1954));

● constitutional obligations;

- the 'floodgates' argument;
- the possible benefits of imposing duties (*Smolden v Whitworth and Nolan* (1997)).

8   Judges have often cited policy when refusing a duty of care:

- liability of lawyers (*Rondel v Worsley* (1969)) – but now see *Arthur J S Hall & Co v Simons & others* (2000) and *Moy v Pettman Smith and Perry* (2005);

- liability of police (*Hill v Chief Constable of West Yorkshire* (1988)) so no duty to victims of crime or to witnesses (*Brooks v Commissioner of Police* (2005)) – but not where there is a positive duty to act (*Reeves v Metropolitan Police Commissioner* (1999)); nor where human rights are involved (*Osman v UK* (2000)) and breach of Article 6 ECHR; but no duty to protect a witness from attack and murder by a defendant in a criminal trial (*Chief Constable of Hertfordshire v Van Colle; Smith v Chief Constable of Sussex* (2008));

- immunity of judges (*Sirros v Moore* (1975));

- alternative ways to compensate, e.g. CICB, MIB;

- rescues (*Salmon v Seafarer Restaurants* (1983));

- specific claims (wrongful life) (*McKay v Essex AHA* (1982));

- where claimant belongs to an indeterminately large group (*Monroe v London Fire and Civil Defence Authority* (1991));

- where claimant is responsible for own misfortune (*Governors of the Peabody Donation Fund v Parkinson* (1984)).

9   At one point Lord Atkin's test was simplified by Lord Wilberforce in *Anns v Merton LBC* (1978) into a two-part test.

a) Is there sufficient proximity between defendant and claimant to impose a *prima facie* duty?

b) If so, does the judge consider that there are any policy grounds which would prevent such a duty being imposed?

10   The *Anns* test was always seen as too broad because:

a) it creates a general duty based only on proximity;

b) it gives judges too much power to decide on policy alone.

11   A long line of cases expressed dissatisfaction with the *Anns* test, e.g. *Governors of Peabody Donation Fund v Sir Lindsay Parkinson* (1985); *Caparo v Dickman* (1990). The test was finally overruled in *Murphy v Brentwood DC* (1990).

12   It was replaced by a three-part test of Lords Oliver, Keith, Bridge in *Caparo* (1932).

   a)   Reasonable foresight (*Fardon v Harcourt-Rivington* and *Topp v London Country Bus (South West) Ltd* (1993)), but see also *Margereson v J W Roberts Ltd, Hancock v JW Roberts Ltd* (1996) compared to the earlier rule in *Gunn v Wallsend Slipway & Engineering Co Ltd* (1989); and food allergies may also be foreseeable (*Bhamra v Dubb* (2010)).

   b)   Proximity (*Hill* (1988) and *John Munroe v London Fire and Civil Defence Authority* (1997)). See also the Court of Appeal in *Sutradhar v Natural Environment Research Council* (2004).

   c)   Is it fair and reasonable to impose duty? (*Hemmens v Wilson Browne* (1993) and *Ephraim v Newham LBC* (1993); and it is not fair, just and reasonable to impose a duty where it conflicts with a duty owed by the defendant to another party (*Mitchell v Glasgow City Council* (2009)).

13   Subsequent cases have approved this 'incremental' approach (*Spring v Guardian Assurance* (1995)); (*Jones v Wright* (1994)).

14   Policy has inevitably remained a major factor (*Hill* (1988)):

   a)   as with public, regulatory bodies; compare *Philcox v Civil Aviation Authority* (1995) and *Perrett v Collins* (1998) – but assumption of responsibility and special knowledge may create liability on public bodies (*Thames Trains Limited v Health and Safety Executive* (2002));

   b)   and immunity from suit for professionals (*Kelley v Corston* (1997) and *Griffin v Kingsmill* (1998));

   c)   and also for public services (*Capital & Counties plc v Hampshire County Council* (1997)) – so a local authority owes no duty to protect tenants from crime (*X v Hounslow LBC* (2009));

   d)   in *Harris v Perry* (2008) it was held that it was impractical for parents to keep children under constant supervision and it would not be in the public interest for the law to require them to do so.

15   The *Anns* test was flawed, but the new test is arguably no better:

   ●   it claims to follow the separation of powers theory;

   ●   but it is more complex and secret, and restricts development.

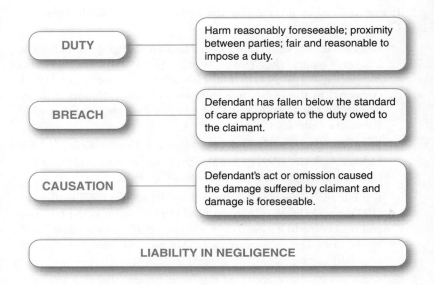

What must be proved for negligence

2.1.2 The duty of care

1 Case law is crucial to identifying duty situations.

2 Negligence is not mere carelessness, so no duty no liability.

3 There must be a 'duty on the facts', not a mere notional duty.

4 The key questions are:

   a) Is the situation or loss of a type to which negligence applies?

   b) Does the defendant owe a duty to the actual claimant?

5 Numerous straightforward situations, e.g. employers/employees; fellow motorists; doctors/patients, manufacturers/consumers, etc.

6 However, courts have also considered many controversial situations.

▶ 2.2 Breach of the duty of care

2.2.1 The Standard of Care and Reasonable Man Test

The reasonable man test

- A breach occurs when the defendant falls below the standard of care appropriate to the duty owed.
- So breach is doing something which a reasonable, prudent man would not do, or omitting to do something that he would do.
- The reasonable man is said to be free from both over-apprehension and over-confidence.

BREACH OF DUTY

Res ipsa loquitur

Plea reversing burden when negligence impossible to prove. Three ingredients:
- at all material times thing causing damage is in defendant's control (*Gee v Metropolitan Railway*);
- no alternative explanation other than negligence (*Barkway v South Wales Transport*);
- accident of a type usually only caused by negligence (*Scott v London & St Katherine's Docks*).

Factors in determining the standard of care

- Foreseeability (*Roe v Minister of Health*).
- Magnitude of risk (compare *Bolton v Stone* and *Hale v London Electricity Board*).
- Social utility (*Watt v Hertfordshire CC*).
- Practicality of precautions (*Latimer v AEC*).
- Common practice (*Brown v Rolls Royce*).
- Children (same standard as child of age, *Morales v Ecclestone*).
- Motorists (standard of learners is same as for experienced drivers (*Nettleship v Weston*)).
- Sport (standard is the standard of reasonable competitors (*Condon v Basi*) or reasonable officials (*Smoldon v Whitworth*)).
- Experts or professionals (standard is measured against a reasonable competent body of professional opinion (*Bolam v Friern Hospital Management Committee*)).

i) Applicable also to professional advice (*Sidaway v Governors of Bethlem Royal & Maudsley Hospitals*).
ii) Some practices are unacceptable even if common (*Re Herald of Free Enterprise*).
iii) Standard for trainees is the same as for experienced professionals (*Wilsher v Essex Area Health Authority*).
iv) But a judge may disregard professional opinion if it is not sustained by logic (*Bolitho v City and Hackney Health Authority*).

1   A breach occurs whenever a defendant falls below the standard of care appropriate to the particular duty owed.

2   The standard is objectively measured by the 'reasonable man' test: 'the omission to do something which a reasonable man would do, or doing

something which a prudent and reasonable man would not do.' Per Alderson B in *Blyth v Birmingham Waterworks* (1865).

3   The reasonable man has been described as 'the "man on the street" or "the man on the Clapham omnibus" . . .'

4   Or, as MacMillan LJ put it in *Glasgow Corporation v Muir* (1943), the test is 'independent of the idiosyncrasies of the particular person whose conduct is in question . . . The reasonable man is presumed to be free from both over-apprehension and over-confidence'.

5   So breach of duty then is merely the same as fault.

6   Factors of policy and expediency are taken into account, e.g.:

●   who can best bear the loss;

●   whether or not the defendant is insured;

●   how the decision might affect future behaviour;

●   the justice of the individual case;

●   how the decision affects society as a whole.

7   Judges have established criteria by which to measure the standard.

2.2.2 Principles in determining the standard of care

1   **Foreseeability**: no obligation for defendant to compensate for incidents beyond his normal contemplation or outside his existing knowledge; compare *Roe v Minister of Health* (1954) with *Walker v Northumberland County Council* (1995).

2   **Magnitude of risk**: the care expected depends on likelihood of risk – compare *Bolton v Stone* (1951) with *Haley v London Electricity Board* (1965).

3   **Social utility**: a risk averting a worse danger may be justified (*Watt v Hertfordshire CC* (1954)), but not any risk at all (*Griffin v Mersey Regional Ambulance* (1998)).

4   **Practicality of precautions**: need not take extraordinary steps or suffer extraordinary cost (*Latimer v AEC* (1953)) – but if defendant is in sufficient control to avoid harm then s(he) is obliged to act (*Bradford-Smart v West Sussex County Council* (2002) on preventing bullying in schools).

5   **Common practice**: usually, but not always, suggests non-negligent practice (*Brown v Rolls Royce* (1966)).

6   Specific classes of people have specific rules.

   a) **Children**: originally not expected to take same care as adults (*McHale v Watson* (1966)), but see now *Morales v Ecclestone* (1991) and *Armstrong v Cottrell* (1993) and see *Orchard v Lee* (2009) for instance on 'boisterous activity in a playground'.

   b) **The disabled and sick**: standard appropriate to disability.

   c) **Motorists**: the same standard applies to all drivers, even learners (*Nettleship v Weston* (1971)) and one becoming ill while driving (*Roberts v Ramsbottom* (1980)), but not if unaware of the illness (*Mansfield v Weetabix Ltd* (1997)).

   d) **People lacking specialist skills**: not expected to show same standard as a skilled person (*Phillips v Whiteley Ltd* (1938)).

   e) **Sport**: standards applicable to reasonable competitors (*Condon v Basi* (1985)), reasonable officials (*Smoldon v Whitworth* (1997)) or reasonable sporting authority (*Watson v British Boxing Board of Control* (2001)). But standard depends on individual circumstances (*Pitcher v Huddersfield Town FC* (2001)) and 'horseplay' may be covered by the same standard as sport (but only where the defendant's conduct amounts to a high degree of carelessness (*Blake v Galloway* (2004)).

7   **Experts and professionals** are not bound by the standards of a reasonable man but those of a reasonable practitioner of that particular skill or profession (*Bolam v Friern Hospital Management Committee* (1957)).

   a) The test also applies to advice and information (*Sidaway v Governors of Bethlem Royal & Maudsley Hospitals* (1985)) and warning of risk (*Chester v Afshar* (2002)).

   b) And to diagnosis (*Ryan v East London & City Health Authority* (2001)).

   c) So professionals need only provide expert witnesses who agree with conduct in question (*Whitehouse v Jordan* (1981)).

   d) Some practices are unacceptable even though common (*Re Herald of Free Enterprise* (1989)).

   e) Trainees must show the same degree of skill as experienced professionals (*Wilsher v Essex AHA* (1988)).

   f) The test applies even if the defendant does not have full professional qualifications (*Adams v Rhymney Valley DC* (2000)).

   g) The rule has been approved since. 'There is seldom any one answer exclusive of all others to problems of professional judgement. A court may prefer one body of opinion to the other; but that is no basis for a conclusion of negligence', per Lord Scarman in *Maynard v West Midlands RHA* (1985).

h) Only a small number of doctors following the practice is sufficient to relieve liability (*De Freitas v O'Brien and Conolly* (1995), where 11 out of 1,000 would have operated).

i) However, the test has been subject to many criticisms:

- it overprotects professionals;
- it allows the professionals to set the standard;
- it is inconsistent with negligence principles generally;
- it can often legitimise quite marginal practices;
- definition of a competent body of opinion is too imprecise;
- the test can lead to professionals closing ranks.

j) Numerous recent cases have challenged its authority:

- *Newell v Goldberg* (1995);
- *Lybert v Warrington HA* (1996);
- *Thompson v James and others* (1996) – failure by GP to follow guidelines in warnings about measles vaccinations, and claimant brain damaged as a result.

k) If the judge feels that the opinion held is not sustained by logic, then it may be disregarded (*Bolitho v City and Hackney Health Authority* (1997)).

2.2.3 Proof of negligence and *res ipsa loquitur*

1   Normally the burden of proof is on the claimant, who has the hard task of collecting evidence.

2   This can be relaxed in two instances:

a) for criminal convictions under s 11 Civil Evidence Act 1968;

b) if the plea of *res ipsa loquitur* is raised.

3   Literally translated this means 'the thing speaks for itself'.

4   Succeeding with the plea means burden of proof is reversed.

5   However, *Wilsher* (1987) suggests that it merely raises a refutable presumption of negligence.

6   It is narrowly construed for fairness – the facts must conform to the criteria in *Scott v London & St Katherine Docks* (1865).

7　There are three essential requirements for the plea to succeed.

   a)　At all material times the thing causing injury or damage must have been in defendant's control. Compare *Gee v Metropolitan Railway Co* (1873) with *Easson v London and North Eastern Railway* (1944).

   b)　The incident has no obvious alternative explanation (*Barkway v South Wales Transport Co Ltd* (1950)).

   c)　The accident is of a type which would not occur if proper care was shown so is of a type commonly caused by negligence (*Scott v London & St Katherine Docks* (1865); *Mahon v Osborne* (1939); and *Ward v Tesco Stores* (1976)).

8　It is debatable whether *res ipsa loquitur* applies in medical negligence but it is often pleaded because of a difficulty in gaining evidence.

9　However, it has been rejected by both the courts and Pearson because of fear of escalating claims and insurance premiums.

2.2.4　Strict liability in negligence

1　*Res ipsa loquitur* formerly applied to foreign bodies in food.

2　Consumer Protection Act (1987) was introduced to comply with EU directives.

- It introduced strict liability on anyone in the distribution chain where the consumer suffers harm.

- Fault liability was removed, but causation is still required.

▶ 2.3 Causation and remoteness of damage

2.3.1　Introduction

1　Once duty and breach are shown it must also be proved that the defendant's act or omission caused the damage.

2　Claimant must prove causal link on a balance of probabilities.

3　This may be difficult if there are multiple causes or the type of damage is unusual.

4　Policy considerations are still crucial to causation.

5　Must show: defendant's act or omission caused loss or injury to claimant (causation in fact); and sufficient proximity between act and damage to fix defendant with liability (causation in law).

Causation in fact

Based on 'but for' test (if harm would not have occurred but for defendant's act/omission, the defendant liable) (*Barnett v Chelsea & Kensington Hospital Management Committee*).

If there are multiple causes:
- defendant may not be liable for all of damage if claimant has pre-existing condition (*Cutler v Vauxhall Motors*);
- multiple concurrent causes may defeat claim (*Wilsher v Essex AHA*), but even one cause may materially contribute to the damage (*Fairchild v Glenhaven*);
- with consecutive causes there is no liability for second event unless it causes extra damage (*Performance Cars v Abraham*), but see *Baker v Willoughby* and *Jobling v Associated Dairies* on under or over compensating the claimant.

CAUSATION

Novus actus interveniens

A new act intervenes and relieves defendant of liability – can be act of:
- claimant (*McKew v Holland & Hannon & Cubitts*);
- nature (*Carslogie Steamship Co v Royal Norwegian Government*);
- third party – compare (*Knightley v Johns* and *Rouse v Squires*)

Remoteness of damage

- For claimant to recover, damage must not be too remote a consequence of the breach.
- Originally measured on direct consequence (*Re Polemis*).
- Now measured on foreseeability (*The Wagon Mound*).
- Only the general type of harm need be foreseen, not the actual extent (*Bradford v Robinson Rentals*).
- The 'thin skull rule' applies – defendant must take claimant as he finds him (*Paris v Stepney BC*).

2.3.2 Causation in fact

1   Based on 'but for' test – Lord Denning in *Cork v Kirby Maclean Ltd* (1952): 'if the damage would not have happened but for a particular fault, then that fault is the cause of the damage; if it would have happened just the same, fault or no fault, the fault is not the cause of the damage . . .'.

2   Often straightforwardly proved by the facts (*Barnett v Chelsea & Kensington Hospital Management Committee* (1969)).

3   However, problems may exist in proving cause:

   a)   it is more about apportioning blame than scientific enquiry;

   b)   level of knowledge/scientific advance may make pinpointing exact cause impossible (*Wilsher v Essex AHA* (1988)).

c) the case law is often contradictory:

- it may be unfair to the claimant (*Hotson v East Berkshire AHA* (1987)) but see *Stovold v Barlows* (1995);

- it may be unfair to the defendant (*McGhee v National Coal Board* (1973));

- occasionally courts adopt a pragmatic/realistic approach (*Chester v Ashfar* (2004)).

4 Multiple causes.

a) Proving a causal link is always difficult if there is more than one cause.

b) The problem occurs in one of three ways:

- claimant has pre-existing condition – defendant may not be liable for all damage (*Cutler v Vauxhall Motors* (1971));

- multiple concurrent causes:

 i)   here if there are many causes and the exact cause cannot be identified then there is no liability (*Wilsher v Essex AHA* (1988));

 ii) there may be liability if the defendant's acts materially increase the risk of harm (*McGhee v NCB* (1973));

 iii) if a number of defendants could cause the same harm then liability is possible for materially increasing the risk of harm (*Fairchild v Glenhaven Funeral Services Ltd & others* (2002));

 iv) more recently the House of Lords held that in this situation apportionment between defendants was appropriate (*Barker v Corus Ltd* (2006));

 v)   but the Compensation Act 2006 reverted to the principle in *Fairchild* for asbestos cases;

 vi) in any case, *Fairchild* only applies where the claimant can clearly show a breach of duty by the defendant (*Brett v University of Reading* (2007) and *Pinder v Cape plc* (2006));

 vii) and there can be no claim where the 'injury' is too slight e.g. 'pleural plaques' (*Johnson v NEI International Combustion Ltd; Rothwell v Chemical and Insulating Co Ltd* (2007));

 viii) but the claimant only needs to show that the increase in risk was material and not minimal *Sienkewicz v Greif* (2011).

- consecutive causes:

  i) if second event caused no extra damage, liability remains with
      first event (*Performance Cars v Abraham* (1962));

  ii) but see *Baker v Willoughby* (1970) and *Jobling v Associated
      Dairies* (1982), which concern neither under nor over
      compensating the claimant.

5   There can be no recovery for a mere loss of a chance of avoiding the
    harm (*Hotson v East Berkshire AHA* (1987)) and *Greg v Scott* (2005),
    although a claim for loss of life expectancy may be possible (*JD v Mather*
    (2012)).

2.3.3 *Novus actus interveniens*

1   Translates as 'a new intervening act', i.e. the chain of causation is broken
    by a subsequent act that the court accepts is the true cause of damage.

2   The effect is to relieve the defendant of liability.

3   It does not apply if the later act is not accepted as the cause of damage
    (*Kirkham v Chief Constable of Greater Manchester* (1990)).

4   Cases fall into three categories.

  a) An intervening act by claimant – more than contributory negli-
      gence since it breaks the chain of causation. Compare *McKew v
      Holland & Hannen & Cubitts (Scotland) Ltd* (1969) with *Wieland
      v Cyril Lord Carpets* (1969).

  b) An intervening act of nature:

      ● rarely succeeds because it means claimant has no remedy;

      ● defendant may succeed if the natural act is unforeseeable and
        independent of his own negligence (*Carslogie Steamship Co v
        Royal Norwegian Government* (1952)).

  c) intervening act of a third party:

      ● the act must be sufficient to break the chain of causation;

      ● it must be foreseeable;

      ● the defendant must not owe a duty to avoid it (compare *Knightley
        v Johns* (1982) with *Rouse v Squires* (1973)).

2.3.4 Remoteness of damage

1   Despite proof of a causal link the claimant may fail to recover if damage
    is said to be too remote a consequence of the breach.

2   It is a legal test based on policy, to avoid overburdening defendant.

3   In the old test the claimant could recover direct consequence loss, even
    if unforeseeable (*Re Polemis and Furness, Withy & Co* (1921)).

4   The test was criticised for its failure to distinguish between degrees of
    negligence. Viscount Simmonds in *The Wagon Mound (No 1)* (1961):
    'It does not seem consonant with current ideas of justice or morality,
    that for an act of negligence, however slight, which results in some
    trivial foreseeable damage, the actor should be liable for all the conse-
    quences, however unforeseeable and however grave, so long as they can
    be said to be direct.'

5   So the test was changed to one of 'reasonable foreseeability' in *The
    Wagon Mound (No 1)* (1961).

6   The type rather than the extent of damage must be foreseen (*Bradford v
    Robinson Rentals* (1967) and now *Margereson v J W Roberts Ltd, Hancock
    v JW Roberts* (1996)).

7   Nor must the precise circumstances be foreseen (*Hughes v The Lord
    Advocate* (1963)).

8   There is a broad view of foreseeability in personal injury (*Jolley v Sutton
    London Borough Council* (2000)), except in *Doughty v Turner Manufac-
    turing* (1964) and *Tremain v Pike* (1969).

    ● But policy reasons may be used to decide that an outcome is reason-
      ably foreseeable (*Corr v IBC Vehicles* (2006) – suicide will not break
      the chain of causation when the psychiatric illness was caused by the
      defendant's negligence) and the fact that a patient is an immediate
      suicide risk means authorities must do everything that can be reason-
      ably expected to avoid it (*Savage v South Essex Partnership NHS
      Foundation Trust* (2008));

    ● Contrast with *Grives v FT Everard and Sons Ltd* (2006).

9   But a narrower approach is taken to property damage:

    ● so in *The Wagon Mound (No 1)* the trial judge agreed some damage
      (fouling) possibly foreseeable, so fire satisfied direct consequence test;

    ● but in *The Wagon Mound (No 2)* the trial judge had suggested that
      fire was possible but too remote, so Privy Council reversed him.

10 The defendant must take the claimant as he finds him – the so-called
    'thin skull rule'.

    ● So the defendant is liable for the full extent of damage where the
      claimant's extra sensitivity caused worse damage (*Paris v Stepney BC*
      (1951) and *Smith v Leech Brain and Co Ltd* (1962)).

- This also applies where likely harm is psychiatric (*Walker v Northumberland County Council* (1994)).
- It also applies if shock is suffered but no physical injury (*Page v Smith* (1995)).
- And it applies if the claimant's impecuniosity (lack of means) may be the feature (*Mattocks v Mann* (1993)).

11 The difference between the two tests appears minimal:

- most reasonably foreseeable consequences are also natural;
- the thin skull rule means that even many unforeseeable consequences are still liable to compensation;
- insurance covers many, if not most, types of loss.

Key Cases Checklist

Duty of care

***Caparo v Dickman* (1990)**
Must show foreseeability of harm, proximity and fair, just and reasonable to impose a duty

Breach of duty

***Blyth v Birmingham Waterworks* (1856)**
Standard is that of the reasonable man
***Bolton v Stone* (1951)**
Should take into account factors such as foreseeability of harm, the magnitude of risk, practicality of precautions etc
***Bolam v Friern Hospital Management Committee* (1957)**
Standard of doctors is that of a competent body of professional opinion

Causation

***Barnett v Chelsea & Kensington Hospital* (1969)**
Must show damage would not have occurred 'but for' defendant's breach
***Fairchild v Glenhaven* (2002)**
But where there are multiple causes a material contribution may be sufficient
***The Wagon Mound* (1961)**
The damage must be foreseeable or is too remote
***McKew v Holland, Hannen & Cubitts* (1969)**
The chain of causation may be broken by a '*novus actus interveniens*'

2.1.1.1

Donoghue v Stevenson [1932] AC 562   (HL)

Key Facts

The claimant claimed to suffer shock and gastro-enteritis after drinking ginger beer from an opaque bottle out of which a decomposing snail had fallen when the dregs were poured.

A friend had bought her the drink and so the claimant could not sue in contract. She was owed a duty of care by the manufacturer despite the fact that she had no contractual relationship.

Key Law

A manufacturer owes a duty of care towards consumers or users of his products not to cause them harm (often referred to as the 'narrow *ratio*' of the case).

Key Judgment

Lord Atkin also identified the means of establishing the existence of a duty of care (the 'neighbour principle'):

'You must take reasonable care to avoid acts or omissions which you can reasonably foresee would be likely to injure your neighbour. Who then in law is my neighbour? . . . persons who are so closely and directly affected by my act that I ought reasonably to have them in my contemplation as being affected so when I am directing my mind to the acts or omissions in question'.

Key Comment

Lord Atkin's judgment also exploded the so-called 'privity fallacy' and is credited with creating a separate tort of negligence. Negligence can be proved by showing:

- the existence of a duty of care owed to the claimant by the defendant;

- a breach of that duty by the defendant falling below the appropriate standard of care;

- damage caused by the defendant's breach of duty that was not too remote a consequence of the breach, i.e. that was a foreseeable consequence of the breach.

2.1.1.11 *Caparo Industries plc v Dickman* [1990] 1 All ER 568

Key Facts

Shareholders in a company bought more shares and then made a successful take-over bid for the company after studying the audited accounts prepared by the defendants. They later regretted the move and sued the auditors, claiming that they had relied on accounts which had shown a sizeable surplus rather than the deficit that was in fact the case. Their case failed.

Key Law

The House of Lords (now the Supreme Court) held that the auditors owed no duty of care to the claimants since company accounts are not prepared for the purposes of people taking over a company and cannot then be relied on by them for such purposes. The court also developed the three-stage test for determining when a duty of care is owed:

● Firstly, it should be considered whether the consequences of the defendant's behaviour were reasonably foreseeable.

● Secondly, the court should consider whether there is sufficient legal proximity between the parties for a duty to be imposed.

● Lastly, the court should ask whether or not it is fair, just and reasonable in all the circumstances to impose a duty of care.

Key Link

The three-part test was approved in *Murphy v Brentwood District Council* [1991] 2 All ER 908, which itself overruled *Anns v Merton London Borough Council* [1978] AC 728, which had produced a simple two-part test for establishing a duty. This test was heavily based on policy and had led to much criticism from judges.

2.1.1.8 *Hill v Chief Constable of West Yorkshire* [1988] 2 All ER 238

Key Facts

The mother of the final victim of the Yorkshire Ripper claimed against the police for their careless and ineffective handling of the case, arguing that her daughter would not have died but for the negligence in the police investigation. The claim failed.

Key Law

The court held that there was insufficient proximity between the police and the public for a duty to be imposed to protect individual members of the public from specific crimes.

Key Comment

This was an obvious policy decision. However, even under the three-part test it would be considered unfair, unjust and unreasonable to impose such a duty on the police.

Key Links

Reeves v Metropolitan Police Commissioner [2000] 1 AC 360 (where police owed a duty to a known suicide risk while he was in custody and could not rely on *volenti* when he did commit suicide).

In *Jain v Strategic Health Authority* [2009] 2 WLR 248 claimants suffered damage to their business, a private nursing home, after the defendant had applied successfully to have the home's registration cancelled. This was later found to have been based on carelessness and overturned. The claim was rejected as a matter of policy since to impose a duty would interfere with the duty the council owed to the residents of registered nursing homes and the general public.

In *Mitchell v Glasgow City Council* [2009] 2 WLR 481 the House of Lords (now the Supreme Court) held that it would not be 'fair, just and reasonable' to impose a duty on a council to warn a tenant about a meeting with his neighbour whom he had complained about and who then killed him.

2.2.1.2 ***Blyth v Proprietors of the Birmingham Waterworks*** **(1856) 11 Exch 781**

Exch Div

Key Facts

A water main was laid with a 'fire plug', a wooden plug in the main that would allow water to flow through a cast iron tube up to the street when necessary. The plug became loose in severe frost and water flooded the claimant's house because the cast iron tube was blocked with ice. The frost was beyond normal expectation.

Key Law

The court held that the defendants had done all they reasonably could have done to prevent the damage, so there was no liability.

Key Judgment

Alderson B stated:

'Negligence is the omission to do something which a reasonable man, guided upon those considerations which ordinarily regulate human affairs, would do, or doing something which a prudent and reasonable man would not do.'

2.2.1.4   *Glasgow Corporation v Muir* [1943] AC 448   HL

Key Facts

A tea urn was being carried through a narrow passage in the defendant's premises where small children were buying ice creams. Some children were scalded when the urn was dropped. Their claim for damages failed.

Key Law

The court assessed liability by using the 'reasonable man' test and held that the damage was not foreseeable and not a risk that the defendant should have guarded against.

Key Judgment

MacMillan LJ explained the objective test:

'The standard of foresight of the reasonable man is an impersonal test . . . independent of the idiosyncrasies of the particular person whose conduct is in question. Some persons are by nature unduly timorous and imagine every path beset by lions; others, of more robust temperament, fail to foresee or nonchalantly disregard even the most obvious dangers. The reasonable man is presumed to be free from both over-apprehension and from over-confidence.'

2.2.2.1 *Roe v Minister of Health* [1954] 2 QB 66   CA

Key Facts

Two patients became paralysed after being injected with nupercaine, a spinal anaesthetic. The nupercaine was sealed in glass ampoules which were stored in a sterilising fluid, phenol. Evidence at the trial showed that the phenol solution had entered the anaesthetic through hairline cracks in the ampoules, contaminating it and causing the paralysis. The claims for damages failed.

Key Law

There was no liability because such an event had not previously occurred and was unforeseeable as a result.

Key Comment

As McBride and Bagshaw point out (*Tort Law* (2nd ed, Pearson Publishing, 2005) pp 38–40):

'if . . . the function of tort law is to determine when someone who has suffered loss at another's hands [is] entitled to sue . . . you will think that tort law failed the patients in Roe . . . the truth is more complicated . . . the patients could not establish that the hospital had committed a civil wrong . . . tort law imposed a duty on the hospital to treat the patients with reasonable . . . care and skill; but the hospital fully discharged that duty . . . No one could have foreseen that treating the patients in the way they were treated would expose them to the risk of paralysis'.

2.2.2.2 *Bolton v Stone* [1951] AC 850   HL

Key Facts

Miss Stone was standing on a pavement by a cricket ground when she was hit by a cricket ball that was hit out of the ground. She was standing 100 yards from where the batsman had struck the ball. The batsman was 78 yards from a 17-foot-high fence over which the ball had been struck. It was also shown that balls had only been struck out of the ground six times in 28 years. The claimant's action in negligence failed.

Key Law

It was held that the likelihood of harm was extremely low and that the cricket ground had done everything reasonably possible to avoid risks of people being hit. There was no breach of duty.

Key Judgment

Lord Radcliffe identified the connection with the 'reasonable man' test:

'unless there has been something which a reasonable man would blame as falling beneath the standard of conduct that he would set for himself . . . there has been no breach of legal duty.'

2.2.2.2   *Haley v London Electricity Board* [1965] AC 778   HL

Key Facts

The defendant's workmen were digging a hole along a pavement and had left a hammer propped up on the pavement to warn passers-by of the presence of the hole. The claimant was a blind man who was passing and whose stick failed to touch the hammer so that he tripped over the hammer and fell heavily, becoming deaf as a result. His claim in negligence was successful.

Key Law

The court held that there was a sufficiently large proportion of blind people in the community for the risk of harm to be great. The cost of the necessary precautions to protect blind people would have been very low. The defendants were liable for negligence.

2.2.2.3   *Watt v Hertfordshire County Council* [1954] 1 WLR 835   CA

Key Facts

A woman was trapped under a heavy vehicle and seriously injured. The fire service called to free her had a special jack for use in such circumstances. This would normally be transported securely in a special vehicle, but this was in use elsewhere. The jack was taken unsecured in another vehicle because of the emergency. When the driver was forced to brake sharply the jack moved, injuring one of the firemen. His claim for damages was unsuccessful.

Key Law

The court held that there was no negligence because the situation was an emergency; those in charge had to balance the nature of the risk against the importance of the emergency. The risk was justified in the circumstances.

2.2.2.4   *Latimer v AEC Ltd* [1953] AC 643   HL

Key Facts

A factory floor became flooded during a torrential rainstorm. The water mixed with oil and grease on the floor so that the surface was slippery and dangerous. Once the water was cleared, sawdust was spread over the floor to make it safe to walk on. There was not enough to cover the whole floor and the claimant slipped on an oily patch and injured his ankle. His action for damages failed.

Key Law

The House of Lords (now the Supreme Court) held that everything reasonable and practicable had been done in the circumstances to avoid risk of harm and, balancing out the possible risks, it was unreasonable to expect the factory to be closed. There was no negligence.

2.2.2.6   *Nettleship v Weston* [1971] 2 QB 691   CA

Key Facts

A learner driver on her third lesson crashed into a lamppost and injured her instructor. The question for the court was whether a lower standard of care should be expected of her because she was a learner driver. She was still found liable.

Key Law

The Court of Appeal found that she was liable despite being a learner driver since exactly the same standard of skill was expected of her as would be expected of a competent driver.

Key Judgment

Lord Denning stated that the law demands from a learner driver

'the same standard of care as of any other driver. The learner driver may be doing his best, but his incompetent best is not good enough. He must drive in as good a manner as a driver of skill, experience and care . . . who makes no errors of judgment . . .'.

Key Comment

It was also identified that this is probably to do with the requirement of compulsory motoring insurance so that the degree of risk associated with the particular type of driver can be reflected in the insurance premium they have to pay.

2.2.2.6 *Smoldon v Whitworth and Nolan* [1997] PIQR P133

CA

Key Facts

In a Colts rugby match, involving players under 19 years of age, the referee was approached by the coach of one team about repeated collapsing of the scrum by players from the other team. The referee did not control the scrums properly and the 17-year-old claimant was seriously injured, leading to paralysis, when the scrum was again collapsed. The claim for damages, arguing that the referee had failed to match the appropriate standard of care, succeeded.

Key Law

The Court of Appeal agreed that the referee had fallen below the standard of care that he owed to the players. This was because rules relating to scrums had been intro-duced for Colts' games specifically to protect young players from spinal injury which was a foreseeable risk and these rules therefore imposed a higher standard of care on the referees in such games.

Key Link

Vowles v Evans [2003] EWCA Civ 318; [2003] 1 WLR 1607, where it was held that a rugby referee owes a duty of care to the players to enforce the rules of the game because the players depended on these rules for avoiding injury.

2.2.2.6   *Orchard v Lee* [2009] EWCA Civ 295   CA

Key Facts

A thirteen-year-old boy caused injury to a lunch break supervisor when he ran backwards in a school playground.

Key Law

The court held that, although some harm was foreseeable, the risk of harm was insufficient on its own to impose liability. Since the school did not prohibit running in the playground, the boy was merely doing what any boy of the same age would do in a designated play area, and did not fall below the standard appropriate to a boy of his age in the circumstances.

2.2.2.7   *Bolam v Friern Hospital Management Committee* [1957] 2 All ER 118   QBD

Key Facts

The claimant suffered from depression and consented to undergo electro-convulsive therapy, a practice which can cause severe muscular spasms. The doctor giving the treatment failed to provide relaxant drugs or any means of restraint and the claimant suffered a fractured pelvis. The claimant maintained that the procedure carried out in this way was negligent but he failed in his action for damages.

Key Law

The court accepted evidence showing that doctors at the time were divided on whether or not to use relaxant drugs during the procedure. The defendant was not negligent because he engaged in a procedure accepted by a competent body of medical practitioners skilled in the particular field.

Key Judgment

McNair J established that a different standard of care was appropriate to doctors:

'In the ordinary case which does not involve any special skill . . . negligence . . . means a failure to do some act which a reasonable man in the circumstances would do, or the doing of some act which a reasonable man in the circumstances would not do . . . But where you get a situation which involves the use of some special skill or competence, then the test as to whether there has been negligence or not is not the test of the man on the top of a Clapham omnibus, because he has not got this skill . . . The test is the standard of the ordinary skilled man exercising and professing to have that special skill . . . Putting it the other way round, a doctor is not negligent, if he is acting in accordance with such a practice, merely because there is a body of opinion that takes a contrary view.'

Key Comment

Brazier and Miola (in 'Bye-bye *Bolam*: A medical Litigation Revolution?' (2000) 8 *Med Law Review* (Spring), pp 85–114) argue that 'Many academic commentators and organisations campaigning for victims of medical accidents perceive [that] the *Bolam* test . . . has been used by the courts to abdicate responsibility for defining and enforcing patient rights.'

2.2.2.7

Bolitho v City and Hackney Health Authority [1998] AC 232

(HL)

Key Facts

A two-year-old boy was in hospital being treated for croup. His airwaves became blocked and, despite the requests of the nurses, the doctor on call failed to attend. The boy suffered a cardiac arrest and brain damage as a result. This could have been avoided if a doctor had intubated the boy and cleared the obstruction. The hospital admitted that the doctor was negligent in failing to attend, but claimed that it was not liable because the doctor would not have intubated even if she had attended, so there would have been no difference in the outcome, and that not intubating was acceptable medical practice.

Key Law

The case was ultimately decided on causation but the House rejected the view that because certain medical opinion would accept the practice of a doctor as reasonable and responsible it was bound to accept that merely because of Bolam.

Key Judgment

Lord Browne-Wilkinson suggested that

'. . . if, in a rare case, it can be demonstrated that the professional opinion is not capable of withstanding logical analysis, the judge is entitled to hold that the body of opinion is not reasonable or responsible' but added 'It is only where a judge can be satisfied that the body of expert opinion cannot be logically supported at all that such opinion will not provide the bench mark by reference to which the defendant's conduct falls to be assessed'.

Key Problem

The House of Lords (now the Supreme Court), taking up the criticism of Bolam expressed by many academic commentators, seems to be suggesting that there are circumstances where the test would not be followed. The problem is that it gives no examples of what circumstances this would occur in.

2.3.2.2   ***Barnett v Chelsea & Kensington Hospital Management Committee* [1969] 1 QB 428**   (QBD)

Key Facts

The claimant went to the casualty ward of the hospital at around 5 am on the morning of New Year's Day, complaining of vomiting and stomach pains after drinking tea. The doctor on duty, in clear breach of his duty, refused to examine him and told him to see his own doctor in the morning. The claimant later died of arsenic poisoning. It was shown that the man would have died even with treatment.

Key Law

On a straightforward application of the 'but for' test the failure to treat was not the factual cause of death so there was no liability.

2.3.2.4

McGhee v National Coal Board [1973] 3 All ER 1008

Key Facts

The claimant worked in a brick kiln and contracted dermatitis, one possible cause being the brick dust to which he was exposed. The claimant argued a breach of duty because the employer did not provide washing facilities.

Key Law

The Board was held liable on the basis that it 'materially increased the risk' of the claimant contracting the disease because of its failure to provide washing facilities, even though it could not be shown that he would have avoided the disease if facilities had been in place.

Key Problem

As the employer was negligent in failing to provide basic health and safety the court felt that it should have the burden of disproving the causal link. The test is more advantageous to a claimant than the basic 'but for' test but potentially unfair on the defendant.

2.3.2.43

Wilsher v Essex Area Health Authority [1988] 3 All ER 871

HL

Key Facts

After a difficult delivery, a baby was mistakenly given too much oxygen by the doctor. The baby suffered retrolental fibroplasias, resulting in blindness. The House of Lords (now the Supreme Court) accepted evidence that excess oxygen was just one of six possible causes of the condition and dismissed the claim.

Key Law

The House of Lords (now the Supreme Court) applied the 'but for' test rigidly. Since the doctor's error was one of six possible causes the blindness could not be said to fall squarely within the risk created by the defendants.

2.3.2.4

Fairchild v Glenhaven Funeral Services Ltd and others; Fox v Spousal (Midlands) Ltd; Matthews v Associated Portland Cement Manufacturers (1978) Ltd and another [2002] UKHL 22; [2002] 3 WLR 89

(HL)

Key Facts

Three joined appeals involved employees who had contracted mesothelioma through prolonged exposure to asbestos dust with a number of different employers. It is currently scientifically uncertain whether inhaling a single fibre or inhalation of many fibres causes the disease, so it was impossible to say accurately which employer caused the disease. Nevertheless, the claims succeeded against the specific employers who were sued.

Key Law

The House of Lords (now the Supreme Court) held that, since greater exposure to the dust means that the chances of contracting the disease are greater, then each employer has a duty to take reasonable care to prevent employees from inhaling the dust and that any of the employers could be liable because they had all materially contributed to the risk of harm. Since the claimants suffered the very injuries that the defendants were supposed to guard against the House was prepared to impose liability on all employers. Because the employers never argued that they should only be liable for a proportion of the damages each employer should be liable to compensate its employee in full, even though the employee may have inhaled more fibres while working for another employee.

Key Comment

The House accepted that sufferers of diseases such as mesothelioma, while inevitably deserving of compensation, are unable to satisfy the normal tests for causation because they are unable to point to a single party who is responsible. The court was prepared to accept the possibility of a claim for three connected reasons:

- Because claimants could only not satisfy the normal tests for causation because of the current state of medical knowledge, although there is no doubt that exposure to asbestos fibres in whatever volume is the cause of the disease.

- As a result, it was fairer to give the defendants the burden of proving that their negligence could not be the actual cause.
- If this approach was not taken it would be almost impossible to make successful claims for the disease, so the employer's duty of care would be made meaningless.

Key Link

In *Barker v Corus* [2006] UKHL 20 the House of Lords (now the Supreme Court) held that damages for exposure to asbestos causing mesothelioma should only be for the share of the risk created by the breach. The Government effectively reversed this position in the Compensation Act 2006. *Sienkiewicz v Greif (UK) Ltd* [2011] UKSC 10 identifies that the *Fairchild* exception can be relied upon whenever the defendant's breach of duty made a material contribution to the risk of the claimant contracting mesothelioma.

2.3.2.4   *Baker v Willoughby* [1970] AC 467   HL

Key Facts

Through the defendant's negligent driving the claimant suffered a permanent disability in his leg which meant that he had to take work on a lower income. Some time later, he was shot in the same leg by an armed robber, which meant that his leg then had to be amputated. The House of Lords (now the Supreme Court) rejected the defendant's claim that he was only liable for damages up to the point of the amputation.

Key Law

The court identified that the loss of earnings was a permanent result of the original injury and unaffected by the amputation.

Key Judgment

Lord Reid explained:

'A man is not compensated for the physical injury; he is compensated for the loss which he suffers as a result. . . . His loss is not in having a stiff leg; it is in his inability to lead a full life . . . to enjoy those amenities which depend on freedom of movement and . . . to earn as much as he used to earn or could have earned if there had been no accident. In this case the second injury did not diminish any of these.'

2.3.2.4

Jobling v Associated Dairies Ltd [1982] AC 794

HL

Key Facts

In 1973, as a result of his employer's negligence, the claimant slipped on the floor of a refrigerator in the butcher's shop where he worked and injured his back, losing 50 per cent of his earning capacity as a result. In 1976 he developed spondylotic myelopathy, a back disorder unrelated to the fall, which meant he could not work at all. The court held that the defendant employer was liable for damages only up to when the condition developed in 1976.

Key Law

The House held that, since the condition would have occurred anyway, the defendant's negligence had only caused the loss of earnings prior to that point. Any later loss of earnings would have occurred anyway, despite the defendant's negligence.

Key Comment

The court, while not overruling *Baker*, was nevertheless very critical of the case.

2.3.2.5

Greg v Scott [2005] UKHL 2; [2005] 2 WLR 268

HL

Key Facts

The claimant consulted his GP about a lump under his arm. The doctor diagnosed fatty tissue and failed to send the claimant to hospital for any further tests, which he should have done because cancer was a foreseeable possibility. Nine months later it was discovered that the lump was a cancer. Medical evidence was accepted that the claimant would have had a 42 per cent chance of being alive and cancer-free in 10 years if the cancer had been diagnosed and treated after the first visit. This had reduced to a 25 per cent chance by the time the nine months had passed.

The claimant unsuccessfully sought damages for the reduction in his prospects of cure and life expectancy.

Key Law

The House held that it would be to develop the law in a way that was inappropriate to allow a claim for a proportion of what would have been awarded if the defendant had been proved to have been the cause of the claimant's premature death. In fact all that could be proved was the loss of a chance of full recovery and the law does not accept this as a basis for showing causation.

Key Link

Hotson v East Berkshire Area Health Authority [1987] 1 All ER 210; *Savage v South Essex Partnership NHS Foundation Trust* [2008] UKHL 74

2.3.2.3

Chester v Ashfar [2004] UKHL 41; [2005] 1 AC 134

(HL)

Key Facts

The defendant neurosurgeon failed to warn the claimant of a 1–2 per cent risk of partial paralysis from the procedure, and which she in fact suffered. The claimant succeeded in her claim for damages because the court accepted that she had proved that if she had been properly informed she would not have undergone the surgery.

Key Law

The House held that the claimant could not satisfy the normal 'but for' test, since it was possible that she may have consented to the operation at a future date. However, the court felt that justice required that in order to give practical force to a doctor's legal duty to warn a patient of the risks involved in surgery it should treat the injury as though it had been caused by the defendant's breach.

2.3.3.4

McKew v Holland & Hannen & Cubitts (Scotland) Ltd [1969] 3 All ER 1621

(HL)

Key Facts

The claimant suffered an injury to his leg caused by the defendants' negligence. For some time after the event, he suffered from a condition which meant that his leg frequently gave way. While in this condition he tried to climb down a steep flight of steps with no handrail, without any help and while carrying his daughter.

He fell when his leg gave way and suffered further serious injuries. The defendants were not held liable for this further injury.

Key Law

The court held that the defendants were not liable for this fall. The claimant's act was a *novus actus interveniens*. He was fully aware of the weakness in his leg and his behaviour was unreasonable.

Key Judgment

Lord Reid explained:

'if the injured man acts unreasonably he cannot hold the defender liable for injury caused by his own unreasonable conduct. His unreasonable conduct is novus actus interveniens. *The chain of causation has been broken and what follows must be regarded as being caused by his own conduct.'*

Key Link

Lord v Pacific Steam Navigation Co Ltd (The Oropesa) [1943] 1 All ER 211, where there was no *novus actus* because the claimant's behaviour was entirely reasonable in the circumstances.

2.3.3.4 *Carslogie Steamship Co v Royal Norwegian Government* [1952] AC 292

 HL

Key Facts

The claimant's ship was damaged in a collision with the defendant's ship through the defendant's negligence. Following a delay for repairs, the ship embarked on a voyage to a different destination, during which it suffered further damage caused by an exceptionally heavy storm. The claimant was not able to gain damages from the defendant for this extra damage.

Key Law

The House accepted that the extra damage was caused by the storm, which was a break in the chain of causation. It would have been unfair to fix the defendant with liability for the full extent of the damage. The storm damage was not a consequence of the collision but was a quite separate occurrence.

2.3.3.4   *Knightley v Johns* [1982] 1 All ER 851

Key Facts

The defendant, through negligent driving, crashed and blocked a tunnel. The police officer in charge at the scene sent a police motorcyclist back against the flow of traffic to block off the tunnel at the other end, in order to prevent further accidents. The police officer was injured when he collided with an oncoming car while rounding a bend. The defendant was not held liable for the police officer's injuries.

Key Law

The court held that the defendant could not be said to have caused this injury. It was the fault of the senior police officer whose ill-considered action broke the chain of causation and was a *novus actus interveniens*.

Key Judgment

Stephenson LJ made a quite significant comment in suggesting that 'Negligent conduct is more likely to break the chain of causation than conduct which is not.'

Key Problem

There is a clear problem for the claimant where the chain of conduct is broken by the act of a third party. If that act is not negligent then the claimant can receive no compensation for the extra harm suffered.

2.3.4.4

Overseas Tankship (UK) Ltd v Morts Dock & Engineering Co (The Wagon Mound (No 1)) [1961] AC 388

(PC)

Key Facts

As a result of the defendant's negligence, oil leaked into Sydney Harbour from its tanker. The oil floated on the water to the claimant's wharf. Welding was taking place in the wharf and the claimant's manager enquired whether there was a risk of the oil igniting. This was considered unlikely since the oil had an extremely high flash point. The welder continued and sparks ignited oil-soaked wadding and set fire to ships being repaired in the wharf; the oil also caused fouling to the wharf. The trial judge had held that since some damage, the fouling, was foreseeable, the defendants were also liable for the fire damage which was a direct consequence of its breach of duty in allowing the spillage. The Privy Council reversed this decision and disallowed damages for the fire damage.

Key Law

The court held that the defendant could not be liable for the fire damage as it was too remote a consequence of the breach of duty. The true test should be based on reasonable foreseeability and, because of the unlikelihood of the oil igniting; the fire damage was not foreseeable to a reasonable man.

Key Judgment

Viscount Simonds explained why the court rejected the former test of direct and natural consequences from Re Polemis:

'if it is asked why a man should be responsible for the natural or necessary or probable consequences of his act the answer is that it is not because they are natural or necessary or probable, but because, since they have this quality, it is judged by the standard of the reasonable man that he ought to have foreseen them.'

Key Link

Re Polemis and Furness, Withy & Co [1921] 3 KB 560

2.3.4.8   *Tremain v Pike* [1969] 3 All ER 1303   (QBD)

Key Facts

The claimant was a herdsman who contracted Weil's disease on his employer's farm, which was infested with rats. This disease is very rare and can only be contracted through direct contact with rats' urine. The claimant argued that this did happen when he handled hay and washed in water that was contaminated with rats' urine. His claim failed.

Key Law

The court accepted that the defendant had negligently let the rat population on his farm grow too high, so that there was risk of injury from rats. Nevertheless, the court held that the defendant was not liable since the court considered that the disease was too rare in humans and so was unforeseeable.

Key Judgment

Payne J suggested that the disease was *'entirely different in kind from the effect of a rat bite or food poisoning'.*

Key Problem

This is a very narrow view of foreseeability, particularly in view of the level to which the claimant was exposed to the rat urine. If injury from the rats was foreseeable then surely injury from the exposure to the urine was an equally fore-seeable cause of harm.

2.3.4.7   *Hughes v The Lord Advocate* [1963] AC 837   (HL)

Key Facts

Post Office employees dug a hole in the road and left a manhole uncovered inside a tent and then left the tent unat-tended. They also left four lit paraffin lamps at the corners of the tent at night as a warning and to avoid people falling in the hole. A boy entered the tent with one of the lamps and when it fell into the hole an explosion caused the boy to suffer burns. The boy's claim succeeded.

Key Law

The House accepted that the precise circumstances in which the injury occurred were quite remote. However, some fire-related damage was a foreseeable consequence of leaving the scene unattended and so it held the defendants liable. Providing damage of the general kind was foreseeable, then this was sufficient.

Key Comment

This is a much broader and, from the claimant's perspective, a much more generous view of foreseeability.

Key Link

Jolley v London Borough of Sutton [2000] 3 All ER 409: see p 94.

2.3.4.8 *Doughty v Turner Manufacturing Co Ltd* [1964] 1 QB 518

Key Facts

The cover on a tank of heated sodium cyanide was improperly secured so that it slid into the liquid in the tank while the claimant was working by it. The cover was made of asbestos and an explosion caused by the mixing of the chemicals and the asbestos badly burned the claimant. The claim for personal injury failed.

Key Law

The Court of Appeal accepted that it was previously unknown that there would be such a chemical reaction. Applying *Wagon Mound* principles, the chemical reaction was thus unforeseeable and the damage was too remote to impose liability on the defendants.

Key Comment

This is a narrow view of the foreseeable circumstances in which an injury might occur. It seems foreseeable that injury of some type could occur if the lid fell into the chemical while the workman was by it. Interestingly, the Court of Appeal chose to apply persuasive precedent from the Privy

Council in *The Wagon Mound* rather than its own previous precedent in *Re Polemis*.

2.3.4.10 *Smith v Leech Brain & Co Ltd* [1961] 3 All ER 1159

QBD

Key Facts

The claimant suffered a burnt lip as a result of being splashed by molten metal while at work, because of his employer's negligence. The burn ulcerated and activated a cancer from which he died three years later. He received full damages rather than just for the burn.

Key Law

The court held that even though the death from cancer was an immediately unforeseeable consequence of the negligence, some form of injury clearly was and the defendants were held liable as a result. While it was accepted that his lip had actually been in a pre-malignant state at the time of the burn, some form of harm from the burn was foreseeable and the court rejected the argument that *Wagon Mound* principles prevented operation of the 'thin skull' rule.

Key Comment

This operates as an exception to the test of reasonable foreseeability. Where the 'thin skull' rule is applicable the test is still one of direct and natural consequences.

3 Negligence: specific duty situations

▶ 3.1 Nervous shock

1   This is a complex area which has both expanded and contracted.

2   It must involve an actual psychiatric condition, e.g. post-traumatic stress disorder; temporary grief or fright is insufficient.

3   Originally cases failed on the 'floodgates' argument and fear of faking (*Victoria Railway Commissioners v Coultas* (1888)).

4   Liability was originally based on the Kennedy test – real and immediate personal danger must be foreseeable (*Dulieu v White* (1901)).

5   The principle was then extended to cover family and close friends (*Hambrook v Stokes* (1925)).

6   It was extended further, to close workmates (*Dooley v Cammell-Laird* (1951)).

7   But it was then limited to claimant being in the area of impact. Compare *King v Phillips* (1953) and *Attia v British Gas* (1987). And no claim possible if outside the area of foreseeable shock (*Bourhill v Young* (1943)).

8   Then an alternative was introduced where the claimant was outside the area of impact but within the area of shock. Compare *Bourhill v Young* (1943) with *Ravenscroft v Rederiaktiebolaget* (1991).

9   There are, in any case, incongruous judgments (*Owens v Liverpool Corp* (1933)).

10   The high point of liability came in *McLoughlin v O'Brian* (1982) – succeeded even though not a witness of the incident, but this came under Wilberforce's two-part test (there was proximity and no policy reason for denying the claim).

11   Rescuers can claim (*Chadwick v BR Board* (1993) and *Hale v London Underground* (1992)), and police at one point succeeded where relatives of Hillsborough victims failed (*Frost v Chief Constable of South Yorkshire* (1996)). Now a rescuer must be a primary victim and at risk to succeed (*White v Chief Constable of South Yorkshire* (1999)), or a genuine

Development of liability

- Originally no action possible because of lack of expertise on psychiatric illness (*Victoria Railway Commissioners v Coultas*).
- Liability first accepted where claimant also at risk of physical injury (*Dulieu v White*).
- Then extended to cover fear for close family when within area of impact (*Hambrook v Stokes*).
- Then to include claimants not within area of impact but within area of shock (*Bourhill v Young*).
- Widest point of liability when claimant not present at scene but present at immediate aftermath and close ties with victim (*McLoughlin v O'Brien*).

Criteria for liability

Contained in *Alcock v Chief Constable of West Yorkshire* and distinguishing between primary and secondary victims – claimants can be:

- present at scene and injured (primary) (*Page v Smith*);
- present at scene and at risk of physical harm (primary) (*Dulieu v White*);
- close tie of love and affection with victim and witnessed unaided the incident or its immediate aftermath (secondary) (*McLoughlin v O'Brien*);
- claimant proves a close tie with the victim and witnessed close-ups of the victim on TV in breach of broadcasting rules (secondary).

Professional rescuers have traditionally been accepted as legitimate claimants (*Chadwick v BR Board*). Now they need to be:

- at risk and thus primary victims also to succeed (*White v Chief Constable of West Yorkshire*);
- or a genuine secondary victim (*Greatorex v Greatorex*).

Claimants who will fail include:

- those suffering pre-accident terror (*Hicks v Chief Constable of West Yorkshire*);
- mere bystanders (*McFarlane v E E Caledonia*);
- workmates of victims (*Duncan v British Coal* and *Robertson & Rough v Forth Road Bridge*);
- when shock develops gradually (*Sion v Hampstead HA*).

NERVOUS SHOCK

Recognised psychiatric illness

- Can be post-traumatic stress disorder or depression.
- Also pathological grief (*Tredget v Bexley HA*).
- But not claustrophobia (*Reilly v Merseyside RHS*).

secondary victim (*Greatorex v Greatorex* (2000)). Merely proving rescuer status is insufficient on its own to claim without being either a genuine primary victim or a genuine secondary victim (*Stephen Monk v P C Harrington UK Ltd* (2008)).

12 Restrictions now exist (*Alcock v Chief Constable of South Yorkshire* (1991)) for secondary victims and there are three key requirements to determine. The claimant must:

- be sufficiently proximate in time and space to the incident;
- have a close tie of love and affection to the victim;
- see or hear the incident or its immediate aftermath (restricted to two hours in *Alcock* but the Court of Appeal has accepted a single traumatic event lasting 36 hours in *North Glamorgan NHS Trust v Walters* (2002).

13 *Alcock* (1991) suggests future successful claims will be based on:

- claimant present at scene and injured (primary victim) (*Page v Smith* (1996)). If psychiatric injury follows a physical injury it will generally be considered foreseeable (*Simmons v British Steel* (2004));
- claimant present at scene and own safety threatened (primary victim) (*Dulieu v White* (1901));
- claimant proves a close tie with the victim and witnessed the incident or its immediate aftermath at close hand (secondary victim) (*McLoughlin v O'Brien* (1981));
- claimant is a rescuer or one of the professional services (*Piggott v London Underground* (1995)), but see *Duncan v British Coal* (1996) and *White* (1999);
- claimant proves a close tie with the victim and witnessed close-ups of the victim on TV in breach of broadcasting rules;
- claimant shows a close tie with the victim and witnessed the catastrophic event involving victim on TV (more debatable).

14 Claims for pre-accident terror have also been rejected (*Hicks v Chief Constable of South Yorkshire* (1992)).

15 Bystanders have no claim (*McFarlane v E E Caledonia* (1994)).

16 Nor do workmates witnessing the incident without sufficiently close ties (*Robertson and Rough v Forth Road Bridge* (1995)).

17 Nor does it apply where the shock happens gradually rather than suddenly (*Sion v Hampstead HA* (1994)).

18 But see the Court of Appeal in *North Glamorgan NHS Trust v Walters* (2002) accepting a single traumatic event lasting 36 hours; and the House of Lords in *W v Essex County Council* (2000) accepting a claim for learning of child abuse after the event.

19 Many cases now focus on:

a) the nature of the psychiatric illness:

- *Reilly v Merseyside RHA* (1994) – claustrophobia and subsequent insomnia was insufficient for a claim;

- *Tredget v Bexley HA* (1994) – death of newborn baby did create liability because the trauma created a psychiatric disorder.

b) causation:

- *Calascione v Dixon* (1994) (no causal link between PTSD and accident);
- *Vernon v Bosley* (1996) (there was a causal link between death of children and pathological grief amounting to a psychiatric disorder).

▶ 3.2 Pure economic loss

1   The courts have always been reluctant to accept claims for pure economic loss, since it is more closely linked to contract law.

2   However, they have kept a distinction between economic loss caused by negligent statements and that caused by negligent acts.

- The distinction was originally seen as mainly one of policy (*Spartan Steel v Martin & Co (Contractors) Ltd* (1973)).
- The purpose being to limit any extension of liability.

3   It was confirmed in *Weller v Foot & Mouth Research Institute* (1966); *Meah v Creamer* (1986); *Pritchard v Cobden* (1988)).

4   Liability was extended in *Dutton v Bognor Regis UDC* (1972).

- Although it was not clear-cut whether this was under *Hedley Byrne* or *Donoghue*.
- The justification for liability was risk to health.

5   Liability was expanded:

- as a result of the two-part test in *Anns v Merton LBC* (1978);
- and also for a possible future threat to health (*Batty v Metropolitan Property Realisations* (1978)).

6   The 'high water mark' was *Junior Books v Veitchi Co Ltd* (1983).

a) There were three key issues:

- claimant nominated defendants to lay their floor in the new printing works, so relied on their skill;
- defendant knew of this reliance by the claimant;
- damage was a direct and foreseeable consequence of the defendant's negligence.

Original position

- No liability for a pure economic loss, eg loss of profit (*Spartan Steels v Martin*).
- Because more appropriate to contract law.

Origins of liability

- Some liability in *Dutton v Bognor Regis UDC* because of risk to health.
- Developed in *Anns v Merton LBC* as a result of Lord Wilberforce's two-part test – proximity and policy.
- Developed further in *Junior Books v Veitchi* because claimant nominated sub-contractors (so no action in contract); defendant knew claimants relied on their skill; damage was direct and foreseeable consequence of their breach.

PURE ECONOMIC LOSS

Modern position

- Many cases expressed dissatisfaction with *Anns*, eg *D & F Estates v Church Commissioners*.
- So two-part test overruled in *Murphy v Brentwood*.
- Artificial divide between property damage and pure economic loss discredited in *Marc Rich v Bishop Rock Marine*.
- Current policy favours private insurance.

b) Lord Brandon dissented because the case extended tortious liability into contract areas.

7   Many later cases expressed dissatisfaction with *Junior Books*:

- *Governors of the Peabody Donation Fund v Sir Lindsay Parkinson* (1984);

- *Muirhead v Industrial Tank Specialists Ltd* (1985);

- *D & F Estates v Church Commissioners* (1988);

- *Reid v Ruth* (1989).

8   The *Anns* two-part test was overruled in *Murphy v Brentwood DC* (1990).

9   This was followed in *Department of the Environment v Thomas Bates & Sons Ltd* (1990).

10   The artificial divide between damage to property and pure economic loss has been further discredited in *Marc Rich & Co v Bishop Rock Marine* (1995).

11   So the present policy favours private insurance rather than tort.

12   However, judges have shown themselves willing to be more relaxed in response to specific policy considerations (*Spring v Guardian Assurance* (1994)) involving negligent references.

▶ 3.3 Negligent misstatement

3.3.1 The origins of liability

1   Tort remedies physical loss and damage, but judges are reluctant to allow recovery for a pure economic loss since it is considered to be more appropriate to contract law.

2   Successful actions originally involved misrepresentations made fraudulently, not those made negligently.

3   Any action would be in the tort of deceit (*Derry v Peek* (1889)).

4   Principle reaffirmed in *Candler v Crane Christmas & Co* (1951).

5   But the impetus for creating liability came from Lord Denning's dissenting judgment in this case: defendants should owe a duty of care to 'any third person to whom they themselves show the accounts, or to whom they know their employer is going to show the accounts so as to induce them to invest money or take some other action upon them . . .'.

6   Lord Denning's judgment was finally approved *obiter* in *Hedley Byrne v Heller & Partners Ltd* (1964).

   a) While the action failed because a valid disclaimer was used, HL accepted a duty of care might exist despite:

   ● the absence of a contractual relationship;

   ● the fact that it would mean imposing liability for economic loss.

   b) HL also laid down criteria for allowing such liability:

   ● existence of a special relationship between the parties;

   ● special skill possessed by person giving advice;

   ● presence of reasonable reliance on the advice.

   c) The basic principles have since been accepted and developed in case law.

3.3.2 The criteria for imposing liability

The special relationship

1   The meaning of 'special relationship' was not fully explained in *Hedley Byrne*, so has become an area for judicial policy.

2   Originally a narrow interpretation was preferred, to include only a relationship where the person was expected to give advice of the kind given.

Origins of liability

- Originally courts hostile to accepting liability for any economic loss, since more appropriate to contract law.
- Same reasoning applied in relation to negligently prepared accounts in *Candler v Crane Christmas & Co.*
- Lord Denning, dissenting, thought there should be liability for negligent preparation of accounts to third parties as well as the client.
- Reasoning accepted in *Hedley Byrne v Heller & Partners* where HL suggested for liability:
  i)   there must be a special relationship;
  ii) person giving advice must have specialist skill of kind needed for advice;
  iii) must be reliance on the advice.

NEGLIGENT MISSTATEMENT

Criteria for imposing duty

Special relationship
- Generally means where person is expected to give advice.
- Has been suggested could include business arrangements (*Howard Marine & Dredging v Ogden & Sons*).
- But generally not social relationships (*Chaudhry v Prabhakar*).
- Can involve surveyors (*Yianni v Edwin Evans*).
- But the position on accountants is less clear-cut (*Caparo v Dickman*).

Possession of special skills
- Duty only exists if defendant has skill in area of advice given (*Mutual Life & Citizens Assurance v Evatt*).
- So no liability for uninformed advice (*Chaudhry v Prabhaker*).

Reasonable reliance on the advice
- No liability unless statement affected claimant's judgement (*JEB Fasteners v Mark Bloom*).
- Policy can affect outcome, eg no liability if advisee a member of too large a class (*Goodwill v British Pregnancy Advisory Service*).
- Defendant must know claimant would rely on advice (*Yianni v Edwin Evans*).
- Such knowledge can even invalidate exclusion clauses (*Harris v Wyre Forest DC* and *Smith v Eric S Bush*).

Current state of the law

HL have since expanded on where a duty will apply in *Caparo v Dickman*.
- advice is required for purpose either specified in detail or described in general terms to defendant;
- purpose is made known, actually or by inference, to advisor at the time advice is given;
- advisor knows, actually or inferentially, that advice will be communicated to person relying on it to use for known purpose, and that advice will be acted upon without further independent advice;
- person relying on advice acts on it to their detriment.

Inconsistent cases

- Person receiving advice was not loss sufferer (*Ross v Caunters*).
- Foreseeability of reliance creates liability (*Ministry of Housing and Local Government v Sharp*).
- Policy dictates liability and ensures a remedy (*White v Jones*).

3   It has later been suggested that any business or professional relationship has potential to be a special relationship (*Howard Marine & Dredging Co Ltd v Ogden & Sons Ltd* (1978)).

4   It is not possible in a purely social relationship unless circumstances show that carefully considered advice was being sought (*Chaudhry v Prabhaker* (1988)).

5   Many cases involve surveyors or valuers. The relationship between surveyors and purchasers of houses might be special although not contractual (*Yianni v Edwin Evans & Sons* (1982)).

6   One complex issue is to whom accountants owe a duty of care:

   a) it has influenced how the existence of the duty is determined;

   b) originally there was held to be no duty, since any duty would be contractual (*Candler v Crane Christmas & Co* (1951));

   c) since *Hedley Byrne* the existence of the duty has been established (*JEB Fasteners v Marks Bloom & Co* (1983));

   d) bidders in a takeover or lenders or investors of any kind cannot rely on the annual audited accounts, so there is no duty on the accountants (*Caparo v Dickman* (1990)).

7   There must be sufficient proximity between the parties to impose a duty (*Raja v Gray*), but simple policy reasons can be used to determine that there is insufficient proximity between parties to impose liability (*West Bromwich Albion Football Club Ltd v El-Safty* (2005)).

The possession of special skill

1   Duty only exists if defendant possesses skill in area of advice given (*Mutual Life & Citizens Assurance Co v Evatt* (1971)).

2   So there is usually no liability for advice of an uninformed and inexpert character, but see *Chaudhry v Prabhaker* (1988).

Reasonable reliance on the advice

1   If a negligent statement did not influence the claimant's judgement then no liability (*JEB Fasteners v Marks Bloom & Co Ltd* (1983) and *Lambert v West Devon Borough Council* (1997)).

2   As with special relationship, reasonable reliance has been a subject for judicial policy (*Caparo v Dickman* (1990)).

   a) So reliance is not automatic in a relationship of trust (*Jones v Wright* (1994)).

   b) But is more likely in contractual situations or those that are near contractual, e.g. pre-contractual arrangements (*Commissioner of Police for the Metropolis v Lennon* (2004)).

c) Neither is there reliance if the claimant belongs to too large a group (*Goodwill v British Pregnancy Advisory Service* (1996)).

3 The defendant must have known or be reasonably expected to have known that the claimant would rely upon the advice (*Yianni v Edwin Evans* (1982)).

4 Foreseeability of reliance can even invalidate exclusions (*Harris v Wyre Forest DC* (1989) and *Smith v Eric S Bush* (1990)).

5 A disclaimer may be declared unreasonable and invalid, but a surveyor can still use one to discharge his duty and avoid liability (*Eley v Chasemore* (1989)).

3.3.3 The current state of the law

1 The property and financial markets boom of the late 1980s led to a large number of cases involving surveyors or accountants.

2 In *Caparo v Dickman* (1990), HL restated principles involved for both special relationships and reasonable reliance.

a) HL preferred an incremental approach to duty of care.

b) HL rejected a general test based on reasonable foresight, and led to a later request for leave to amend the statement of claim in *Morgan Crucible plc v Hill Samuel Bank Ltd* (1991).

c) HL explained that a duty will apply where:

● the advice is required for a purpose, either specified in detail or described in general terms to the defendant;

● the purpose is made known, actually or by inference, to the advisor at the time the advice is given;

● the advisor knows, actually or inferentially, that the advice will be communicated to the person relying on it to use for the known purpose;

● the advice will be acted upon without further independent advice;

● the person relying on the advice acts on it to their detriment.

3 This is a narrow approach, reflecting the move away from *Anns*. Later cases have given further advice on when a duty exists. CA in *James McNaughten Papers Group Ltd v Hicks Anderson & Co* (1991) identified areas for consideration:

a) the purpose for which the statement was made;

b) the purpose of communicating the statement;

c) the relationship between the advisor, the recipient of the advice and any third parties;

d) the size of the class to which the recipient belongs;

e) the knowledge and experience possessed by the advisee;

f) whether it was reasonable to rely on the advice.

4   Significantly, however, the narrowing in *Caparo* is at odds with EU law, which requires harmonisation of company law, including the principle that a company's auditors owe a duty of care to third parties who suffer financial loss as a result of negligence.

5   Subsequent cases suggest some relaxation of the law (*Henderson v Merrett Syndicates Ltd* (1994)); (*Aiken v Steward Wrightson Members Agency Ltd* (1995)); (*N M Rothschild and Sons Ltd v Berensons and others* (1995)).

3.3.4 Cases inconsistent with the general principle

1   Some cases do not conform because the person relying on the advice is not the one suffering loss (*Ross v Caunters* (1980)).

2   Liability occurs because it is reasonably foreseeable that the party relies on the advice, and indeed that such a party exists (*Ministry of Housing & Local Government v Sharp* (1971)).

3   Following *Henderson* there may still not be liability if there is no assumption of responsibility, or if the evidence shows the contrary (*McCullagh v Lane Fox and Partners* (1995)).

4   Policy determines liability in such cases to prevent a party being unreasonably denied any remedy (*White v Jones* (1995) and *Gorham v British Telecommunications Plc* (2000)).

5   Debatable whether duty exists under *Donoghue v Stevenson* principles (*Spring v Guardian Assurance Plc* (1994)).

▶ 3.4 Omissions

Generally no liability for non-feasance (a failure to act), because of difficulty of proving causation and too harsh on defendant.
- contractual duty (*Stansbie v Troman*);
- duty based on special relationship (*Home Office v Dorset Yacht Co*);
- or for failure to control a third party (*Haynes v Harwood*);
- or for failure to control land (*Goldman v Hargreave*).

Rules now in S*mith v Littlewoods Organisation*.

OMISSIONS

1   The general rule is for no liability for omissions (non-feasance).

2   The reasons are fairly obvious:

- causation is significantly harder, if not impossible, to prove;

- it imposes too onerous an obligation on the defendant.

3   Exceptions have developed that Lord Goff has listed in *Smith v Little-woods Organisation Ltd* (1987).

- A contractual or other undertaking (*Barnet v Chelsea & Kensington Hospital Management Committee* (1969)); (*Mercer v SE & Chatham Railway* (1922)); (*Stansbie v Troman* (1948)); but see *Hill v Chief Constable of W Yorkshire* (1998).

- A special relationship between the defendant and a third party (*Home Office v Dorset Yacht Co* (1976) and *Barrett v Ministry of Defence* (1993)), but there is a possibility of *volenti* (*Selfe v Ilford District Hospital Management Committee* (1970)). A special relationship may result from a statutory duty (*D v East Berkshire Community Health NHS Trust* (2005)).

- A failure to exercise control over a third party (*Haynes v Harwood* (1935)), as where sporting officials have a duty to act (*Vowles v Evans and another* (2003)).

- A failure to control land or dangerous things. Compare *Cunningham v Reading FC* (1978) with *Goldman v Hargrave* (1966).

Key Cases Checklist

```
                        ┌─────────────────────┐
                        │     Negligence      │
                        └─────────────────────┘
```

Nervous shock

Reilly v Merseyside Regional Health Authority **(1994)**
Must be a recognised psychiatric illness caused by a single traumatic event

Page v Smith **(1996)**
Primary victims are those present at the scene and at risk of some harm

Alcock v Chief Constable of South Yorkshire **(1992)**
Secondary victims must show close tie of love and affection with primary victim and be present at scene or immediate aftermath, and witness event with own unaided senses

Omissions

Smith v Littlewoods **(1987)**
Liability for failure to act only if there is a duty to act

Economic loss

Murphy v Brentwood District Council **(1991)**
Generally no liability for pure economic loss caused by negligent actions

Hedley Byrne v Heller & Partners **(1964)**
But can be for economic loss caused by negligently made statements if made by a person with expertise in the matter who knows that the advice is relied on

---

3.1.3   *Victoria Railway Commissioners v Coultas* **(1888) 13 App Cas 222**   PC

Key Facts

The claimant suffered no physical injury but claimed to suffer psychiatric injury when involved in a train crash.

Key Law

The claim was refused because there was insufficient medical understanding of the nature of psychiatric injury at that time and there was no evidence of physical injury.

Key Problem

Claims for nervous shock were originally rejected not just because of the lack of understanding of psychiatric injury, but also because of the 'floodgates' argument. The judge feared that allowing the claim would open up a 'wide field of imaginary claims'.

3.1.4   *Dulieu v White & Sons* [1901] 2 KB 669

Key Facts

The claimant was the pregnant wife of a publican. She suffered nervous shock and her baby was born prematurely after a horse and van that had been negligently driven burst through the window of the pub where she was washing glasses. Her claim was successful even though she had suffered no physical injury.

Key Law

The court held that the defendant was liable because the claimant was within the zone of impact of physical injury and some damage was therefore foreseeable. Kennedy J devised the test for claiming damages for psychiatric injury (to become known as the 'Kennedy' test: a claimant might recover damages if the claimant feared real and immediate danger to himself as a result of the sudden shock).

Key Judgment

Kennedy J stated that: *'Shock, when it operates through the mind, must be a shock which arises from a reasonable fear of immediate personal injury to oneself'.*

3.1.5   *Hambrook v Stokes Bros* [1925] 1 KB 141

Key Facts

A woman saw a runaway lorry going downhill towards where she had left her three children. She then heard that there had indeed been an accident involving a child. She suffered nervous shock and died.

Key Law

The court extended claims for nervous shock to include those within the area of shock, i.e. those who while not in danger themselves feared for the safety of somebody who was.

Key Comment

The court distinguished the 'Kennedy' test. The judge considered that it would be unfair not to compensate a mother who had feared for the safety of her children when she could have claimed if she only feared for her own safety.

3.1.7   *Bourhill v Young* [1943] AC 92 HL

Key Facts

A pregnant Edinburgh fishwife claimed to have suffered nervous shock after getting off a tram, hearing the impact of a crash involving a motorcyclist, and later seeing his blood on the road. She then gave birth to a stillborn child. Her claim failed.

Key Law

The House of Lords (now the Supreme Court) held that, as a stranger to the motorcyclist, she was outside of the area of foreseeable shock. This then identifies the law on nervous shock in relation to bystanders. If they are not within the zone of danger and have no relationship with the primary victim then the damage they suffer is not foreseeable.

3.1.10   *McLoughlin v O'Brian* [1982] 2 All ER 298 HL

Key Facts

A woman was summoned to a hospital about an hour after her children and husband were involved in a car crash. One child was dead, two were badly injured, all were in shock and they had not yet been cleaned up. She suffered nervous shock as a result and her claim succeeded.

Key Law

The House of Lords (now the Supreme Court) held that since the relationship was sufficiently close and the woman was present at the 'immediate aftermath' she could claim. Lord Wilberforce identified a three-part test for secondary victims that was approved later in *Alcock*.

3.1.12

Alcock v Chief Constable of South Yorkshire [1992] 4 All ER 907

Key Facts

At the start of a football match police allowed a large crowd of supporters into a caged pen as the result of which 95 people in the stand suffered crush injuries and were killed. Since the match was being televised much of the disaster was shown on live TV. A number of claims for nervous shock were made. These varied between those present or not present at the scene, those with close family ties to the dead and those who were merely friends. The House of Lords (now the Supreme Court) refused all of the claims.

Key Law

The House of Lords (now the Supreme Court) held that none of the claimants identified the factors that must be proved in order to make a successful claim as a secondary victim:

- The proximity in time and space to the negligent incident – the claimant must have been present at the scene or its immediate aftermath (limited to two hours following *McLoughlin*).

- The proximity of the relationship with a party who was a victim of the incident – the claimant must have a close tie of love and affection with a primary victim.

- The cause of the nervous shock – the claimant must show that he suffered nervous shock as a result of witnessing or hearing the horrifying event or its immediate aftermath.

Key Problem

The development of the law on secondary victims has been to develop controls based on public policy that limit the potential for a successful claim, the justification being the 'floodgates' argument. Claims were denied here even though the relationship with the primary victim was a family one. It is also possible that the proximity to and the gruesomeness of the incident makes it foreseeable that a bystander could suffer psychiatric injury in which case there is a contradiction with the reasoning for granting remedies to primary victims and many bystanders are being unfairly denied a remedy.

3.1.13

Page v Smith [1996] 3 All ER 272

Key Facts

Page was involved in a car accident caused by the defendant's negligence. He suffered no physical injury but did suffer a recurrence of 'chronic fatigue syndrome' (ME) from which he had suffered before. He recovered damages for nervous shock.

Key Law

The House of Lords (now the Supreme Court) held that: firstly the illness in question was a recognised psychiatric injury; secondly that Page was indeed a genuine primary victim (present at the scene and at risk of foreseeable physical injury); thirdly that the 'thin skull' rule applied and that it did not matter that the single traumatic event led to injury that Page was more likely to suffer because of a pre-existing condition.

Key Problem

The situation for primary victims differs from that of secondary victims. The 'thin skull' rule applies to primary victims but a secondary victim would be expected to show 'reasonable phlegm and fortitude' – so a secondary victim with Page's condition would be unable to claim.

Key Link

Stephen Monk v PC Harrington UK Ltd [2008] EWHC 1879 (QB) – cannot be a primary victim if at no point would the claimant have considered himself to be at risk of foreseeable harm.

3.1.11

White v Chief Constable of South Yorkshire [1999] 1 All ER 1

Key Facts

Police officers who were present at the Hillsborough disaster as rescuers claimed to have suffered post-traumatic stress disorder. Their claim succeeded in the Court of Appeal as *Frost*. The House of Lords (now the Supreme Court) rejected their claim.

Key Law

The House of Lords (now the Supreme Court) held that no claim was possible since the police officers could not be classed as primary victims since they were never in any danger. The Lords also identified that there is no longer any presumption that a rescuer is a primary victim. A rescuer can only claim if he can show that he was at risk of foreseeable physical injury, and is therefore a genuine primary victim.

Key Comment

The Law Lords were also worried about the effect on public opinion if they awarded damages to police officers from Hillsborough when all the relatives of the dead had been denied claims.

Key Link

Frost v Chief Constable of West Yorkshire Police [1998] QB 254.

3.1.12

North Glamorgan NHS Trust v Walters [2002] EWCA Civ 1792

 CA

Key Facts

Doctors negligently failed to diagnose that a tiny baby required a liver transplant, despite reassuring his mother that he would survive. He then suffered a major fit and both were taken to a London hospital for the child to have a liver transplant. On arrival it was discovered that he had irreversible and severe brain damage. The life support system was switched off and the baby died minutes later in his mother's arms, the whole episode lasting 36 hours. The mother claimed successfully for pathological grief. The defendants appealed on the grounds that the psychiatric injury was not brought about as a result of witnessing a single shocking event but the Court of Appeal rejected this argument.

Key Law

The Court of Appeal held that the whole period from when the baby suffered the fit to when it died was 'a single horrifying event' and was part of a continuous chain of events.

Key Problem

The result seems to conflict quite sharply with the principle of single shocking event and the use of the 'immediate aftermath' test from *Alcock*. The Court of Appeal did in fact though distinguish from those cases where there is a slow realisation of the consequences of the shocking event.

3.1.17

Sion v Hampstead Health Authority [1994] 5 Med LR 170

 CA

Key Facts

A father suffered psychiatric injury after watching his son over the space of 14 days gradually deteriorate and then die, when there was the possibility of the death resulting from medical negligence. He was unsuccessful because the psychiatric injury was not the result of the sudden appreciation of a single traumatic event.

Key Law

Nervous shock must result from a single traumatic event. There is no claim for an injury suffered over a long period of time.

3.1.19

Reilly v Merseyside Regional Health Authority (1994) 23 BMLR 26

 CA

Key Facts

A couple became trapped in a lift as the result of negligence and suffered insomnia and claustrophobia as a result. There was held to be no liability for nervous shock.

Key Law

It was held that claims for nervous shock must involve an actual, recognised psychiatric condition capable of resulting from the shock of the incident, and recognised as having long-term effects. Claustrophobia was not accepted as a recognised psychiatric injury for the purposes of nervous shock.

3.1.19

Vernon v Bosley [1997] 1 All ER 577   CA

Key Facts

A father had witnessed his children being drowned in a car that was being negligently driven by the children's nanny. He recovered damages for nervous shock that was held to be partly the result of pathological grief and bereavement, but partly also the consequence of the trauma of witnessing the events.

Key Law

A secondary victim can claim if the psychiatric injury caused by the sudden traumatic event, even though it is based on profound grief if also linked to clinical depression.

3.1.19

Calascione v Dixon (1993) 19 BMLR 97   CA

Key Facts

The defendant caused the death of a 20-year-old in a motorcycle accident. The mother of the young man then suffered nervous shock following the inquest and a private prosecution.

Key Law

It was held that the nervous shock must be in fact caused by the single traumatic event. In other words, there must be a causal link between the event and the damage suffered. There was none here and so no liability.

3.2.2

Spartan Steel v Martin & Co (Contractors) Ltd [1973] 1 QB 27   CA

Key Facts

The defendant cut an electric cable, causing loss of power to the claimant, who made steel alloys. A 'melt' in the claimant's furnace when the power cut occurred had to be destroyed or it would have set and wrecked the furnace.

The claimant also lost profit on further 'melts' that it could have made during the power cut. The claimant successfully claimed for physical damage and lost profit from the 'melt' in the furnace, but was refused the further loss of profit.

Key Law

The loss was foreseeable. However, the court held that it was not possible to recover for pure economic loss caused by a negligent act since policy dictated that the loss was better borne by the insurers than by the defendants alone.

Key Judgment

Lord Denning explained:

'It seems to me better to consider the particular relationship in hand, and see whether or not, as a matter of policy, economic loss should be recoverable or not'.

3.2.8   *Murphy v Brentwood District Council* [1991] 2 All ER 908   (HL)

Key Facts

A council approved plans for a concrete raft on which properties were built. The raft was inadequate and later moved causing cracks in the walls and gas pipes to break. The claimant lost £35,000 from the value of his house and sought damages.

Key Law

The court held that, in the absence of any injury, loss was purely economic, and could not be recovered. Local authorities will not be liable for the cost of repairing dangerous defects unless injury occurs as well. The court also overruled *Anns*.

3.3.1.6   *Hedley Byrne v Heller & Partners Ltd* [1964] AC 465   (HL)

Key Facts

The claimant, an advertising company, was asked to produce a campaign for a small company. Because it had not previously dealt with that company it sought a credit reference from the company's bank, which gave a satisfactory reference without checking on the company's current financial standing. The claimant produced the campaign but then the company went into liquidation and so the claimant could not be paid for its work. The claimant sued the bank for its negligently made advice but failed because the bank had included a disclaimer of liability in its credit reference.

Key Law

The House *obiter* approved Lord Denning's dissenting judgment from *Candler v Crane Christmas & Co* and held that it is possible to recover for a purely financial loss caused by a negligently made statement if certain conditions are met.

Key Judgment

Lord Reid explained:

'A reasonable man, knowing that he was being trusted or that his skill and judgment were being relied on, would . . . be held to have accepted some responsibility for his answer being given carefully, or to have accepted a relationship with the inquirer which requires him to exercise such care as the circumstances require'.

Key Link

Candler v Crane Christmas & Co [1951] 2 KB 164.

3.3.2 | *Mutual Life and Citizens Assurance Co Ltd v Evatt* **[1971] AC 793** (PC)

Key Facts

The claimant asked an insurance company agent to give advice about the products of another company with which he planned to invest. The advice was inaccurate and the claimant lost money.

Key Law

The court held that there was no duty owed in the circumstances because the defendant had not held himself out as being in the business of giving the type of advice asked for.

3.3.2   *Chaudhry v Prabhaker* **[1988] 3 All ER 718**   CA

Key Facts

The claimant asked a friend, with some experience of cars, to find her a good second-hand car. When it was later discovered that the car had been in an accident and was not completely roadworthy the claimant successfully sued her friend.

Key Law

The court held that the relationship for the purpose of the advice operated in a similar way to principal and agent and so was sufficient to impose a duty of care on the person giving the advice.

Key Problem

This is a strange result as it is generally accepted that no duty is owed in a purely social relationship.

3.3.2   *Smith v Eric S Bush* **[1990] 2 WLR 790**   HL

Key Facts

A building society valuation identified that chimney breasts had been removed, but the valuer failed to check whether the bricks above were properly secured. They were not and after the purchase they collapsed and the purchaser sued successfully.

Key Law

The court held that there was a duty of care because, even though the contract was between the building society and valuer, it was reasonably foreseeable that the purchaser would rely on it.

3.3.2

Goodwill v British Pregnancy Advisory Service [1996] 2 All ER 161

Key Facts

The defendant failed properly to advise a patient of the possibility that his vasectomy could automatically reverse itself. The claimant had become pregnant after relying on the man informing her that he had had a vasectomy.

Key Law

The court held that a doctor can not be fixed with liability to the future partners of patients who they have performed a vasectomy on. The class is potentially too wide and unforeseeable. The court rejected the link drawn with *White v Jones*.

3.3.3.5

Henderson v Merrett Syndicates [1994] 3 All ER 506

Key Facts

Insurance underwriters lost huge sums because of negligent management of the syndicates of which they were members and needed to prove that the managing agents owed them a duty in tort as well as contractual duties.

Key Law

The court held that there was a duty because of an assumption of responsibility by the defendants. The court added this requirement to the list for establishing liability from *Caparo v Dickman* (1990):

- the advice must be required for a purpose described at the time to the defendant at least in general terms;
- this purpose must be made known actually or by inference to the party giving the advice at the time it is given;
- if the advice will subsequently be communicated to the party relying on it, this fact must be known by the adviser;
- the adviser must be aware that the advice will be acted upon without benefit of any further independent advice;
- the person alleging to have relied on the advice must show actual reliance and consequent detriment suffered;

- the person giving the advice must have assumed responsibility.

Key Link

Caparo v Dickman [1990] 2 AC 605

3.3.4.4   ***White v Jones* [1995] 1 All ER 691**   HL

Key Facts

Solicitors failed to draw up a will before the testator's death and the intended beneficiaries consequently lost their inheritance.

Key Law

The court held that a duty was owed to the beneficiaries even though the contractual relationship was with the testator, and since a will can be changed a beneficiary is not necessarily ensured the inheritance. Nevertheless, the House was prepared to identify both a special relationship in the circumstances and reliance.

3.4.3   ***Smith v Littlewoods Organisation Ltd* [1987] 1 All ER 710**   HL

Key Facts

The defendant bought a cinema to demolish and rebuild as a supermarket and then left it empty. Vandals broke in and set fire to it. The fire spread and caused damage to the claimants' properties.

Key Law

The court held that there was no liability. The defendant could not be responsible for acts of strangers of which it had no knowledge.

Key Judgment

Lord Goff in the House of Lords (now the Supreme Court) stated:

'In such a case it is not possible to invoke a general duty of care; for it is well recognised that there is no general duty of care to prevent third parties from causing such damage'.

Key Comment

Lord Goff also identified the situations in which a party could be liable for an omission – where the defendant owes a duty to act:

- because of a contractual or other undertaking;
- because of a special relationship with the claimant;
- because of damage that is done by a third party who is within his control;
- because he has control of things on his land or other dangerous things.

3.4.3

Home Office v Dorset Yacht Co Ltd [1970] AC 1004

 HL

Key Facts

Seven Borstal boys on a training camp in Poole, five of whom had escaped before, escaped when the warders, against their instructions, were all asleep. The boys caused considerable damage to yachts in the harbour. The claim for damages against the Home Office was successful.

Key Law

The Home Office was held liable for its employees' failure to control the offenders in their charge because its employees had failed in their duty to restrain the boys and protect the public from them.

3.4.3

Goldman v Hargrave [1967] 1 AC 645

 PC

Key Facts

A 100-foot-high tree on the defendant's land was struck by lightning and ignited. The defendant cleared land around the tree, felled it and cut the burning tree into sections to burn out. When a high wind developed the fire from the tree spread to neighbouring property causing extensive damage. The defendant was liable.

Key Law

The court acknowledged that the defendant had done nothing positive to cause the spread of fire or increase the risk of damage. Nevertheless, he failed to do something which he could have done with little extra cost or effort than he had already made, put the fire out. On this basis, he was negligent.

4 Occupier's liability

Parties to action

- **Defendants:**
  occupiers are those in control of premises at material time (*Wheat v Lacon*).
- **Claimants 1957 Act:**
  visitors include: invitees, licensees, people entering under a contract, people with a legal right to enter.
- **Claimants 1984 Act:**
  non-visitors include: trespassers, people using private rights of way (*Holden v Wright*), people entering under National Parks and Access to Countryside Act.
- **Claimants common law:**
  those using public rights of way.

Scope of duty in 1957 Act

- **Common duty of care:**
  by s 2(1) occupier owes same duty to all visitors.
- **Standard of care:**
  by s 2(2) occupier must take reasonable steps to ensure visitor safe for legitimate purpose of visit.
- **Avoiding the duty:**
  i) warnings are acceptable if effective to keep the visitor safe (*Rae v Mars*);
  ii) exclusions are possible by agreement or otherwise, but not, eg for sub-contractors, or those with legal right to enter;
  iii) contributory negligence can reduce damages (*Sayers v Harlow UDC*);
  iv) *volenti* is possible if risk is genuinely accepted (*White v Blackmore*).

OCCUPIER'S LIABILITY

Liability under 1984 Act

- Based on common duty of humanity (*Herrington v BR Board*).
- Available for personal injury only.
- Under s 1(3) duty if aware of danger, and knows or believes the non-visitor is in danger, and risk is one occupier should guard against.

Special cases

Children:
- by s 2(3) premises must be safe for child of that age;
- there should be no allurements (*Glasgow Corporation v Taylor*); occupier can expect parents to care for young children (*Phipps v Rochester Corporation*).

Those exercising a trade:
- by s 2(3) must guard against risks associated with their trade (*Roles v Nathan*);
- but occupier can still be liable (*Salmon v Seafarers Restaurant*).

Liability for acts of independent contractors:
no liability if reasonable to hire out work, competent contractor chosen, and work inspected if necessary (*Haseldine v Daw*).

▶ 4.1 Liability to lawful visitors under the 1957 Act

4.1.1 Introduction

1   Occupier's Liability Act 1957 – covers liability to visitors.

2   1984 Act covers liability to non-visitors (mainly trespassers).

3   Both Acts only cover damage resulting from state of premises – other damage is covered by negligence (*Ogwo v Taylor* (1987)).

4.1.2 Definition of occupier (potential defendants)

1   There is no real statutory definition so common law test applies: who has control of premises? (*Wheat v Lacon* (1966)).

2   Dual occupation possible – identity of the defendant depends on the nature of the interest, etc. (*Collier v Anglian Water Authority* (1983)).

3   In an action a lawyer's main concern is who has means to be sued.

4   There is no need for proprietary interest or possession, only control, so different from trespass (*Harris v Birkenhead Corporation* (1976)).

4.1.3 Definition of premises

1   No complete definition in either Act, so common law applies.

2   It obviously includes houses, buildings, land, etc. but also:
   - ships in dry dock (*London Graving Dock v Horton* (1951));
   - vehicles (*Hartwell v Grayson* (1947));
   - lifts (*Haseldine v Daw & Son Ltd* (1941));
   - aircraft (*Fosbroke-Hobbes v Airwork Ltd* (1937));
   - and even a ladder (*Wheeler v Copas* (1981)).

3   The 1957 Act in s 1(3)(a) preserves the common law ('fixed or movable structure, including any vessel, vehicle or aircraft . . .').

4.1.4 Potential claimants

1   The 1957 Act simplified complex common law classes of entrant. These were:

- invitee – enters in material interest of occupier, e.g. a shop customer, a friend visiting;

- licensee – mere permission, e.g. a person taking a short cut;

- a person entering under a contract, e.g. a painter (duty depended on contract) – a subcontractor is only a licensee;

- a person entering by legal right, e.g. meter readers, police executing warrants, but also private and public rights of way;

- trespassers – no permission and no rights.

2   The different classes were owed different duties so s 1(2) 1957 Act was replaced with 'common duty of care' to 'visitors', including:

- licensees and invitees – implied licensees must show licence created by occupier's conduct (*Lowery v Walker* (1911)) and an implied licence will not include a claimant's reckless actions that lead to his injury *Harvey v Plymouth CC* (2010);

- those entering under a contract – where the contract provides for greater protection it will be owed;

- those entering by legal right.

3   Visitor does not include:

- private rights of way (*Holden v Wright* (1982));

- those entering under an access agreement under the National Parks and Access to Countryside Act;

- trespassers (all covered by the Occupier's Liability Act 1984);

- public rights of way, covered by the common law (*McGeown v Northern Ireland Housing Executive* (1994)).

4.1.5 The scope of the Act (the common duty of care)

1   By s 2(1), 'An Occupier of premises owes the same duty, the common duty of care to all his visitors except insofar as he is free to do and does extend, restrict, modify or exclude his duty.'

2   By s 2(2) duty is to 'take such care as in all circumstances . . . is reasonable to see that the visitor will be reasonably safe in using the premises for the purpose for which he is invited . . .'. Higher duty may be owed by a professional occupier (*Ward v Tesco Stores Ltd* (1976)) than by an ordinary homeowner (*Fryer v Pearson* (2000)).

3   Three key points apply.

a) The standard of care is the same as for negligence, the standard of reasonableness (*Esdale v Dover* (2010)) – no need to guard against the unforeseeable (*Bolton v Stone* (1951)), so no liability for 'pure accidents' (*Cole v Davis-Gilbert and the Royal British Legion* (2007)).

b) Duty only exists while the visitor carries out authorised activities.

c) The visitor must be kept safe, not the premises, so the Act elaborates on certain classes of visitor (*Searson v Brioland* (2005)).

4.1.6 Liability to children

1   Section 2(3) allows for 'children to be less careful than adults' and 'premises must be reasonably safe for a child of that age . . .'.

2   So the standard of care owed to a child is measured subjectively.

3   This is because an unthreatening object to an adult may be dangerous to a child (*Moloney v Lambeth LBC* (1966)).

4   Occupiers must not lead children into temptation (the 'allurement principle') (*Glasgow Corporation v Taylor* (1922)).

5   However, allurement is not definite proof of liability (*Liddle v Yorkshire (North Riding) CC* (1944)).

6   It had been held that there is no liability where there is an allurement but the type of damage sustained is not foreseeable (*Jolley v London Borough of Sutton* (1998)) CA, but HL (2000) subsequently held that if damage is foreseeable then there is liability even if the way in which it is caused is not foreseeable.

7   Parents may be expected to be responsible for very young children (*Phipps v Rochester Corporation* (1955)).

4.1.7 Liability to persons entering to exercise a calling

1   By s 2(3)(b) a person carrying out a trade 'will appreciate and guard against any special risks ordinarily incident to it . . .'.

2   So tradesmen are expected to avoid the risks associated with their trade (*Roles v Nathan* (1963)).

3   An employer may still be liable for failing to provide safe systems of work (*General Cleaning Contractors v Christmas* (1953)).

4   The fact that the visitor has a skilled calling is not proof *per se* of the occupier's liability (*Salmon v Seafarer Restaurants Ltd* (1983)).

4.1.8 Liability for the acts of independent contractors

Under s 2(4) there is no liability for 'faulty execution of any work or construction, maintenance or repair by an independent contractor ...' providing:

a)   it was reasonable to entrust the work (*AMF International Ltd v Magnet Bowling Ltd* (1968));

b)   a competent contractor was hired (*Ferguson v Welsh* (1987)):

- an occupier may be liable where a contractor is not insured (*Bottomley v Todmorden Cricket Club* (2003));

- so duty also to check that contractor is insured (*Gwilliam v West Hertfordshire Hospitals NHS Trust* (2002));

- but not if there are other accepted means of assessing the independent contractor's competence to carry out the work (*Naylor (t/a Mainstream) v Payling* (2004));

c)   if necessary the occupier checked work was carried out properly – compare *Haseldine v Daw* with *Woodward v Mayor of Hastings* (1945).

4.1.9 Avoiding the duty

1   **Warnings**

a)   By s 2(4) warning relieves liability if 'in all circumstances it was enough to enable the visitor to be reasonably safe'.

b)   What is sufficient warning is a question of fact in each case.

c)   A warning may be insufficient and a barrier be necessary instead (*Rae v Mars (UK) Ltd* (1990)).

d)   Genuine warnings, e.g. 'Danger: steps slippery when wet' must be distinguished from attempts to use the defence of *volenti*, e.g. 'Persons enter at their own risk', and exclusions, e.g. 'No liability accepted for accidents, however caused'.

e)   If the danger is obvious to all the occupier can assume that the visitor will take care (*Staples v West Dorset DC* (1995)).

2 **Exclusion:**

   a) Under s 2(1) exclusions are allowed 'by agreement or otherwise . . .', so can exclude by a term of the contract or by a communicating notice (*Ashdown v Samuel Williams* (1957)).

   b) Restrictions on the principle include:

   - excluding liability to persons entering by a legal right is not possible;

   - nor is excluding liability when bound by a contract to admit strangers to a contract (subcontractors);

   - the Occupier's Liability Act 1957 imposes a minimum standard, so one argument is that excluding liability should not be possible or trespassers will have greater rights than lawful visitors;

   - exclusions may well fail against children;

   - s 1(3) of UCTA applies in business premises.

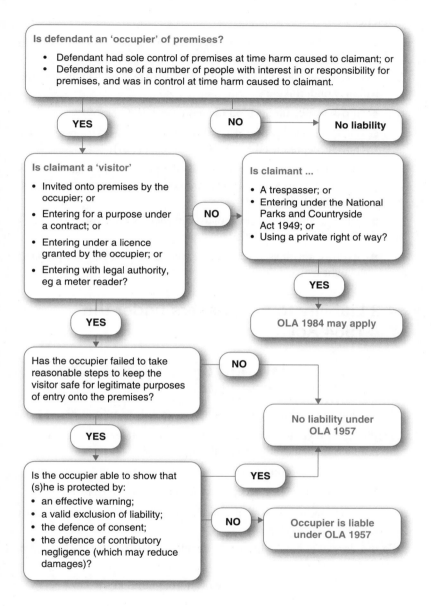

Assessing liability under the Occupier's Liability Act 1957

3   **Defences**

   a) Contributory negligence under the Law Reform (Contributory
       Negligence) Act 1945 when appropriate.

   b) *Volenti non fit injuria* (s 2(5)) allows that there is no liability for risks
       willingly undertaken:

       ● if risk is fully understood (*Simms v Leigh RFC* (1960));

       ● mere knowledge of a risk is insufficient to raise defence – must
         have accepted it (*White v Blackmore* (1972));

       ● But there is no obligation on an occupier to guard against a risk
         that is obvious where the claimant chooses to run that risk (*Evans
         v Kosmar Villa* (2008));

       ● where claimant has no choice then there is no consent (*Burnett v
         British Waterways* (1973));

       ● express warnings of claimant entering at own risk are probably
         caught by UCTA.

▶ 4.2 Liability to trespassers under the 1984 Act

4.2.1 Common law and the duty of common humanity

1   The Occupier's Liability Act 1984 applies mainly to trespassers.

2   Traditionally no real duties were owed at common law except to refrain
    from inflicting damage intentionally or recklessly:

   a) so no man traps (*Bird v Holbreck* (1828));

   b) some deterrents were accepted (*Clayton v Deane* (1817));

   c) and the law was harsh on children (*Addie & Sons (Colliers) Ltd v
       Dumbreck* (1927)).

3   So the duty of common humanity developed (*BR Board v Herrington*
    (1972)).

4   The 1984 Act was passed because of shortcomings in the law.

4.2.2 When the Act applies

1   Like the common duty of humanity, the Act imposes a minimum
    standard.

2   Under s 1(1)(a) the duty to non-visitors is for 'injury . . . due to state of premises or things done or omitted to be done on them' but not a dangerous activity of the claimant (*Siddorn v Patel* (2007)).

3   Therefore it does not cover damage to property.

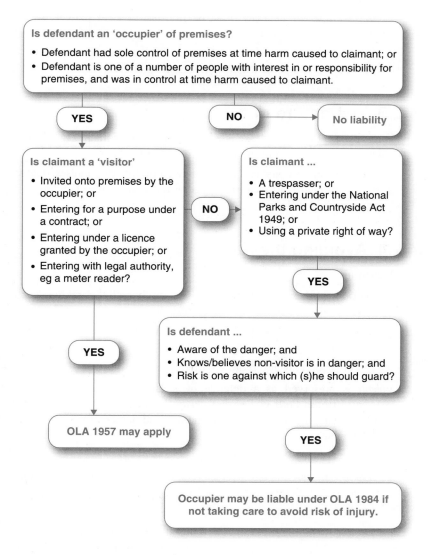

Assessing liability under the Occupier's Liability Act 1984

4   'Occupier' and 'premises' are defined as in the 1957 Act.

5   Under s 1(3) the occupier owes a duty if:

    a)   (s)he is aware of the danger, so no liability if the occupier is unaware of the danger or has no reason to suspect danger (*Rhind v Astbury Water Park* (2004));

    b)   (s)he knows or believes that the non-visitor is in danger, so no liability if the occupier has no reason to suspect presence of trespasser (*Higgs v Foster* (2004));

    c)   the risk is one against which (s)he should guard.

4.2.3 The nature of the duty

1   Duty by s 1(4) is to 'take such care as is reasonable in all the circumstances to prevent injury . . . by reason of danger'.

2   Standard of care is objective and influenced by type of premises, degree of risk, practicality of precautions, age of trespasser, etc. (*Tomlinson v Congleton BC* (2003)).

4.2.4 Avoiding the duty

1   **Warnings**

    a)   Section 1(5) says the duty can be discharged by taking 'such steps as are reasonable in the circumstances'.

    b)   Warnings are enough for adults (*Westwood v Post Office* (1973)).

    c)   But children may also require barriers.

2   *Volenti* is preserved as a defence by s 1(6) (*Scott and Swainger v Associated British Ports & British Railways Board* (2000)). Defence only applies if claimant appreciates both nature and degree of risk (*Ratcliffe v McConnell* (1999)).

3   **Exclusion clauses**

    a)   There is no reference to exclusion clauses, but there is in 1957 Act.

    b)   UCTA cannot apply (it never applied to trespassers in the common law before the Act).

    c)   As it is a minimum standard there should be no exclusions, but public policy may prevent lawful visitors being worse off than trespassers in non-business premises.

Key Cases Checklist

Occupier's Liability Act 1957 (lawful visitors)

***Glasgow Corporation v Taylor* (1922)**
The occupier must expect children to be less cautious than adults, has a higher standard of care, and must avoid 'allurements'

***Phipps v Rochester Corporation* (1955)**
But can expect parents to be responsible for very young children

***Roles v Nathan* (1963)**
The occupier can rely on the skill and knowledge of people entering to exercise a trade or calling to avoid risks associated with the work

***Haseldine v Daw* (1941)**
The occupier is not liable for the work done by independent contractors if it was reasonable to hire them, a competent contractor is chosen and the work is checked if the nature of the work allows

***Staples v West Dorset DC* (1995)**
The occupier may use warning signs to avoid liability but has no need when the danger is obvious to a reasonable man

***White v Blackmore* (1972)**
Consent is only a defence where the visitor freely accepts the actual risk

Definition of 'occupier'

***Wheat v Lacon* (1966)**
A person who is in actual control of the premises when the damage occurs

Occupier's liability

Occupier's Liability Act 1984 (trespassers)

***BR Board v Herrington* (1972)**
Introduced the 'common duty of humanity' through common law

***Tomlinson v Congleton BC* (2003)**
The Act can apply if the danger is due to the state of the premises, and is the sort of risk that the defendant should have guarded against and one that the trespasser in fact chose to run

***Ratcliffe v McConnell* (1999)**
Volenti applies and liability is avoided if the claimant freely accepted the actual risk of harm

4.1.2.1 *Wheat v E Lacon & Co Ltd* [1966] AC 552

Key Facts

A pub manager was allowed to rent out rooms in his private quarters even though he was not the owner. An action arose because a paying guest fell on an unlit staircase, although as it was later identified, a stranger had removed the bulb so there was no liability on either the pub manager or the brewery.

Key Law

The House of Lords (now the Supreme Court) held that an occupier was someone in 'actual control of the premises at the time when the damage was caused'. This meant that both the landlord and the manager could potentially be liable.

4.1.5.3 *Cole v Davis-Gilbert and the Royal British Legion* [2007] All ER (D) 20 (Mar)

Key Facts

The claimant suffered a broken leg after stepping on a hole hidden by grass on a village green. The hole was used for inserting a maypole during annual fêtes. She sued the owner of the village green arguing that, as an occupier, he had a duty to keep visitors safe, and also the British Legion which had erected the maypole and filled the hole after a fête 21 months before.

Key Law

The Court of Appeal held there was no duty on the owner to inspect the green for holes, as even a daily inspection could not guarantee that there would be no holes as the green was used by many people for many different purposes. Even if the British Legion owed a duty to properly fill the hole, the duty could not last indefinitely, and not for 21 months after its last use.

Key Comment

Lord Justice Scott Baker observed in his judgment that 'sometimes accidents are just pure accidents'. This reinforces the principle that the scope of the duty only extends to guarding against foreseeable risks, not unexpected or unlikely risks.

4.1.6.4   *Glasgow Corporation v Taylor* [1922] 1 AC 44   (HL)

Key Facts

A seven-year-old boy was poisoned when he ate berries in an area of botanical gardens which was not fenced off in any way. The subsequent negligence claim was successful.

Key Law

The court held that occupiers must anticipate that children are less cautious than adults and that the berries amounted to an 'allurement'. Occupiers must take greater care of children than they would of adults.

Key Link

S 2(3) Occupier's Liability Act 1957: occupiers 'must be prepared for children to be less careful than adults . . . the premises must be reasonably safe for a child of that age'.

4.1.6.7   *Phipps v Rochester Corporation* [1955] 1 QB 450   (QBD)

Key Facts

A five-year-old boy was injured one evening when he fell in a nine-foot-deep trench dug by the defendants' workers, near which children often played. The claim for compensation failed.

Key Law

The court held that the occupier (the local council) was not in breach of its duty of care as parents of young children have a duty to prevent them from coming into contact with danger.

Key Judgment

Devlin J stated:

'Even if it be prudent, which I do not think it is, for a parent to allow two small children out in this way on an October evening, the parents might at least have satisfied them-selves that the place to which they allowed these little chil-dren to go held no dangers for them . . . defendants are entitled to assumed that parents would behave in this natu-rally prudent way, and are not obliged to take it on them-selves, in effect, to discharge parental duties'.

4.1.6.6   *Jolley v London Borough of Sutton* [2000] 3 All ER 409

HL

Key Facts

Two 14-year-old boys were injured on an abandoned boat on the Council's land. Children regularly played in the boat and it was an obvious danger but the Council had failed to remove it for two years. The boys had been injured while jacking up the boat and trying to repair it. The Court of Appeal had held that there was no liability since the circumstances in which the injuries had occurred was unforeseeable. The House of Lords (now the Supreme Court) reversed this decision.

Key Law

The House of Lords (now the Supreme Court) held that, as long as the boat created a foreseeable risk of injury, then the precise circumstances in which the injury occurred was not material in imposing liability.

Key Link

Hughes v Lord Advocate [1963] AC 387

4.1.7.2   *Roles v Nathan* [1963] 1 WLR 1117

CA

Key Facts

Two chimney sweeps, who were cleaning flues in a factory, died after inhaling fumes. There was no liability because they had been warned by the occupier of the danger of working in the chimney while the furnace was lit but had ignored the advice.

Key Law

The occupier may assume that professional visitors will guard against risks that are within their professional knowledge.

4.1.8

Haseldine v Daw & Sons Ltd [1941] 2 KB 343

Key Facts

The claimant was killed following the negligent repair of a lift on the occupier's premises. The occupier had hired reputable contractors for a highly technical procedure and successfully defended the claim on this basis.

Key Law

There was no liability because the technical nature of the repairs meant that the occupier was not equipped to check the work and could rely on the skill and expertise of the contractor.

Key Link

S 2(4)(b) Occupier's Liability Act 1957

The section identifies that an occupier can avoid liability if it is reasonable for him to entrust the work to an independent contractor, and that he has taken reasonable steps to ensure that a competent contractor has been hired and that the work has been carried out properly.

4.1.8

Woodward v Hastings Corporation [1945] KB 174

Key Facts

A child was injured on school steps that had been left in an icy state when they had been cleared of snow by contractors. The claim for damages against the occupier succeeded.

Key Law

Liability stayed with the occupier since checking on the standard of the work was straightforward because of the type of work.

Key Judgment

In commenting on the occupier's responsibility Lord Denning identified that: *'there is no esoteric quality in the nature of the work which the cleaning of a snow covered step demands'*.

 4.1.8

Gwilliam v West Hertfordshire NHS Trust [2002] 3 WLR 1425   CA

Key Facts

The hospital trust held a fund raising fair on its premises and hired a 'splat wall' from a firm, Club Entertainments, that was also responsible for operating it. (A 'splat wall' is a wall to which a person wearing a Velcro suit will stick after bouncing from a trampoline.) The wall was poorly assembled by the firm and the claimant fell, injuring herself. Club Entertainments was bound under the contract with the trust to have public liability insurance but this had expired four days before the fair so when the claimant sued the trust for damages she was unsuccessful.

Key Law

Lord Woolf CJ and Lord Justice Waller held that, while ensuring that contractors were insured was part of the duty of hiring competent contractors, the duty had not been breached here and the contractors had the duty of ensuring that the claimant was safe to use the 'splat wall'.

Key Link

Bottomley v Todmorden Cricket Club [2003] EWCA Civ 1575.

4.1.9.1

Staples v West Dorset DC (1995) 93 LGR 536   CA

Key Facts

The claimant slipped on wet algae on a high wall at Lyme Regis, injuring himself. His claim against the council was unsuccessful.

Key Law

The court held that the danger should have been obvious and there was therefore no additional duty to warn of the danger.

4.1.9.3

White v Blackmore [1972] 3 All ER 158   CA

Key Facts

The claimant, who was a competitor in a 'jalopy race', was killed while standing in front of a rope barrier to a spectators' enclosure. A car crashed into the barrier and caused it to catapult him into the air. A prominently displayed notice excluded liability. A claim failed on his behalf.

Key Law

The court held that he was an implied licensee, but the defence of *volenti non fit injuria* under s 2(5) of the 1957 Act was inapplicable because the claimant could not have consented to inadequate safety arrangements and was unaware of the full risk. However, the exclusion clause was effective.

Key Link

Evans v Kosmar Villa (2008) 1 All ER 530.

4.2.1.3

British Railways Board v Herrington [1972] AC 877   HL

Key Facts

A six-year-old was badly burned when straying onto an electrified railway line, through vandalised fencing. It was well known that the fences were often broken and that small children played near the line and the railway board regularly repaired it.

Key Law

The House, using the Practice Statement, overruled the previous law in *Addie v Dumbreck* (1929) and established the 'common duty of humanity'. This was a limited duty owed to child trespassers when the occupier knew of the danger, and of the likelihood of the trespass, and had the skill, knowledge and resources to avoid an accident.

Key Problem

This duty would obviously operate in fairly limited circumstances and was not without criticism or difficulties. Because of some of the impracticalities of the rule, the 1984 Act was passed.

Key Link

Robert Addie & Sons (Collieries) Ltd v Dumbreck [1929] All ER 1.

Child trespassers were injured on industrial premises but denied a remedy by the rule that occupiers owed no duty of care to trespassers other than not to deliberately cause them harm.

4.2.3.2   *Tomlinson v Congleton BC* [2003] 1 AC 46

Key Facts

A local authority owned a park in which there was a lake. It posted warning signs prohibiting swimming and diving because the water was dangerous, but the council knew that the signs were generally ignored. The council decided to make the lake inaccessible to the public but delayed start on this work because of lack of funds. The claimant, who was aged 18, dived into the lake, struck his head and suffered a severe spinal injury and was paralysed as a result. His claim under the 1984 Act was rejected by the trial judge but succeeded in the Court of Appeal. The House of Lords (now the Supreme Court) then upheld the appeal by the Council.

Key Law

The Court of Appeal had held that all three aspects of s 1(3) were satisfied as it felt that the gravity of the risk of injury, the frequency with which people were exposed to the risk, and the fact that the lake acted as an allurement all meant that the scheme to make the lake inaccessible should have been completed with greater urgency, although it did acknowledge the contributory negligence of the claimant. The House of Lords (now the Supreme Court), in accepting the council's appeal, based its decision on three reasons: that the danger was not due to the state of the premises, that it was not the sort of risk that the defendant should have to guard against but one that the trespasser in fact chose to run, and that the council would not have breached its duty even in the case of a lawful visitor since the practicality and financial cost of avoiding the danger was beyond what should be expected of a reasonable occupier.

Key Judgment

Lord Hoffmann stated that:

'A duty to protect [against] self-inflicted harm exists only in cases where there is . . . some lack of capacity, such as the inability of children to recognise danger'.

4.2.4.1   *Westwood v The Post Office* [1974] AC 1   HL

Key Facts

The claimant was injured when he took an unauthorised break at work and fell through a defective trapdoor. A sign 'Only the authorised attendant is permitted to enter' on the door of a motor room was held sufficient warning for an intelligent adult.

Key Law

The court held that there was a valid warning under s 1(5) and so there could be no liability.

Key Comment

There is still a question as to whether such warnings would succeed in the case of children who may be unable to read or may not fully understand the warning.

4.2.4.2   *Ratcliffe v McConnell* [1999] 1 WLR 670   CA

Key Facts

A warning notice at the shallow end of a swimming pool read: 'Deep end shallow dive'. The pool was always kept locked after hours and the claimant knew that entry was prohibited at this time. He was a trespasser and so when he was injured while diving into the shallow end his claim failed.

Key Law

The court held that the claimant was fully aware of the risk and that by s 1(6) the defence of *volenti non fit injuria* thus applied. The claimant had freely accepted the risk of harm.

5 Nuisance

Private nuisance – definition and parties

Definition:

continuous, unlawful (unreasonable), indirect interference with a person's enjoyment of land or rights over it.

Potential claimants:
- holder of legal/equitable title;
- landowner not in possession;
- occupier suing for benefit of those affected;
- tenant but not family (*Hunter v Canary Wharf*).

Potential defendants:
- creator of nuisance (*Southport Corporation v Esso Petroleum*);
- person authorising nuisance (*Tetley v Chitty*);
- person who adopts nuisance (*Sedleigh Denfield v O'Callaghan*);
- landlords can be liable to tenants.

Private nuisance – ingredients

Unreasonable use of land
- Locality is important, so what may be a nuisance in a residential area need not be in an industrial area (*Sturges v Bridgman*).
- Nuisance must be continuous (*Bolton v Stone*), although liability possible for an isolated incident arising from a continuous state of affairs (*Spicer v Smee*).
- Locality unimportant if claimant suffers damage (*Halsey v Esso Petroleum*).
- Claimant's over-sensitivity to the nuisance may defeat a claim (*Robinson v Kilvert*), but see *Network Rail v Morris* (2004).
- Malice can make a legitimate activity unreasonable (*Christie v Davey*) and a deliberate act of malice can be nuisance (*Emmet v Hollywood Silver Fox Farm*).
- A person can 'adopt a nuisance naturally present' (*Leakey v National Trust*).

Indirect interference:
- fumes (*Bliss v Hall*);
- vibrations (*Sturges v Bridgman*).

Enjoyment of land
- Pure recreational use not protected (*Bridlington Relay v Yorks Electricity Board*).

NUISANCE

Public nuisance

Something affecting a reasonable class of Her Majesty's citizens materially or in reasonable comfort and convenience of life.

Involves highway and can be:
- obstructions (*Thomas v NUM*);
- projections (*Noble v Harrison*);
- conditions (*Griffiths v Liverpool Corporation*);

but must involve special damage (*Castle v St Augustine Links*).

Private nuisance – defences

- Statutory authority (*Hammersmith Railway v Brand*).
- Planning permission (*Gillingham BC v Medway (Chatham) Dock Ltd*).
- Twenty years prescription (*Sturges v Bridgman*).
- Consent (*Kiddle v City Business Properties*).
- Act of a stranger (*Sedleigh Denfield v O'Callaghan*).
- Public policy (*Miller v Jackson*).

▶ 5.1 Private nuisance

5.1.1 The definition, character and purpose of the tort

1   Defined as 'continuous, unlawful and indirect interference with a person's enjoyment of land or some right over, or in connection with it'.

2   It only applies to an 'indirect' interference – direct is trespass.

3   It concerns prevention more than compensation.

4   It concerns the relationship between neighbours.

5   There are three key elements to neighbourhood:

   ● continuity – involving a recurring state of affairs;

   ● people should be free to use their land as they wish, so long as it does not harm their neighbours;

   ● neighbours are subject to many trivial disputes, so there is a risk of the courts being flooded with claims.

6   Only 'unreasonable' interference is a nuisance:

   ● so there is no protection against interference classed as reasonable;

   ● but if classed as unreasonable it is irrelevant whether it was reasonable for the defendant to engage in such behaviour.

7   The test is: what conduct is sufficient to justify legal intervention?

8   The court must strike a balance between conflicting interests and this now involves balancing the rights of the individual against that of the wider community even where violation of human rights (Article 8) is involved (*Hatton v UK* (2003); *Dennis v MoD* (2003); *Marcic v Thames Water Utilities Limited* (2003)).

5.1.2 Who can sue in nuisance

1   Nuisance usually affects occupiers, so traditionally a claimant is the holder of a legal or equitable title – but might include:

   a) a landowner out of possession;

   b) an occupier suing for the benefit of others affected;

   c) a tenant, but not his/her family:

      ● limiting a landlord's responsibility for the state of property (*Habinteng Housing Association v James* (1994));

- so Law Commission Report No 238, 1996 recommends updating the implied covenant of fitness for human habitation in the Landlord and Tenant Act 1985;

- at one point an occupier's family harassed by offensive telephone calls was included (*Khorasandjian v Bush* (1993)), but overruled by *Hunter v Canary Wharf* (1997).

5.1.3 The ingredients of the tort

There are three key elements:

a) unlawful use of land;

b) indirect interference with land;

c) indirect interference with the claimant's use or enjoyment of his/her land.

The unlawful (unreasonable) use of land

1   Interference alone is insufficient – it must be unlawful.

2   Unlawful means unreasonable so, in balancing competing interests, the question is whether in all of the circumstances it is reasonable for the claimant to suffer the particular interference (*Barr v Biffa Waste Services Ltd* (2012)).

3   In assessing the defendant's conduct the court is analysing fault (so there must be foreseeable damage), but in a more flexible way than with negligence – so a defendant might be excused liability for not having the resources to avoid the nuisance (*Solloway v Hampshire County Council* (1981)), but see *Hurst & another v Hampshire County Council* (1997), CA.

4   Many key factors are used to assess what is unreasonable.

   a) The locality:

   - The activity may be a nuisance in a residential area but not in an industrial one (*Sturges v Bridgman* (1879), where vibrations were a nuisance to a doctor's waiting room).

   - So it can include a common facility in the wrong area (*Laws v Florinplace* (1981)).

   - The customary use of the area may be a factor (*Sturges v Bridgman* (1879)).

   - Locality may be irrelevant if damage is suffered (*St Helens Smelting Co v Tippin* (1865)).

   - Courts may in any case try to reach a compromise (*Dunton v Dover DC* (1977)).

b) The duration of the interference:

- The interference must be continuous (*Bolton v Stone* (1950)).

- An isolated incident can be a nuisance if arising from a continuous state of affairs (*Spicer v Smee* (1946)).

- The cause could be over a long time span (*Cambridge Water Co v Eastern Counties Leather plc* (1994)).

- But very short time spans have been accepted (*Crown River Cruises Ltd v Kimbolton Fireworks Ltd* (1996)).

c) The seriousness of the interference:

- if the claim is for interference with use or enjoyment, the test is whether it is 'an inconvenience materially interfering with the ordinary comfort of human existence, not merely according to elegant or dainty modes and habits of living, but according to plain, sober and simple notions . . .' (Knight-Bruce VC in *Walter v Selfe* (1851)).

- Where the claimant suffers physical damage the use of land is unreasonable (*Halsey v Esso Petroleum* (1961), where smuts from a refinery affecting the claimant's car were a nuisance even though in an industrial area).

- This does not apply if protected by public policy (*Miller v Jackson* (1977)).

- It does not apply if the use of land is an absolute right (*Stephens v Anglian Water Authority* (1987)).

- It does not apply if the activity is seen to be to the public benefit (*Ellison v Ministry of Defence* (1997)).

d) The sensitivity of the claimant – if a claimant's own use of land is hypersensitive to the interference he may fail (*Robinson v Kilvert* (1889)). But the Court of Appeal in *Network Rail Infrastructure Ltd v CJ Morris* (2004) has now suggested that there may now be no need to apply such a test.

e) Malice and the conduct of the defendant:

- Malice does play a part in nuisance.

- A deliberately harmful act will normally be a nuisance (*Hollywood Silver Fox Farm v Emmet* (1936)).

- An act of revenge in response to unreasonable behaviour will normally be a nuisance (*Christie v Davey* (1893)).

- Sometimes merely selfish or unthinking behaviour is sufficient (*Tutton v Walter* (1986)).

- Where the defendant does not cause the problem, but, knowing about it, allows it to continue, is sufficient to be considered nuisance (*Leakey v National Trust* (1980)).

f) The state of the defendant's land:

- A defendant cannot ignore things that may cause interference (*Goldman v Hargrave* (1967) and *Leakey v National Trust* (1980)).

- A defendant has a duty to prevent the spread of things that may cause nuisance (*Bradburn v Lindsay* (1983)).

- But only to do what is reasonable in relation to reasonably foreseeable hazards (*Holbeck Hall Hotel Ltd v Scarborough BC* (2000)).

Indirect interference with land

1   Nuisance has included:

- fumes drifting over land (*Bliss v Hall* (1838));

- the loud noise of guns used to frighten breeding silver foxes (*Hollywood Silver Fox Farm v Emmet* (1936));

- vibrations from machinery (*Sturges v Bridgman* (1879));

- hot air rising to an upstairs flat (*Robinson v Kilvert* (1889));

- pollution of rivers (*Pride of Derby Angling Association v British Celanese* (1953)).

The use and enjoyment of land

1   Judges have limited the extent of 'enjoyment' in nuisance.

2   So there is no right to protect pure pleasure or aesthetics (*Bridlington Relay v Yorkshire Electricity Board* (1965)) and, in the USA, *Amphitheatres Inc. v Portland Meadows* (1948).

3   Confirmed in *Hunter and another v Canary Wharf Ltd* (1997).

4   A functional use supporting pure entertainment or leisure can create liability (*Crown River Cruises Ltd v Kimbolton Fireworks Ltd* (1996)).

5   So lowering the tone of the neighbourhood is not usually actionable, but see *Laws v Florinplace* (1981).

6   If personal injury is involved the claimant must have a proprietary interest (*Malone v Laskey* (1907)), and see also *Hunter v Canary Wharf* (1997).

5.1.4 Who can be sued in nuisance

1   The creator of the nuisance, who does not have to be the occupier (*Southport Corporation v Esso Petroleum* (1953)).

2   A person authorising the nuisance. Compare *Tetley v Chitty* (1986) with *Smith v Scott* (1973).

3   A person who adopts the nuisance:
    - either of a stranger or trespasser (*Sedleigh Denfield v O'Callaghan* (1940));
    - or of a previous occupier (*Anthony and others v The Coal Authority* (2005));
    - or of a natural occurrence (*Leakey v National Trust* (1980)).

4   Landlords can be liable to tenants:
    a) for a negligent failure to repair under the usual covenants; or
    b) under the Defective Premises Act 1972; or
    c) from want of repair under the rule in *Wringe v Cohen* (1940).

5.1.5 Defences

1   Statutory authority:
    - this is the most effective modern defence, since so many activities are licensed (*Hammersmith Railway v Brand* (1869) and *Allen v Gulf Oil Refining Ltd* (1980));
    - not available if a discretion is improperly exercised (*Metropolitan Asylum District Hospital v Hill* (1881));
    - where statute provides another remedy a nuisance action is not available (*Marcic v Thames Water Utilities Limited* (2003));
    - not available for negligence (*Home Office v Dorset Yacht Co* (1970));
    - unlike Parliament, planning authorities cannot authorise a nuisance except where they have statutory authority to do so. Compare *Wheeler v Saunders* (1995) and *Gillingham BC v Medway (Chatham) Dock Ltd* (1993) and see also *Watson v Croft Promosport* (2009) – the issue is whether the character of the land has changed (*Coventry v Lawrence* (2012)).

2   Prescription: this is a defence unique to nuisance – 20 years without complaint and the right to complain lapses (*Sturges v Bridgman* (1879)).

3   Act of a stranger or trespasser, but not if adopted (*Sedleigh Denfield v O'Callaghan* (1940)).

4   Consent: e.g. tall building (*Kiddle v City Business Properties Ltd* (1942)).

5   The common enemy rule: each landowner can protect against a common enemy e.g. flooding (*Arscott v Coal Authority* (2004)).

6   Public policy:

● both sides should be considered (*Miller v Jackson* (1977));

● usefulness is insufficient excuse (*Adams v Ursell* (1913)).

7   Coming fresh to the nuisance is no defence (*Bliss v Hall* (1838)).

5.1.6 Remedies

1   Damages.

a) Test of remoteness is the same as in *The Wagon Mound (No. 2)* (1961) – foreseeability.

b) Claimant can recover for physical loss, depreciation in value, and business loss.

2   Injunction:

a) an order to prevent the nuisance from continuing (*Kennaway v Thompson* (1981));

b) it can be coupled with damages.

3   Abatement of the nuisance:

a) can involve entering the defendant's property;

b) but can lead to a counter injunction (*Stanton v Jones* (1995));

c) and is not always possible (*Burton v Winters* (1993)).

5.1.7 Relationship with other torts

1   Relationship with trespass to land:

a) the difference is between direct and indirect interference.

b) repeated trespasses can be nuisances (*Bernstein v Skyways* (1940)).

2   Relationship with *Rylands v Fletcher* (1868):

a) one involves non-natural use of land, the other involves unreasonable use (but the distinction is now blurred – see *Arscott*);

b) before *Cambridge Water v Eastern Counties Leather* (1994) there was no requirement for damage to be foreseeable in R v F;

    c) nuisance can be committed by a non-occupier, unlike *R v F*;

    d) *R v F*, at least in theory, involves strict liability;

    e) *R v F* covers isolated escapes, nuisance is a continuous state of affairs.

3   Relationship with negligence:

    a) negligence requires the existence of a legal duty;

    b) no claim in negligence for interfering with enjoyment;

    c) nuisance is about creating a balance, but the merest damage in negligence can justify a claim.

▶ 5.2 Public nuisance

5.2.1 Definition

1   Unlike private nuisance it extends beyond immediate neighbours.

2   It has been defined as 'something which affects a reasonable class of Her Majesty's citizens materially or in the reasonable comfort and convenience of life'.

5.2.2 Ingredients of the tort

1   A substantial class of people must be involved before an action is possible (*Attorney General v PYA Quarries* (1957)).

2   A claimant must have suffered a special loss over and above other subjects (*Tate & Lyle Industries v GLC* (1983)).

3   Public nuisances can also be crimes by statute.

4   Public nuisance often involves the highway:

    a) obstructions to the highway, e.g. pickets (*Thomas v NUM* (1985));

    b) projections on the highway, e.g. overhanging tree branches providing special damage is caused (*Noble v Harrison* (1926));

    c) condition of the highway; council may have a duty to maintain it (*Griffiths v Liverpool Corporation* (1967)) subject to limitations, e.g. no general common law duty to salt roads (*Sandhar v Department of Transport* (2004)).

5   Special damage must occur which can be:

a) personal injuries (*Castle v St Augustine Links* (1922) and *Corby Group Litigation v Corby BC* (2008) – so it is clearly different from private nuisance in this respect);

b) damage to goods (*Halsey v Esso Petroleum* (1961));

c) financial loss (*Rose v Miles* (1815));

d) loss of trade connection.

▶ 5.3 Statutory nuisance

1   Parliament has declared certain activities nuisance by statute.

2   They are usually part of public health reform and so prejudicial to health more than prejudicial to land, e.g. Clean Air Act 1956.

3   They provide a means of stopping the nuisance and save the victim the cost and inconvenience of civil action.

4   They are quasi-criminal and enforced by local authorities through the use of abatement notices.

5   Offenders failing to comply are then tried in the Magistrates' Court.

Key Cases Checklist

Ingredients of the tort

***St Helens Smelting v Tipping* (1865)**
Locality is important in determining whether there has been unreasonable use of land when enjoyment is interfered with but not when there is damage done

***Robinson v Kilvert* (1889)**
No nuisance where the claimant is over sensitive

***Christie v Davey* (1893)**
Malice can contribute to a nuisance

***Crown River Cruises Ltd v Kimbolton Fireworks Ltd* (1996)**
Nuisance usually requires a continuous act

Claimants

***Hunter v Canary Wharf* (1997)**
A nuisance action can only be brought by a person with proprietary rights in the land affected

Private nuisance

Defendants

***Leakey v The National Trust* (1980)**
Can be a person who adopts the nuisance

***Marcic v Thames Water* (2003)**
Not a public body where this conflicts with a statutory duty

Defences

***Sturges v Bridgman* (1879)**
20-year prescription starts when the nuisance starts

***Sedleigh Denfield v O'Callaghan* (1940)**
No liability for the act of a stranger unless aware of it and failing to do anything to remedy it

***Allen v Gulf Oil* (1980)**
Statute often authorises a nuisance

***Wheeler v Saunders* (1996)**
Planning permission is only a defence if it changes the character of the area

Public nuisance

Public nuisance

***Attorney-General v PYA Quarries Ltd* (1957)**
Public nuisance is one which affects the reasonable comfort and convenience of a class of Her Majesty's subjects

***Castle v St Augustine Links* (1922)**
But the claimant must suffer special damage

5.1.2.1

Hunter and another v Canary Wharf [1997] 2 All ER 426

 HL

Key Facts

Families of tenants made unsuccessful claims in private nuisance for dust and interference with television reception caused by the erection of a very large building near to their homes.

Key Law

The court held that there was an interference with recreational facilities only, not with the health or physical well-being of the claimants. The House also held that the claimants could not in any case bring an action as they had no proprietary interest in the land.

Key Judgment

Lord Goff explained:

'an action in nuisance will only lie at the suit of a person who has a right to the land affected'.

5.1.3.4

St Helens Smelting Co v Tipping (1865) 11 HL Cas 642

 HL

Key Facts

The claimant owned property near to the defendant's copper smelting works and claimed in nuisance for damage to hedges and trees caused by the toxic smuts and interference with his quiet enjoyment of his land. He succeeded.

Key Law

The court held that the nuisance was actionable because, even though it involved an industrial area, damage had been caused.

Key Judgment

Lord Westbury LC stated:

'With regard to . . . personal inconvenience and interference with one's enjoyment . . . whether that may . . . be . . . a

nuisance, must undoubtedly depend . . . on . . . the place where the thing complained of actually occurs . . . when an occupation is carried on . . . and the result . . . is a material injury to property, then there unquestionably arises a very different consideration'.

5.1.3.4 *Laws v Florinplace Ltd* [1981] 1 All ER 659

Key Facts

Ten residents in a suburban area, enjoying what was described as an 'attractive village atmosphere', successfully sought an injunction against a sex shop and video club that had opened in their area.

Key Law

The court held that even if the defendant changed the name of the business and its name and its displays, it was still arguable that the repugnance caused to the residents by their awareness of the business could be an interference amounting to a nuisance.

5.1.3.4 *Robinson v Kilvert* (1889) 41 ChD 88

Key Facts

The claimant stored paper in premises where the defendant manufactured cardboard boxes in the basement. The heat necessary for the manufacture damaged the brown paper and the claimant unsuccessfully sought damages in nuisance.

Key Law

The court held that the heating was not a nuisance since it was not of a sort that would cause damage in the case of the ordinary uses of the premises. Damage was only caused because the brown paper was very susceptible to variations in temperature.

5.1.3.4

Christie v Davey [1893] 1 Ch 316

Ch
Div

Key Facts

The claimant gave music lessons and the defendant, his next-door neighbour, became annoyed by the constant noise from the music lessons next door. The defendant reacted by banging on the walls, beating trays and shouting.

Key Law

The court held that the noises were made maliciously and deliberately to annoy the claimant. They were an unreasonable use of land and the claimant was granted an injunction.

Key Link

Hollywood Silver Fox Farm Ltd v Emmet [1936] 2 KB 468.

5.1.3.4

Halsey v Esso Petroleum Co Ltd [1961] 2 All ER 145

QBD

Key Facts

The claimant won a claim for nuisance from the noise from the defendant's depot, the nauseating smell and also in relation to the damage which acid smuts caused to her washing and to her car.

Key Law

The court held that they were all private nuisance except for the damage to the car, which was a public nuisance. The defendant's use of land was unreasonable.

Key Judgment

Veale J stated:

'the law must strike a fair and reasonable balance between the rights of the plaintiff on the one hand to the undisturbed enjoyment of his property, and the right of the defendant on the other hand to use his own property for his own lawful enjoyment'.

5.1.3.4

Crown River Cruises Ltd v Kimbolton Fireworks Ltd [1996] 2 Lloyd's Rep 533

QBD

Key Facts

A barge was set alight by flammable debris resulting from a firework display which lasted only 20 minutes. The owners claimed successfully in negligence and it was also accepted that the action in private nuisance was also possible.

Key Law

The court held that an action for nuisance was possible because the barge owners had a licence to occupy the site.

Key Problem

The very limited duration of the display seems to run contrary to the principle of continuity required for nuisance, e.g. *Bolton v Stone* (1951).

5.1.3.4

Holbeck Hall Hotel Ltd v Scarborough BC [2000] 2 All ER 705

CA

Key Facts

The claimant's hotel stood near to a cliff by the sea. The defendant, the local council, owned the land between the hotel and the cliff top. After a long period of steady erosion a major landslip undermined the foundations of the hotel so that it had to be demolished. On appeal, the council was held not to be liable in nuisance.

Key Law

The Court of Appeal held that, since the council was unaware of the danger of the landslip, which could not merely be presumed from the previous erosion, it neither adopted nor created the nuisance.

Key Judgment

Stuart-Smith LJ explained that:

'It is the existence of the defect coupled with the danger that constitutes the nuisance; it is knowledge . . . of the nuisance that involves liability for continuing it when it could have been abated'.

5.1.4.3   *Leakey v The National Trust* **[1980] QB 485**   CA

Key Facts
....
Following heavy rain, a large natural mound of land on a hillside, known as the Burrow Mump, slipped and damaged the claimant's cottage. The defendant was held liable in nuisance.

Key Law
....
The court found the defendant liable because it was aware of the possibility of the landslide happening and did nothing to prevent it.

Key Comment
....
The case shows what a close link there is between nuisance and negligence. The type of duty depends on the facts of the case.

5.1.4.2   *Tetley and others v Chitty and others* **[1986] 1 All ER 663**   QBD

Key Facts
....
The defendant council rented land to another party on which to run go-kart racing. Local residents succeeded in gaining an injunction.

Key Law
....
The court held the council liable because it was already aware of the excessive noise that the activity would cause and had accepted responsibility for the nuisance by granting the lease.

5.1.5.1 *Marcic v Thames Water plc* [2003] UKHL 66; [2003] 3 WLR 1603

HL

Key Facts

Because of the substantial rise in the number of houses in an area the sewers, which had not been modified, became inadequate to cope with the amount of sewage, even though the defendant maintained them properly. The sewers flooded periodically and the claimant, rather than using statutory enforcement measures, installed a flood defence and claimed for damages in nuisance and for interference in family life in breach of Art 8 of the European Convention on Human Rights. Both claims failed.

Key Law

The House held that there was no actionable nuisance since the common law would be unable to impose obligations on a water authority which were inconsistent with a statutory scheme and in this instance the right of complaint was to the Director-General of Water Services. There was no breach of Human Rights legislation since Art 8 of the European Convention does not guarantee absolute protection of residential properties but must balance out the rights of individuals and the rights of the public generally.

5.1.5.2 *Sturges v Bridgman* (1879) 11 ChD 852

CA

Key Facts

Eight years after he moved in, a doctor built a consulting room at the bottom of his garden. Vibrations from the defendant's machinery in the neighbouring property disturbed the claimant and prevented him from listening to his patients' chests etc. His claim succeeded.

Key Law

The court held that the defence could not apply because the twenty-year period for prescription would only begin when the nuisance commenced, here when the consulting room was built.

5.1.5.6   *Miller v Jackson* [1977] QB 966   CA

Key Facts

A new housing estate was built by a cricket club that had been used for 70 years. Balls constantly came into the claimant's garden during matches and he succeeded in claims in both nuisance and negligence, but was denied the injunction that he sought.

Key Law

The court held that while there was a plain interference with the claimant's enjoyment of his land it recognised that the remedy could not be granted because it would interfere with a public utility of importance to the community.

Key Judgment

Lord Denning dissented on the decision because, as he said, playing cricket 'is a most reasonable use of land'. On refusing to grant the injunction, he said *'I recognise that the cricket club are under a duty to use all reasonable care . . . but I do not think the cricket club can be expected to give up the game of cricket altogether'.*

5.1.5.3   *Sedleigh Denfield v O'Callaghan* [1940] AC 880   HL

Key Facts

A workman had placed grating for trapping leaves too close to a culvert pipe on the defendant's land. The defendant knew about it.

After a severe storm the pipe became blocked, and his neighbour's land was flooded. His neighbour succeeded in his nuisance claim.

Key Law

On appeal, the court held that the defendant was liable because he was aware of the nuisance but failed to do anything to remedy it and so had adopted the nuisance. The defence of act of a stranger was not applicable in the circumstances.

Key Judgment

Lord Wright said:

'The responsibility which attaches to the occupier because he has possession and control of the property cannot logically be limited to the mere creation of the nuisance. It should extend to ... if, with knowledge, he leaves the nuisance on his land'.

5.1.5.1   *Allen v Gulf Oil Refining Ltd* [1980] QB 156

Key Facts

The claimants sued for nuisance caused by a refinery. An Act authorised the defendants to purchase land for the construction of a refinery but made no mention of its use. The claim failed.

Key Law

The court held that the statutory authorisation for construction of a refinery necessarily implied its use as a refinery. The defence of statutory authority succeeded.

5.1.5.1   *Wheeler v J J Saunders Ltd* [1996] Ch 19

Key Facts

The defendant, a pig farmer, was granted planning permission to expand by building two more pig houses each containing 400 pigs. One pig house was only 11 metres from the cottage of a neighbour, who then successfully claimed in nuisance.

Key Law

The defendant's appeal on the defence of planning permission failed because the defence was said to operate only in respect of those nuisances that Parliament had authorised.

Key Judgment

Peter Gibson LJ explained that planning permission can only be a defence where as the result of the permitted activity *'there will be a change in the character of the neighbourhood'*.

Key Link

Gillingham Borough Council v Medway (Chatham) Dock Co [1993] QB 343.

See also *Watson v Croft Promosport* [2009] EWCA 15, where planning permission to convert a disused aerodrome into a motor racing circuit did change the character of the area and so was reasonable, but the Court of Appeal limited the use of the race track to 40 days annually.

5.1.6.2   *Kennaway v Thompson* [1981] 3 WLR 311   CA

Key Facts

The claimant built a house near to a lake where speedboat racing had taken place for many years. He succeeded in his claim for nuisance created by the excessive noise.

Key Law

At first instance the claimant was awarded £1,600 in damages. On appeal he was granted an injunction restraining the use of the lake for speedboat races to certain days with certain noise limits.

5.2.2.1   *Attorney-General v PYA Quarries Ltd* [1957] 2 QB 169   CA

Key Facts

Houses neighbouring a quarry suffered from dust and vibrations.

The Attorney-General successfully sought injunctions on behalf of the County Council and the District Council.

Key Law

The court rejected the defendant's argument that the nuisance was not sufficiently widespread to amount to a public nuisance.

Key Judgment

Romer LJ stated:

'any nuisance is "public" which materially affects the reasonable comfort and convenience of life of a class of Her Majesty's subjects'.

5.2.2.5

Castle v St Augustine Links (1922) 38 TLR 615

QBD

Key Facts

A taxi driver was hit in the eye by a sliced golf ball. The golf links straddled the highway so the risk of harm was great and it was shown that golf balls regularly came off the course and onto the road. The claim in public nuisance succeeded.

Key Law

The court accepted that the regularity of the occurrence was a significant interference with the public's use of the highway and the claimant had suffered special damage so the nuisance was proved.

6 Strict liability

Ingredients of rule

A bringing on to land and accumulating:
- no liability for things naturally present (*Giles v Walker*);
- or for natural accumulations (*Ellison v Ministry of Defence*);
- escape need not be by thing brought on to land (*Miles v Forest Rock Granite*).

A thing likely to do mischief it it escapes:
- escape need not be probable (*Musgrove v Pandelis*);
- nor the thing dangerous in itself (*Shiffman v Order of St John*);
- but escape causes foreseeable harm (*Hale v Jennings*).

A non-natural use of land:
- domestic use is usually natural (*Sokachi v Sas*);
- unusual volume or quantity suggests non-natural use – *The Charing Cross case*.

Thing escapes and causes damage:
- either from land in defendant's control to that not in his/her control (*Read v Lyons*);
- or from circumstances within defendant's control to ones not in his/her control (*British Celanese v A H Hunt*);
- damage is foreseeable (*Cambridge Water v Eastern Counties Leather*).

Parties to an action

Potential defendants.
- If *Read v Lyons* is followed will be owners or occupiers of land thing escaped from.
- If *British Celanese v Hunt* is taken will be people in control of circumstances escape happened from.

Potential claimants.
- If *Read v Lyons* is followed then owners/occupiers of land thing escapes to.
- If British Celanese then claimant does not need a proprietary interest in land.
- See also *Crown River Cruises v Kimbolton Fireworks*.

RYLANDS v FLETCHER

Problems with rule:
- Number of defences.
- Requirement of foreseeability.
- *Read v Lyons*.
- Non-natural use.
- No real strict liability for dangers.

Defences
- Consent (*Peters v Prince of Wales Theatre*).
- Common benefit (*Dunne v North West Gas Board*).
- Act of stranger (*Perry v Dendricks Transport*).
- Act of God (*Nicholls v Marsland*).
- Statutory authority (*Green v Chelsea Waterworks*).
- Contributory negligence (*Eastern Telegraph v Capetown Tramways*).

▶ 6.1 The rule in *Rylands v Fletcher*

6.1.1 The definition, purpose, and character of the rule

1   First defined by Blackburn J in Court of Exchequer Chamber in the case: 'the person who, for purposes of his own, brings on his land, and collects and keeps there anything likely to do mischief if it escapes, must keep it in at his peril, and, if he does not do so, he is *prima facie* answerable for all the damage which is the natural consequence of its escape.'

2   Lord Cairns in HL added requirement of non-natural use of land.

3   The tort is said to be one of strict liability, but it is possible to argue it as a type of nuisance used to cover isolated escapes.

● There are many defences available, so it is strict liability only in the sense that the claimant need not prove fault.

● If the use of land is natural an action will fail.

● It was previously distinguished from nuisance which required foreseeability, where *Rylands v Fletcher* did not.

● Now *Cambridge Water Co v Eastern Counties Leather plc* (1994) suggests that foreseeability is required. This is confirmed in *Transco plc v Stockport Metropolitan Borough Council* (2003).

● Judges have limited strict liability by restricting the use of the rule – to escapes from land only (*Read v Lyons* (1947)) and to 'special use of land bringing with it increased danger to others' (*Rickards v Lothian* (1913)), and see also *Cambridge Water* and *Crown River Cruises v Kimbolton* (1996).

● Claimants have recovered even though not occupiers of land, so it is not a straightforward extension of nuisance.

6.1.2 The ingredients of the rule

1   There are four key ingredients to the tort:

   a) a bringing on to land;

   b) of a thing which is likely to do mischief if it escapes;

   c) which amounts to a non-natural use of land;

   d) the thing actually escapes, causing damage.

A bringing on to land

1   If thing is naturally present on land there can be no liability (*Giles v Walker* (1890) and *Pontardawe RDC v Moore-Gwyn* (1929)).

2   There is no liability where the thing naturally accumulates (*Ellison v Ministry of Defence* (1997)).

3   But nuisance may be possible (*Leakey v National Trust* (1980)).

4   The person bringing the thing on to the land need not be the owner or occupier of the land (*Charing Cross Electricity Supply Co v Hydraulic Power Co* (1914) (*The Charing Cross Case*)).

5   The defendant must have had a purpose for bringing the thing on to the land, but it need not have been for his/her benefit. Compare *Smeaton v Ilford Corporation* (1954) with *Dunne v North Western Gas Board* (1964).

6   The escape can be of something other than the thing brought on to the land (*Miles v Forest Rock Granite Co* (1917), where explosives used in blasting caused rock to escape).

A thing likely to do mischief if it escapes

1   Escape need not be probable (*Musgrove v Pandelis* (1919)).

2   The thing need not be dangerous in itself (*Shiffman v Order of St John* (1936), where the thing was a flag pole).

3   It must be a source of foreseeable harm if it does escape (*Hale v Jennings Bros.* (1938), where a 'chairoplane' car flew off the ride in a fairground).

4   Even people have been held as dangerous (*AG v Corke* (1933)).

A non-natural use of land

1   This was added by Lord Cairns in HL: 'if the defendants, not stopping at the natural use of their close, had desired to use it for any purpose I may term a non-natural use . . . and in consequence . . . the water came to escape . . . it appears to me that which the defendants were doing they were doing at their own peril'.

2   It was developed and explained by Lord Moulton in *Rickards v Lothian* (1913): 'not every use of land brings into play this principle. It must be some special use bringing with it increased danger to others, and not merely by the ordinary use of land or such as is proper for the general benefit of the community'.

3   Non-natural use is a fluid concept inevitably changing with technological developments.

4   It is 'extraordinary' use rather than 'artificial' use.

5   Domestic use is usually natural, e.g. *Sokachi v Sas* (1947) – fire; *Collingwood v Home & Colonial Stores Ltd* (1936) – electricity; *Rickards v Lothian* (1913) – water pipes.

6   Sometimes also applies to commercial premises (*Peters v Prince of Wales Theatre (Birmingham) Ltd* (1943)).

7   Unusual volume or quantity indicates non-natural use (*The Charing Cross* case).

8   Technical developments may be non-natural while at an innovative stage (*Musgrove v Pandelis* (1919)).

9   Context may also make them non-natural (*Mason v Levy Autoparts of England* (1967)).

10   If a public benefit is gained from the activity it may make it a natural use (*British Celanese v A H Hunt* (1969)).

11   Things connected with war may be a natural use even in peace time (*Ellison v Ministry of Defence* (1997)).

12   Some activities will be seen as a non-natural use despite being of public benefit, e.g. use of chemicals (*Cambridge Water* (1994)).

The thing must actually escape and cause damage

1   Blackburn's original rule was not rigidly restricted to neighbouring landowners (he probably intended a general liability for dangerous activities).

2   The rule was limited by Lord MacMillan in *Read v Lyons* (1947): 'the rule derives from a conception of mutual duties of adjoining landowners'.

3   It was also limited by Lord Simons in *Read v Lyons* by defining escape as 'from a place where the defendant has occupation or control over land to a place which is outside of his occupation or control'.

4   However, escape is also defined as 'from a set of circumstances over which the defendant has control to a set where he does not' by Lawton J in *British Celanese v A H Hunt* (1969).

6.1.3 The parties to an action

1   A defendant in an action will be either:

● according to Lord Simon in *Read v Lyons* an owner or an occupier who satisfies the four requirements; or according to Lawton J in *British Celanese* a person where the escape is from a set of circumstances under his control to one which is not. And see *Hale v Jennings Bros* (1948).

2   Possible claimants also vary according to the judge:

- Blackburn J suggested there is no need for the claimant to have a proprietary interest.

- Lord MacMillan in *Read v Lyons* said there is.

- Lawton J in *British Celanese* was not prepared to limit the rule that much, so that a claimant could even be a party who has suffered personal injury.

- Recently a claim has succeeded where the escape was from the defendant's control of the highway on to the claimant's land (*Rigby v Chief Constable of Northamptonshire* (1985)).

- Another successful claim is an escape from accumulations in a vessel escaping on to other vessels (*Crown River Cruises Ltd v Kimbolton Fireworks Ltd* (1996)).

6.1.4 Recoverable loss and remoteness of damage

1   According to Lord MacMillan, recovery is only possible for damage to land occupied by the claimant or his chattels on that land.

2   Lawton J suggests claims for personal injury are also possible (*Hale v Jennings* (1938)).

3   A successful action for economic loss is less likely (*Weller v Foot and Mouth Disease Research Unit* (1966)).

4   The tort is not actionable *per se*, so damage must be proved.

5   So there is no liability for mere interference with enjoyment of land as there is in nuisance (*Eastern & SA Telegraph Co v Cape Town Tramways Co* (1902)).

6   By *Cambridge Water v Eastern Counties Leather plc* (1994) the defendant must know or ought reasonably to foresee that damage of the relevant kind might be a consequence of the escape (this is remoteness as in negligence and seems inconsistent with strict liability). And the point is affirmed in *Transco plc v Stockport MBC* (2003).

6.1.5 Possible defences

1   **Consent:** e.g. occupiers of tall buildings (*Peters v Prince of Wales Theatre* (1943)).

2   **Common benefit:** no liability if source of danger is kept for both defendant and claimant (*Dunne v North West Gas Board* (1964)).

3   **Act of a stranger:** if stranger over whom defendant exercises no control causes the escape then no liability (*Perry v Kendricks Transport Ltd* (1956)), but see *Mehta v Union of India* (1987).

4   **Act of God:** will only succeed for conditions of nature 'which no human foresight can provide against', e.g. extreme weather conditions (*Nichols v Marsland* (1876)).

5   **Statutory authority:** if the escape is a direct result of carrying out the duty (*Green v Chelsea Waterworks Co* (1894)).

6   **Contributory negligence:** damages reduced if claimant is partly at fault for the escape (*Eastern & SA Telegraph Co v Cape Town Tramways* (1902)).

6.1.6 Problems with the rule

1   Often seen merely as an extension of nuisance, so there is no general strict liability for hazardous activities.

2   The principle has been constantly limited in scope:

   ● requirement of non-natural use;

   ● *Read v Lyons* reasoning on escape;

   ● the breadth of defences available;

   ● the requirement of foreseeability in *Cambridge Water*;

   ● reluctance to expand the principle in *Crown River Cruises*.

3   Has doubtful modern relevance:

   ● most instances could be covered by negligence;

   ● rarely used now, and rarely successfully;

   ● since *Cambridge Water* the Australian High Court has abolished the rule saying it was effectively swallowed up by negligence (*Burnie Port Authority v General Jones Pty Land* (1994));

   ● many areas concerning hazards are now covered by statute (*Blue Circle Industries plc v Ministry of Defence* (1998)).

Origins and common law actions

Liability began in Middle Ages:
- scienter – keeping a dangerous animal that escapes and causes harm;
- cattle trespass – damage caused by escaping livestock.

Liability still under many torts:
- trespass to goods (*Manton v Brocklebank*);
- private nuisance (*Rapier v London Tramways*);
- *Rylands v Fletcher* (*Brady v Warren*);
- negligence (*Birch v Mills*);
- very appropriate if Act ineffective (*Draper v Hodder*).

ANIMALS

Animals Act (defences)

- S 5(1) – damage due entirely to fault of victim (*Sylvester v Chapman*).
- S 5(2) – victim voluntarily accepted risk (*Cummings v Grainger*).
- S 5(3) – animal either not kept for protection or, if so, then reasonable to do so (*Cummings v Grainger*).
- S 10 – contributory negligence.

Animals Act 1971 – liability

Dangerous species:
- defined in s 6(2) – animal not commonly domesticated in UK and with characteristics that, unless restricted, likely to cause severe damage or any damage caused likely to be severe;
- dangerous is a question of fact in each case (*Behrens v Bertram Mills Circus*);
- keeper is strictly liable;
- a keeper is either the owner or head of a household in which a person under 16 is the owner.

Non-dangerous species:
- duty is under s 2(2);
- keeper liable if:
  i) damage of a kind animal is likely to cause unless restrained, or if caused by animal is likely to be severe;
  ii) likelihood or severity of damage is due to characteristics of individual animal or species, or of species at specific times;
  iii) keeper knows of characteristics.

▶ 6.2 Liability for animals

6.2.1 Introduction

1   The origins of liability are in medieval law:

   a) animals were a major source of wealth so attitudes differed;

   b) animals had a separate system because they are mobile (a 'will of their own').

2   There were two basic actions in the common law:

a) scienter (knowingly keeping a dangerous animal that escaped and caused harm);

b) cattle trespass (damage caused by escaping livestock).

3   The Animals Act 1971 replaced these, retaining the essentials.

4   Other torts can be used where the Act does not apply.

5   The Pearson Committee found that animals are responsible for 50,000 injuries annually, but few actions are brought.

6.2.2 Common law torts

1   If the requirements of any tort are met an action is possible e.g.:

● trespass to goods (*Manton v Brocklebank* (1923));

● trespass to land (*League Against Cruel Sports v Scott* (1985));

● private nuisance (*Rapier v London Tramways* (1893));

● *Rylands v Fletcher* (*Brady v Warren* (1900));

● defamation, e.g. a parrot taught to repeat insulting untruths;

● assault and battery, e.g. a dog trained to attack;

● with more widespread application, negligence for a failure to control an animal where some risk of harm is foreseeable (*Gomberg v Smith* (1962) and *Birch v Mills* (1995));

● negligence is useful in respect of non-dangerous species where the Act may prove ineffective (*Draper v Hodder* (1972));

● so a duty to take reasonable precautions against foreseeable risks exists (*Smith v Prendergast* (1984)), but there is no liability where there is only a remote possibility of an injury (*Whippey v Jones* (2009)).

2   Liability can exist simultaneously in more than one tort (*Pitcher v Martin* (1937)).

6.2.3 The Animals Act 1971

Dangerous species (*ferae naturae*)

1   By s 6(2) a dangerous species is one:

i) which is not commonly domesticated in the UK;

ii) where fully grown animals usually have such characteristics that they are likely, unless restricted, to cause severe damage, or any damage they cause is likely to be severe.

2   Under s 2(1) the 'keeper' of a dangerous species is liable.

3   Dangerous is a question of law not fact (*Behrens v Bertram Mills Circus* (1957)).

- So it could include species domesticated in other countries.
- Few native species correspond to the category.
- Dangerous even if unlikely to do harm if possible harm would be severe (*Tutin v Chipperfield Promotions* (1980)).
- So liability is strict.

4   Keeper is defined in s 6(3) as:

i)   an owner or possessor; or

ii)   the head of a household of which a member under 16 possesses the animal.

NB. It is possible to have more than one keeper.

5   Dangerous Wild Animals Act 1976 requires licensing of animals, and third party insurance.

Non-dangerous species (*mansuetae naturae*)

1   There is a rather complex duty under s 2(2). Keeper is liable if:

a)   the damage is of a kind which the animal is likely to cause unless restrained, or which if caused by the animal is likely to be severe;

b)   the likelihood or severity of damage was due to unusual characteristics of the individual animal, or common in species only at particular times;

c)   those characteristics were known to the keeper, or a person having charge of the animal who is a member of the household and is under 16.

2   The subsection requires proper interpretation, which is to consider each part in turn (*Curtis v Betts* (1990)).

- So, by s 2(2)(a) damage need not be caused in the way which is likely (*Smith v Ainger* (1990)).
- s 2(2)(a) might include infectious animals.
- s 2(2)(b) distinguishes between permanent and temporary characteristics, and between species and breed (*Smith v Ainger* and *Cummings v Grainger* (1977)).
- Being trained to be aggressive need not be a characteristic involving liability (*Gloster v Chief Constable of Greater Manchester*

Police (2000)) and a horse bucking is a normal characteristic of a horse at any time (*Freeman v Higher Park Farm* (2009)).

- 'Likelihood of damage' refers to the individual animal.

- 'Likely to be severe' refers to the possible injury (*Cummings v Grainger* and *Curtis v Betts*).

- 'Knowledge' in s 2(2)(c) means actual knowledge.

- Implied knowledge may be negligence (*Draper v Hodder*).

- There must be a causal link between the characteristics of the animal and the damage it inflicts (*Jaundrill v Gillett* (1996)).

- The House of Lords has suggested that the keeper may be liable where behaviour of animal is reasonably foreseeable even though the keeper is not at fault (*Mirvahedy (FC) v Henley and another* (2003)).

Defences

1 By s 5(1) a keeper is not liable for damage 'due wholly to the fault of the person suffering it' (*Sylvester v Chapman* (1935)) and accepting a risk knowingly can mean damage is wholly the fault of the claimant so s 5(1) and s 5(2) can be applied simultaneously (*Dhesi v Chief Constable of West Midlands Police* (2000)).

2 By s 5(2) there is no liability 'for a person who has voluntarily accepted the risk' (*Cummings v Grainger* (1977), where a woman entered a scrap yard already afraid of the Alsatian dog guarding it).

3 By s 5(3) the keeper is not liable to a trespasser if the animal was not kept for protection of property, or if it was it was reasonable to do so (*Cummings v Grainger*), but see now also the Guard Dogs Act 1995.

4 By s 10 can apportion damages if contributory negligence shown.

Trespassing livestock

1 Section 11 defines livestock as 'cattle, horses, asses, mules, hinnies, sheep, pigs, goats, poultry and deer in the wild state'.

2 'Cattle trespass' is replaced by s 4, imposing liability if animals stray and:

- damage is done to land or property;

- or

- expenses incurred in keeping them until restored to the owner.

3 Possible defences are:

- s 5(1) if the damage is wholly due to the fault of the claimant;

- s 10 apportionment for contributory negligence;

- s 5(5) if driving livestock on to highway only liable if negligent;

- s 5(6) there is no general duty to fence the land, but if there is a customary duty then a failure to fence provides a defence (compare *Tillet v Ward* (1882) with *Matthews v Wicks* (1987));

- s 7 power to detain straying animal until damage is paid for. Must notify police within 48 hours; can sell after 14 days.

Liability for injury to livestock by dogs

1 By s 3 a keeper is liable if a dog kills or injures livestock.

2 No need to show abnormal characteristics, so greater protection than for people.

3 Straying of livestock on to land where a dog is entitled to be may be a defence under s 5(4).

4 Defences under s 5(1) and s 10 are also available.

5 By s 9 it is legal to kill a dog if it is to protect livestock.

   - The dog must be worrying and there is no other way of dealing with it, or it has not left the vicinity.

   - Must be entitled to protect livestock and must notify the police within 48 hours.

Animals straying onto the highway

1 Prior to the Act there was no liability.

2 Section 8(1) abolished immunity and introduced liability in negligence.

3 By s 8(2) no liability for putting animals on unfenced land if:

   i) the land is common, or a customary right not to fence, or town or village green;

   ii) there is a right to put the animal there.

4 Duty is only to do what is reasonable, not, for example, to fence a moor.

5 Registration of Commons Act 1971 requires registration of rights to graze on common.

Remoteness of damage

1 Not dealt with by the Act, so common law applies.

2 Liability for animals is like *Rylands v Fletcher* – this was excluded from the *Wagon Mound* foreseeability test, so probably the direct consequence test applies instead.

3 Section 2(1) in any case refers to liability being for 'any damage'.

4 By s 2(2) for non-dangerous species damages are limited to those resulting from unusual characteristics known to the keeper.

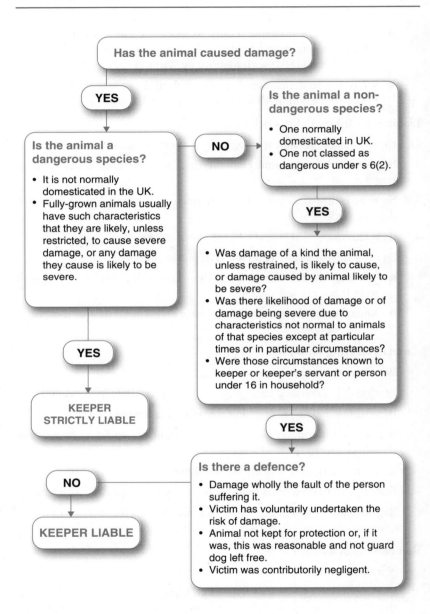

Diagram illustrating liability for dangerous and non-dangerous species under the Animals Act 1971

Key Cases Checklist

> *Rylands v Fletcher* (1868)
>
> *Giles v Walker* (1890)
> No liability for things naturally present on the land
>
> *Rickards v Lothian* (1913)
> A domestic water supply is not a non-natural use of land
>
> *Mason v Levy Auto Parts* (1967)
> But potentially dangerous things stored in extremely large quantities are
>
> *Read v Lyons* (1947)
> The thing must escape from land over which the defendant has control to land over which he has no control
>
> *Hale v Jennings* (1948)
> It is arguable whether the tort extends to personal injuries
>
> *Cambridge Water v Eastern Counties Leather* (1994)
> There must be foreseeable damage as the result of the escape
>
> *Perry v Kendricks Transport* (1956)
> Act of a stranger is a common defence
>
> *Green v Chelsea Waterworks* (1894)
> As is statutory authority

6.1.1.3   *Rylands v Fletcher* (1868) LR 1 Exch 265; LR 3 HL 330

CE and HL

Key Facts

The defendant, a mill owner, hired contractors to create a reservoir on his land to supply water to the mill. The contractors carelessly failed to block off disused mineshafts which, unknown to the contractors, were connected to other mine works on adjoining land. When the reservoir was filled it flooded these neighbouring mines, causing damage.

Key Law

While the facts did not fit easily into the law of nuisance as the case did not involve continuity, it was held that there could be liability for the accumulation of things that were not naturally present on the land which escaped and caused damage. Lord Cairns in the House of Lords (now the Supreme Court) added the requirement that the accumulation must amount to a 'non-natural' use of land for there to be liability.

Key Judgment

Blackburn J in the Court of Exchequer explained the rule in the following way:

'We think that the true rule of law is, that the person who, for purposes of his own, brings on his land and keeps there anything likely to do mischief if it escapes, must keep it in at his peril, and, if he does not do so, he is prima facie answerable for all the damage which is the natural consequence of its escape.'

Key Comment

It is generally agreed that the judges were creating an entirely new legal principle. A possible reason is that judges then were from the landed elite and resented the new wealth of the industrialists so wished to create a strict liability rule to prevent industrial pollution.

6.1.2   *Giles v Walker* (1890) 24 QBD 656   `QBD`

Key Facts

A claim for damage resulting from the defendant allowing weeds growing on his land to accumulate and spread to his neighbour's land was unsuccessful.

Key Law

There was held to be no liability for things not naturally present on the land. The rule requires artificial accumulation.

6.1.2   *Miles v Forest Rock Granite Co (Leicestershire) Ltd* (1918) 34 TLR 500 CA   `CA`

Key Facts

The claimant brought a successful claim for injury suffered when rocks flew onto the highway from the defendant's land where blasting was being carried out.

Key Law

Even though it was the explosives that had been brought onto land rather than the rock itself, which was naturally present, it was the blasting that had actually caused the rock to escape. It was held that in such circumstances it need not be the actual thing brought onto land that escapes.

6.1.2   *Musgrove v Pandelis* [1919] 2 KB 43   KB

Key Facts

A car was kept in a garage with a full tank of petrol. When the petrol caught fire and the fire spread to the next door neighbour's house, although the fire was unlikely it was accepted that it would certainly cause mischief if it escaped.

Key Law

Because of the small number of cars in existence at the time, the practice was held to be a non-natural use of land.

Key Problem

This demonstrates the unpredictability of the rule since the same practice would not be considered non-natural use of land today, with the modern extent of car ownership.

6.1.1.3   *Rickards v Lothian* [1913] AC 263   PC

Key Facts

An unknown person turned on water taps and blocked plugholes on the defendant's premises so that damage was caused in the flat below. The defendant was held not liable.

Key Law

There was held to be no liability not just because the defendant could successfully use the defence of act of a stranger but more importantly because a domestic water supply was not a non-natural use of land.

Key Judgment

As Lord Moulton explained:

'It is not every use . . . that brings into play the principle . . . It must be some special use bringing with it increased danger to others and must not be the ordinary use of the land or such a use as is proper for the benefit of the community'.

6.1.2

Mason v Levy Auto Parts of England [1967] 2 QB 530

QBD

Key Facts

The defendant stored large quantities of scrap tyres on his land. These were then ignited and the fire spread to the claimant's premises, causing great damage, and the claim under the rule was successful.

Key Law

The judge identified that storage of such large quantities of combustible material, the casual way in which they were stored and the character of the neighbourhood were all factors in determining that there was a non-natural use of the land.

Key Comment

The case illustrates that it is the context in which the thing is accumulated as much as the thing itself that can determine that there is a non-natural use of land and possible liability.

6.1.2

Read v Lyons [1947] AC 156

HL

Key Facts

A factory inspector was inspecting a munitions factory and was injured, along with a number of employees, one man dying, when some of the shells exploded. Her claim for damages failed.

Key Law

The House of Lords (now the Supreme Court) held that the rule did not apply because there was 'no escape at all of the relevant kind'.

Key Judgment

Viscount Simon explained that an escape in *Rylands v Fletcher* (1868) means *'an escape from a place where the defendant has occupation or control over land to a place which is outside his occupation or control'*.

6.1.2

British Celanese v A H Hunt (Capacitors) Ltd **[1969] 1 WLR 959**

(QBD)

Key Facts

The defendant stored strips of metal foil on its land, for use in manufacturing electrical components. Some strips of foil blew off the defendants' land and onto an electricity substation, causing power failures to the claimant's factory. A claim was brought under negligence, private nuisance, public nuisance and under *Rylands v Fletcher* (1868) and the claim under the latter was dismissed.

Key Law

The court held that the use of land was natural. This was partly because there were no unusual risks associated with the storage of the foil and partly because of the benefit derived by the public from the manufacture, so the rule could not apply.

Key Judgment

Lawton J identified also that escape means:

'from a set of circumstances over which the defendant had control to a set of circumstances where he does not'.

Key Problem

It has been suggested that this interpretation of 'non-natural' is very similar to the idea of unreasonable risk in negligence, making the tort indistinguishable from negligence.

6.1.3.1 | *Hale v Jennings Bros* [1948] 1 All ER 579

Key Facts

A stallholder on a fairground was injured when a car from a 'chair-o-plane' ride became detached from the main assembly while it was in motion and crashed to the ground. The owner of the ride was liable even though both parties occupied the same ground.

Key Law

The court held that there was liability because risk of injury was foreseeable if the car came loose and because there was an escape from the defendant's control.

Key Problem

This clearly conflicts with the meaning of escape given in *Read v Lyons*, and extends the range of potential claimants.

Key Link

Hunter v Canary Wharf [1997] AC 655.

This is a major case in private nuisance that suggests that the rule may not extend to claims for personal injury.

6.1.4.6 | *Cambridge Water Co v Eastern Counties Leather plc* [1994] 2 WLR 53

Key Facts

The defendant owned a tannery and used a solvent to degrease the animal skins. Sometimes this solvent spilled onto the concrete floor and over a period of time it seeped into the ground and eventually filtered through into a bore-hole more than a mile away owned by the claimant Water Company and from which water for domestic consumption and use was extracted. The solvent contaminated the water and the claim for damages was unsuccessful.

Key Law

The House of Lords (now the Supreme Court) held that storage of chemicals could always be regarded as a non-natural use of land but that, since the contamination could not be foreseen by a reasonable person, there could be no liability.

Key Judgment

Adding the requirement of foreseeability to the essential elements of a claim under the tort Lord Goff identified that *'foreseeability of damage of the relevant type should be regarded as a prerequisite of liability . . . under the rule'*.

Key Problem

The addition of foresight of harm is a fault-based concept making the tort indistinguishable from negligence, casting doubt on whether the tort is in fact strict liability and making a successful claim almost impossible to bring.

6.1.4.6

Transco plc v Stockport MBC [2003] UKHL 61; [2003] 3 WLR 1467

 HL

Key Facts

The defendant council built a block of multi-storey flats in which, without any negligence, the water pipes supplying the flats burst and water then escaped eventually causing an embankment to collapse, exposing the claimant's gas main and posing an immediate and serious risk. The claimant took immediate remedial action and unsuccessfully sought to recover the cost.

Key Law

The House held that the claim could not succeed because it did not involve a non-natural use of land. The judges reviewed the law and identified *obiter* that *Rylands v Fletcher* (1868) is still good law and approved the views expressed in *Cambridge Water* (1994) that it is a specific type of private nuisance, requiring foreseeable harm and that it is thus unavailable in claims for personal injury.

Key Judgment

Lord Bingham did cast doubt on the concept of non-natural use of land:

'I think it is clear that ordinary user is a preferable test to natural user, making it clear that the rule . . . is engaged only where the defendant's use is shown to be extraordinary and unusual . . . I also doubt whether a test of reasonable user is helpful, since a user may well be quite out of the ordinary but not unreasonable'.

6.1.5.1   *Peters v Prince of Wales Theatre (Birmingham) Ltd* [1943] KB 73   CA

Key Facts

The claimant rented a kiosk in a theatre. His stock was damaged by water from the defendant's sprinkler system. His claim failed.

Key Law

It was held that the water supply was a natural use of land in context and for the benefit of both parties so that the claimant consented to the risk, and there was no liability for the escape.

6.1.5.3   *Perry v Kendricks Transport Ltd* [1956] 1 WLR 85   CA

Key Facts

The defendant parked its bus on its parking space after draining the petrol tank. When an unknown person removed the petrol cap a child was then injured when another child threw in a lit match, igniting the fumes in the tank. The claim for personal injury failed.

Key Law

The court accepted that the rule could apply and also that an action for personal injury was possible under the rule. However, the damage was caused by an act of a stranger. It considered that the claimant had the burden of proof to show that such an eventuality was foreseeable. There was a valid defence and no liability.

6.1.5.5

Green v Chelsea Waterworks Co (1894) 70 LT 547

CA

Key Facts

The defendants were obliged by statute to provide a water supply. The water supply was inevitably pressurised and when a burst pipe occurred water escaped, causing damage to the claimant whose action for damages was unsuccessful.

Key Law

The court held that from time to time burst pipes were an inevitable consequence of the statutory duty, which provided an obvious defence, and there could be no liability without proof of negligence.

Key Judgment

Lindley LJ commented that the rule:

'is not to be extended beyond the legitimate principle on which the House of Lords (now the Supreme Court) decided it. If it were extended as far as strict logic might require, it would be a very oppressive decision'.

6.2.2.1

Draper v Hodder [1972] 2 QB 556

CA

Key Facts

A child was savaged by a pack of Jack Russell terriers that were rushing from their owner's house next door. They had never acted this way before, so there could be no liability under the Animals Act 1971. The claimant was successful under negligence.

Key Law

The court held that it was known that the breed of dog characteristically attacks in packs so there was foreseeable risk of harm and negligence.

6.2.3

Tutin v Mary Chipperfield Promotions Ltd (1980) 130 NLJ 807

Key Facts

The claimant was injured when she was thrown off a camel during a camel race at the Horse of the Year Show. She succeeded in her negligence claim but failed under the Animals Act 1971.

Key Law

The court accepted that the camel was a member of a dangerous species within the definition in s 6(2) of the Act, even though this conflicted with a previous decision in *McQuaker v Goddard* [1940] 1 KB 687 which held that a camel is not a dangerous species because there is nowhere in the world where a camel is wild. The court applied that part of s 6(2) 'that any damage that they may cause is likely to be severe'. However, the action would fail because the claimant by agreeing to take part in the race had voluntarily accepted the risk of harm within the meaning of s 5(2) of the Act.

Key Link

For definition of dangerous see s 6(2) Animals Act 1971.

6.2.3

Cummings v Grainger [1977] 1 All ER 104

CA

Key Facts

The owner of a scrap yard allowed an untrained Alsatian to roam free at night. The dog savaged a woman who entered with her boyfriend who worked there. The woman's claim for damages under the 1971 Act was unsuccessful.

Key Law

The claim failed because, under s 5(2), the woman had voluntarily accepted the risk of harm, she knew the dog was dangerous and was frightened of it, and also because, at that time, under s 5(3), it was held to be reasonable to keep a guard dog in a scrap yard in the East End of London.

Key Judgment

Lord Denning identified that the case was one where:

'the keeper of the dog is strictly liable unless he can bring himself within one of the exceptions . . . because the three requirements . . . are satisfied . . . Section 2(2)(a): . . . if it did bite anyone the damage was "likely to be severe". Section 2(2)(b): this animal was a guard dog . . . on the defendant's own evidence it used to bark and run around in circles . . . characteristics . . . not normally found in Alsatian dogs except . . . where they are used as guard dogs. Section 2(2)(c): those characteristics were known to the defendant'.

Key Link

The Guard Dogs Act 1995 – which would probably have produced a different result since it is now a criminal offence for guard dogs to roam premises without a handler.

6.2.3

Curtis v Betts [1990] 1 All ER 769   CA

Key Facts

The claimant was an 11-year-old boy who succeeded in his action for personal injury. The boy was bitten on the face by a 70 kg bull mastiff dog called Max whom he knew well and whom he had called as he was passing the car that Max was being put into. Evidence showed that a characteristic of bull mastiffs was defence of territory and also that Max regarded the car as his own territory.

Key Law

The court held that no defences under s 5 or contributory negligence applied and, although Max was considered to be a docile animal, that the damage he was likely to cause if unrestrained was likely to be severe. The court also held that s 2(2) (b) should be interpreted to mean that there should be a causal link between the characteristics of the animal and the type of damage suffered.

Key Judgment

Slade LJ said:

> *'Lord Denning MR in Cummings v Grainger described s 2(2) as "very cumbrously worded" and giving rise to "several difficulties". I agree. Particularly in view of the somewhat tortuous wording of the subsection, I think it desirable to consider each of the three requirements separately and in turn'.*

6.2.3   ### *Mirvahedy v Henley* [2003] UKHL 16; [2003] 2 AC 491

 HL

Key Facts

The defendant kept horses in a field. Something frightened the horses and they escaped eventually onto a major road. There was then a collision between one of the horses and the claimant's car, in which the claimant suffered personal injury. The defendant's appeal in the House of Lords (now the Supreme Court) was unsuccessful. The key issue was the characteristics of the animals.

Key Law

The House of Lords (now the Supreme Court), by a majority of three to two, held that s 2(2)(b) applied. Even though the behaviour of the horses was unusual for the species for the most part, it was nevertheless normal for the species in the particular circumstances.

Key Judgment

Lord Walker gave the reason for imposing liability:

> *'It is common knowledge (and was known to the appellants in this case) that horses, if exposed to a very frightening stimulus, will panic and stampede, knocking down obstacles in their path . . . and may continue their flight for considerable distance. Horses loose in that state . . . are an obvious danger on a road carrying fast moving traffic. The appellants knew these facts; they could decide whether to run the risks involved in keeping horses . . . Although I feel sympathy for the appellants, who were held not to have been negligent in the fencing of the field, I see nothing unjust or unreasonable in the appellants having to bear the loss'.*

Key Comment

The problem with this interpretation of s 2 is that it means that almost any circumstances in which a domestic animal causes harm could be classed as characteristics only exhibited at particular times. This would have the effect of extending liability to almost unlimited proportions.

Key Link

Freeman v Higher Park Farm [2008] EWCA Civ 1185, where bucking was held to be a normal characteristic of a horse and that horses do not buck at any particular time.

6.2.3 *Dhesi v Chief Constable of the West Midlands Police, The Times*, 9 May 2000

Key Facts

Police had tracked the claimant, who was armed with a hockey stick, after a violent confrontation. When the claimant hid in bushes he was repeatedly warned that the dog would be set free unless he came out. The claimant was bitten when trying to escape from the dog, but was unsuccessful in his claim for personal injury.

Key Law

The court held that the claimant had caused his own injury and had accepted the risk of being injured through his actions. There was a valid defence under both s 5(1) and s 5(2) and no liability.

Trespass to land

Definition and purpose of tort

Defined as: intentional unlawful entry or direct interference with land in another's possession.

Actionable *per se*, so no proof of damage needed.

Purpose of action can be:
- to remove intruders;
- to settle disputes over title;
- to seek compensation for loss or damage;
- to recover land when unlawfully ejected.

TRESPASS TO LAND

Claimants and types of trespass

Claimants:
- based on possession;
- so lessees and mortgagees can sue;
- and a squatter can sue against someone with less title (*Graham v Peat*);
- but not a possessor against someone with superior title (*Delaney v TP Smith*);
- nor a lodger against a landlord (*White v Bayley*).

Types of trespass:
- requires direct entry onto land (*Perera v Vandiyar*);
- but need not be defendant who enters (*Smith v Stone*);
- can be active interference (*Basely v Clarkson*);
- or static interference (*Kelsen v Imperial Tobacco*);
- and can be only temporary (*Woolerton & Wilson v Richard Costain*);
- or the merest touching (*Westripp v Baldock*).

Defences and remedies

Defences:
- customary right to enter
- (*Mercer v Denne*);
- common law right to enter (*Clissold v Cratchley*);
- statutory right to enter;
- *volenti*;
- necessity;
- licences.

Remedies:
- injunction and/or damages;
- distress damage feasant;
- declaration (*Acton BC v Morris*).

Definition of land

- *Cujus est solum ejus est usque ad coelum et ad inferos* – includes air space above and soil below.
- Covers air space to a reasonable extent (*Kelsen v Imperial Tobacco*).
- Does not cover air to extent of preventing air traffic (*Lord Bernstein of Leigh v Skyways*).
- Can prevent unlawful use of a public road over a person's land (*Harrison v Duke of Rutland*).
- Can include the boundary of the land (*Westripp v Baldock*).
- Most air rights now covered by CAA, and undersoil rights also by statute.

▶ 7.1 The origins and character of trespass

1   Trespass is as old as the common law itself.

2   It was necessary so claimants could bring their own action where the distinction between civil and criminal law was unclear.

3   Derives from the Latin: *trans* (through) and *passus* (a pace).

4   It is most accurately used in conjunction with land.

5   But there are torts of trespass to the person and to goods also.

6   It is used generally to refer to an interference.

7   It is actionable *per se* (so without proof of damage).

8   Originally it was only actionable if it arose directly as a consequence of the defendant's direct and positive act.

9   Indirect interference or omission would be an action on the case (forerunner of negligence) when damage had to be shown.

▶ 7.2 Trespass to land

7.2.1 Definition, character and purpose of the tort

1   Developed from the writ *quare clausum fregit* by way of the taking of an enclosed area.

2   Defined as the intentional or negligent, unlawful entry upon or direct interference with the land in another 's possession.

3   The tort is actionable *per se*, so no proof of damage needed.

4   Damages are payable if there is any loss.

5   It can be intentional, but also by a person who enters lawfully, but then carries out an unlawful act.

6   There may be many purposes of suing:

   ● to remove unwanted intruders;
   ● to settle disputes over title;
   ● to seek compensation for loss or damage;
   ● to recover land from which claimant was unlawfully ejected.

7   The action can be by a possessor rather than an owner.

7.2.2 Potential claimants

1   If the tort were based only on title a tenant could not claim. If it was based on pure possession then an owner might not claim.

2   So, an action is in favour of the person in possession at the time the trespass is committed, as against the wrongdoer.

3   So 'possession is title as against a wrongdoer . . .'.

4   An action is available to lessees, mortgagees, etc., and possession need not be legal, i.e. a squatter may sue a trespassing third party (*Graham v Peat* (1861)).

5   But not the superior owner (*Delaney v T P Smith & Co* (1946)).

6   Possession means exclusivity, so a lessee can sue a lessor, but a lodger may not sue the landlord (*White v Bayley* (1861)).

7   However, a licensee may gain a proprietary interest as in estoppel.

7.2.3 Actions amounting to a trespass

1   Acts/non-acts must be direct; indirect interference is actionable, as nuisance or negligence (*Lemon v Webb* (1894), and *Esso Petroleum Co v Southport Corporation* (1956)).

2   There must be an entry on to the land (*Perera v Vandiyar* (1953)).

3   It need not be the defendant who enters (*Smith v Stone* (1647)).

4   So, it might be rocks or balls thrown, but not rubbish blown by the wind (compare *Smith v Stone* (1647) with *Esso v Southport Corp* (1956)).

5   Any presence can be a trespass, e.g. walking, standing, riding.

6   So it can be active interference (*Basely v Clarkson* (1681)).

7   It can also be a static intrusion (*Kelsen v Imperial Tobacco Co* (1956)).

8   Can be merely temporary (*Woolerton & Wilson v Richard Costain Ltd* (1970), where a crane swung over the claimant's land).

9   The merest contact can be trespass (*Westripp v Baldock* (1938)).

10 A trespass can occur even if the original entry was lawful.

7.2.4 Definition of land in trespass

1   There is no single concept. Traditional proposition is *cujus est solum ejus est usque ad coleum et ad inferos* (the action extends to the air above the land and the sub-soil beneath it).

2   It can be the land, any part of the land, any structure on the land.

3   It can even be the boundary (*Westripp v Baldock* (1938)).

4   Most underground rights are now under statutory authority.

- Rights can extend under roads to include unlawful use of the road (*Harrison v The Duke of Rutland* (1893) and *Hickman v Maisey* (1900)).

- But cannot extend to adjoining land (*Randall v Tarrant* (1955)).

- But can include the strata underneath the land through which pipelines pass (*Bocardo v Star Energy UK* (2010)).

5   Air space:

a)   Overhanging signs have been trespass (*Kelsen v Imperial Tobacco* (1956) and *Gifford v Dent* (1926)).

b)   Wire cables (*Wandsworth Board of Works v United Telephones* (1864)).

c)   Cranes (*Woolerton & Wilson v Richard Constain* (1970)).

d)   But not balloons flying overhead (*Pickering v Rudd* (1815) and *Saunders v Smith* (1838)).

e)   Aircraft are unlikely to amount to a trespass (*Lord Bernstein of Leigh v Skyways General Ltd* (1977), where there was no liability in trespass when aerial photographs were taken of Lord Bernstein's estate).

f)   Aircraft in any case have free passage under the Civil Aviation Act 1982.

7.2.5 Trespass *ab initio*

1   A common law doctrine – if a person enters land lawfully then does an act inconsistent with his rights, then the entry is deemed unlawful from the beginning despite his original lawful entry.

2   Needed to stop abuses by lawful visitors (*Oxley v Watts* (1785)).

3   It may be ineffective if a lawful purpose remains (*Elias v Pasmore* (1934)).

4   Possibly the doctrine is no longer in existence according to CA (*Chic Fashions Ltd v Jones* (1968)).

7.2.6 Defences

1   A customary right to enter (*Mercer v Denne* (1905), where the defendant was prevented from building on his beach because fishermen had an ancient right to dry their nets on it).

2   A common law right to enter, which is lost if the person entering goes beyond his legal rights (*Clissold v Cratchley* (1910)).

3   Statutory right to enter, e.g. police under PACEA 1984; meter readers by Rights of Entry (Gas and Electricity Boards) Act 1954.

4   *Volenti non fit injuria* (where visitors are allowed on to land).

5   Necessity, e.g. someone rescuing a child from a burning building (*Rigby v Chief Constable of Northamptonshire* (1985)).

6   Licences – constantly given e.g. shops etc. – valid only while terms of licence are complied with.

7.2.7 Remedies

1   If claimant is in possession (s)he can sue for damage resulting from infringement and injunction to prevent further trespass. But an injunction cannot be applied generally to any land that the trespass may occur on in the future, only that which is already the subject of a trespass (*Sec of State for the Environment v Meier* (2010)).

2   If defendant is in possession, claimant can sue for ejectment for recovery of land, possibly with mesne profits.

3   Damages may be:

   a)   nominal and exemplary;

   b)   related to actual deterioration;

   c)   related to the cost of repossession.

4   Other remedies:

   a)   distress damage feasant – keeping an object causing damage;

   b)   declaration – if rights are uncertain (*Acton BC v Morris* (1953)).

	Private nuisance	Public nuisance	*Rylands v Fletcher*	Trespass to land
Claimants	Person with proprietary interest in land	A member of a class of Her Majesty's citizens	A person harmed by the escape	Person in possession of land
Defendants	Landowner, creator, person adopting nuisance	Person creating nuisance	Person in control of land from which thing escapes	Person carrying out the trespass
Duration of interference	Must be continuous	Single interference is enough	Single escape is enough	A single trespass is enough
Directness of interference	Must be indirect	Could be direct or indirect	Could be direct or indirect	Must be direct
Need to prove fault	Requires unreasonable use of land – which is indirect	Fault need not be proved	*Cambridge Water* says foreseeability required – suggests fault	Actionable *per se* – so no need to prove fault
Locality of interference	Relevant unless damage caused	Could be relevant, e.g. to losing client connection	Could be relevant in deciding what is non-natural	Not relevant
Availability of damages	Physical harm, personal injury to proprietor, economic loss	Physical harm, personal injury, economic loss	Physical loss and personal injury	Any damage related to the trespass – and no need to show damage

Defences	Statutory authority, prescription, consent, act of stranger, public policy, over-sensitivity of claimant	General defences	Consent, common benefit, act of a stranger, or God, statutory authority, contributory negligence	Customary right to enter, common law right, statutory right, consent, necessity, licence
Whether also a crime	No – unless statutory	Yes – can be	No	Yes – possible under some statutes

The similarities and differences between the torts relating to land

Key Cases Checklist

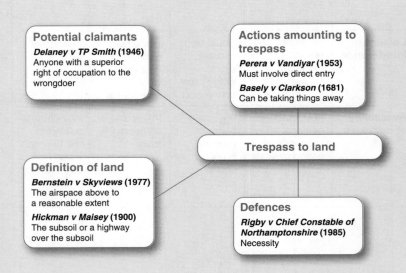

Potential claimants

Delaney v TP Smith (1946)
Anyone with a superior right of occupation to the wrongdoer

Actions amounting to trespass

Perera v Vandiyar (1953)
Must involve direct entry

Basely v Clarkson (1681)
Can be taking things away

Trespass to land

Definition of land

Bernstein v Skyviews (1977)
The airspace above to a reasonable extent

Hickman v Maisey (1900)
The subsoil or a highway over the subsoil

Defences

Rigby v Chief Constable of Northamptonshire (1985)
Necessity

7.2.2.5   ***Delaney v T P Smith & Co* [1946] KB 393**   CA

Key Facts

By an oral agreement, the claimant was to acquire a tenancy of the defendant's property. Before the lease was executed the claimant secretly entered the premises. The defendant then ejected the claimant, who unsuccessfully sued for trespass.

Key Law

The court held that, since the agreement had not been reduced to writing, the defendant still had superior rights of occupation.

Key Judgment

Tucker LJ said:

'no doubt . . . a plaintiff need only in the first instance allege possession. This is sufficient to support his action against a wrongdoer, but . . . not . . . against the lawful owner'.

7.2.3.2   ***Perera v Vandiyar* [1953] 1 WLR 672**   CA

Key Facts

The claimant was a tenant in the defendant's property. His gas and electricity meters were situated in the defendant's cellar. When the defendant switched off both supplies and the claimant was left for two days without heat or light, he claimed damages unsuccessfully.

Key Law

The court held on appeal that, while there was a clear interference with the claimant's premises, there was no direct entry, which would be an absolute requirement for trespass.

7.2.3.6   *Basely v Clarkson* (1681) 3 Lev 37   CP

Key Facts

The defendant cut and carried away some grass from his neighbour's strip of land. The claimant alleged trespass.

Key Law

The court held that this was trespass even though it was carried out by mistake. However, the defendant had offered 2 shillings (10p) in full satisfaction, which was accepted as discharging the issue.

7.2.4.5   *Lord Bernstein of Leigh v Skyviews & General Ltd* [1977] QB 479   QBD

Key Facts

A company specialising in aerial photographs flew over the claimant's land, took photographs, and then tried to sell them to him. It was held not to be a trespass.

Key Law

It was held that the claimant did have rights over the airspace above his property but that these should only extend to a height 'reasonably necessary for the enjoyment of the land'.

Key Link

The Civil Aviation Act 1982 confirms this. Aircraft are generally immune from actions for trespass except where things fall from an aircraft or where aircraft make unauthorised landings.

7.2.4.5   *Kelsen v Imperial Tobacco Co Ltd* [1956] 2 QB 334   QBD

Key Facts

The defendant's advertising hoarding overhung the neighbouring land by 8 inches. An injunction to remove the sign succeeded.

Key Law

The court held that there was a trespass because the sign invaded the claimant's airspace.

 7.2.4.4

Harrison v Duke of Rutland [1893] 1 QB 142

Key Facts

The Duke commonly held grouse shoots on his land. Protesters gathered on the highway next to his land and tried to scare off the grouse. The Duke's action for trespass succeeded.

Key Law

The court held that since the highway ran over the Duke's land it gave him rights over it and the defendants were liable because they used the highway improperly.

Key Link

Bocardo v Star Energy UK [2010] UKSC 35.

7.2.4.4

Hickman v Maisey [1900] 1 QB 752

Key Facts

The defendant used the highway to spy on the claimant's race horses in training and find out information on their performance before they entered races. The claimant's action succeeded.

Key Law

The court held that there was a trespass since the defendant was using the adjoining highway for improper purposes. The highway could be freely used but not when it abused a landowner 's rights.

7.2.5.3   *Elias v Pasmore* [1934] 2 KB 164   KB

Key Facts

The police entered premises and seized some documents lawfully under a warrant, but also some not covered by the warrant. The claim for trespass in relation to the documents unlawfully seized was accepted but the claim of trespass *ab initio* failed.

Key Law

The court held that the principle could not apply since it would have made the police liable for breaking the door to carry out the warrant.

7.2.6.5   *Rigby v Chief Constable of Northamptonshire* [1985] 2 All ER 985   QBD

Key Facts

Police officers fired CS gas into the claimant's shop where a dangerous armed psychopath was hiding. This ignited powder and caused the shop to burn down. The police successfully raised a defence of necessity to the claimant's action for trespass.

Key Law

The court accepted that the defence was uncertain in scope but accepted that it applied in relation to the trespass because there was a life-threatening situation. (However, the police were found negligent for not providing effective fire-fighting cover.)

8 Torts concerning goods

Trespass to goods

Defined as – direct, immediate, intentional interference with personal property belonging to another.

- Interference must be direct (*Fouldes v Willoughby*).
- Contact with goods must be intentional (*Ranson v Kitner*).

Claimants are those entitled to immediate possession.

Conversion

More complex because it involves ownership as well as possession.

Defined as – intentional, wrongful interference of substantial nature with claimant's possession or rights to possession, or dealing with goods in manner inconsistent with rights of owner.

Can be:
- wrongly taking with intention to keep goods permanently;
- destroying or misusing goods (*Moorgate Mercantile v Finch*);
- selling goods;
- refusing to return goods when asked (*Arthur v Anker*).

TRESPASS TO GOODS

Remedies

Trespass:
- damages or
- injunction.

Conversion:
- delivery of goods plus damages for consequential loss;
- or full value of goods plus consequential loss.

Torts (Interference with Goods) Act 1977

Made a number of changes to the law.
- The right to sue for negligent loss by a bailee is conversion.
- Created general liability for interference and remedies.
- Contributory negligence was removed as a defence.
- Rules introduced regarding disposal of unclaimed goods.
- Claiming sum for improvements to goods whilst in wrongful possession made possible by the Act.
- Old rule that defendant not allowed to plead a third party had better title to the goods than claimant was reversed.

▶ 8.1 Trespass to goods

8.1.1 Introduction

1   Trespass, meaning interference, is one of the oldest areas of tort.

2   Trespass to goods developed alongside trespass to land and to the person, and was similar but protected personal property.

3   Medieval law became outdated and in need of reform, so updated and clarified in Torts (Interference with Goods) Act 1977, but not entirely, so some common law still remains, adding confusion.

8.1.2 Trespass to goods

1   One of the original two torts to do with goods.

2   Defined as 'direct, immediate interference with personal property belonging to another person'.

3   Claimants are those entitled to immediate possession.

4   Interference must be direct (*Fouldes v Willoughby* (1841)).

5   The interference must be intentional in the sense that contact with the goods is intentional (*Ranson v Kitner* (1888)).

6   Traditionally actionable *per se* (without proof of damage), but this probably does not survive (*Letang v Cooper* (1965)).

7   Under s 11(1) Torts (Interference with Goods) Act 1977 the defence of contributory negligence is not available.

8   Wheel clamping can be a trespass unless the claimant voluntarily undertook the risk of the clamping (*Vine v Waltham Forest London Borough Council* (2000)), where the claimant had not seen warning signs and did not appreciate the consequences of trespassing.

8.1.3 Conversion

1   Trespass to goods is a fairly simple tort; conversion is complex.

   a) This is because it involves ownership as well as possession.

   b) As it takes many forms it is often said to defy easy definition.

2   Broadly defined as 'intentional, wrongful interference of a substantial nature with the claimant's possession or right to possession of the goods'; or 'dealing with goods in a manner inconsistent with the true owner's rights'. So it might occur even where the defendant has no knowledge that the goods belong to the claimant (*Lewis v Avery* (1972)).

3   There are a number of examples of conversion:

- wrongfully taking the goods with the intention of keeping them permanently, or at least for some time;

- selling the goods or assisting in their disposition (*Parker v British Airways Board* (1982));

- destroying or misusing the goods (*Moorgate Mercantile Co v Finch* (1962));

- refusing to return the goods once their return has been demanded (*Arthur v Anker* (1996)) (wheel clamping).

4   Conversion does not cover intangible rights unless those rights are sufficiently connected with a chattel (*OGB v Allan Ltd* (2007)).

5   After the Act a verbal statement denying the claimant's title is not conversion.

6   Again the Act removes contributory negligence as a defence.

8.1.4 Other common law provisions

1   The Act abolished a third common law action (part of conversion).

2   In all three torts there was no remedy for a claimant who did not have possession or an immediate right to possession of the goods.

3   So common law developed an action on the case (as in land) to challenge interference with the claimant's reversionary interest in the goods.

8.1.5 The Torts (Interference with Goods) Act 1977

1   The Act tried to remove overlaps and ambiguities with common law.

2   It did make a number of changes to the law:

- the right to sue for negligent loss by a bailee is conversion;

- created general liability for interference and remedies;

- contributory negligence was removed as a defence;

- rules were introduced regarding disposal of unclaimed goods;

- claiming a sum for improvements made to the goods whilst in wrongful possession was made possible by the Act;

- the old rule that the defendant was not allowed to plead that a third party had better title to the goods than the claimant was reversed.

8.1.6 Remedies

1   In trespass to goods the claimant may recover damages or obtain an injunction.

2   Conversion has been modified by the Act with two possibilities:

● delivery of the goods, plus damages for consequential loss;

● if this is not possible or appropriate the claimant can have the full value of the goods, plus damages for any consequential loss.

▶ 8.2 Product liability

8.2.1 Introduction

1   Product liability is only one aspect of consumer protection.

2   Its origins are in contract law:

a) *caveat emptor* traditionally applied;

b) effective consumer protection began with the Sale of Goods Act 1893, which implied terms as to quality of the goods into contracts.

3   Otherwise only limited opportunities existed to sue in tort in respect of dangerous goods.

4   Suing in contract had obvious shortcomings:

● remedies were only available to the parties to the contract;

● damages limited to loss of bargain, reliance loss, restitution.

5   So a doctrine of tortious liability for defective goods developed.

8.2.2 Common law liability for defective products in tort

1   Came from Lord Atkin's judgment in *Donoghue v Stevenson* (1932): 'a manufacturer of products . . . he intends to reach the ultimate consumer in the form in which they left him with no reasonable possibility of . . . examination . . . and knowledge that absence of reasonable care . . . will result in an injury to consumer's life or property, owes a duty to the consumer to take reasonable care'.

Common law liability

- Comes from case of *Donoghue v Stevenson*.
- 'Manufacturers' now includes wholesalers, retailers, etc
- Claimants are 'ultimate consumers', e.g. include people receiving gifts (*Stennet v Hancock*).
- Must show breach of duty as well as duty (*Grant v Australian Knitting Mills*).
- Must show causation (*Evans v Triplex Safety Glass*).
- Can recover for defects but not pure loss of value (*Muirhead v Industrial Tank*)

Consumer Protection Act 1987

Introduced to give effect to EU Directive 85/374. Civil liability is imposed in s 2(1).

Defendants:
- producers – including manufacturers, those abstracting the product or adding to it in an industrial process;
- importers, suppliers (e.g. retailers) and 'own branders';
- anyone else in chain of manufacture or distribution.

Products covered:
- goods – anything growing or any ship, aircraft, vehicle;
- products – goods, parts of other products, but not buildings and nuclear power.

Defects covered:
- if safety is not such as persons are generally entitled to expect.

Types of damage covered:
- death and personal injury, loss or damage to property;
- but not damage under £275, business property, damage to the defective property itself.

Limitation:
- within three years of becoming aware of defect, damage, or identity of defendant;
- ten years from date of knowledge for latent damage.

Possible defences:
- product complies with statute or EU law;
- defect did not exist when supplied;
- not supplied in course of business;
- defendant did not supply product;
- state of technological or scientific knowledge when goods supplied.

PRODUCT LIABILITY

Criticisms of Act

- Does not apply to all products, defects or damage.
- Strict limitation period.
- Does not apply to disputes pre-1988.
- Too many defences.
- More like negligence than strict liability.

2   Not concerned with quality of goods, but the damage they cause:

- damage must be physical, not purely economic (*Murphy v Brentwood DC* (1990));

- concerns over quality are contested in contract law.

3   At first applied to foodstuffs only, but later extended to anything manufactured (*Grant v Australian Knitting Mills* (1936) – liability when underpants still containing a chemical caused dermatitis in the wearer).

4   Potential defendants are 'manufacturers' – a narrow concept, but expanded to include wholesalers, retailers, repairers, hirers, and assemblers (if under a duty to inspect the goods).

5   Potential claimants are any 'ultimate consumers'.

- Again this is a broad concept including anyone who the 'manufacturer' should see as being affected by his/her actions.

- It can be people receiving goods as presents, borrowing goods, or innocent bystanders (*Stennet v Hancock* (1939)).

6   Bringing an action is the same as for negligence:

a)   The claimant must show a duty of care, breach, and a causal link with the damage suffered.

b)   Breach is, for example, a failure in the production process (*Grant v Australian Knitting Mills* (1936)) – and can include failing to do anything about a known fault (*Walton v British Leyland* (1978)). Detailed knowledge of manufacturing processes is beyond the capability of most consumers, placing a very heavy burden of proof, so the doctrine *res ipsa loquitur* may be appropriate.

c)   Causation will also only be proved if:

- there is no other cause for the defects in the product, so the chain of distribution can be a problem for the claimant (*Evans v Triplex Safety Glass* (1936));

- there is no negligent inspection of the goods by claimant which should have revealed the defect (*Griffiths v Arch Engineering Co* (1968)).

d)   Can recover for damage caused by defects in goods (*Aswan Engineering Establishment Co v Lupdine Ltd* (1987)).

e)   Cannot recover a pure loss of value in the goods themselves (*Muirhead v Industrial Tank Specialities Ltd* (1985)).

7   Clearly the two most important problems of the tort are:

- the difficulty of proving causation;

- the difficulty of establishing fault.

- The Thalidomide cases (settled out of court) are evidence of this.

8.2.3 The Consumer Protection Act 1987

Introduction

1 The Act was the UK's response to EU Directive 85/374 on product liability requiring harmonisation of member states' law.

2 The Act is both criminal and civil in content:

- in the regulatory sense it has been supplemented by the Product Safety Regulations 1994 (again responding to EU law), and criminal sanctions possibly provide more effective control of defective products;

- civil liability in the Act is in s 2(1): 'where any damage is caused wholly or partly by a defect in a product, every person to whom subsection 2 applies shall be liable'.

Who can be sued under the Act?

1 Potential defendants are listed in s 2(2).

a) Producers – defined in s 1(2) and including:

- the manufacturer, ie the manufacturer of the final product; manufacturers and assemblers of component parts; and also producers of raw materials;

- a person who 'wins' or 'abstracts' products, e.g. someone who extracts minerals from the ground;

- a person carrying out an industrial or other process which adds to the essential characteristic of the product, e.g. freezing vegetables.

b) Importers, suppliers and 'own-branders', also defined in s 2(2) and liable to the consumer in certain circumstances:

- importers (by s 2(2)(c) includes anybody who in the course of business imports a product from outside the EU);

- suppliers (retailers or equivalent, usually only liable in contract law, but by s 2(3), where it is impossible to identify a 'producer' or importer, supplier is liable if consumer asked supplier to identify producer, within a reasonable time of the damage suffered, because it is impractical for consumer to identify producer, and supplier has failed to identify or refuses to identify it (so businesses must keep records of their suppliers));

- own-branders (by s 2(2)(b) these are, for example, supermarket chains who, while not producers, hold themselves out as producers by declaring a product as their own brand. They must indicate that someone else is producing the goods for them in order to avoid liability under the Act).

2   Anyone in chain of manufacture and distribution is potentially liable.

- Liability is joint and several, so consumer can sue the person with the most money or best insurance cover.
- Liability is strict so fault need not be proved.

Products covered by the Act

1   Product is defined in s 2(1) as 'any goods or electricity and (subject to subsection (3)) includes a product which is comprised in another product, whether by virtue of being a component part, raw material or otherwise'.

2   Goods are defined in s 45(1) as 'substances, growing crops, and things comprised in land by virtue of being attached to it and any ship, aircraft or vehicle'.

3   Certain things are exempted from the scope of the Act:

- buildings (because they are immovable – though building materials can fall within the Act);
- nuclear power;
- agricultural produce which has not undergone an industrial process – the problem being what is an industrial process?, e.g. butchery in the light of the BSE and CJD problems.

Defects covered by the Act

1   Defect is defined in s 3(1) as 'if the safety of the product is not such as persons generally are entitled to expect, taking into account all the circumstances'.

2   Courts take into account various circumstances to define safety:

- manner in which and purposes for which product has been marketed, its get-up, use of any mark in relation to the product and any instructions, or warnings to do or refrain from doing anything in relation to the product;
- what can reasonably be expected to be done with the product (*Abouzaid v Mothercare (UK) Ltd* (2001));
- time when product was supplied by its producer to another.

3   Market can be important (e.g. toys and children) as can use of warnings, so the way the consumer uses the product can relieve liability (e.g. fireworks not to be used indoors).

4   Defects in production or design which render the product unsafe will result in liability under the Act, but the consumer may cause the damage by improper use.

5   Time can be another important factor because knowledge is always increasing. So, if knowledge has changed should a producer recall all products sold however long ago in the past?

Types of damage the Act applies to

1   The Act covers death, personal injury, and loss or damage to property caused by unsafe products.

2   Some limitations are put on this, so no damages possible for:

   ●   small property damage under £275, so a consumer would need to use contract law;

   ●   business property, so property must be intended for private use, occupation or consumption;

   ●   loss or damage to the defective product itself.

Limitation

1   Claimant must begin proceedings within three years of becoming aware of the defect, damage or identity of the defendant or, if damage is latent, the date of knowledge of the claimant provided that is within the ten-year period.

2   Court has discretion to override three-year period in personal injury.

3   In all cases there is an absolute cut-off point for claims of ten years from the date that the product was supplied.

Defences

1   Defences are contained in s 4 of the Act, including:

   ●   compliance with statutory or EU obligations, so defect is an inevitable consequence of complying with law, e.g. a chemical ingredient required by law which turns out to be dangerous;

   ●   defect did not exist when supplied by the defendant, including, for example, animal rights campaigners 'doctoring' baby food, or defect arises in subsequent product but was not in component;

   ●   product was not supplied in the course of a business;

   ●   defendant can show (s)he did not actually supply the product;

   ●   state of technical or scientific knowledge at relevant time was not such that defendant could be expected to have discovered the defect (*A v National Blood Authority* (2001), where screening test for infected blood was not available until 1991 but virus known of from 1988). This is controversial and inconsistent with other EU countries, which follow the Directive's wording of when the product was put into circulation.

Some criticisms of the Act

1   The Act is a step forward in a few ways:

- it has put producers on their guard, and increased knowledge of the need for appropriate checking and quality control;

- as a result there is a greater likelihood of product recall;

- it gives consumers more chance of an action because they have a greater range of potential defendants to choose from.

2   However, the Act has several shortcomings:

- it does not apply to all products, or all defects, or all damage;

- the limitation period is very strict;

- the Act does not apply to products supplied before 1988;

- the number of defences make it hard for claimants to succeed;

- causation is still a requirement and the standard of care is very similar to negligence, making it too similar to negligence, and not enough like strict liability which it is supposed to be.

Key Cases Checklist

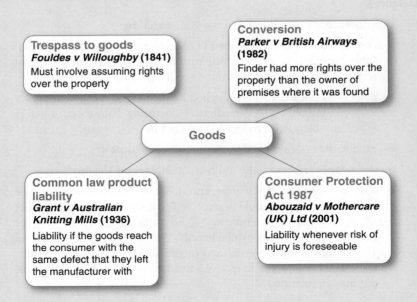

Trespass to goods
Fouldes v Willoughby **(1841)**
Must involve assuming rights over the property

Conversion
Parker v British Airways **(1982)**
Finder had more rights over the property than the owner of premises where it was found

Goods

Common law product liability
Grant v Australian Knitting Mills **(1936)**
Liability if the goods reach the consumer with the same defect that they left the manufacturer with

Consumer Protection Act 1987
Abouzaid v Mothercare (UK) Ltd **(2001)**
Liability whenever risk of injury is foreseeable

8.1.2.4   *Fouldes v Willoughby* (1841) 8 M & W 540   CE

Key Facts

The claimant boarded the defendant's ferry with two horses. The claimant was alleged to have behaved improperly and so to induce him to leave the ferry the defendant took hold of the horses and led them ashore. The claimant's action failed.

Key Law

The requirements of the tort were that the interference should be both direct and intentional. The court held that the defendant did not intend to interfere with the rights of the owner of the horses or assume any rights over them himself and so the action failed.

8.1.3.3   *Parker v British Airways Board* [1982] QB 1004   CA

Key Facts

The claimant found a gold bracelet in an airport lounge and handed it in together with his name and address. The true owner could not be found and the defendant air company sold it. The claimant then tried to claim the proceeds but the company refused.

Key Law

The court rejected the argument that the airport should have more right to the property than the finder because the real owner was more likely to make enquiries of them. The fact that the defendant had a procedure for lost property was insufficient to establish rights over things found on its premises and it was liable for conversion and was bound to return the property to the finder.

8.2.2.3

Grant v Australian Knitting Mills [1936] All ER Rep 209

Key Facts

The claimant contracted a painful skin disease from chemi-cals in underpants that he had bought. The chemicals were a part of the manufacturing process and the processes used to remove them had failed to do so.

Key Law

The court applied the basic principle in *Donoghue v Stevenson* (1932) in the claim against the manufacturer in making the defendant liable.

Key Judgment

Lord Wright stated:

'The garments were made by the manufacturers for the purpose of being worn exactly as they were worn . . . in Donoghue . . . the essential point . . . was that the article should reach the consumer or user subject to the same defect as it had when it left the manufacturer. That this was true of the garment is . . . beyond question'.

8.2.3

Abouzaid v Mothercare (UK) Ltd [2001] EWCA Civ 348

Key Facts

The claimant was injured in the eye when he was fastening elastic straps to secure a sleeping bag to a pushchair. The plastic slipped through his fingers and the buckle hit him in the eye. He claimed under the Act.

Key Law

The court held that the product was defective within the meaning of the Act because the design meant that the risk of injury was possible without the manufacturers giving any warning that it might occur.

9

Trespass to the person

Assault

- Intentionally and directly causing the victim to fear an imminent battery, so based on impression caused rather than what defendant will actually do.
- Can be threatening behaviour (*Read v Coker*).
- Can be a prevented battery (*Stephens v Myers*).
- Words traditionally insufficient without gestures:
  i) can disprove assault (*Tuberville v Savage*);
  ii) words can be duress in contract law (*Barton v Armstrong*);
  iii) now words are enough for assault in crime (*R v Ireland, R v Burstow*).
- Defences are consent, necessity, and self-defence.

False imprisonment

- Requires total bodily restraint (*Bird v Jones*).
- No action possible if a means of escape exists (*Wright v Wilson*).
- Liability possible where claimant unaware of the restraint (*Meering v Graham White Aviation*).
- No liability merely because claimant must pay to escape (*Robinson v Balmain Ferry*).
- No liability where employer has legitimate expectation that employee will complete shift (*Herd v Weardale Steel, Coal and Coke*).
- Defences include: consent, mistaken arrest, lawful arrest – and rules on arrest apply.

Battery

- Intentional, direct, unlawful physical contact with the claimant's body.
- If contact is not intentional then negligence appropriate (*Letang v Cooper*).
- Requires direct contact, but indirect has been accepted in the past (*Gibbons v Pepper, Nash v Sheen*), even where another party makes contact (*Scott v Shepherd*).
- There is some controversy over whether hostility is required – compare *Wilson v Pringle* with *Collins v Wilcock*.
- Medical treatment without consent is battery (*Re F*) but consent need not be informed (*Sidaway v Governors of Bethlem & Maudsley Hospitals*).
- Defences include:
  i) consent (*Simms v Leigh RFC*);
  ii) necessity (*Leigh v Gladstone*);
  iii) self-defence (*Revill v Newbury*);
  iv) inevitable accident (*Stanley v Powell*);
  v) lawful arrest.

TRESPASS TO THE PERSON

Harassment

- Action now under s 3 of Protection from Harassment Act 1997.
- Where there is a course of conduct that is unreasonable (*Green v DB Group Services*).

▶ 9.1 Assault

9.1.1 Definitions

1   The old view was that assault was an incomplete battery.

2   Modern definition is intentionally and directly causing a person to fear being victim of an imminent battery (*Letang v Cooper* (1965)).

9.1.2 Ingredients of the tort

1   Assault is free-standing, so intention refers to the impression it will produce in claimant, not as to what defendant intends to do. Compare *R v St George* (1840) with *Blake v Barnard* (1840).

2   No harm or contact is required (*I de S et Ux v W de S* (1348)).

3   Requires active behaviour, so merely barring entry is no assault (*Innes v Wylie* (1844)).

4   However, threatening behaviour can be assault (*Read v Coker* (1853)).

5   An attempt to commit a battery which is thwarted is still an assault (*Stephens v Myers* (1830)) – but there is no assault if it is impossible to carry out a battery since there could be no apprehension of it (*Thomas v National Union of Mineworkers* [1986]).

6   Traditionally words alone were not an assault:

   ● but could disprove an assault (*Tuberville v Savage* (1669));

   ● and a threat on its own can be assault (*Read v Coker*);

   ● and in contract law, words can amount to duress if the threat is sufficiently serious (*Barton v Armstrong* (1969));

   ● more recently, in crime, words alone and even silence have been accepted as assault (*R v Ireland; R v Burstow* (1998)).

7   The claimant must be fearful of an impending battery. Compare *Smith v Superintendent of Woking* (1983) with *R v Martin* (1881).

9.1.3 Defences

1   Consent (as in sports).

2   Self-defence (e.g. threatening an attacker).

3   Necessity (frightening people away from possible harm).

▶ **9.2 Battery**

9.2.1 Definitions

1   There are a number of possible definitions:

- the defendant intentionally and directly applies unlawful force to claimant's body – so cannot include negligent conduct (*Letang v Cooper* [1965]) – but force is irrelevant in, for example, medicine;

- the defendant, intending the result, does an act which directly and physically affects the claimant, but still implies damage;

- has been said to include the 'ordinary collisions of life', but this is very unlikely (*Wilson v Pringle* (1987)).

9.2.2 Ingredients of the tort

1   Intention is a fairly recent requirement – without it an action should be brought in negligence (*Fowler v Lanning* (1959)).

2   Traditional distinction was between direct and indirect contact:

- but now between intention and negligence (*Letang v Cooper* (1965));

- although in traditional cases indirect damage was often accepted (*Gibbons v Pepper* (1695));

- often where negligence might have seemed more appropriate (*Nash v Sheen* (1953));

- and even where other parties have actually caused the harm (*Scott v Shepherd* (1773)).

3   Usually no liability for omissions in trespass, only positive acts (*Fagan v Metropolitan Police Commissioner* (1969)).

4   Hostility is a recent requirement, with traditional foundations:

- Lord Holt CJ in *Cole v Turner* (1704) suggested that 'the least touching of another in anger is a battery';

- restated in *Wilson v Pringle* (1987);

- but conflicting with Lord Goff's test in *Collins v Wilcock* (1987) of whether the contact is acceptable in the conduct of daily life.

5   Medical treatment without consent has always been battery:

- a view reaffirmed by Lord Goff in *Re F* (1990) **and** *Re T* (1992);

- and in *T v T* (1988) the court refused to follow *Wilson v Pringle*;

- so where patient has full capacity s(he) can refuse life-sustaining treatment even where it leads to death (*Ms B v An NHS Hospital Trust* (2002));

- so consent is clearly an issue in medical treatment, but it is arguable what level of information is required for consent to be valid (*Sidaway v Governors of Bethlem Royal and Maudsley Hospitals* (1985));

- and patients are more likely to sue in medical negligence than in battery, according to the basic principle in *Bolam v Friern Hospital Management Committee* (1957).

6   The House of Lords in *Wainwright v Home Office* (2003) (where strip searches were not carried out in accordance with Prison Rules) has identified that there is no general tort of invasion of privacy.

9.2.3 Defences

1   *Volenti non fit injuria* – consent:

- in legitimate sporting injuries (*Simms v Leigh RFC* (1969));

- but not if inflicted outside proper rules (*Condon v Basi* (1985));

- in medical treatment consent invalid if patient is not broadly aware of type of treatment, etc. (*Chatterton v Gerson* (1981));

- if the patient is informed of the type of treatment but not the true extent of the risk there is no liability since English law has no doctrine of informed consent (*Sidaway v Governors of Bethlem Royal and Maudsley Hospitals* (1985)).

2   Necessity: justified if it is to prevent greater harm, e.g. death (*Leigh v Gladstone* (1909)).

3   Self-defence:

- only if reasonable force used (*Lane v Holloway* (1968));

- and it is reasonable to fear imminent attack and reasonable to use force in the circumstances *Ashley v Chief Constable of Sussex Police* (2008);

- a trespasser may defeat the defence where unreasonable force is used against him (*Revill v Newbery* (1996)).

4   Parental chastisement:

- a traditional right of parents to punish their naughty children;

- without reasonable force it may be tortious;

- it may not in any case have survived the Children Act.

5   Inevitable accident: possible if injury is unavoidable and beyond defend-ant's control (*Stanley v Powell* (1891)).

6   Lawful ejectment of a trespasser: depends on using reasonable force (*Revill v Newbery* (1996)).

7   Lawful arrest:

- by a police officer under s 24 PACE;

- by a citizen subject to the common law rules;

- in either case the arrest must be by reasonable force.

▶ 9.3 False imprisonment

9.3.1 Definition and ingredients of the tort

1   This tort is committed where the defendant imposes intentionally and directly a total restraint on the liberty of the claimant.

2   It is usually associated with wrongful arrests in the modern day, either by police or by security guards, store detectives, etc.

3   The restraint must be total (*Bird v Jones* (1845)).

4   The extent of the restraint could be large, but not, for example, a country.

5   No action if a safe means of escape exists (*Wright v Wilson* (1699)).

6   The restraint must be directly applied, but if it is not an action is still possible in negligence (*Sayers v Harlow UDC* (1958)). A police cordon could be false imprisonment (*Austin v Commissioner of Police for the Metropolis* (2005)).

7   There may even be liability where the claimant is unaware of the restraint (*Meering v Graham White Aviation* (1919)).

8   Or even if claimant is unconscious (*Murray v MOD* (1988)).

9   Not actionable merely because claimant is obliged to pay to get free, where he is contractually bound by a voluntary arrangement (*Robinson v Balmain New Ferry Co* (1910)).

10   Not actionable if an employer legitimately expects an employee to stay until end of shift (*Herd v Weardale Steel, Coal and Coke Co* (1915)).

11   It is an unlawful arrest which is made for a purely civil offence (*Sunbolf v Alford* (1838)).

12 It is false imprisonment to keep a prisoner past the lawful release date (*Cowell v Corrective Services Commissioner* (1989) and *R v Governor of Brockhill Prison ex parte Evans* (2000)) but holding prisoners in their cells for longer than normal because of a prison officers' strike was held to be negligence not trespass *Iqbal v Prison Officers Association* (2009).

13 But less convincingly false imprisonment where prisoners are maintained in a condition at odds with the prison rules. See the debate between CA in *Wheldon v Home Office* (1990) and DC in *R v Deputy Governor of Parkhurst Prison* (1990).

9.3.2 Defences

1   *Volenti non fit injuria* – consent, e.g. lawyer locked in cell with client.

2   Mistaken arrest – available to police only, if they act reasonably.

3   Lawful arrest:

●   powers defined in Police and Criminal Evidence Act 1984 (as amended by s 110 Serious Organised Crime and Police Act 2005);

●   a police officer can arrest on suspicion;

●   private citizens (security guards, store detectives) must be sure an arrestable offence has been or is being committed.

4   There are also common law rules on arrest.

●   An arrest must be made using reasonable force (*Treadaway v Chief Constable of the West Midlands* (1994)).

●   The arrest must not itself be an actionable trespass (*Hsu v Commissioner of the Police of the Metropolis* (1996)).

●   The person must be informed of reasons for arrest (*Christie v Leachinsky* (1947)).

●   In a citizen's arrest the person must be taken to a police station within reasonable time (*John Lewis & Co v Tims* (1952)) (or in arrest by police as soon as is reasonably practicable).

●   An unreasonable period of detention can be as little as 15 minutes (*White v WP Brown* (1983)).

●   PACE (1984) includes a code of conduct for police.

5   So arrest or detention should not offend the codes of practice or in any way be oppressive.

▶ 9.4 Intentional indirect harm

1   Originally if trespass was unavailable a novel action was needed.

2   To get over the problem of harm being direct rather than indirect courts accepted other principles:

 ● a duty not to deliberately cause harm (*Bird v Holbrook* (1828));

 ● an action for indirect but intentional harm (1828); *Wilkinson v Downton* (1897) and *Janvier v Sweeney* (1919).

3   Negligence now applies to most actions not covered by trespass. The House of Lords in *Wainwright v Home Office* (2003) has identified that *Wilkinson v Downton* should 'disappear' within negligence except where actual psychiatric injury has been caused.

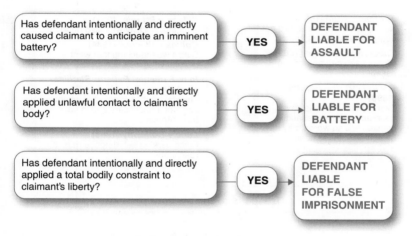

The different ways of committing trespass to the person

▶ 9.5 Harassment

1   Section 3 Protection from Harassment Act 1997 has introduced a statutory tort entitling victims of harassment to compensation (originally aimed at 'stalking').

2   The tort requires a 'course of conduct' – so must be at least two occurrences.

3   Conduct can be anything that a reasonable person would think amounts to harassment (*Howlett v Holding* (2006)).

4   This has now developed in the context of employers' liability for the protection of people who suffer bullying and other abuse in the work-place (*Green v DB Group Services (UK) Ltd* (2006)).

5   The course of conduct must be sufficiently serious for harassment to succeed (*Ferguson v British Gas Trading Ltd* (2009)).

6   Foreseeability of harm is not an essential element (*Jones v Ruth* (2011)).

Key Cases Checklist

Assault

Read v Coker (1853)
Requires physical actions that are threatening

Thomas v NUM (1986)
No assault if claimant could not apprehend imminent harm

Tuberville v Savage (1669)
Words used can negate the assault

R v Ireland; R v Burstow (1998)
Silent telephone calls have been accepted as assault in criminal law so words may now be sufficient for assault in tort

Battery

Letang v Cooper (1965)
Force must be applied directly and intentionally so not negligently

Wilson v Pringle (1987)
Said that hostility was also needed

Collins v Wilcock (1984)
Said it was touching that went beyond what was acceptable

In re F (Mental Patient: Sterilisation) (1990)
Medical treatment possible without consent if necessary and in patient's best interests

Lane v Holloway (1968)
Force used in self-defence must be reasonable

Trespass to the person

False imprisonment

Bird v Jones (1845)
Requires total bodily restraint with no means of escape

Meering v Graham White Aviation (1919)
Can occur even though claimant unaware of the imprisonment

Herd v Weardale Steel, Coal and Coke (1915)
No false imprisonment where there is a contractual duty to remain

Hsu v Commissioner of Police for the Metropolis (1997)
Lawful arrest is a defence but only if carried out reasonably

Wilkinson v Downton

Wilkinson v Downton (1897)
A claim is possible for harm intentionally but indirectly caused

Wainwright v Home Office (2003)
But claim not possible unless there is evidence of specific intent to cause physical or psychiatric harm

9.1.2.4

Read v Coker (1853) 13 CB 850   CP

Key Facts

The claimant owed the defendant rent. When the defendant told the claimant to leave the premises, the claimant refused. The defendant then ordered some employees to escort the claimant from the premises. These men surrounded the claimant, rolled up their sleeves and told him that if he did not leave they would break his neck. Held that there was an assault.

Key Law

The Court of Common Pleas held that there was a threat of violence with an ability to carry out the threat, indicated by the rolling up of sleeves but not by the words alone. This amounted to an actionable assault.

Key Judgment

Byles Serjt. explained that:

'To constitute an assault, there must be something more than a threat of violence . . . There must be some act done denoting a present ability and an intention to assault.'

9.1.2.4

Thomas v National Union of Mineworkers [1986] 1 Ch 20   Ch Div

Key Facts

During the miners' strike in 1984–85 working miners suffered abuse from striking miners as they were taken into the colliery in buses. Their claim for an injunction to prevent the picketing failed.

Key Law

The court held that there could be no assault since there was no possibility of the striking miners reaching the working miners as they were in buses at the time of the abuse. As such they could not have been put in any apprehension of an imminent battery.

9.1.2.6 *Tuberville v Savage* (1669) 1 Mod Rep 3   CP

Key Facts

During an argument with the claimant the defendant put his hand on his sword and said: 'If it were not Assize time I would not take such language from you.' The claim of assault failed.

Key Law

The court held that there was no assault because, while words alone cannot amount to an assault, they can make clear that an assault is not intended. The words here showed that the claimant had no intention to harm the claimant at that particular time so the claimant could not fear an impending battery.

9.1.2.6 *R v Ireland; R v Burstow* [1998] AC 147 HL   HL

Key Facts

This involved joined criminal appeals on whether silence can amount to assault. In both cases the victim had suffered psychiatric harm and Ireland made numerous silent telephone calls. Burstow was in effect a 'stalker', who engaged in a long campaign of silent telephone calls and anonymous letters to a young woman with whom he had briefly gone out three years previously. The case resulted in successful convictions.

Key Law

The House was first of all prepared to accept the psychiatric injuries as 'actual bodily harm' which was a necessary element of the criminal charges. It also accepted that a person who uses silence in order to produce apprehension of immediate violence in others is guilty of assault.

Key Problem

The case is generally taken now to mean that words alone can amount to assault. However, it is a criminal case and until such time as a tort case develops *Read v Coker* (1853) is still good law.

9.2.1.1

Letang v Cooper [1965] 1 QB 232 CA

Key Facts

The claimant was sunbathing in the grounds of a hotel near to where cars were parked. The defendant negligently reversed over her legs, injuring her. The woman claimed three years later, which fell outside the limitation period for negligence, so she claimed in trespass instead but was unsuccessful.

Key Law

The court held that while there was direct harm caused to the woman by the defendant's negligence, there was no intention to harm her and both were required for battery. Lord Denning felt that there was no overlap between trespass and negligence although Lord Diplock felt that there could be.

Key Judgment

Lord Denning explained:

'The plaintiff . . . must also allege that he did it intentionally or negligently. If intentional, it is . . . assault and battery. If negligent and causing damage, it is . . . negligence.'

9.2.1.1

Wilson v Pringle [1987] 2 All ER 440 CA

Key Facts

The claimant, a 13-year-old boy, suffered injuries to his hip when a school friend, as a practical joke, pulled his bag off his shoulder causing him to fall. His claim for damages failed.

Key Law

The court referred to the words of Holt CJ in *Cole v Turner* (1704) Holt KB 108 where he stated that 'the least touching of another in anger is a battery', and held that hostility was a necessary element of an actionable battery. Since the harm occurred during ordinary horseplay this element was missing and the claim failed.

Key Problem

This view would appear to narrow the scope of battery dramatically. It would make it impossible for instance to bring battery actions against doctors who engage in treatment without the consent of the patient but who clearly would not be acting with hostility.

Key Link

Collins v Wilcock [1984] 3 All ER 374.

9.2.2.2   *Nash v Sheen* [1953] CLY 3726   QBD

Key Facts

The claimant went to the defendant's hairdressing salon and asked for a 'permanent wave'. Instead she was given a 'tone rinse'. This not only dyed her hair an unpleasant colour but also caused a painful rash all over her body. The defendant was liable in battery.

Key Law

The court held that the defendant had applied the tone rinse to the claimant's scalp without any consent. The essential elements of a direct intentional interference were present so there was liability.

9.2.2.4   *Collins v Wilcock* [1984] 3 All ER 374   DC

Key Facts

A woman police officer was trying to take the name and address of a woman suspected of soliciting. When the suspect went to leave, the officer took hold of her arm but did not arrest her.

Key Law

The court held that, since the woman was not being arrested at the time the officer intentionally restrained her, which may otherwise have made the officer's action lawful, there was a battery.

Key Judgment

Lord Goff said:

'since her action went beyond the generally acceptable conduct of touching a person to engage his or her attention, it must follow . . . that her action constituted a battery'.

Key Comment

Lord Goff's definition of battery appears to be much more sensible and capable of general application than that of the Court of Appeal in *Wilson v Pringle* (1987).

9.2.2.5

Re T (an adult) (refusal of medical treatment) [1992] 3 WLR 782

Key Facts

The claimant was injured in a car crash and needed an emergency Caesarean section when she prematurely went into labour. As a result she needed a blood transfusion. She was a Jehovah's Witness, and refused the transfusion on religious grounds but the doctors gave it anyway. Her action in battery failed.

Key Law

The Court of Appeal accepted that in the case the patient was delirious at the time of refusal and was acting under undue influence by her mother, so that there was an emergency situation and the doctors in giving the transfusion had acted in her best interests. The court, however, accepted the absolute right of a competent patient to refuse treatment even to the point of death.

Key Judgment

Lord Donaldson MR stated that:

'An adult patient who . . . suffers from no mental incapacity has an absolute right to choose whether to consent to medical treatment, to refuse it or to choose one rather than another of the treatments being offered.'

9.2.2.5 — *In re F (Mental Patient: Sterilisation)* [1990] 2 AC 1

Key Facts

A 30-year-old woman in a mental institution had a mental age of about four or five but had become sexually active with another inmate. It was felt that if she became pregnant this would be disastrous for her. As contraception was inappropriate in the circumstances, the doctors applied to the court for a compulsory sterilisation. The treatment was allowed.

Key Law

The House held that, despite the inability of the claimant to consent, the sterilisation would be allowed because it was in her best interests, and it based its view on the principle of necessity.

Key Comment

The majority of judges in both the House of Lords (now the Supreme Court) and the Court of Appeal felt that the treatment would have been lawful without seeking a declaration from the courts. Nevertheless the issues in medical battery are often complex and it is important that individual cases should be referred to the courts.

Key Link

Re S (Adult: refusal of medical treatment) [1992] 3 WLR 806; *Re C (Adult: refusal of medical treatment)* [1994] 1 WLR 290.

9.2.3.1 — *Condon v Basi* [1985] 2 All ER 453

Key Facts

The claimant suffered a broken leg in a football game after a particularly reckless and dangerous tackle by the defendant. His claim in negligence succeeded.

Key Law

The court rejected the defendant's argument that the mere fact of participation in a sport automatically indicated an acceptance of the risk of harm that would relieve a defendant of any duty of care. The tackle fell out of the normal risks associated with the game and could not come within the defence of *volenti*.

Key Comment

It must be remembered that this is in fact a negligence case. However, the principles on consent are just as appropriate when applied to battery in a sporting context.

9.2.3.3   *Lane v Holloway* **[1968] 1 QB 379**   CA

Key Facts

A strained relationship existed between some neighbours. When one of them, the defendant, came home drunk and rowdy one night he was told by the woman next door to be quiet. He replied 'Shut up you monkey faced tart'. This then led to a fight between the defendant and the woman's husband. The defendant made a friendly and ineffectual shove at the husband who then beat him in the face so that he required 19 stitches. This attack was out of proportion to the gestures of the drunken man and the defence of self-defence failed.

Key Law

The court held that for the defence to apply, only reasonable force was appropriate. The reaction here was out of proportion to the verbal provocation by the claimant and the defence failed.

Key Link

Ashley v Chief Constable of Sussex Police (2008) UKHL 25.

9.3.1.3   *Bird v Jones* **(1845) 7 QB 742**   QB

Key Facts

The claimant wanted to cross Hammersmith Bridge. The footpath was closed and cordoned off for people to watch a regatta so he was invited by police officers to return the way that he had come. He refused and lost his subsequent action for false imprisonment.

Key Law

The court held that for the tort to apply there must be a total bodily restraint. Since there was a way of him getting away there was no unlawful restraint and no actionable trespass.

Key Judgment

Coleridge J suggested:

'it is one part of the definition of freedom to be able to go whither-soever one pleases; but imprisonment is something more than the mere loss of this power; it includes the notion of restraint within some limits defined by a will or power exterior to our own.'

9.3.1.7 *Meering v Graham White Aviation* (1919) 122 LT 44

Key Facts

The claimant was questioned in relation to thefts from his employer. Unknown to him, two men were posted at the door to prevent him from leaving. His claim for false imprisonment succeeded.

Key Law

The court held that knowledge of the imprisonment was not an essential element of the tort and therefore as the claimant had been held without lawful cause there was indeed a false imprisonment.

9.3.1.9 *Robinson v Balmain New Ferry* [1910] AC 295

Key Facts

The claimant had entered an enclosed wharf in order to board the ferry from Sydney to Balmain. Payment of a penny was made on exiting the wharf. The claimant in fact missed the ferry and as the next ferry was not due for another 20 minutes, he wished to exit. The gate manager would not allow him to exit without paying a penny, which he refused to do. His claim for false imprisonment failed.

Key Law

The court held that there was no false imprisonment because by passing through the turnstiles the claimant had agreed to be bound by the contractual terms.

9.3.1.10 *Herd v Weardale Steel, Coal and Coke Co* [1915] AC 67

HL

Key Facts

The claimants, who were miners, had entered the mine but towards the start of their shift, decided that they were being asked to do work that was too dangerous so they asked to be returned in the cages to the surface. The employers refused and they were not allowed out until the end of their shift. Their action for false imprisonment failed.

Key Law

The court held that there was no false imprisonment since the men had already contracted to stay down the mine for a specific time and the employer was not obliged to use the lift until then. This was a reasonable condition for release.

9.3.2.4 *Hsu v Commissioner of Police of the Metropolis* [1997] 3 WLR 402

QBD

Key Facts

The claimant, who was a hairdresser, refused to allow police officers without a warrant to enter his house. He was grabbed, handcuffed, and then thrown into a police van where he was punched, kicked, and verbally abused. He was finally released from custody wearing only his jeans and flip-flops and had to walk two miles home where he found his door open and property stolen. At hospital he was found to have extensive bruising and blood in his urine. His complaint to the Police Complaints Authority succeeded and he sued successfully in trespass to the person.

Key Law

The court found that there was no lawful justification for his detention and the police had not used reasonable force.

9.4.2 *Wilkinson v Downton* [1897] 2 QB 57 QBD

Key Facts

The claimant suffered severe shock after the defendant had told her as a joke that her husband had been seriously injured in an accident. Her claim for damages succeeded.

Key Law

The court held that, since there was no direct interference, an action in trespass was not possible. However, the court found that there was an intentional act that was calculated to cause harm indirectly for which the defendant must be liable, since it was reasonable to assume that the harm was of a type that could be expected of a reasonable person in the circumstances.

9.4.3 *Wainwright v Home Office* [2003] UKHL 53; [2003] 3 WLR 1137 HL

Key Facts

A mother and son, the claimants, visited a prisoner in prison and were subjected to full strip searches, which were not authorised under the prison rules, in order to check for drugs. The mother suffered emotional distress as a consequence but the son suffered post-traumatic stress disorder. The claimants alleged that the searches were an invasion of their privacy and also that the rule in *Wilkinson v Downton* (1897) applied. Their actions for damages failed.

Key Law

The House of Lords (now the Supreme Court) first of all rejected the idea that there was a common law tort of invasion of privacy. Secondly, it held that the rule in *Wilkinson v Downton* (1897) could not apply without proof of a specific intention to cause either physical or psychiatric injury.

Key Comment

Mention was made in the case of the Protection from Harassment Act 1997. This requires a course of action of at least two incidents so the rule in *Wilkinson v Downton* still survives for single incidents that are intentional but cause damage indirectly.

9.5.5

Ferguson v British Gas Trading Ltd [2009] EWCA Civ 46

Key Facts

The claimant, a customer of British Gas, changed to a different supplier. British Gas continued to send her bills for gas it had not supplied and later sent several letters threatening to cut off her gas supply, to start legal proceedings against her and to inform a credit rating agency. Despite her contacting the company several times, the sending of the bills and threatening letters continued.

These were generated by a computer rather than an individual. The claimant alleged harassment.

Key Law

The Court of Appeal held that the company's conduct was sufficiently serious to amount to harassment, and there was no policy reason to treat a corporation differently to an individual.

Key Comment

The court held that, although conduct must be serious for a claim under s 3 of the Act, the fact of parallel criminal and civil liability is not significant in determining civil liability.

10 Torts affecting reputation

Classifications

Libel:
- permanent form, e.g. in writing, but also films (*Youssoupoff v MGM Pictures*);
- wax effigy (*Monson v Tussauds*);
- actionable *per se*.

Slander:
- transitory form, e.g. spoken;
- requires proof of damage unless suggesting:
    i) an offence involving prison;
    ii) incompetence in a trade, profession or employment

Ingredients of the tort:

Publication:
- involves making statement to a third party;
- so includes when defendant knows that someone other than claimant will open a letter (*Theaker v Richardson*);
- and things like graffiti (*Byrne v Deane*);
- but not where claimant shows a letter to a third party (*Hinderer v Cole*);
- nor remarks in a sealed letter (*Huth v Huth*).

Of a defamatory statement:
- judge decides whether statement is capable of being defamatory and jury whether it is in fact;
- must lower esteem of claimant in the minds of right-thinking people (*Sim v Stretch*);
- can be any derogatory remarks (*Cornwell v Daily Mail*);
- or can be by innuendo (*Monson v Tussauds* and *Tolley v Fry*);
- but not if implying honesty (*Byrne v Deane*).

Referring to the claimant:
- false statement must refer to claimant;
- which may even be through a fictional name (*Hulton v Jones*);
- but cannot include a class that is too broad and vague (*Le Fanu v Malcolmson*).

Which causes serious harm to the claiment's reputation –s1 Defamtion Act 2013

DEFAMATION

Defences

Truth –s2 Defamation Act 2013
- the truth can never be defamatory;
- burden is on defendant to show statement is true (*Archer v The Star*);
- can be complex where general rather than specific allegations made (*Bookbinder v Tebbitt*).

Honest opinion: s5 Defamtion Act 2013
- Statement was matter of honest opinion
- An honest person could have held the opinion
- Which is based on fact

Responsible publication on matters of public interest:
- Must be of public interest ***London Artists v Littler***
- Defendant must have acted responsibly ***Telnikoff v Matusevich***

Absolute privilege:
- applies in Parliament and court and fair reporting of either, and to client.
- applies to memos, references, reports on Parliament not in *Hansard*;
- can be defeated if malice shown.

Unintentional defamation:
- where defendant does not know of defamation – now in ss 2–4 1996 Act.

Innocent dissemination:
- where defamation repeated innocently (*Vizetelly v Mudies Select Library*).

Volenti:
- where defendant has in effect invited publication (*Moore v News of the World*).

▶ 10.1 Defamation

10.1.1 The categories of defamation

1   The main tort developed to protect reputation.

2   As such it can be made in a number of ways, but there are two specific categories: libel and slander.

3   The general distinction is between 'permanent' and 'transitory':

- libel has been called a written form and slander a spoken form;
- this view is no longer adequate because of modern technology;
- the difference owes more to origins than real justification;
- it has been discarded by most commonwealth jurisdictions;
- this was recommended in the UK by the Faulkes Report;
- but the Defamation Act 1996 did not address this issue;
- and nor does the Defamation Act 2013.

4   The two categories do have two important distinctions:

a)   Libel can be crime as well as tort (*R v Lemon* (1977)).

b)   Libel is actionable per se; for slander damage must be shown except in some limited circumstances:

- imputation of an offence involving imprisonment;
- imputation of unfitness or incompetence in a trade, profession, office or calling (and now by Defamation Act 1952 for any employment provided claimant could be harmed as a result);
- imputation of a contagious disease now requires proving special damage under s14 Defamation Act 2013.

5   The difference between permanent and transitory is not always obvious, but there are acknowledged situations:

- a written defamation is obviously libel;
- films are libels (*Youssoupoff v MGM Pictures Ltd* (1934));
- radio and television broadcasts are libel under the Defamation Act 1952 and the Broadcasting Act 1990;
- by s 4 Theatres Act 1968 a defamation in a public performance of a play is also libel;
- wax effigy in a museum is libel (*Monson v Tussauds* (1894));

- a red light hung outside a woman's house could be libel;
- the spoken word in general is slander;
- gestures in general are slander;
- tapes are probably slander because they can be wiped;
- but other recordings, such as CD and vinyl, whether made in studios or from live performance, are less easy to categorise.

10.1.2 The definition and ingredients of the tort

Definition

1   Defined as 'the publishing of a defamatory statement which refers to the claimant and which has no lawful justification'.

2   Section 1 Defamation Act 2013 adds another element, that the defamation has caused serious harm to the claimant's reputation.

3   Each separate element of the tort must be proved.

Publication

1   This involves communicating the statement to a third party.

2   Each repeat is a fresh publication and therefore actionable, so there can be many defendants to a defamation action.

3   Publication could include:

- a postcard (as it is assumed it will be seen by a third party);
- every sale of a newspaper;
- every lending of a book from a library;
- a letter addressed to the wrong person;
- a letter the defendant knows someone besides the claimant might open (*Pullman v Hill* (1891) and *Theaker v Richardson* (1962));
- graffiti that cannot be removed (*Byrne v Deane* (1937));
- making a remark so that it is overheard;
- the defendant can also be liable for the consequences of a defamatory statement that (s)he knows will be repeated (*Slipper v BBC* (1991));
- it is uncertain whether repeating the remark through internal mail amounts to fresh publication.

4   In the following there is generally no publication:

- a statement made only to the claimant who then shows it to a third party (*Hinderer v Cole* (1977));

- communication between spouses only;

- a letter addressed only to the claimant;

- remarks contained in a sealed letter (*Huth v Huth* (1915));

- an 'innocent dissemination' (*Vizetelly v Mudie's Select Library Ltd* (1900));

- an internet search engine has been held not to be a publisher *Metropolitan International Schools Ltd v Designtechnica Corp* (2009).

The defamatory statement

1   Defamation trials traditionally involved a jury but there is a presumption against the use of juries in the Defamation Act 2013.

2   The judge must decide whether the words in fact are defamatory: 'a statement which tends to lower the plaintiff in the minds of right-thinking members of society generally, and in particular to cause him to be regarded with feelings of hatred, contempt, ridicule, fear and dis-esteem' (Lord Atkin in *Sim v Stretch* (1935)).

3   So defamatory remarks depend entirely on context and include:

- vulgar abuse (*Cornwell v Daily Mail* (1989));

- derogatory remarks (*Savalas v Associated Newspapers* (1976) and *Roach v Newsgroup Newspapers Ltd* (1992));

- references to a person's moral character (*Stark v Sunday People* (1988)).

4   Implying honesty is not defamatory (*Byrne v Deane* (1937)); nor are statements that lead to sympathy rather than scorn (*Grappelli v Derek Block Holdings Ltd* (1981)).

5   'Innuendo' can also be defamation:

- so, words can defame because of their juxtaposition with other things (*Monson v Tussauds* (1894) and *Cosmos v BBC* (1976));

- or by containing hidden meaning (*Tolley v Fry & Sons Ltd* (1931) and *Cassidy v Daily Mirror* (1929));

- although a complaint of such a meaning can bring other evidence into court (*Allsopp v Church of England Newspaper Ltd* (1972)).

Referring to the claimant

1   The claimant must show that the statement referred to him/her:

- this is easy if (s)he is named:
- it is sufficient if claimant can show people might think it refers to him/her;
- this may be shown even if a fictional name is used (*Hulton & Co v Jones* (1910));
- or if two people have the same name (*Newstead v London Express Newspapers Ltd* (1940));
- or with cartoons (*Tolley*).

2   Vague generalisations about a broad class are difficult to relate to a particular claimant.

- Class defamation is possible if a claimant can show (s)he is identifiable as a member of the class. Compare *Knupffer v London Express Newspapers Ltd* (1944) with *Le Fanu v Malcolmson* (1848).

10.1.3 Defences

Without lawful justification

1   'Without justification' refers to the existence or not of a defence.

2   Traditional common law defences have been added to by statute.

3   Each is complex and usually applies in specific circumstances.

Truth under s 2 Defamation Act 2013

1   Introduced by s 2 Defamation Act 2013 (replacing justification).

2   This is a complete defence, since truth can never be defamatory.

3   It is not straightforward because the burden of proof is on the defendant to show that the allegation was true (*Archer v The Star* (1987)).

4   Problems arise where the defendant makes a general rather than a specific allegation (*Bookbinder v Tebbitt* (1989)).

5   By s 4 Defamation Act 2013 the defence will not fail merely because every charge is not true.

6   However, there are important exceptions to this principle (*Charleston v Mirror Group* (1996)).

7   Possible on revealing spent conviction if no malice is shown.

Honest opinion

1   Under s 5 Defamation Act 2013 this defence replaced fair comment.

2   Fair comment mainly protected the press in expressing opinions of public interest but honest opinion applies more generally.

3   The basis of honest opinion would be:

● The statement was a matter of honest opinion.

● The statement formed the basis of the opinion.

● An honest person could have held the opinion based on current facts or privileged information.

4   The opinion must be based on facts (*Kemsley v Foot* (1952)).

Responsible publication on matters of public interest

1   Defence introduced by s 6 Defamation Act 2013.

2   So the statement must involve something of public interest (*London Artists Ltd v Littler* (1969)).

3   The defendant must have acted responsibly in publishing the statement – under the previous defence of fair comment this would have been measured objectively (*Telnikoff v Matusevitch* (1992)).

4   Acting responsibly would be measured against:

● the nature of the publication and its context;

● the seriousness of the imputation conveyed by the statement;

● the relevance of the imputation conveyed by the statement to the matter of public interest concerned;

● the importance of the matter of public interest concerned;

● the information the defendant had before publishing the statement; and

● what the defendant knew about the reliability of that information;

● whether the defendant sought the claimant's views on the statement before publishing it and whether an account of any views the claimant expressed was published with the statement;

● whether the defendant took any other steps to verify the truth of the imputation conveyed by the statement;

● the timing of the statement's publication.

Absolute privilege

1   In certain situations freedom of speech is essential.

2   These are given absolute protection of the freedom and include:

- statements made in either House of Parliament (Bill of Rights 1688), which can now be waived under s 13 Defamation Act 1996;

- official reports of parliamentary proceedings, i.e. *Hansard*;

- judicial proceedings (which covers judge, jury, lawyers, parties, and witnesses, but not the public) (*Mahon and another v Rahn and others* (2000));

- 'fair, accurate and contemporaneous' reports of judicial proceedings (s 3 Law of Libel Amendment Act 1888 for the press and now s 9(2) Defamation Act 1952 for broadcasters);

- communications between lawyer and client;

- communications between officers of state.

3   And under s 9 Defamation Act 2013 is extended to courts outside of the UK and courts set up by the United Nations.

Qualified privilege

1   This is complex and different from absolute privilege since it concerns the communication itself, rather than the occasion when it is made.

2   So it can be defeated by showing malice. Compare *Horrocks v Lowe* (1974) with *Angel v Bushel Ltd* (1968).

3   But it applies in a number of situations:

- in exercise of a duty, e.g. a comment made in a reference;

- in protecting an interest, e.g. a comment made in internal memos within a business;

- in the fair, accurate and contemporaneous reports of parliamentary proceedings, i.e. not in *Hansard* (*Reynolds v Times Newspapers* (1998));

- in fair reporting of judicial proceedings (under the Defamation Act 1996 this includes all court and official proceedings or official proceedings worldwide);

- in fair and accurate reporting of public meetings (*Turkington and others v Times Newspapers* (2000));

- a complex list under s 7 Defamation Act 1952 also includes:

    i)   those privileged without an explanation under Part 1 of the Schedule, e.g. public proceedings in Commonwealth Parliaments;

ii) those privileged subject to an explanation under Part 2 of the Schedule, e.g. fair and accurate reports of trade associations.

4   And under s 9 Defamation Act 2013 is extended to fair and accurate reports of proceedings of courts outside of the UK.

NB in either case if malice is proved it defeats the defence.

Unintentional defamation

1   This applies under s 4 Defamation Act 1952 where a defendant is unaware of the defamatory nature of remarks made.

2   It remedies situations like those in *Hulton* and *Cassidy*.

3   The statement must have been innocently made.

4   Defendant may offer amends by suitable apology, payment into court, supported by affidavit saying why publication was innocent (*Nail v News Group Newspapers* (2005)):

● if accepted there can be no further action;

● if not the defendant may still have a defence if (s)he shows:

i) publication was innocent and no negligence in making it;

ii) offer of amends was made as soon as possible;

iii) the statement was made without malice.

5   The defence was criticised by the Faulkes Committee.

6   Now under ss 2–4 Defamation Act 1996 there is a rebuttable presumption of innocent publication.

Innocent dissemination

1   Protects producers of mechanical reproduction or distribution if they can show that:

● they were innocent of knowledge of the defamation;

● there was nothing to alert them to the defamation;

● their ignorance of the defamation was not negligence.

Volenti non fit injuria

1   Consent to the publication may defeat a claim.

2   It may apply because claimant has passed material on (*Hinderer v Cole*).

3   It may apply because claimant has invited publication (*Moore v News of the World* (1972)).

Accord and satisfaction

1   Applies if the claimant gives up the right to sue in return for a payment and/or apology.

10.1.4 Remedies

Injunctions

1   Interim injunctions are granted to prevent publication/broadcast.

2   However, this is often accused of 'gagging' free speech.

Damages

1   There are three types in defamation actions:

   ● **nominal:** if case is proven but little or no damage is suffered;

   ● **contemptuous:** awarded where, even though the claimant wins the case, the jury feel the action should not have been brought (*Dering v Uris* (1964), where damages of $\frac{1}{2}$d were awarded);

   ● **exemplary:** used to punish defendant, so damages high.

2   Traditionally there were many criticisms concerning damages while defamation actions were heard by juries which also decided on damages:

   ● that juries awarded them at all;

   ● that judges in other civil actions (e.g. personal injury) are restrained in the damages they may award;

   ● that juries were inconsistent in their awards and awarded excessive sums (*Lord Aldington v Tolstoy and Watts* (1989) – £1,500,000); (*Donovan v Face* (1992) – £100,000 damages nearly ruined the magazine);

   ● overlarge sums could be reduced, e.g. *Sutcliffe v Private Eye* (1989), where damages of £650,000 were reduced to £6,000. But the jury's award were not interfered with unless they exceeded what any jury could have considered reasonable (*Kiam II v MGN Ltd* (2002));

   ● but all of these problems have been remedied by s 13 Defamation Act 2013, which creates a presumption against the use of juries.

10.1.5 Reform of defamation law

1   The Faulkes Committee in 1975 suggested many reforms:

   ● ending the distinction between libel and slander;

- altering the defence of justification to one of truth;

- improving the defence of fair comment so it only fails if the comment is not actually a true opinion;

- qualified privilege to be defeated if the maker takes advantage of the privilege rather than only if there is malice;

- simplifying the procedural requirements for unintentional defamation;

- making exemplary damage awards impossible;

- allowing actions for defaming the dead;

- reducing the limitation period to three years;

- making legal aid available;

- giving judges the responsibility for awarding damages.

2   Later suggestions for simplified procedures followed.

3   The Defamation Act 1996 attempted to partly reform the law, but made fairly minimal reforms which included:

- creating a new fast-track system for claims under £10,000 to dispose quickly of small cases;

- introducing a new 'offer of amends' defence for newspapers in the case of unintentional defamation;

- certain cases to be heard by a judge alone;

- reducing the limitation period to one year.

4   The Defamation Act 2013 answers many of the criticisms above and makes more far-reaching changes as indicated in earlier sections.

10.1.6 Justifications and criticisms of the tort

1   Justified because we are each entitled to protect our reputation.

2   However, this right must be balanced with freedom of speech:

- so the truth, however damaging, must not be suppressed;

- but the common criticism of defamation law is that it does so.

3   The UK has been very out of line with human rights principles:

- inconsistent with US law – 1st amendment to the Constitution;

- out of line with Art 10 European Convention on Human Rights:

  'Everyone has the right to freedom of expression. This right shall include freedom to hold opinions and to receive information and ideas without interference by public authority and regardless of frontiers';

- this was recognised before incorporation by Human Rights Act 1988 (*Rantzen v Mirror Group Newspapers* (1996)). See *Steel and Morris v UK* (2005) for breach of Article 6 and Article 10;

- but the Act should remedy this.

4   It also favours the rich, since legal aid is unavailable.

- this can be avoided by bringing an action under malicious falsehood (*Joyce v Sengupta* (1993));

- costs are very prohibitive (*Taylforth v Metropolitan Commissioner & The Sun Newspaper* (1994));

- as a result actions always seem to involve the press and the famous.

5   The defence of privilege can also cause practical problems, but these can be overcome by claiming negligence instead (*Spring v Guardian Assurance plc* (1994)).

6   The law also fails to protect the dead, whose actions die with them.

▶ 10.2 Malicious falsehood and deceit

10.2.1 Deceit

1   In deceit a defendant makes a false statement to the claimant, or a class of people including the claimant, knowing it is false, or being reckless, intending that the claimant will rely on it for his/her conduct, and the claimant does rely on it and suffers damage.

2   A successful claimant can recover for both physical injury and financial loss (*Burrows v Rhodes* (1899)).

3   The tort can also apply to misrepresentations in contract.

10.2.2 The ingredients of deceit

The making of a false statement

1   The false statement must concern a material fact, not a mere opinion (*Bisset v Wilkinson* (1927)).

2   This does not apply if it is based on specialist knowledge (*Esso v Marden* (1976)).

3   It may be a false statement of fact to misrepresent an opinion or knowledge not actually held (*Edgington v Fitzmaurice* (1885)).

4   A false statement includes failing to correct a true statement that becomes false (*With v O'Flanagan* (1936)).

The ingredients of deceit

Defendant makes a false statement:
- so it must be a statement of fact, not opinion (*Bisset v Wilkinson*);
- but can be failing to correct a true statement that becomes false (*With v O'Flanagan*).

Defendant knows that the statement is false:
- so makes the statement deliberately, or without belief in its truth, or reckless as to its truth (*Derry v Peek*);
- and an employer can be vicariously liable for the false statements of his/her employee, or a principal for those of his/her agent.

Defendant intends claimant to act upon the statement:
- which must be by the person defendant intends (*Peek v Gunley*);
- though the statement need not be made to the claimant (*Langridge v Levy*).

The claimant must rely on the false statement:
- and show detriment by acting on it (*Smith v Chadwick*).

Claimant must suffer damage as a result:
- and can claim for direct consequence loss (*Doyle v Olby (Ironmongers)*).

DECEIT AND MALICIOUS FALSEHOOD

The ingredients of malicious falsehood

Defendant makes a false statement about claimant:
- so it must refer to claimant to be actionable (*Cambridge University Press v University Tutorial Press*).

The statement is made to a third party:
- similar requirement to publication in defamation that claimant's reputation harmed.

The statement is made with malice:
- so must involve absence of just cause or belief (*Joyce v Motor Surveys*).

The statement is calculated to cause damage to claimant:
- so requires specific references to claimant (*White v Mellin*).

Claimant suffers damage or loss:
- which can be general, but must be foreseeable, and special damage need not be proved.

Knowledge that the statement is false

1   The test is in *Derry v Peek* (1889), where false statement was made:

- knowingly; or

- without belief in its truth; or

- reckless as to whether it was true or not.

2   If a servant acting in the course of his employment commits deceit then the master is vicariously liable.

3   The same is likely to be true of agents and their principals.

4   And where the misrepresentation is made on behalf of another party if all other elements of the tort are satisfied (*Standard Chartered Bank v Pakistan National Shipping Corporation (Nos 2 and 4)* (2002)).

Intention that the statement should be acted upon

1   The defendant must intend the statement to be acted upon.

2   Only people in the class that the defendant intended to act upon the statement can sue (*Peek v Gurnley* (1873)).

3   So the representation need not be made personally to the claimant (*Langridge v Levy* (1837)).

4   The mere fact that it is foreseeable that the claimant may act on the statement is not enough (*Caparo v Dickman* (1990)).

Reliance on the statement

1   The claimant must show detriment caused by acting on the statement (*Smith v Chadwick* (1884)).

2   It need not be the only reason that he acted as he did.

Damage suffered by the claimant

1   The claimant must suffer damage e.g. economic loss, personal injury, property damage, distress (*Archer v Brown* (1984)).

2   Any losses that are a direct consequence of the deceit are recoverable (*Doyle v Olby (Ironmongers) Ltd* (1969)).

3   And damages for loss of a chance are also available in deceit (*4 Eng v Harper* (2008)).

10.2.3 Malicious falsehood

1   Also known as injurious falsehood, a generalisation of specific cases (*Ratcliffe v Evans* (1892)) with origins in slander of title – questioning a person's title to land and making it less saleable.

2   In the 19th century it extended to include slander of goods.

3   It now includes protecting personal business interests (*Kaye v Robertson* (1991) and *Joyce v Sengupta* (1993)).

4   There must be a false statement about the claimant, made to a third party, and made maliciously, calculated to cause the claimant damage, and actually causing damage to the claimant.

10.2.4 The ingredients of the tort

A false statement about the claimant

1   The statement must be false, so trade puffs are not actionable, but false statements running down competitors' goods may be (*De Beers Abrasive Products Ltd v International General Electric Co of New York* (1975)).

2   A statement not referring to the claimant is not actionable even if it causes damage (*Cambridge University Press v University Tutorial Press* (1928)).

A statement made to a third party

1   A similar requirement to publication in defamation.

2   Third parties must be turned off the claimant before (s)he suffers loss.

Malice

1   Claimant must prove that the statement was made with malice.

2   Malice need not necessarily involve dishonesty.

3   It must involve the absence of just cause or of belief in the statement (*Joyce v Motor Surveys Ltd* (1948)).

Calculated to cause damage to the claimant

1   Calculated means foreseeable.

2   So specific references rather than general ones are necessary. Compare *Lyne v Nicholls* (1906) with *White v Mellin* (1895).

Damage suffered by the claimant

1   The claimant must show actual loss.

2   Loss can be general rather than, for example, loss of a specific customer.

3   Damage can include property damage and financial loss.

4   The test for remoteness is foreseeability.

5   The claimant need not prove special damage:

- if the statement is in written or permanent form and calculated to cause financial loss; or

- calculated to cause the claimant a financial loss in respect of a claimant's office, profession, calling, trade, or business at the time of publication (s 3(i) Defamation Act (1952)).

6   Suing in defamation instead can be advantageous (*Fielding v Variety Incorporated* (1967)).

Key Cases Checklist

Defamation

Monson v Tussauds (1894)
Libel is defamation in permanent form e.g. a waxwork effigy

Theaker v Richardson (1962)
There must be a publication to a third party which could be where someone who might be expected to open mail does so

Hulton & Co v Jones (1910)
The defamation must refer to the claimant but it is sufficient that it is reasonable to suppose that acquaintances might think it refers to him

Tolley v Fry (1931)
Defamation can be by innuendo or by implication

Byrne v Deane (1937)
The statement must lower the estimation of the claimant in the minds of right-thinking people so following the law would not lower that estimation

Knupffer v London Express Newspapers Ltd (1944)
Class actions usually fail unless the claimant is individually recognisable

Bookbinder v Tebbitt (1989)
The truth can never be defamatory

Kemsley v Foot (1952)
Fair comment is a defence where it is genuine opinion based on facts and in the public interest

Reynolds v Times Newspapers (2001)
Qualified privilege defence depends on ten key factors

Torts Affecting Reputation

Deceit

Derry v Peek (1889)
Liability possible where defendant made a false representation knowingly, without belief in its truth, or reckless as to whether it was true or not

Malicious falsehood

Kaye v Robertson (1991)
The false statement must be made maliciously and calculated to cause the claimant financial loss

10.1.1.5

Monson v Tussauds Ltd [1894] 1 QB 671

QBD

Key Facts

A man accused of murder was released on a 'not proven' verdict by a Scottish jury. The defendant produced a wax effigy of the man and placed it at the entrance to the Chamber of Horrors.

Key Law

The court held that the effigy on its own did not amount to defamation but its juxtaposition with other tableaux in the Chamber of Horrors indicated that he was in fact guilty and thus did. Libel is defamation in permanent form and the court held that the waxwork was sufficiently permanent to be libel.

10.1.1.5

Youssoupoff v MGM Pictures Ltd (1934) 50 TLR 581

CA

Key Facts

A film about the life of Rasputin suggested that he had seduced a Princess Natasha, one of the Russian Royal family, who was recognisable as the claimant.

Key Law

The court held that even though the film did not suggest that the princess was at all responsible for the seduction, the suggestion was still sufficient to damage her social standing. The film was accepted as defamation in permanent form and was thus libel.

Key Comment

Now attitudes have changed and Defomation Act 2013 has repealed the Slander of Woman Act 1891.

10.1.2

Theaker v Richardson [1962] 1 WLR 151

Key Facts

A member of a local council wrote a letter to another member of the council in which he called her a 'lying, low down brothel keeping whore and thief'. The claimant's husband opened and read the letter. The claimant's action for libel succeeded.

Key Law

The court identified that there was a publication since it was reasonable to assume that the husband, who was the claimant's election agent, might open it, thinking it was an election address.

10.1.2

Hulton & Co v Jones [1910] AC 20

Key Facts

A humorous fictitious article in a newspaper about the London to Dieppe motor rally suggested that the central character called Artemus Jones and described as a church-warden from Peckham had engaged in an affair. The claimant, also called Artemus Jones, who was a barrister from Wales, sued successfully for libel.

Key Law

The court held that it was not necessary to show that the defamation was intended to refer to the claimant, only that people who knew him might easily believe that the article referred to him.

10.1.2

Tolley v Fry & Sons Ltd [1931] AC 333

Key Facts

An advertising poster for Fry's chocolate bars included a caricature of a famous amateur golfer of the time with a bar of chocolate sticking out of his back pocket. He sued successfully in libel because he was disturbed that his amateur status would be compromised because people would think that he had been paid.

Key Law

The court held that the advert was defamation by innuendo; the suggestion of breaching amateur rules was implied.

10.1.2   *Byrne v Deane* [1937] 1 KB 818

Key Facts

After a tip-off from an informer, police had removed an illegal gambling machine from a golf club. Later a poem appeared on the notice board which included the words 'he who gave the game away may he byrne in hell'. The claimant argued that the spelling was an accusation that he was the informer and suggested disloyalty on his part. His claim failed.

Key Law

While there was a publication, the court held that the words were not defamatory since the inference in the poem was that the claimant had done his duty as a law-abiding citizen, which could not lower his estimation in the minds of right-thinking people.

Key Judgment

Greene LJ was of the opinion that *'to say of a man that he has put in motion the proper machinery for suppressing crime is a thing which . . . cannot, on the face of it, be defamatory'*.

10.1.2   *Cassidy v Daily Mirror Newspapers Ltd* [1929] 2 KB 331

Key Facts

Mrs Cassidy sued successfully when a picture was taken of her husband at the races, accompanied by a young woman who was described in the caption as being recently engaged.

Key Law

The court held that by innuendo the photograph implied that the young woman was Mr Cassidy's fiancé and that Mr and Mrs Cassidy were not married, which had caused and could cause her friends to doubt her moral character. It was therefore defamatory.

Key Judgment

Russell LJ explained that:

'Liability for libel does not depend on the intention of the defamer, but on the fact of the defamation.'

Scrutton LJ added:

'If newspapers ... publish statements which may be defamatory ... without inquiry as to their truth, in order to make their newspaper more attractive, they must take the consequences if ... their statements are found to be untrue.'

10.1.2   *Knupffer v London Express Newspapers Ltd* [1944] AC 116

HL

Key Facts

An article about the Young Russian Party described it as unpatriotic and being willing to help Hitler. Knupffer was head of the British branch of the party which had only 24 members. His claim failed.

Key Law

The court held that, since the party was in fact international, no individual could be easily identified in the article and reasonable people would not think that it referred to the claimant in particular.

Key Judgment

Lord Atkin explained:

'The reason why a libel published of a large or indeterminate number of persons described by some general name generally fails to be actionable is the difficulty of establishing that the plaintiff was, in fact, included in the defamatory statement.'

Key Comment

Actions alleging defamation of a class of people will almost always fail unless the class is so small that it is possible to recognise the individual claimant in the class, e.g. 'Footballers are corrupt villains' would fail, but 'The goal-keepers at Badborough United are renowned for taking money to lose matches' might succeed.

10.1.2

Vizetelly v Mudie's Select Library Ltd [1900] 2 QB 170

Key Facts

A mobile library failed to prevent circulation of a book containing defamatory material after receiving a warning about its content.

Key Law

The defendants were liable because they had ignored the warnings and had failed to establish that they published innocently. The court accepted, however, that there could be a defence of innocent dissemination which would be available if defendants could show that:

- they were unaware that the book contained defamatory material when they distributed it;
- there was nothing suspicious to alert them to the presence of the defamatory material.

10.1.3

Bookbinder v Tebbitt [1989] 1 All ER 1169

Key Facts

During an election campaign the defendant referred to the policies of a local council as 'a damn fool idea'. The policy in question was overprinting stationery with 'Support Nuclear Free Zone'. The defendant was unsuccessful in his defence of justification.

Key Law

The court would not allow the defendant to introduce evidence of the council's overspending, so the words in context were incapable of supporting the specific allegation made by the defendant.

10.1.3   *Telnikoff v Matusevitch* **[1992] 4 All ER 817**   HL

Key Facts

In an article in the *Telegraph* the claimant criticised the BBC Russian Service for over-recruiting employees from ethnic minority groups. The defendant then replied in a letter to the paper accusing the claimant of being racist and anti-Semitic. The defendant successfully pleaded fair comment in the claimant's action.

Key Law

The House of Lords (now the Supreme Court) felt that the defendant had to show that he was commenting since many people might not have seen the original article and would not necessarily know to what he was referring. On this basis the defence could only be defeated by the claimant showing malicious intent on the part of the defendant, which he had not done. The claimant had also failed to disprove that the defendant had an honest belief in the view expressed.

10.1.3   *Kemsley v Foot* **[1952] AC 345**   HL

Key Facts

A former leader of the Labour Party, while a junior MP, wrote an article in response to an article, attacking it as 'one of the foulest pieces of journalism perpetuated in this country for many a long year'. The article itself appeared under the headline 'Lower than Kemsley', a reference to another newspaper. The proprietor of that newspaper argued that in the light of the attack in the article the reference to his paper reflected badly on it and was defamatory.

Key Law

The old defence of fair comment succeeded because the article was genuine comment, supported by factual information, and was in the public interest. The headline was used as a comparison. There was no negligence on their part.

Key Comment

The defence is now replaced by responsible publication of matters of public interest.

10.1.3

Reynolds v Times Newspapers [2001] 2 AC 127

(HL)

Key Facts

The claimant had been leader of the Irish parliament and was trying to promote the Northern Ireland peace process. A political crisis arose so he resigned and withdrew his party from the governing coalition. *The Sunday Times* then published an article which the claimant felt suggested that he had both misled the Irish Parliament and withheld information from it. The newspaper failed to print an apology so he claimed for libel. The newspaper sought to rely on the defence of qualified privilege but was unsuccessful.

Key Law

The Court of Appeal held that qualified privilege can be argued by the press when (i) the paper has a moral, social or legal duty to inform the public of the matter in question; and (ii) the public has a corresponding interest in receiving the information; and (iii) the nature, status and source of the material and the circumstances of the publication are such as to warrant the protection of privilege. On appeal the House of Lords (now the Supreme Court) decided that there was no general category of qualified privilege for political information. Despite arguments based on Art 10 of the European Convention on Human Rights, the standard test of duty to disseminate and duty to receive should be applied. They held that ten matters were critical:

- the seriousness of allegation;
- whether or not it was of public concern;
- the source of the information;
- whether steps were taken to verify it;
- the status of the information;
- the urgency of the issue;
- whether comment was sought from the claimant;

- whether the claimant's comments were included in the article;
- the tone of the article;
- the circumstances and timing of publication.

Since the article here was highly critical and the defendants had never sought the claimant's side of the story they had no privilege.

10.2.2   *Derry v Peek* (1889) 14 App Cas 337   HL

Key Facts

A tram company was licensed by Act of Parliament to operate horse-drawn trams. The Act also allowed use of mechanical power by gaining a certificate from the Board of Trade. The company applied for a certificate and at the same time issued a prospectus to raise further share capital. Honestly believing that the certificate would be granted, the company falsely represented in the prospectus that it was able to use mechanical power. In fact the application was denied and the company fell into liquidation. The claimant had invested on the strength of the representation in the prospectus and lost money. His action for damages failed.

Key Law

The court held that there was insufficient proof of fraud, the allegation of which was simply rebutted by showing an honest belief in the statement. There was no reason for the company to suppose that their application for a certificate would be refused.

Key Judgment

Lord Herschell defined the action as requiring actual proof that the false representation was made:

'. . . knowingly or without belief in its truth or recklessly careless whether it be true or false'.

Key Link

4 *Eng v Harper* (2008) EWCH 915 which identifies that damages for loss of a chance are also available in deceit.

| 10.2.3.3 | *Kaye v Robertson* [1991] FSR 62 | |

Key Facts

A famous television actor, Gorden Kaye, was injured. Journalists from the *Sunday Sport* entered the actor's room, interviewed him and took photographs, even though he was in no fit state to consent. They then published the photographs and a story about his injuries, falsely stating that the story was produced with the actor's permission. His action for malicious falsehood succeeded although a claim for invasion of privacy failed.

Key Law

The court accepted that the ingredients of the tort were made out. The defendant had made a false statement about the claimant to third parties by publishing the story and photographs. It was malicious in having been done while he was too ill to realise. The loss to the claimant was that it prevented him from marketing the story himself and receiving payment for it.

Key Link

Wainwright v Home Office [2003] UKHL 53; [2003] 3 WLR 1137.

11 Employment-related torts

Purpose, criticisms

Justified because:
- employer has some control;
- employer selects employee;
- employer can stand loss;
- employer must have public liability insurance;
- ensure claimant has an action.

Criticised because:
- employer liable for something (s)he did not do;
- ignores fault principle.

VICARIOUS LIABILITY

Other liability

Independent contractors, if hired for purpose (*Ellis v Sheffield Gas Consumers*) or non-delegable duty by statute or common law.

Crimes of employees, if part of employment (*Lloyd v Grace Smith*), or sufficient connection between employment and crime (*Lister v Hesley Hall*).

For loaned cars, to give claimant a remedy (*Morgans v Launchbury*).

Testing employee status

Tortfeasor must be employee for employer to be liable:
- originally based on control test (nature and degree of detailed control) (*Performing Rights Society v Mitchell*);
- then based on integration test – the more integrated into organisation the more likely to be an employee (*Stevenson, Jordan & Harrison v MacDonald & Evans*);
- and finally based on the economic reality test (*Ready Mixed Concrete v Minister of Pensions*):
  i) agreement to provide skill for wage;
  ii) employer exercises degree of control;
  iii) nothing inconsistent with employment and weigh up all factors, e.g. ownership of tools, payment of tax and NI, method of payment, self-description, etc.
- Some workers not so straightforward, e.g. casual workers (*Carmichael v National Power*), outworkers (*Nethermere (St Neots) v Taverna*).

Did tort occur in course of employment?

Employer only liable if tort in course of employment.

In course of employment:
- authorised act (*Poland v Parr*);
- ignore express order (*Limpus v London General Omnibus*);
- carelessly undertakes work (*Century Insurance v Northern Ireland Transport Board*);
- uses unauthorised help (*Rose v Plenty*);
- over-enthusiastic (*Bayley v Manchester, Sheffield & Lincolnshire Railways*).

Not in course of employment:
- act not within scope of employment (*Beard v London General Omnibus*);
- on a frolic (*Hilton v Thomas Burton*);
- giving unauthorised lifts (*Twine v Beans Express*);
- exceeding proper limits of job (*Makanjuola v Metropolitan Police Commissioner*);
- driving to work unless paid to (*Smith v Stages*).

▶ 11.1 Vicarious liability

11.1.1 Origins, purposes and criticisms

1   Not a tort, but imposing liability on someone other than tortfeaser.

2   Originally based on the idea of control, which was appropriate to the 19th-century master and servant laws.

3   Rarely appropriate now other than to employment.

4   Sometimes criticised for being unfair because:

   ● employer is made liable for something (s)he has not done; and it directly contradicts the fault principle.

5   But there are a number of justifications:

   ● traditionally an employer did have control;

   ● the employer is responsible for choice of staff;

   ● the employer is better able to stand any loss, e.g. from profit;

   ● employers must in any case insure for public liability;

   ● it may be impossible to trace the person actually responsible (which may be appropriate, e.g. in medical cases).

6   While vicarious liability has been accepted in sexual harassment (*Brace-bridge Engineering Ltd v Derby* (1990)) and racial harassment (*Jones v Tower Boot Co Ltd* (1997)), it has been rejected in claims against councils for physical abuse by carers (*Trotman v North Yorkshire County Council* (1998)), but accepted in claims against education authorities where staff fail to diagnose and make effective provision for special needs such as dyslexia (*Phelps v Hillingdon LBC* (2000)).

7   Liability is only for a tort by an employee acting in the course of employment, so there are three key questions:

   a) Was the person committing the tort an employee?

   b) Was the tort committed in the course of employment?

   c) Was the act a tort?

11.1.2 Was the tortfeaser an employee?

1   There have been numerous methods of testing employment.

2   The original test was the control test from master/servant law:

   a) measured by 'nature and degree of detailed control' (*Performing Rights Society v Mitchell* (1924));

b) four key factors to be considered: selection, wages, control, and dismissal (Lord Thankerton in *Short v Henderson* (1946));

c) it is sometimes almost impossible to apply, e.g. medicine;

d) but it may be appropriate to borrowed workers (*Mersey Docks & Harbour Board v Coggins & Griffiths* (1947)) or where hirer rather than employer gives detailed instructions (*Hawley v Luminar Leisure plc* (2005)).

3 Lord Denning introduced the 'integration' or 'organisation test' in *Stevenson, Jordan & Harrison v MacDonald & Evans* (1952) (the more the worker is integrated into the organisation the more likely (s)he is employed) (*Whittaker v Minister of Pensions and National Assistance* (1967)).

4 The modern test is that of Mackenna J in *Ready Mixed Concrete Ltd v Minister of Pensions* (1968) (the 'economic reality' or 'multiple' test):

● three conditions were identified:

  i) employee agrees to provide skill in return for a wage;

  ii) employer exercises a degree of control;

  iii) nothing in terms inconsistent with employment.

● there are many factors to take into account, but are not definitive: ownership of tools, tax and NI liability, method of payment, self-description, etc.

5 Certain types of worker do not conform easily to any test:

● casual workers (*O'Kelly v Trust House Forte* (1983) and, more recently, *Carmichael v National Power plc* (2000));

● outworkers (*Nethermere (St Neots) v Taverna* (1984)), usually considered self-employed;

● labour-only subcontractor (*Lane v Shire Roofing Co* (1996)), usually seen as self-employed;

● hospital workers – compare *Hillyer v St Bartholomew's Hospital* (1909) with *Cassidy v Minister of Health* (1951).

11.1.3 Was the act in the course of employment

1 Generally a question of fact, but based on policy so inconsistent.

2 If the employee commits the tort in the course of employment then the employer can be vicariously liable.

3   If the tort happens outside of the course of employment or the employee is on a 'frolic of his own' the employer is not liable.

4   There is generally said to be liability for:

i)   authorised wrongful acts; and

ii)   authorised acts carried out in a wrongful way.

5   Employer is obviously liable for (i) when instructing the employee to act wrongfully, but can also be liable if the employee has implied authority to commit the tort (*Poland v Parr* (1927)).

6   Authorised acts carried out wrongfully include situations where the employee is engaged in his/her own work, but:

● ignores an express prohibition (*Limpus v London General Omnibus Co* (1862), which involved racing buses against instructions and injuring a third party);

● uses an unauthorised method of work (*LCC v Cattermoles (Garages) Ltd* (1953));

● acts carelessly (*Century Insurance v Northern Ireland Road Transport Board* (1942), where an explosion was caused while delivering petrol after lighting a cigarette);

● uses unauthorised help (*Rose v Plenty* (1976), where liability arose because the employer was seen to gain a benefit);

● causes the tort by excess of enthusiasm (*Bayley v Manchester, Sheffield, & Lincs. Railway* (1873); *Fennelly v Connex South Eastern Ltd* (2001));

● where individual employee breaches a statutory duty making a claim possible under s 3 Protection from Harassment Act 1997 (*Majrowski v Guy's and St Thomas' NHS Trust* (2006).

7   Acts that are outside of employment or 'frolics' include:

● carrying out an act not within the scope of the employee's work (*Beard v London General Omnibus Co* (1900));

● diverting away from the proper work on 'a frolic' (*Hilton v Thomas Burton (Rhodes) Ltd* (1961));

● giving unauthorised lifts (*Twine v Beans Express* (1946));

● acting in excess of the proper bounds of the work (*Makanjuola v Metropolitan Police Commissioner* (1992)).

8   The tests are confusing because cases with apparently similar facts will differ in whether liability is imposed.

9   An employer can be liable purely because (s)he derives a benefit from the employee's wrongful act (*Rose v Plenty* (1976)).

10   Whether an employer is liable for torts of employees travelling to and from work depends on whether the travel is part of the work or paid for (*Smith v Stages* (1989)).

11   An important recent development is that dual vicarious liability is now possible (*Viasystems (Tyneside) Ltd v Thermal Transfer (Northern) Ltd, S & P Darnwell Ltd and CAT Metalwork Services* (2005)).

11.1.4 Liability for the torts of independent contractors

1   Hirer generally not liable, because of the absence of control.

2   However, there are possible exceptions:

   a) if employed for the tort (*Ellis v Sheffield Gas Consumers* (1953));

   b) if there is a non-delegable duty by statute, e.g. to provide and ensure wearing of safety equipment;

   c) if there is a non-delegable duty under common law (*Honeywill & Stein v Larkin* (1984)).

11.1.5 Liability for the crimes of employees

1   There is not usually liability for crimes which give rise to civil liability also (*Warren v Henleys* (1948)).

2   Liability is possible where the crime is part of the employment:

   ● as in theft (*Morris v Marten* (1966));

   ● and fraud (*Lloyd v Grace Smith* (1912)).

3   The House of Lords in *Lister v Hesley Hall Ltd* (2001) has accepted that liability for crimes is possible where there is sufficient connection between the employment and the crime e.g. child abuse by carers, teachers etc. on employer's premises and the 'close connection' test used in *Dubai Aluminium v Salaam* (2003) and *Mattis v Pollock* (2003).

4   The test succeeds where the activity leading to the tort is of a type common to the employment (*Andrew Gravil v Richard Carroll and Redruth Rugby Club* (2008)) and has applied where a Roman

Catholic priest sexually assaults a young person *Maga v Roman Catholic Church* (2010) and *JGE v The Trustees of the Portsmouth Roman Catholic Diocesan Trust* (2012), but there is no vicarious liability where the tortfeasor merely takes advantage of e.g. a uniform out of work time to commit the tort (*N v Chief Constable of Merseyside Police* (2006)).

11.1.6 The employer's indemnity

1   At common law an employer can recover from an employee under the principle of subrogation (*Lister v Romford Ice & Cold Storage Co* (1957)).

2   But this can cause problems so insurance companies usually operate a gentleman's agreement.

11.1.7 Vicarious liability of lenders of cars

1   Vicarious liability can result from the lending of cars (*Britt v Galmoye* (1928)).

2   This can be because the lender gains a benefit (*Ormrod v Crosville Motor Co* (1953)).

3   Or it can simply be to ensure that the injured party has a remedy (*Morgans v Launchbury* (1973)).

▶ 11.2 Employers' liability

11.2.1 Origins

1   Employment was traditionally seen as a contractual relationship based on freedom of contract, with no remedies available in tort.

2   In the 19th century there were three major barriers to workers' claims:

- *volenti* – worker was said to consent to the dangers of work;
- contributory negligence – a complete defence at that time;
- 'common employment' – no liability if a 'fellow servant' caused the injury.

3   Most industrial safety law developed in statute.

4   Common law was generally hostile to workers.

5   Eventually the scope of the three defences was reduced:

- after *Smith v Baker* (1891)) *volenti* only available if the claimant freely accepted risk;

- Law Reform (Contributory Negligence) Act 1945 made the defence a partial one, only affecting the amount of damages;

- by *Groves v Lord Wimbourne* (1898) the 'fellow servant' rule was not available to breach of statutory duty, and the Law Reform (Personal Injury) Act 1948 abolished the rule.

6   Other major developments included:

a) employers became liable for defective plant and equipment in the Employer's Liability (Defective Equipment) Act 1969;

b) the Workmen's Compensation Act 1897 introduced an insurance principle; later applied to all employees in the Employment Liability (Compulsory Insurance) Act 1969;

c) *Wilsons & Clyde Coal v English* (1938) identified a non-delegable duty of an employer to his employees.

7   Now the area involves common law, statute, and EU law in Directives implemented as 'the six pack' set of Regulations 1992.

Aspects of the non-delegable common law duty

Four key elements:
• Must provide competent fellow employees:
  i)   must be competent to carry out work (*General Cleaning Contractors v Christmas*);
  ii) and be well behaved (*O'Reilly's case*);
  iii) and not 'harass' colleagues (s 3 Protection from Harassment Act 1997 and *Majrowski v Guy's & St Thomas' NHS Trust* (2006)).
• Must provide safe plant and equipment:
  i)   must provide it and maintain it (*Smith v Baker*);
  ii) now superseded by statute and EU law.
• Must provide safe premises, but only need do what is reasonable to make them safe (*Latimer v AEC*).
• Must provide a safe system of work:
  i)   both provide system and ensure it is used safely (*Bux v Slough Metals*);
  ii) although employees are expected to be aware of dangers associated with their skill (*Roles v Nathan*).
Duty has now extended to cover preventing psychiatric harm (*Walker v Northumberland CC*).

EMPLOYERS' LIABILITY

Defences

Volenti (consent):
• but only if employee accepts actual risk (*Smith v Baker*);
• unavailable if employee had no choice but accept risk (*Baker v T E Hopkins*);
• possible if employee sole cause of own misfortune (*Ginty v Belmont Building Supplies*).

Contributory negligence:
• rare but damages can be reduced if employee contributes to harm (*Jones v Livox Quarries*);
• even for death (*Davies v Swan Motor Co*);
• and 100% is possible (*Jayes v IMI (Kynoch)*).

Character of the duty:
• duty is entirely non-delegable (*Wilson & Clyde Coal v English*); and is to do what is reasonable (*Latimer v AEC*);
• extends to ancillary activities (*Davidson v Handley Page*); but not to property (*Deyong v Shenburn*);
• only reasonable trade practices are acceptable (*Cavanagh v Ulster Weaving*);
• employer must take into account possible extent of injury to employee (*Paris v Stepney BC*);
• and can take into account practicality of any precautions (*Charlton v Forrest Printing Ink*);
• duty is to prevent foreseeable accidents (*Bradford v Robinson Rentals*).

11.2.2 Employers' non-delegable duty

1   The duty includes four key elements, but is an expanding area:

- the duty to provide competent fellow employees;
- the duty to provide safe plant and equipment;
- the duty to provide safe premises;
- the duty to provide a safe system of work.

2   Now the duty also extends to protecting the general health and safety of the employee, including psychiatric health.

The duty to provide competent fellow employees

1   All employees should be competent to carry out their contractual duties (*General Cleaning Contractors Ltd v Christmas* (1953)).

2   An employer should ensure the good behaviour of staff (*Hudson v Ridge Manufacturing Co* (1957)), but is not responsible for unknown characteristics (*O'Reilly v National Rail & Tramway Appliances* (1966)).

3   Actions are rare nowadays because the employer is usually caught by vicarious liability, but it is useful when the employee's act causing injury or damage is outside the scope of employment.

4   Now an employer can be vicariously liable also under the Protection from Harassment Act 1997 (*Majrowski v Guy's & St Thomas' NHS Trust* (2006)).

The duty to provide safe plant and equipment

1   The duty is not only to provide safe equipment but to properly maintain it (*Smith v Baker* (1891)).

2   And the system for using equipment must not damage the health or safety of the employee (*Alexander v Midland Bank* (2000)).

3   An employer can avoid liability if the employee misuses equipment (*Parkinson v Lyle Shipping Co Ltd* (1964)).

4   The duty is now possibly superseded by the Employer's Liability (Defective Equipment) Act 1969, but the Act itself has been subject to conflicting interpretation (*Coltman v Bibby Tankers* (1988) (compare CA and HL) and *Knowles v Liverpool Corporation* (1993)).

The duty to provide safe premises

1   The duty is to do what is reasonably practicable to ensure premises are safe (*Latimer v AEC* (1957)).

2   This may include premises other than the employer's (*Wilson v Tyneside Cleaning Co* (1958)).

3   There may also be liability under the Occupier's Liability Act 1957.

The duty to provide a safe system of work

1   The duty has two key aspects:

   ● creating a safe system of work in the first place;

   ● ensuring proper implementation of the system.

2   The duty is to provide an effective system to meet the danger (*General Cleaning Contractors Ltd v Christmas* (1953)), so the employer may be liable for a failure to warn of the danger (*Pape v Cumbria CC* (1992)).

3   There is also a duty to ensure the system is carried out (*Bux v Slough Metals* (1974)).

4   Providing a safe system may include the method of using equipment (*Mughal v Renters* (1993)), so employer may need to:

   ● train employees to use equipment safely (*Mountenay (Hazzard) v Bernard Matthews* (1993));

   ● and rotate work properly (*Mitchell v Atco* (1995));

   ● and guard against foreseeable dangers of the work (*Cook v Bradford Community Health NHS Trust* (2002)).

5   The system should not cause undue stress to the employee (*Walker v Northumberland CC* (1994)).

6   An employer cannot rely on an unsafe practice merely because it is a common practice (*Re Herald of Free Enterprise* (1989)).

7   Employees may be expected to be aware of risks associated with the work they do (*Roles v Nathan* (1963)).

8   Much of the duty here has probably now been superseded by, e.g. the duty to undertake risk assessment under the 'six pack'.

11.2.3 Developments in the common law duty

1   Judges have recently expanded boundaries of duty to include:

   ● a duty to protect an employee's general health and safety (*Johnstone v Bloomsbury Health Authority* (1991));

- a duty to protect the psychiatric health of the employee (*Walker* following *Petch v Commissioners of Customs and Excise* (1993)), but this depends on the presence of foreseeable harm – extensive guidelines are now in *Sutherland v Hatton* (2002) and *Barber v Somerset County Council* (2004) – and merely referring the employee for counselling may be insufficient to discharge the duty (*Daw v Intel Corporation (UK) Ltd* (2007));

- a duty not to negligently prepare references for an employee (*Spring v Guardian Assurance* (1995));

- a duty to protect the employee from harassment (*Majrowski v Guy's & St Thomas' NHS Trust* (2006)).

11.2.4 The character of the duty

1   The duty is entirely personal and non-delegable (*Wilson & Clyde Coal v English* (1938)).

2   The duty is only to do what is reasonable, not to provide a guarantee of safety (*Latimer v AEC* (1953)).

3   The duty extends to all reasonable and ancillary activities (*Davidson v Handley Page Ltd* (1945)).

4   The duty does not extend as far as protecting property (*Deyong v Shenburn* (1946)).

5   An employer can only rely on a trade practice that is reasonable (*Cavanagh v Ulster Weaving Co* (1960)).

6   But an employer should consider the possible extent of the injury (*Paris v Stepney BC* (1951)).

7   An employer may take into account the practicality of any precautions (*Charlton v Forrest Printing Ink Co Ltd* (1978)).

8   The duty is to prevent accidents that are reasonably foreseeable (*Bradford v Robinson Rentals* (1967)), but not unforeseeable (*Doughty v Turner Manufacturing Co Ltd* (1964)).

11.2.5 Defences

1   *Volenti* (consent).

- This only has limited use since *Smith v Baker* (1891).

- But it is possible if employee accepts actual risk (*ICI v Shatwell* (1965)).

- It cannot be claimed where the employee had no choice but to act (*Baker v T E Hopkins* (1959)).
- By policy unavailable for breach of a statutory duty (*ICI v Shatwell* (1965)).
- But it is possible if a claimant is the sole cause of his/her own misfortune (*Ginty v Belmont Building Supplies Ltd* (1959)).

2   Contributory negligence.

- Can be a defence to any of the duties.
- However, employees are treated more leniently by the courts (*Caswell v Powell Duffryn Collieries* (1940)).
- This is because the duty is to protect employees from their own carelessness (*General Cleaning Contractors v Christmas* (1953)).
- Damages are reduced if employees have contributed to their own injuries (*Jones v Livox Quarries Ltd* (1952)).
- This applies even if death resulted (*Davies v Swan Motor Co Ltd* (1949)).
- One hundred per cent contributory negligence is possible (*Jayes v IMI Kynoch Ltd* (1985)).

▶ 11.3 Breach of a statutory duty

11.3.1 Introduction

1   Many regulatory statutes impose a duty and create civil liability.

2   An action is similar to negligence, but differs in significant ways:

- the standard of care is fixed by the statute;
- the duty can be strict, or the burden of proof may be reversed, either being advantageous to a claimant;
- such statutes are regulatory, so usually impose criminal sanctions, and the existence of civil liability is debatable;
- in America breach of the statutory duty can be proof of negligence, but in England it is treated as a separate tort.

3   As a result both are commonly pleaded at the same time.

4   Civil liability is more obvious where the Act modifies common law.

5   Other Acts are harder to determine, so the area is dependent on statutory interpretation and so is unpredictable.

6   Industrial safety law is the most common example.

7   A number of questions must be considered.

Nature of liability

- Regulatory statutes sometimes create civil liability as well as imposing criminal sanctions.
- Action for breach of statutory duty similar to negligence, though standard is set by statute and duty sometimes strict.
- Often hard to decide whether statute does create civil action so requires statutory interpretation.

BREACH OF A STATUTORY DUTY

Defences

Volenti – available only if:

- claimant's wrongful act puts defendant in breach (*Ginty v Belmont Building Supplies*);
- vicarious liability is an issue (*ICI v Shatwell*).

Contributory negligence:

- reluctantly accepted (*Casswell v Powell Duffryn Collieries*);
- but 100 per cent possible (*Jayes v IMI (Kynoch)*).

Essential elements of liability

Must ask six questions:

Was Act intended to create civil liability?

- Obvious if statute gives guidance, e.g. HASAW 1974.
- But if silent, use test in *Lonrho v Shell Petroleum*:

    i) Presume if Act creates obligation enforceable in only one manner then no other;

    ii) unless obligation benefits a particular class, or creates public right and claimant suffers damage different to rest of public.

- Wording vital (*Monk v Warbey* and *Atkinson v Newcastle Waterworks*).

Is claimant owed a duty of care?

- Must show duty owed as individual or as member of class (*Hartley v Mayoh*).
- Must show Parliament intended to create private law rights (*X (Minors) v Bedfordshire County Council*).

Is duty imposed on defendant?

- Must consider precise words of statute (*R v Deputy Governor of Parkhurst Prison ex parte Hague*).
- No duty, no civil liability.

Has defendant breached duty?

- No single standard, so court must construe from words of statute.
- Subject to dictates of policy (*Ex parte Island Records*).
- If specific words used then standard clear (*Chipchase v British Titan Products*).
- 'Must' and 'shall' usually means liability is strict (*John Summers & Sons v Frost*).

Did breach cause damage?

- 'But for' test applies.

Was damage of type contemplated in Act?

- No liability if type of damage not contemplated in statute (*Gorris v Scott*).
- So damage must not be too remote (*Young v Charles Church*).

11.3.2 The essential elements of liability

Is the statute intended to create civil liability?

1   Claimant must show that the Act creates an action for damages.

2   This is straightforward if the Act gives specific guidance, e.g. Health and Safety at Work Act 1974.

3   Problems can occur if the statute is silent on the issue.

4   Courts must always give effect to the intention of Parliament.

5   The modern test is Lord Diplock's in *Lonrho Ltd v Shell Petroleum Co* (1982):

   a) court presumes that if Act creates obligation enforceable only in specific manner, then not enforceable in any other manner;

   b) but there are two exceptions:

     ● when an obligation is to benefit a particular class;

     ● when provision creates public right but claimant suffers particular, direct, and substantial damage different from the rest of the public.

6   This test is criticised because of two problems:

   a) it gives the court discretion in determining class;

   b) there is no set distinction between a statute creating a public right and one just prohibiting what was formerly lawful.

7   Courts consider various factors in determining Parliament's intent:

   ● civil action more likely to be possible if wording precise. Compare *Monk v Warbey* (1935) with *Atkinson v Newcastle Waterworks* (1877);

   ● failure to mention a specific penalty (*Cutler v Wandsworth Stadium Ltd* (1949));

   ● some groups are well-established classes (*Groves v Lord Wimbourne* (1898));

   ● action is more likely with an identifiable group (*Thornton v Kirklees MBC* (1979));

   ● there must be a direct link with purpose of statute (*McCall v Abelsz* (1976));

   ● the purpose must be for the benefit of that class (*R v Deputy Governor of Parkhurst Prison ex parte Hague* (1992)).

Is the claimant owed a duty of care?

1   Action only succeeds if claimant shows he is owed duty as an individual or as a member of a class (*Hartley v Mayoh & Co* (1954)), so an action by a relative might fail (*Hewett v Alf Brown's Transport* (1992)) possibly because the risk is unforeseeable (*Maguire v Harland & Wolff plc* (2005)).

2   There is a wide scope for establishing the existence of a duty (*Garden Cottage Foods v Milk Marketing Board* (1984) and *Atkinson v Croydon Corporation* (1938)).

3   But HL has restated the need to show that Parliament intended to create private law rights (*X (minors) v Bedfordshire County Council; (M (a minor) v Newham London Borough Council; Keating v Bromley LBC* (1995)).

Is a duty imposed on the defendant?

1   Must consider precise words of statute (*Ex Parte Hague* (1992)).

2   If there is no duty on the defendant there can be no civil action.

3   And a civil action is never possible where the court feels that the duty is intended to be enforced by other means (*Cullen v Chief Constable of the Royal Ulster Constabulary* (2003)).

Has the defendant breached a statutory duty?

1   No single standard of care, so court must construe statute.

2   Has been subject to inconsistency and the dictates of policy – Lord Denning in *Ex Parte Island Records* (1978): 'you might as well toss a coin in order to decide the cases'.

3   If the words are specific, the standard is self-evident (*Chipchase v British Titan Products Co Ltd* (1956)).

4   When words like 'must' or 'shall' are used, liability is likely to be strict (*John Summers & Sons v Frost* (1955)).

5   But the standard is often vaguely stated (*Brown v NCB* (1962)).

Did the breach of duty cause the damage?

1   Tested as negligence by the 'but for' test.

2   So there must be a direct causal link between the breach and the damage (*King v Sussex Ambulance NHS Trust* (2002)).

3   Defendant can be liable if duty also to ensure claimant complies with provision (*Ginty v Belmont Building Supplies Ltd* (1959)).

Was the damage of a type contemplated in the statute?

1   Liability is not possible if the type of damage was not contemplated in the statute (*Gorris v Scott* (1874)).

2   So it must not be too remote (*Young v Charles Church* (1997)).

11.3.3 Defences

1   *Volenti non fit injuria*:

   a) not normally available on policy grounds;

   b) but may be:

   ● where the claimant's wrongful act put the defendant in breach (*Ginty* (1959)); or

   ● where the claimant tries to claim vicarious liability as an issue (*ICI Ltd v Shatwell* (1965)).

2   Contributory negligence:

   a) only accepted reluctantly as regulations are often meant to protect workers from their own carelessness: 'employees' sense of danger will have been dulled by familiarity, repetition, noise, confusion, fatigue, and preoccupation with work . . .' (*Caswell v Powell Duffryn Collieries* (1940));

   b) but it is possible if claimant is genuinely at fault (*Jayes v IMI (Kynoch) Ltd* (1985)).

Key Cases Checklist

Vicarious liability

Ready Mixed Concrete v Minister of Pensions and National Insurance (1968)
The tortfeasor must be employed according to the 'economic reality' test

Poland v Parr (1927)
The employer is responsible for all authorised acts

Rose v Plenty (1976)
And prohibited acts where the employer gains a benefit

Twine v Beans Express (1946)
Butnot where the employee is on a 'frolic on his own'

Lister v Hesley Hall (2001)
Employer can be liable for employee's crimes where there is a close connection with the employment

Viasystems (Tyneside) Ltd v Thermal Transfer Ltd (2005)
Dual vicarious liability is possible

Employment-related torts

Employer's liability

Wilsons & Clyde Coal Co Ltd v English (1938)
The employer owes a non-delegable duty of care to provide safe colleagues, plant and equipment, premises, and systems of work

Sutherland v Hatton and others (2002)
And now has a duty to protect the employee's psychiatric health if he is aware of the employee's susceptibility to stress

Baker v T E Hopkins (1959)
The employee can only consent to risks he is aware of and freely accepts

Jones v Livox Quarries (1952)
Employer's contributory negligence

Breach of a statutory duty

Lonrho Ltd v Shell Petroleum Co Ltd (No. 2) (1982)
Civil remedy not generally available if the statute provides a different sanction unless provison protects a class of individuals or claimant suffered damage above what the public would expect

11.1.2.2

Mersey Docks & Harbour Board v Coggins and Griffiths (Liverpool) Ltd [1947] AC 1

Key Facts

The Harbour Board hired out a crane to stevedores and a driver to operate it for them. In the contract between the Board and the stevedores the Board would still pay the driver and only they had the right to dismiss him, but during the contract he was employed by the stevedores. The crane driver negligently injured a person in the course of his work and the Harbour Board was held liable.

Key Law

The court held that the Harbour Board was the crane driver's employer at the material time since it was in control of him and could not show that liability for his actions had shifted to the stevedores since, although they could tell him what to do, they were not in a position to tell him how to operate the crane.

Key Judgment

Lord Porter explained the control test:

'To ascertain who is the employer at any particular time . . . ask who is entitled to tell the employee the way in which he is to do the work upon which he is engaged . . . it is not enough that the task to be performed should be under his control, he must control the method of performing it.'

11.1.2.4

Ready Mixed Concrete (South East) Ltd v Minister of Pensions and National Insurance [1968] 2 QB 497

QBD

Key Facts

Under a new contract drivers were bound to have vehicles in the company colours and logo that they also bought on hire purchase agreements from the company. They also had to maintain the vehicles according to set standards and could only use the lorries on company business. Hours were flexible, however, and pay was subject to an annual minimum rate according to the concrete hauled. The contract also permitted them to hire drivers in their place.

The case concerned who was liable for National Insurance contributions: the company or one of its drivers.

Key Law

The court held that the terms of the contract were inconsistent with a contract of employment and the driver was self-employed.

Key Judgment

McKenna J developed the 'economic reality' test:

'(i) The servant agrees that in consideration of a wage or other remuneration he will provide his own work and skill in the performance of some services ... (ii) he agrees, expressly or impliedly, that in the performance of that service he will be in the other's control in a sufficient degree to make that other master; (iii) the other provisions of the contract are consistent with it being a contract of service.'

11.1.3.5   *Poland v Parr* **[1927] 1 KB 236**   (CA)

Key Facts

The employee was a carter who assaulted a boy in order to stop him from stealing from his employer's wagon. The boy fell under the wagon and was injured as a result.

Key Law

The court held that, while the act was excessive and thus tortious, since the employee was only protecting the employer's property, and by implication he had authority to do so, the employer would be vicariously liable for the employee's act.

Key Judgment

Atkin LJ explained:

'Any servant is, as a general rule, authorised to do acts which are for the protection of his master's property.'

11.1.3.6   *Rose v Plenty* [1976] 1 WLR 141   CA

Key Facts

A milkman used a child helper despite the express instructions of his employer not to allow people to ride on the milk floats. The boy was then injured through the milkman's negligent driving.

Key Law

The court held that the milkman was carrying out his work in an unauthorised manner but was still in the course of his employment because the employer benefited from the work done by the boy.

Key Judgment

Lord Denning explained that:

'An employer's express prohibition . . . is not necessarily such as to exempt the employer from liability, provided that the act is done not for the employee's own purpose, but in the course of his service and for his employer's benefit.'

11.1.3.6   *Century Insurance Co Ltd v Northern Ireland Transport Board* [1942] AC 509   CA

Key Facts

The driver of a petrol tanker was delivering to a petrol station. He lit a cigarette and carelessly threw down the lit match, causing an explosion and extensive damage. The employer was held liable.

Key Law

The court held that the driver was in the course of employment because he was engaged in his primary activity, delivering petrol, and was merely doing his work in a negligent manner.

11.1.3.7   *Twine v Beans Express* [1946] 1 All ER 202

Key Facts

A hitchhiker was injured through the negligence of a driver who was expressly forbidden to give lifts. The employers were not liable.

Key Law

The court held that the driver was doing something outside of his contract in giving free lifts and that the express prohibition was also a limiting factor on the scope of his employment.

11.1.3.11   *Viasystems (Tyneside) Ltd v Thermal Transfer (Northern) Ltd* [2005] EWCA Civ 1151

Key Facts

A fitter's mate who was seconded by his employers to other contractors negligently flooded a factory floor.

Key Law

The court held that, because both employers were both entitled and obliged to control the worker to prevent negligent acts, both could be vicariously liable for his actions.

11.1.5.3   *Lister v Hesley Hall Ltd* [2001] 2 All ER 769

Key Facts

The claimants were residents in a school for children with emotional difficulties. They were all sexually abused over time by the warden who was later convicted of criminal charges. The claimants sought damages against the school on the basis that it had actual or constructive knowledge of the abuse and failed to prevent it.

Key Law

The House of Lords (now the Supreme Court) rejected the test in *Trotman v North Yorkshire County Council* (1999) LGR 584 and held that the appropriate test was whether there was sufficient connection between the employment and the torts carried out by the employee. Here the torts were carried out on the school's premises and at times when the employee should have been caring for the claimants. The court accepted that there was an inherent risk of abuse that the employer should have guarded against so that vicarious liability was appropriate in the circumstances.

Key Comment

Rosalind Coe (in *Lister v Hesley Hall Ltd* (2002) 65 MLE 270) suggests '*Lister* has inevitably raised concerns as to the application of the "close connection" test, provoking comment that . . . Litigants, their advisers and insurers will all be concerned as to the boundaries of the decision and will turn to the judgments of the House for guidance. Unfortunately they will find limited assistance.'

Key Link

Mattis v Pollock [2003] EWCA Civ 887 (involving a nightclub bouncer) and *Gravill v Carroll and Redruth Rugby Club* [2008] EWCA Civ 689 (involving a rugby player) have both applied the Principle and *Maga v Roman Catholic Church* (2010) EWCA Civ 256 and *JGE v The Trustees of the Portsmouth Roman Catholic Diocesan Trust* (2012) EWCA Civ 938 (applied the test in the case of sexual assaults by Roman Catholic priests). *N v Chief Constable of Merseyside Police* [2006] EWHC 3041 (QB) (involving an off-duty police officer still in uniform) did not because he had merely taken advantage of his uniform.

11.1.5.2   *Lloyd v Grace Smith & Co* [1912] AC 716

Key Facts

Solicitors employed an unsupervised conveyancing clerk. The clerk fraudulently induced a client to convey her property over to him.

Key Law

The court identified that the clerk was engaged in the job that he was hired to do and that the fraud occurred because he was given insufficient supervision by his employers, who were thus liable.

11.1.6.1

Lister v Romford Ice & Cold Storage Ltd [1957] AC 555

(HL)

Key Facts

A lorry driver negligently knocked over his father who was acting as his driver's mate. The father claimed compensation from the employers whose insurers on settling the claim exercised their rights of subrogation under the insurance contract by suing the driver.

Key Law

The House of Lords (now the Supreme Court) accepted that this was possible.

Key Problem

The case was very strongly criticised, not least because it destroys the purpose of imposing vicarious liability. Because of this insurers are reluctant to exercise their rights in such an unfair way.

11.1.7.3

Morgans v Launchbury [1973] AC 127

(HL)

Key Facts

A wife let her husband use her car, knowing that he was going out drinking after he promised her that he would not drive while drunk. The husband drank too much, so he let a friend drive him home who was also drunk and uninsured, and who caused an accident. The Court of Appeal imposed vicarious liability on the wife so that a claim could be made against her insurance.

Key Law

Lord Denning held that the fact the wife had given permission to her husband to use the car was enough to make her responsible. The House of Lords (now the Supreme Court) rejected this argument because it was impossible to pinpoint the exact basis on which to fix liability in the circumstances and it was not for judges to interfere with the interrelationship between liability and insurance.

11.2.1.6   *Wilsons & Clyde Coal Co Ltd v English* [1938] AC 57   (HL)

Key Facts

Colliery owners tried to delegate their responsibilities and liability under various industrial safety laws to their manager by contractually making him entirely responsible for safety. When a miner was injured the owners tried to avoid liability on this basis.

Key Law

The court held the colliers liable on the basis that their personal liability could not be delegated to a third party, who was in any case an employee. The duty of care included: the duty to provide competent working colleagues; safe plant and equipment; a safe place of work; and a safe system of work.

11.2.2   *Bux v Slough Metals* [1974] 1 All ER 262   (HL)

Key Facts

In compliance with health and safety regulations an employee was provided with safety goggles but would not use them because he claimed that they misted up. The employer knew this. The employee was then injured by a splash of molten metal.

Key Law

The court held the employer liable for failing to ensure that the goggles were worn, identifying that the duty is not just to provide safe working systems but to ensure that they are followed.

Key Link

Pape v Cumbria CC [1992] 3 All ER 211 where there was breach of a duty to warn that not wearing gloves could lead to dermatitis.

11.2.2

Walker v Northumberland CC [1995] 1 All ER 737

QBD

Key Facts

A senior social worker had already suffered a nervous breakdown as a result of work-related stress. On returning to work he had been promised that his workload would reduce but was actually faced with a huge backlog of work from his absence. The result was that he suffered a second breakdown causing him to leave work permanently after he was dismissed on sickness grounds. His claim was successful. Leave for an appeal to the Court of Appeal was granted but the case was settled beforehand for £175,000.

Key Law

The court held that the employer was liable because after the first breakdown it was aware of his susceptibility to stress and failed to reduce his workload or the pressure associated with it, and thus placed him under even more stressful conditions.

Key Judgment

Colman J explained the development:

'It is clear law that an employer has a duty to provide his employee with a safe system of work and to take reasonable steps to protect him from risks which are reasonably fore-seeable . . . there is no logical reason why risk of psychiatric damage should be excluded from the . . . duty.'

11.2.3.1

Sutherland v Hatton and others [2002] EWCA Civ 76

CA

Key Facts

This case was in fact a number of joined appeals on stress-related illnesses at work. Two claimants were teachers; one was a local authority administrator and one was a factory worker. All were claiming that they were forced to stop work because of stress-related psychiatric illnesses caused by their employers.

Key Law

The appeals were decided on whether the injuries were foreseeable but the court also issued important guidelines on stress claims:

- the basic principles of negligence must apply including the usual principles of employers' liability;

- the critical question for the court to answer is whether the type of harm suffered was foreseeable;

- foreseeability depends on what the reasonable employer knew or ought reasonably to have known;

- an employer can assume that an employee can cope with the normal pressures of the work unless the employer has specific knowledge that an employee has a particular problem;

- the same test should apply whatever the employment;

- the employer should take steps to prevent possible harm when possibility of harm would be obvious to a reasonable employer;

- the employer will be liable if he then fails to take steps that are reasonable in the circumstances to avoid the harm;

- the nature of the employment, the employer's available resources, and the counselling and treatment services provided are all relevant in determining whether the employer has taken effective steps to avoid the harm, and in any case the employer is only expected to take steps that will do some good;

- the employee must show that the employer's breach of duty caused the harm, not merely that the harm is stress-related;

- where there is more than one cause of the harm the employer will only be liable for that portion of damages that relates to the harm actually caused by his breach of duty;

- damages should take account of any pre-existing disorder.

Key Comment

Andrew Collender QC in 'Stress in the work place' *New Law Journal* 22 February, 2003 pp 248 and 250 discusses a problem recognised by the court:

'whilst it is possible to identify some jobs that are intrinsically physically dangerous, it is rather more difficult to identify which jobs are intrinsically so stressful that physical or psychological harm is to be expected more often than in other jobs'.

Key Link

Barber v Somerset CC [2004] UKHL 13: a further appeal to HL from one of the appeals in *Hatton*.

 ### *Baker v T E Hopkins* [1959] 3 All ER 225

Key Facts

Workmen were put in danger by being exposed to petrol fumes in a confined space when the fumes overcame the men. A doctor attempted to rescue the men but died himself through exposure to the fumes. The employer tried to claim *volenti* but failed.

Key Law

The court held that the defence could not apply. The doctor had not agreed to the specific risks involved. He was trying to do his best for the unconscious men and did not consent to the risk of death.

Key Judgment

The Court of Appeal explained the application of the defence by referring to the judgment of Cardozo J in an American case, *Wagner v International Railway Co*:

'*Danger invites rescue. The law does not ignore these reactions . . . in tracing conduct to its consequences. It recognises them as normal. It places their effects within the range of the natural and the probable.*

The wrong that imperils life . . . is a wrong also to the rescuer.'

11.2.5.2 *Jones v Livox Quarries Ltd* [1952] 2 QB 608 CA

Key Facts

An employee was injured in a collision caused by the defend-ant's negligent driving while he was riding on the towbar of a traxcavator despite the express prohibition of his employer.

Key Law

The court held that the employee had contributed to his own injury by ignoring safety instructions and reduced his damages by 5 per cent.

Key Judgment

Lord Denning said:

'*contributory negligence does not depend on a duty of care [it] does depend on foreseeability . . . as . . . negli-gence requires . . . foreseeability of harm to others . . . contributory negligence requires . . . foreseeability of harm to oneself'*.

11.3.2 *Lonrho Ltd v Shell Petroleum Co Ltd (No 2)* [1982] AC 173 HL

Key Facts

The claimant argued that it suffered damage following a breach by the defendant of an Order in Council on trading with an illegal regime, in Southern Rhodesia. The order provided criminal sanctions.

Key Law

The court held that there was no civil liability intended in the order so the claim failed. Lord Diplock also established the modern test for determining whether there is civil liability: it should be presumed that if the Act creates an obligation enforceable in a specific manner then it is not enforceable in any other manner, i.e. the presence of criminal sanctions usually indicates that there is no civil liability. Two excep-tions are: where an obligation or prohibition is imposed by the Act to benefit a particular class of individuals; and where a provision in the Act creates a public right but the claimant suffered substantial damage different from that common to the rest of the public.

Key Problem

It has been argued that this gives the court too much discretion in determining how to define a particular class, and there does not appear to be a particular principle to determine the distinction between a statute creating a public right and one merely prohibiting what was previously lawful.

11.3.2

Cullen v Chief Constable of the Royal Ulster Constabulary [2003] 1 WLR 1763

Key Facts

Cullen was arrested then, under s 15 Northern Ireland (Emergency Provisions) Act 1987, was denied the right to see a solicitor. He was later given access to a solicitor and pleaded guilty to criminal charges. He sought damages for the delay in access to a solicitor.

Key Law

The trial judge and the Northern Ireland Court of Appeal held that the police had reasonable grounds to delay access and although they had breached the statutory requirement to give the claimant reasons for this delay at the time this did not give rise to an action in tort. The House of Lords (now the Supreme Court) upheld the decision and also identified that there was no civil law duty because judicial review was available. The House also commented that there was no issue under the Human Rights Act 1998 as there was no breach of Art 5 or Art 6 of the European Convention on Human Rights.

12 Remedies and limitation periods

▶ 12.1 Damages

12.1.1 The purpose and character of damages in tort

1 The purpose of damages in tort is to put the claimant in the position (s)he would have been in if the tort had not occurred.

- So at least one element of damages (general damages) is speculative (a prediction of what would have happened).
- The obvious danger is that the claimant is either under-compensated or over-compensated.

2 So tort damages is an artificial remedy in many situations since it is only a monetary award.

3 There are different types of damages with different effects.

12.1.2 Non-compensatory damages

1 **Nominal damages** can be awarded if there is no actual loss, but a tort has been committed, e.g. trespass to land.

2 **Contemptuous damages** are awarded when the court thinks the action was unnecessary, e.g. with technical defamations.

3 **Exemplary damages** are designed to punish the tortfeasor:

- common elsewhere, e.g. personal injury actions in USA;
- but have restricted use in England and Wales;
- *Rookes v Barnard* (1964) identified three possible categories:
  i) where government servants act in an oppressive, arbitrary or unconstitutional manner (see House of Lords in *Kuddus v Chief Constable of Leicestershire* (2001)) which may reveal 'malice, fraud, insolence, cruelty or the like' (*Muuse v Sec of State for Home Department* (2010));

ii)   where the defendant's conduct is calculated to profit from the tort, e.g. in some libel actions;

iii) where statute expressly allows, e.g. Copyright Act 1958.

Purpose and character

Purpose is to put claimant financially in position as if tort had not occurred, so includes an assessment of future loss.

Contemptuous (exemplary) damages are only possible where:
- Government servants act oppressively;
- defendant's conduct calculated to profit from tort;
- statute expressly allows, e.g. Copyright Act 1958.

Injunctions

- Discretionary.
- Usually prohibitory.
- Can be interlocutory or final.

REMEDIES

Problems with damages

- Inaccurate, unfair and inefficient.
- Favour rich because of future loss.
- Bereavement is limited to certain relatives and is not given to cohabitees.
- Need to show fault, so claimants who cannot lose.
- Insurance companies dictate outcome.
- Lump sum nature need not benefit claimant.
- Delays in system put many claimants off.
- Claimants get less than their claims are worth in settlements.
- Enforcement proceedings are often needed.
- Costly to run, e.g. Pearson said 85% of claim.

Personal injury and death

PI damages of two types:
- special damages up to date of trial;
- future losses, e.g. loss of earnings, and a sum appropriate to pain, suffering and loss of amenities.

Pain, suffering and loss of amenities is based on a fixed quantum for each injury.

Loss of earnings is calculated by multiplying a multiplicand (claimant's earnings) by a multiplier (a number of years).

Possible also to have interim awards, provisional awards and strict settlements where the claimant's condition may deteriorate.

Death claims are of two types:
- on behalf of the deceased's estate under Law Reform (Miscellaneous Provisions) Act 1934;
- on behalf of dependants (and including a sum for bereavement) under Fatal Accidents Act 1976.

Economic loss and property damage

Calculated on:
- loss of property;
- cost of transporting replacements;
- loss of foreseeable profit;
- loss of use until replaced;
- reduction in value.

12.1.3 Economic loss and damage to property

1   Usually compensated as 'special damages'.

2   Usually little problem in calculating such losses.

3   With an economic loss the claimant must be restored as closely as possible to the position if the tort had not occurred.

4   Property damage is calculated according to:

●   loss of the property and its value at the time of loss;

●   cost of transporting replacement property if appropriate;

●   loss of reasonably foreseeable profit;

●   loss of use until the time the property is replaced;

●   reduction in value if damaged but not lost, i.e. repair costs.

12.1.4 Damages in personal injury claims

1   This is divided into two groups.

a) Special damages:

●   this is pecuniary loss up to the date of trial;

●   can include medical care, equipment, loss of earnings, etc.;

●   but only such expenses as the court considers reasonable, so private medical care may well be refused.

b) General damages or future damages:

●   includes pecuniary losses, e.g. future earnings, medical costs, costs of care and special facilities;

●   and also non-pecuniary loss, e.g. pain, suffering and loss of amenities (and in the case of death, bereavement).

2   Non-pecuniary losses are difficult to quantify:

●   peculiarities might include, for example, a person in a coma will gain no award for pain and suffering;

●   awards are based entirely on arbitrary calculations.

3   Loss of earnings are quantified by multiplying:

●   a **multiplicand** – the claimant's annual net loss (any earnings less deductions for, for example, private insurance, sick pay or other benefits etc.); by

- a **multiplier** – notional figure representing the number of years the court feels the award should cover (since the award is made as a lump sum and can be invested, the maximum is 18), less deductions for known illnesses which may cause retirement.

4   Interest to trial is payable on all awards of damages.

5   If it is hard to assess extent of injury, or if claimant's condition may deteriorate, a split trial with interim damages in the case of the first, or provisional damages in the case of the second is possible, or a structured settlement.

12.1.5 The effect of death in tort claims

1   If the claimant dies following the tort, to be fair his action survives.

2   There are two possible actions:

- on behalf of deceased's estate in Law Reform (Miscellaneous Provisions) Act 1934 (similar to a personal injury action);

- on behalf of dependants (a limited group) in Fatal Accidents Act 1976 – includes losses following death, and bereavement.

12.1.6 Problems associated with damages

1   Tort damages are considered inaccurate, unfair and inefficient.

2   They are unfair because the rich receive better compensation than the poor, because their future damages are higher.

3   Certain damages, e.g. bereavement, are available to a restricted range of claimants only, and the level is set low and is arbitrary.

4   Damages discriminates against claimants unable to show fault.

5   Insurance companies can decide the outcome of actions.

6   The lump sum nature of an award can be detrimental to the claimant and only benefits lawyers.

7   Delay caused by procedure often causes claimants to give up, which is what the Woolf reforms tried to address.

8   In out-of-court settlements claimants can be forced to accept much lower sums than they actually deserve.

9   Claimants may still need to use enforcement proceedings where the defendant does not pay up.

10 The system of compensation is inefficient – the cost of administering the tort system prior to Woolf was 85 per cent of damages gained.

▶ 12.2 Injunctions

1   This is an equitable remedy.

2   It is therefore at the court's discretion and not easy to obtain.

3   The clear purpose in seeking such a remedy is to prevent continuation of the tort, e.g. appropriate to the economic torts.

4   The most common form is prohibitory, ie the defendant must refrain from doing something (the tort complained of).

5   An injunction in tort is awarded in one of two ways:

   ● interlocutory – an interim measure sought in advance of trial of the issue, e.g. preventing continued repetition of a libel pending trial;

   ● final – where all the relief needed is contained in the order itself, e.g. an order against pickets.

▶ 12.3 Basic limitation periods

12.3.1 The purpose of limitation periods

1   Unfair on defendant to leave him too long without suing.

2   Difficulty of preserving evidence.

3   Encourages claimant to get on with the case.

12.3.2 Basic periods

1   The general period:

   ● is contained in s 2 Limitation Act 1980;

   ● and is six years from the date on which the action accrues.

2   Damages for personal injury and death:

   ● contained in s 11(4);

   ● and is three years from the date on which the action accrued or the date of knowledge, whichever is the later;

- in fatal accidents where death occurs within three years of the accrual, personal representatives have a fresh limitation period running from the date of death or knowledge of the death (s 11(5)).

3   Latent damage.

- Here there are different rules under Latent Damage Act 1986.

- The action must arise from damage which has lain dormant.

- The period is six years from the date of accrual or three years from the 'starting date' (date of knowledge), with a 15 years 'longstop bar'.

4   Disabilities.

- If a person suffers a disability in law, e.g. a minor lacking capacity, the disability is taken into account.

- Time runs from ceasing of disability, e.g. a minor time barred at 24.

12.3.3 The date of knowledge in personal injury

1   This is defined in s 14.

2   It means knowledge of certain facts, so is the date when:

- the claimant first knew the injury was significant;

- the claimant knew the injury was attributable in whole or part to the defendant's act or omission;

- the claimant first knew the identity of the defendant;

- the claimant knew facts supporting a claim of vicarious liability.

3   Significant injury is one where the claimant considered it sufficiently serious to justify beginning proceedings against a defendant not disputing liability and who could pay.

4   Knowledge means of facts, not law, which the claimant could discover on his/her own or with the help of experts.

12.3.4 Power to disapply the limitation period

1   It is an important power of court in s 33 in cases of death and personal injury.

2   The court must consider certain factors:

- the length of and reasons for the claimant's delay;
- the effect of delay upon the cogency of evidence;
- the defendant's conduct after the cause of action, e.g. responses to a claimant's reasonable requests for information;
- the duration of any disability of a claimant arising after accrual;
- promptness of claimant once aware of possibility of action;
- steps taken by claimant to gain expert advice, and advice given;
- in *A v Hoare and conjoined appeals* (2008) the House of Lords accepted that the discretion to extend the limitation period could be used in the case of deliberate assaults, in this case sexual abuse.

Index

Out After Dark

HUGH LEONARD

Methuen

1 3 5 7 9 10 8 6 4 2

Published in 2002 by Methuen Publishing Ltd
215 Vauxhall Bridge Rd, London SW1V 1EJ

First published in 1989 by André Deutsch
Published in 1990 by Penguin Books

Copyright © 1989 by Hugh Leonard
The right of Hugh Leonard to be identified as author of this work has been asserted
by him in accordance with the Copyright, Designs and Patents Act 1988

Methuen Publishing Limited Reg. No. 3543167

A CIP catalogue record for this book is available from the British Library

ISBN 0 413 77148 2

Printed and bound in Great Britain by
Cox & Wyman Ltd, Reading, Berkshire

For the Big Three -
Ray, Gerry and (again) Zorro

A confessional passage has probably never been written that didn't stink a little of the writer's pride in having given up pride.

J.D. Salinger

Prologue

Ambrose Flood had a model railway, but none of us ever saw it, for it was under the floorboards of his bedroom. It was a Tube train, and Ambrose, who was literal-minded, believed that it should accordingly be kept underground or at least out of sight. Once, when I expressed doubt that the thing existed, he hustled me down to his house on Carysfort Road and brought me upstairs. He pressed a switch, and at once I could hear a humming and a rattling from under the linoleum. The noise travelled in a circle beneath the bed and the wardrobe and past the window and wash-hand stand and was accompanied by a faint, intermittent 'beep-beep'.

'Do Tube trains have whistles?' I asked him.

'Poetic licence,' Ambrose said.

He and I nodded whenever we met, but for the most part that was all. His cronies were Cloggy Lacey and Holy God Furlong. Cloggy was so called because when young he had had adenoids and spoke as through an obstruction; Holy God derived his nickname from his favourite expletive, employed promiscuously either to express amazement or simply to fill a void in conversation. The three were bachelors. They drank, played golf, swam, fished, strolled on the hill or Vico Road and went to plays and concerts at the town hall. Nothing like marriage or parenthood had ever scarred their lives with milestones. Their faces had a kind of priest-like serenity: unruffled, clear, unbothered with time. The town was theirs; they may not have ruled it, but in a sense they

1

owned it. They took part in nothing, sat on no committees, knocked on no doors. What they did do was observe and, to use their own expression, argufy, and if I tell a little of their story here it is because to know them is to know our town. Strangely, considering the tranquillity of their lives, none of them made old bones, and with the death of the last – Cloggy – two months ago as I write this, it was as if the street lamps in Castle Street had blinked out.

They were all three of them reasonably well-read, although Cloggy could not hold a candle to his elder brother, Jimmy, who read the *Iliad* in Greek, hidden behind a copy of *Ireland's Own* lest he be suspected of affectation. Cloggy himself was a railway clerk; Holy God was a maker of gloves; and Ambrose stayed at home – living on what means, I have no idea. They had little regard for the trappings of progress. None of them, for example, ever learned to drive a car: such a departure might have implied that in their lives there was room for improvement, that they did not already inhabit their private, perfect, self-made Fiddler's Green. They disdained to be at the world's beck and call: only illness, an accident or a funeral could dent the immutable pattern of their days, which so gracefully slipped into weeks, months and seasons. Some years ago, I wrote a television play about them and called it *The Virgins*. In Dalkey, to keep a secret is to be guilty of a crime against nature, and one evening when all three were drinking in the Queen's an acquaintance broke the news to them with a muttered: 'I hear tell that the queer fella' (myself) 'has writ a play about yous.'

He might more effectively have tried to elicit casual chatter from a bishop during a canonisation. The pint tumblers did not waver on their slow odyssey from bar-top to lips, and there was little or no small change left out of a minute before the three pairs of eyes turned towards him.

Ambrose said: 'About us?'

Cloggy said: 'You're coddin'.'

Holy God said: 'Holy God.'

Their informant went on to tell them – basing the gist of it on the theorem that no one in our town ever said anything good about anyone who was not yet dead – that the play would parade their lives for the world to make mock of, and if they had a tittle of sense they would watch it, then camp on their solicitors' doorstep and sue the author for slander, libel and God knew what else. What I have encompassed in a single sentence took two John Jamesons to say in fits and starts, but what it amounted to was that the injured parties would make a mint.

'Begod, we might look at it, so,' Cloggy said at length. 'When is it on the goggle box?'

'Sunda' evenin'.'

Holy God said *'When?'* in some disbelief.

Cloggy said: 'Shag that for a lark.'

Ambrose said: 'Can't be did. Sure on Sundays we drink in Finnegan's.'

This last was uttered with the amused incredulity of a pope replying to a suggestion that he had a lie-in on Good Friday morning. Not even the lure of infinite riches could keep them out of Finnegan's on Sundays any more than it could deflect them from the Druid's Chair on Mondays, the Club on Wednesdays, or where they were now, the front bar of the Queen's, on Fridays. They were not the world's messenger boys, to go here and there at its bidding. In the upshot, they missed the play and, as far as I know, could not even find time to inquire from friends who saw it as to the full iniquity of the libel.

My title, *The Virgins*, may have been inaccurate, for it was said that in his youth Ambrose had been 'implicated' with an American woman. It had ended badly; one story went that she had refused him, another that she had turned out to be already married. Whatever the reasons, he was thereafter done with women and carried the hurt around with him, as he did a small box that had most of its blue velvet lining rubbed off from

3

fondling and contained a ring with a modest diamond which he had purchased in the Happy Ring House in O'Connell Street. On evenings when the drink took him in a certain way, he would stare broken-heartedly into the box for minutes on end. No one knew why he had not returned the ring for a refund, and if you attempted to ask others about his blighted romance, the only answer you got was a deep sigh and a cryptic 'Ah, sure poor Ambrose.'

On the first evening I returned home after an exile in London, I saw him, Cloggy and Holy God in their Friday hidey-hole, the Queen's. They gave me the kind of wink coupled with a 'Howyah' and a nod which suggested that it had been two days instead of nine years since they had clapped eyes on me. Ambrose had put on weight and was pasty-faced. At school, he had been handsome in a sullen way, with limp blond hair and stork's legs that seemed all the longer because he wore the shortest short trousers in the town. He was an only child, and his parents indulged him; he had the most pristine football boots, the pearliest-handled six-gun and – what we all envied – a bushranger side-of-the-head hat with a chinstrap. He was the kind of superior boy I craved to be; now he seemed broody and dull. Holy God, in contrast, wore the confident smile a company director might bestow on a nervous stockholder. He was big, pink-faced and barrel-chested, with a full head of corrugated white hair; he walked his dog with the air of a country gentleman. I liked Cloggy best of the three, for he had never been known to say a defamatory word about another being. He was small and brown-haired; he wore spectacles, and with age his face took on the worried, wrinkled appearance of a walnut. With them in the Queen's was a girl named Jo Ann, who came over to where I was sitting and asked if it was true that I had come home for good. After we had talked for a while, she looked back at Ambrose, Holy God and Cloggy. 'Aren't they a hoot?' she said. 'They invite me out for a jar so's people will think they're terrible men for the women.' Then, fondly: 'God help me, I'm in shocking danger!'

The trio had in the beginning been a quartet, and the fourth member was named Rory Cafferky. It took me some time to find out what had happened to him. It was Rory who provided the adventure they preferred to enjoy at second-hand, if at all. As young lads, they robbed orchards and, with even greater daring, hooted after girls in the street. Very occasionally, the girls would call their bluff by hooting back at them, whereupon Ambrose, Holy God and Cloggy would go red and hurry around the nearest corner, each blaming the others for making a show of him, while Rory would brazenly stroll over to the girls whose turn it now was to scurry away.

His daring scandalised and fascinated the three. He acquired an invisible wheelbarrow which he trundled around Dun Laoghaire, asking ladies to hold shop doors open for him and it as he wheeled it through. Often, caught off-guard, they did so and stared at him as, half-stooped over and with fingers clasped around shafts that were not there, he would say "Thank you" and go past them at a half run. Once, in the Carnegie Library, an assistant paid him the ultimate compliment of saying: 'You can't bring that thing in here.' When he became tired of the invisible wheelbarrow, he abandoned it for a more elaborate toy. He would get off a bus with the others and, as they were about to start down Marine Road either for a walk on the pier or to see the picture at the Pavilion, he would say 'Excuse me a minute, lads,' dip into his pocket and take out a key. With half of Dun Laoghaire looking on, he would jab it into midair and turn it. He then proceeded to open a door that only he could see. It was a heavy door; he grunted, strained and went red with the effort. By now a crowd had gathered. He reached in, took hold of a bellrope that was no more visible than the wheelbarrow had been, and gave it a single almighty tug. The great vibration of the bell caused him to reel for a moment, then he recovered, pitted his shoulder against the door, heaved it shut and used the key to lock it again. Ambrose, Holy God and Cloggy had watched the performance from the

5

asylum of the porch of St Michael's Church, with Holy God intoning over and over, lest the other two forget, which was unlikely: 'We're not with him, we're not with him.'

Adolescence marked a watershed: Rory went after girls; the others steered clear. They were Irish bachelors. They treated their homes as comfortable inns; their mothers – or, in Cloggy's case, a doting sister – cooked for them, darned, washed and ironed their shirts, made the beds, scrubbed, polished and even wallpapered, asking for no more in return than the housekeeping on Friday. The three stayed single because they were sensible men who saw no reason why they should hobble themselves for life to creatures to whom a contented smile on a man's face was a foe to be routed. When Ambrose was crossed in love Cloggy and Holy God saw it as a blessed escape. 'He had somebody's good prayers,' one told the other.

Rory had gone his own way; they saw him infrequently. Once, while they were out walking on the Vico Road, he drove past them with a bit of stuff beside him, the car bonnet pointed towards Bray five miles away.

'Going to a hop at the Arcadia,' Ambrose said.

'Will you go 'long out of that,' Holy God said. 'Is it coals to Newcastle? He's taking her up the mountains.'

He paused for a moment, allowing a picture to form in his brain, then did a little dance of lust at the image of Rory and the bit of stuff flattening the crab-grass above Glencree, and the pair of them in their skins or next door to it.

Cloggy was silent. He did not go in for scandal. He looked patiently at the calm sea below, thinking of later on and the few pints he would enjoy as a reward for all the exercise and the fresh air.

For a time, no one knew for certain how Rory made his living except that he had a gift for robbing Peter on the pretence of paying Paul. A pretence was all it was, for he kept no promises, paid no debts. One might as well expect an egg to go back the way it had come. He liked to think of himself as a loveable rogue, a gleam of romance in a drab world; those who had done business with him called him a chancer or, less charitably, a hook. One of his sidelines was smuggling anything from butter to Durex across the six-counties border. In the beginning, he travelled cautiously, at night and by unapproved roads. Later, he bought himself a second-hand Rolls Royce that had been vandalised into a station wagon. Thereafter, he used the main roads and in full day, crossing the border with a cigar clenched between his teeth and a lordly wave that told the customs men that God was passing.

There are people who are born unlucky and remain so for life, who in moments of despair may be heard informing the heavens that if they owned a duck it would surely drown. Rory was the opposite. For him, thin ice never broke, and policemen were always looking the other way. Like the hero in the weekly follower-upper at the Picture House, he unfailingly broke free from his bonds an instant before the blazing roof crashed in. Others, less favoured, muttered peevishly that there was no justice, that hookery paid, and honesty was an also-ran. Rory seemed invulnerable, and so the shock was all the more profound one day in 1961 when Cloggy, on the train home from work, unfurled his *Evening Herald* and saw on the front page the headline: DALKEY MAN DROWNED ON HOLIDAY. A blurry photograph of Rory, taken at a dress dance, grinned up at him.

Rory had no claims to fame, or even infamy, but in Ireland there is an unwritten code of journalism which holds that when an Irishman dies abroad and from unnatural causes it is the equivalent of a hundred Asians perishing when a ferry boat overturns. (If the demise occurs in Britain, the news receives even greater prominence – there are those who claim to have seen a headline in the *Irish Times* that said: IRISH GIRL KILLED BY ENGLISH TRAIN.) Thus a place on the front page was, quite simply, Rory's by birthright. He had died while swimming in Sardinia, of all places. A friend, one Sharon Drexel (23), had sat on a rock overlooking the sea, preferring to sunbathe than swim. She heard shouts, saw him struggling, but even as she looked on he was gone.

The lads were devastated, Cloggy most of all, for he and Rory had shared a passion for swimming. They had competed every year in the race from Coliemore Harbour to Dalkey Island and back, fighting a four-knot current. If Rory had drowned, Cloggy thought, such a fate could be his, too. The lads met that evening and exchanged astonishments. What the hell had brought Rory to foreign parts, they asked, and, come to that, where was Sardinia when it was at home? They went back to Ambrose's house and looked it up in his school atlas, but it yielded no clue. Was Brittas Bay not good enough for Rory, Holy God wanted to know. And if he was all that mad keen to globe-trot, Cloggy said, why else did the Isle of Man exist? As for her nibs, Sharon Drexel, they had never heard of her. The name, Ambrose said, sounded English. Probably, Holy God said, she was a right good thing.

This gave them a new topic: the state of Rory's soul and its present whereabouts. They pulled at what-ifs and buts like three bored dogs tugging at a piece of rag, then Ambrose said gloomily: 'There's no jar in the house, lads.'

'We ought to drink to him that's gone,' Holy God said.

Ambrose nodded and put the atlas back on the shelf, tucked in between Knight's geometry and Hall's algebra. They walked up to the Club (it was a Wednesday) and gave Rory a two-minute silence while their pints went from grey to black under the tap. Next morning, Ambrose went to the parish priest and asked that a novena of masses be said for the repose of the deceased's soul. The offering was ten pounds and each of the lads chipped in three pounds six and eightpence.

That was in 1962. By sheer chance, I was a witness to the end of the story eight years later, or at least to the beginning of the end of it. There was in our town a restaurant where the food was middling when the owner was sober and vile when he was not. It was a last-ditch haunt of Cloggy, Ambrose and Holy God whenever a long-suffering publican asked them if they had no homes to go to and refused their pleas for 'a bang of the latch' — a last quick pint that would fuel them down the road. They were drinking red wine at the table by the window. My wife was abroad, visiting relatives, and I was alone, as was a bearded man across the room. As the waitress, a blonde girl named Pat Moran, passed, he attempted to grasp her arm, but missed.

He called out after her, his accent English, the tone grandiose with drink: 'I requested the favour of a brandy. Might I now be served?'

Pat veered in mid-course. She was an easygoing sort who did not mind a drunk, but had no patience with messers unless they happened to be Dalkey messers. She took a bill from a spike, put it on a saucer, brought it to the man's table and slapped it down.

'I did not ask for "*l'addition*",' he said. 'I ordered a brandy.' He saw another opportunity to speak French and added, '*Un cognac.*'

She said: 'You were told, and you're being told again. We can't sell spirits, we haven't a licence.'

'Brandy is not a—' he said, but she was already gone from him. He addressed the air: 'Then might one be permitted a glass of port?'

He sat, scowling. Ambrose, Cloggy and Holy God had been looking on, interrupted in whatever topic they were pulling and hauling at, and now Ambrose kicked the ball back into play. 'Where was I?' he asked, but before he could remember Cloggy said: 'Wouldn't your man there put you in mind of Rory Cafferky?'

'Who?' Ambrose said.

Holy God said: 'Not at all.'

'That fellow?' Ambrose said. 'He's pissed.'

'I know he's pissed,' Cloggy said, becoming testy. 'What's that got to do with whether he looks like Rory? For Jasus' sake, will you be germane?'

(It was at this point that I began to take notes.)

'Rory got drowned,' Holy God said.

Cloggy said wearily: 'I know he got drowned. We had the mass said, hadn't we? That's proof he was drowned. What I'm saying is that Jembo there looks like him. Rory could have had a cousin, couldn't he? Family resemblance. What's wrong with that?'

'*The Prisoner of Zenda*,' Ambrose said.

'Exactly.'

Holy God seemed unconvinced. He picked up their empty wine bottle and waved it at Pat, signalling for more. She made a face. Wait, she was saying, until the drunk is gone. Without warning, Cloggy lurched to his feet, said 'I'm going to ask him', and started across the room.

'Cloggy, no.'

'Aw, holy God.'

We saw Cloggy talking to the man, who seemed slow on the uptake. He stared at Cloggy and said: 'Hafferty?'

'Cafferky.'

The drunk caught hold of Cloggy's jacket and, using it as a climbing net, pulled himself erect. He stood swaying, blinking at the new perspective as if from a mountain top.

'The name is Leeds,' he said. 'As in Yorkshire. J. G. Leeds.'

He pulled three bunched-up pound notes from his pocket, tossed them any-old-which way on the table, and went out. He seemed in a hurry. Cloggy returned to the others.

'It wasn't him.'

'You wouldn't be told, would you?' Holy God said.

'I wonder where he is,' Ambrose said.

'Gone,' Cloggy said. 'You just saw him.'

'Not him,' Ambrose said. 'I mean Rory.'

'Ah, Jasus,' Holy God moaned. 'Not religion.'

Of a sudden, it came to me that I must seem friendless and miserable sitting there alone and eavesdropping on others. I got up to leave just as Ambrose, a sentimentalist, was declaring that God would not have permitted Rory to drown without allowing

10

him time for an act of contrition. Even a quick ejaculation, he said, would have done the needful. Holy God pooh-poohed the theory. The Almighty, he said, did not intervene. In fact, there was a school of thought that held that God was a mass of ions.

'Of what?' Cloggy asked.

'Ions, Cloggy. Energy. Vapour. Steam.'

'God is steam?' Cloggy said, getting worked up.

'It is a matter,' Holy God said, 'of astrophysics. You would want to ask a Jesuit.'

I paid my bill, nodded to the three and left. There was no sign of J. G. Leeds. The time was a few minutes past midnight, and the street lamps went out with a suddenness that was almost a sound. It was an April night, the sky mad with stars.

Had I remained in the restaurant, I would have seen for myself what all Dalkey was told about within days. Cloggy continued to take umbrage at the assertion that the deity was a mass of steam. Holy God went on acting the know-it-all, his face and voice magisterial. Finally, Cloggy snarled: 'If God is gas, what's the Blessed Virgin, then? Drizzle?' Before the others, appalled by such coarseness, could answer, he said: I'm going to the jacks,' and went out in a temper. A moment later, there was a cry of 'Jasus' from the hall followed by the world's end of a crash.

'Struck dead!' Holy God said and led the rush into the hall.

Cloggy, who had slithered backwards down the stairs on his face, was trying to stand up. The light bulb in the hall was missing or had gone out, and it was only when Pat brought out one of the candles from the dining room and Cloggy recovered the power of narrative speech as an alternative to effing and blinding that anyone understood what had happened.

J. G. Leeds had not, after all, left the building. He had gone upstairs in search of the lavatory and had either fallen down or lain down on the top landing. Cloggy, in a temper and taking the stairs two at a time, had stepped on him in the dark and slid back the way he had come, banging his knee and bending the frame of his glasses. It was not until he had been examined and removed from the danger list that J. G. Leeds was attended to. Ambrose and Holy God sat him up and shook him until he began to groan.

'Where do you live?' Holy God asked.

'Wha'?'

'Tell us where you live, and we'll get you home.'

'He can't stay here,' Pat said.

'*Will* you *tell* us *where* you *live*?' Holy God said in a sing-song, shaking him in rhythm with the words.

J. G. Leeds began to stutter until at last the truth hiccupped out, and his accent was no longer English: 'Rory Cafferky, 10 Infant of Prague Terrace, Dalkey.'

A bed was found in Ambrose's house, and next morning when Cloggy and Holy God called around the born-again Rory Cafferky had the greenish look of a copper dome, but was otherwise his unabashed old self. He was shaving as they stood behind him, like angels come to deliver a soul to judgment. He had faked his death, he said, because there was a warrant out for his arrest on a charge of smuggling. The girl mentioned in the newspaper had been his accomplice. 'I got on the soft side of her,' he said. 'Old Sharon was a decent skin.'

'I'm sure,' Holy God all but sneered. 'What happened to her?'

Rory gave a shrug that told them don't-care as much as don't-know. He said: 'She gave a sworn statement to the police, so she could hardly go back on it and do the dirty on me.' The tone of his voice suggested that somewhere, somehow he had given her good cause to do the dirty on him.

He had stopped off in the town, he said, on his way to Connemara for a break. It was the long way around, but a tender heart had drawn him back to the scenes of his youth, even if the likelihood that the police were still on the look-out for him meant that he was already on the wing. Nowadays, he told them, he lived in Northern Ireland as J. (for Jeremy) G. Leeds and called himself an entrepreneur.

'You pronounce the word well, mind,' Cloggy said with a stone face on him. 'Very French.'

Rory either missed the coolness or chose to ignore it. 'So what's new with the three of you?' he asked.

'What is new,' Holy God said, 'is the matter of the expenditure of ten pounds for a mass for the repose of your soul.'

When Rory realised that they had indeed had a mass said for him, he was obliged to put the razor down lest he cut himself from laughing. Cloggy, Holy God and Ambrose, who had had a council of war over his lying-in-state the night before, waited, expressionless, until he was done. 'Still, lads,' he said, 'it was damn nice of yous.' He tried to pull his lips into a tight straight line, but it failed to hold. 'Damn nice.'

'We want our ten quid back,' Cloggy said.

'Yous what?'

'You rooked us,' Ambrose said mildly, 'so it's a matter of principle.'

'Yous rooked yourself,' Rory said.

'We want it back,' Holy God said.

Rory tried to make light of it. 'Are you sure that Ambrose wouldn't like to charge me for bed and breakfast as well?'

When he saw the set of their faces, he shrugged and went to where his trousers were hanging on a chair. He was wearing the boxer shorts he had slept in, and his thing peered through the front. Cloggy, Ambrose and Holy God looked away demurely. Naked at the Men's Bathing Place or the Forty Foot was permissible; in a house it was another matter.

Rory went through the pockets and found a pound note and some change. 'Don't worry,' he said. 'I'm not broke. I'm staying at the Royal Marine, and I left my travellers' cheques in the hotel safe.' He began to pull his trousers on. 'Tell yous what. Why don't I get the money. Then we can have a jar for old time's sake at the Queen's, and yous can see me off to Galway.'

'Proper order,' Holy God said as the three watched Ambrose's garden gate squeal shut behind him. 'It may be only a tenner, but it's one bit of hookery he won't be let get away with, not if we have to follow a crow for it.'

It would have been better for Holy God if he had taken flying lessons, for of course that was the last they saw of Rory Cafferky – at least for a couple of years. In the matter of the ten pounds, there was, as Ambrose had said, a principle at stake: he had made fools of them, if only in their own eyes; and, quite apart from paying a priest to say a dud mass, there was the waste of wit, argument and conjecture over where his soul had gone. Rory, however, had at least one principle of his own, and it was never to pay a debt – its smallness in this case made it all the more vital that the ideal be preserved.

When he next came south on a flying visit – and he appears fleetingly every year or so – he espied his three old friends in some pub or other. He hailed them with the amnesia of roguery. They turned their backs on him, drank up and went elsewhere. He was not forgiven or again spoken to.

Ambrose, Holy God and Cloggy all died in their late fifties and in that order. Ambrose had been in indifferent health for years, but his passing was the envy of all who knew him. He got up early one winter morning, found that the *Irish Independent* had arrived, made tea in the kitchen and took it and the newspaper back to the warmth of bed. And there, glasses on the tip of his nose, he went out like a tiptoe.

Holy God died of a heart attack, Cloggy more painfully. We miss all three.

When I was twenty-two and a rebellious teenager (we mature late in Ireland), I wrote the first and only chapter of a novel to be called, devastatingly, *Sex on Thursdays*.

It was not as sensational in intent as the title might suggest: quite simply, when the annual mission – the Retreat, we called it – came to our town, the preachers invariably chose Thursdays for the homily on immodest and immoral behaviour, for it was then that domestic servants had their evening off and could attend church. In those well-ordered days when feminism had still to cut its milk teeth, no one questioned the bland assumption that girls up from the country and in service were so much ripe fruit, helpless on the bough and palpitating for damnation.

Everyone enjoyed the Thursday sermon. On that one evening in the year the parishioners could hear sex being talked about without worrying that it might be a sin to listen. Plain speaking was *de rigueur*. The Jesuits, when they came to Dalkey, were too effete for a town that liked its religion to be the spiritual equivalent of a bowl of stirabout or lashings of bacon and spuds. 'Too much old codology,' my mother once daringly said under her breath – and the Franciscans extolled charity and compassion, neither of which virtue has ever commended itself to the Irish ethos. The star performers were the Redemptorists, who promised the impure of heart an eternity on the hottest hob of hell. 'And, as for those who touch their *bodies* . . .!' a missionary would hiss, his own eyes like burning coals, and the entire congregation crooned in an ecstasy of terror.

The idea for the book was the imaginary collision of two quite unconnected events. One of these was the birth of twins to a girl whose name, Honor, was in the circumstances inappropriate, given that the father was unknown, unhonoured (except in the punning sense) and conspicuously unsung. She was not, by the way, a domestic servant, and so the title, *Sex on Thursdays*, was a rank imposture. She was an attractive girl, with shapely legs superb in stockings that had come out of a bottle, with only slightly askew pencil-drawn seams – this was in 1949, when clothes were still rationed. Whenever I passed her on Hyde Road as she trundled a rickety pram with a small bald head protruding from either end, I pictured myself pencilling her stockings on for her, and my lower abdomen tied itself in such tumescent knots that I was obliged to hang on for modesty's sake to the Fannings' pebble-dashed wall. What was worse, her seeming unconcern at the world's opinion suggested that she might actually have enjoyed her misfortune and spiced my fantasies with images of such unbridled abandon that I went on clinging to the wall, until old Fanning appeared at his front window and made feck-off gestures of great savagery.

Our town is only nine miles from O'Connell Bridge, and so, even in those backward times, we considered ourselves not unworldly. Sex, as we all knew, was the worst sin of all, but a single biological mishap could be borne stoically. Twins, however, were not to be glossed over. Quality is commonly deemed to be more important than quantity, but our then parish priest did not apply this criterion to illegitimate births. Contrary to both good taste and theology, he got it into his head that, in Honor's case, the sin was doubled.

Not only was Father Kearney a man of the cloth, but that cloth was of a deep-dyed, if metaphoric, green. Just as Napoleon declared that every French soldier carried in his cartridge case the baton of a Marshal of France, so the good Father believed that every young Irishman went through life with a Miraculous Medal

16

in one hand and a hurling stick in the other. For a godly man who thought the best of his fellow creatures, especially if they happened to be Irish, it was the bitterest of pills to reflect that probably the twins' father was, like their mother, one of his parishioners. (Honor, when interrogated on the subject, merely smiled and hummed a bar or two of an old come-all-ye). He ended up by not swallowing the pill at all, for, within a week of the double christening – done discreetly at St Joseph's, Glasthule, a mile away – he had devised what we would nowadays call a scenario. A post-war tourist boom had set in, and, counting on his fingers, Father Kearney reasoned that the twins had been conceived early the previous August: therefore the father could not have been other than an English visitor.

He even managed, on no evidence at all, to pinpoint the scene of the crime. Early in 1939, work had begun on a new scenic road between Dalkey and Killiney Hills; then, a year and five hundred yards later, the war brought the project and the road to a dead end. Because it wound sharply uphill, it was nicknamed the Burma Road, and, then as now, it stopped on the edge of a meadow with woods beckoning darkly beyond. Honor Prendergast's virginity had ended, Father Kearney confided in an apocalyptic whisper, on or fornenst the Burma Road.

Within days, he convened an emergency meeting of the prefects of the Men's Confraternity and revealed how he intended that no other young girl would share the fate that had befallen the happily unhappy Honor. A pair of iron gates would be erected where the Burma Road began, and these would be padlocked every day at sunset. The ways of the Almighty, Father Kearney told the confraternity, were mysterious, and if the Prendergast twins had been permitted to come into the world, it was for the good and sufficient reason that others of their kind might thereby he kept out of it. God, he said, almost rubbing his hands with excitement, was a queer harp.

Mr Mundow, who collected offerings at the fourpenny door on

Sundays and was to Dalkey what the captain of the Swiss Guards was to the Vatican, could and did outdo Father Kearney when he came to aphorisms. Iron gates, he said, pithily, did not grow on trees.

'We will raise funds,' Father Kearney said calmly. 'A concert.'

A committee was promptly formed, with one of the curates as its chairman. The town hall was booked and posters were printed announcing an All Star Concert. Artistes were engaged, including Mrs Quinn's Irish Dancers, a spoons player, a gipsy harpist named Silvio, Miss McGuinness the soprano, and a housepainter who called himself Sallynoggin's Al Jolson. The main items would be a one-act comedy entitled *The Young Man from Rathmines* and an actual opera singer out from Dublin.

The play, so the curate told his committee, was a howl: all about this flibbertigibbet of a young one who throws over the man she is engaged to, a good Catholic, and titivates herself in hopes that the new lodger, when he arrives, will go wild out over her. Maybe he will even marry her. At the end, he comes in, and when she sees that he is only a black she screams and faints. The committee laughed, and Scurty White, who had built White's Villas, said 'The divil's cure to her, Father', while carefully tearing bits of cigarette paper from his lower lip. The curate told them that the play not only had a strong moral but would also end the first half of the evening on a cheerful note.

The second half would consist of the opera singer and no one else. This was partly in deference to his renown – he was described on the posters as '(Star of Stage and Radio)' – but also because, alone of all the artistes, he had insisted on being paid. 'If he wants blood money,' the curate said with a small forgiving but unforgetting smile, 'we'll make sure he earns it.'

Such is the contrariness of Dalkey that no matter how worthy a cause is it will have its detractors. If a golden chariot with an angel in it were to descend, however briefly, from heaven into Castle Street, it would set off again with 'M. O'B. = J. F.' written on the side in purple pencil and tin cans tied to the back bumper. And so it was a matter for sadness, but not surprise, that a small group of dissidents existed in the matter of the iron gates. It was in vain that Father Kearney preached from the altar that the gates would be a bulwark, not only against the tide of English summer visitors, all of them only after the One Thing, but also the one or two local youths, if they existed, in whom by some freak of nature an alien lust had taken root and festered. Actually, as far as the second category went, he had erred on the side of understatement, for there were at least a dozen of us.

Outwardly, we insisted that the gates would be a violation of basic human rights (we paraphrased bits from Hollywood films in which James Stewart and the like made stumbling speeches ending with 'Well, I guess that's kinda what ya call democracy'). The truth was not nearly so idealistic. We each nursed the frail and private hope that somehow the Burma Road might prove to have erotic properties conducive to the loss of a virginity that persisted in clinging to us like stickybacks. In entertaining so implausible a theory, we were not simple-minded, merely desperate.

We met nightly as conspirators in the Roman Café in Dun Laoghaire, monopolising three tables for an entire evening, so that now and again the son of the *padrona* would appear with an unconvincing snarl to say: 'Two hours . . . glass-a hot-a milk . . . fourpence . . . smart-a fellas.'

Probably, the matter would have dribbled away in empty talk had it not been for Mikie Nixon, a pale little whisper of a fellow in whom, for some reason, any attempt at standing still would being about a fit of staggering. He had grown up brotherless, but with six sisters, and in consequence hated all females on sight. He was the only one in our group who, with utter sincerity, saw Father Kearney's grand design as an infringement of what in years to come would be called civil liberties. Mikie, not to put too fine a point on it, frightened us. He was by our lights unnatural. Not only had a dirty thought never entered his head, but mere talk was not in itself good enough for him: the zealot wanted action as well. Were we, he wished to know, men or mice? If the former, we should make our anger known by a protest outside the town hall on the night of the concert. His idea was that we would carry placards.

The first image to enter my own head was of my mother and my mad aunt Mary crossing the street to pay their one-and-threepence admission and catching sight of me walking up and down, publicly defending the Burma Road's status as a fornicating amenity. In my mind's eye, I saw my mother's face and a wave of faintness washed over me. Other foreheads gleamed beside mine. 'We'll be read off the altar,' someone said.

Mikie Nixon's pale eyes became spears of sleet. He was on the point of telling us that we were cowards and good for damn all else but talk, which of course was true, when a fellow named Looby said with a show of smooth reason that Mikie's plan was masterly, ingenious and a credit to him. Then, with the diffidence of a man in hobnails walking on a brand-new Navan carpet, he put it to the meeting that no strategy devised by mortal man was so flawless that it could not be improved upon. He was sure that Mikie would not take it amiss if a modification or two were added.

We all mumbled gravely at the fairness of this: all of us, that is, except Mikie, whose sixth sense whispered that the same Navan carpet was about to be pulled from under him. We talked, streamlining his master-plan here, beautifying it there, until the Roman Cafe's electric sign flickered out. By then, the plan had been refined to the point where, instead of carrying placards, we would bang loudly on the windows of the town hall while the concert was on and then run for our lives. Mikie was outraged. He attempted to make a speech from among the cafe's dustbins, but we all suddenly said 'Look at the time' or 'It's all hours, I'm destroyed' or 'The last shaggin' bus is gone, I'll have to hoof it', and fanned out in all directions, compounding betrayal with desertion.

The Irish have always fatally combined a passion for conspiracy with an inability to keep a secret. That, in tandem with a natural apathy, has put paid to an assortment of rebellions down the centuries, and our own modest endeavour was not fated to break the mould. To begin with, on the night of the concert no more than half of our number turned up at the bandstand in Dillon's Park. One of these, to our surprise, was an unsmiling Mikie Nixon, who, it was agreed by all, was a decent skin, whatever else.

We straggled up Coliemore Road and into Castle Street. A distant grumble of laughter confirmed that *The Young Man from Rathmines* was, as the curate had predicted, a howl. We paused, six or seven of us, at the gate of the old tramyard. 'We'll wait for the opera singer,' Mikie said.

'No,' Tony Dowd said (everyone in Dalkey had, and still has, a nickname, and his, for reasons lost in time, was Doodah). 'It's too cold to hang around. We'll do it now and have it over with.'

Without waiting for argument, Doodah went swiftly past the Queen's public house and vanished into the laneway that ran alongside the town hall. We had hardly begun to follow him when he reappeared, his walk now eating its heart out to become a run. 'Polis,' he said out of the corner of his mouth as he went past, and sure enough two smiling policemen emerged from the lane.

Some of us, without breaking step, executed an instantaneous about-wheel, while the others crossed the street wearing the kind of determined look that betokened urgent business in a far place. Later, by the long way round, we found our way back to Dillon's Park and crowded into the little sweetshop at the entrance where, such was her girth, there was hardly room enough for Miss Dillon on her own. There we reflected that our rebellion, like all that had gone before, had been blighted by loose tongues at best and informers at worst. Mikie Nixon did not appear, and we assumed that he had gone home in disgust. We were mistaken: what we had all along failed to realise was that through his veins flowed not merely the blood of a fanatic but of a martyr.

While the rest of us were in retreat, he had somehow slipped past the policemen and entered the town hall by the door at the rear. Still unnoticed, he ducked into the backstage lavatory and bolted the door. There he remained throughout the interval, making no sound when the knob was rattled. He heard someone curse, then another voice told someone to use the laneway or the gentlemen's in the Queen's. A few minutes later, the second half of the concert began. The curate introduced the opera singer, saying that he needed no introduction; there was a chord on the piano; the audience applauded, and Mikie heard a tenor voice starting in on 'She moved through the fair'.

Mikie waited a minute and then pulled the lavatory chain.

Some water closets are well-mannered and flush demurely; this was not one of them. The arm with the iron ball attached fetched the roof of the cistern an appalling clout, whereupon water gushed out with the noise of ten simultaneous cases of asthma and five of whooping cough. Mikie had no idea as to whether the sound travelled out as far as the audience, but that the tenor heard it was evident from a kind of soprano wobble that entered his voice on the last word of 'As the swan in the evening moves over the lake.'

Milkie sat on the rim of the bowl and waited for the cistern to refill, but he became impatient after a minute or two and once again pulled the chain. The iron ball rose and dropped repeatedly with a sound like falling kettles. Through the door a voice hissed at him to be quiet, saying 'There's a man out here trying to sing a song.' For answer, Mikie redoubled his efforts, yanking on the chain like a pocket-sized Quasimodo.

Within the lavatory, the noise was so deafening that the cause of it did not realise that the tenor had by now fallen silent. As we learned from eye-witnesses, he signalled to the pianist to rest from her labours, then himself leant on the piano, favoured the audience with a smile of suave forbearance and waited for the bedlam to cease.

Instead, it worsened, for people backstage began to hammer on the door of the lavatory. Shouting was heard. The climax came when Mikie's frenzy reached a pitch where the cistern itself shattered and slabs of vitreous china crashed to the floor, one of them hitting him on the head. Bloody, but unbothered, he now found himself holding the chain, to which were attached sundry bits of rusty metal, the ballcock and the iron ball. He began to swing the chain, using the ball to attack the door as if it were Sports Day in medieval times and he were a knight of old pulverizing an opponent's shield. By now, the audience had become restive. Four hundred eyes looked at the tenor, and he, still leaning on the piano, looked back at them. A voice from the back of the hall asked him if his mother knew he was out. Another wanted to know if he would work for a farmer. Slow hand-clapping began, and this was accompanied by a chant of 'Sing the song . . . sing the song.'

The impoverished nature of the lyrics did not inhibit their popularity, and the volume grew as new voices joined in. Respectable people in the front seats attempted to quell the noise, but in doing so only provided an accompaniment. For some minutes, the tenor's smile had become thinner than of yore, and now he and it decided to depart together. He bowed with elaborate irony and was answered by a storm of whistling and catcalls. In the wings, he confronted the curate, who was looking helplessly at the lavatory door.

'They told me about Dalkey,' he said cryptically. 'And now I know.'

He took his overcoat and silk scarf down from the dressing-room nail and went out into the dark. He was not seen again, any more than he himself ever saw his fee.

As for Mikie, he held out for a few minutes longer until a walking silo of a man known as the Horse Heenan was brought backstage. He bade everyone stand clear, then turned away from the W.C. door as if disowning it, only to knock it clear off its hinges with a terrible backward kick that explained how he had earned his nickname. A groan, not of fury but of revulsion, went up as Mikie stood revealed. Water from the broken cistern had escorted the blood from his scalp wound down his face and over his shirt front. In places, the mixture had combined with dirt from the cistern lid to create a flan of brown mud, deepening to a runny black. He resembled an earthquake victim who had been dug out after a week. The gruesomeness was only embellished by the entrails of the cistern which now hung limply from his hand. People looked away. Even the Horse Heenan blenched.

To any sensible being it was obvious that Mikie was not, after all, a saboteur, but an unfortunate who had been horribly injured in some way, and the noise was his delirious attempt to attract assistance. At any rate, and to his astonishment, no one attempted to lay hands on him. Rather, the onlookers backed fastidiously away, stamping on each other's feet as he scuttled bloodily past them and was swallowed up by the Dalkey night, ballcock and all.

As for the concert, after urgent consultation with Father Kearney, the curate came out to still the uproar and announced that, in response to public demand, those performers on whom the audience had doted in Part One and had not already gone for their buses home, would reappear and endear themselves still further. This was the signal for sullen mutterings and an hour of encores, rounded off with a raffle and a community sing-song. There was, of course, no question of reprising *The Young Man from Rathmines*, a howl though it had been. 'Sure they'll all know the surprise at the end when the golliwog comes on.' Father Kearney said, thereby displaying a grasp of dramaturgy such as lay at the very heart of Aristotle's *Poetics*.

In spite of the noise from the lavatory and the defection of the tenor, the concert was accounted a great success. Which is to say that, as far as the parish priest was concerned, its artistic merits or lack of them were not at issue. There was nothing that Father Kearney liked better than a bar of a song, and he could gaze as if mesmerised for tens of minutes on end at Irish dancers, the maniacal thudding of whose silver-buckled, patent-leather shoes more than compensated for their corpselike rigidity from the knees up. What gave him matter for concern was an awareness that the human mind was the seat of both art and religion, and in that confined space there was the danger that the one might become mistaken for the other. It was safest all around to smile and say that what the know-it-alls affected to look upon as art was known by plump and plain everyday people to be no more than old codology. In short, there was no such thing. The success of the concert resided wholly in its having been a Good Cause, and to enquire if the audience had had their money's worth was as impudent as daring to ask if the ten o'clock short Mass on Sunday had been prettily done.

At the end of the tale, the gates were never erected on the Burma Road. Father Kearney was an unworldly man, and the last thought to enter his head was that the county council might not fall over itself to permit a holy priest to block off a quiet road here and a bosky avenue there in the name of purity. An official letter arrived at the presbytery containing extracts from various by-laws. These – and fair was fair, Father Kearney conceded – upheld the right of couples, mixed or unmixed, to walk abroad after dark. It was, regrettably or not, a free country. To his bafflement, however, the thooleramawns who had drafted the by-laws had omitted to insert a clause making it an offence for strollers in public places at night-time to slow down to a standstill except in certain designated areas, such as under lighted street lamps. It was only thanks to God's all-loving mercy, the priest was heard to say, that such crass ham-handedness had not resulted in Honor Prendergast having had triplets.

None of us believed for an instant that the Council would prove a match for Father Kearney. We expected him to continue blithely on his way, scattering his critics from him as a dog shakes away water after a swim. In our part of the world it was held to be incontrovertible proof of divine intervention in human affairs that court actions against members of the clergy usually came to grief. Unfortunately, another snag arose, and this one was insoluble. No one could be found who, in return for a 'God bless you and sure you'll have your reward in heaven', would agree to padlock the gates every evening, winter and summer, and open them again at dawn. Father Kearney asked for volunteers, jovially saying that he expected to be knocked down in the rush. Weeks passed, and he remained vertical.

As for the profits from the concert, they quickly burned a hole in his soutane. First, the youngest Fagan girl whose father was in the fever ward at Loughlinstown was crying her eyes out for a First Communion dress. Next, after a week as a part-time postman, Liamy Cleary had fecked a postal order, and it was either nine months' goal or find the mailboat fare to Holyhead. Then there was the real emergency of the younger curate's bicycle falling to pieces on his way to a sick call. Every day, new hungers came like mice to nibble away at the money, until finally, tormented by seeing his dream vanishing – not in one decent, brutal awakening, but piecemeal – Father Kearney splurged what was left on an old folks' outing to Glendalough and, for those who could hoist themselves into it, St Kevin's Bed. Thereafter, the Burma Road gates assumed the roseate and unsubstantial glow of the Heavenly Gates themselves.

As for Mikie Nixon, when he arrived home two of his sisters fainted, and the other four washed him down lovingly, cleansed the blood from his clothes and put him to bed before his father could come home from a whist drive in Sallynoggin and take a strap to him. I met a lady at a party last Christmas who told me that Mikie had died some months previously in Australia. 'He wasn't the marrying kind,' she said, then blushed and added 'He was a bachelor gay.' She had never, I am sure, heard 'gay' used in a sexual sense; but the blush told me that she might just as well have done.

When, as a twenty-two-year-old, I began to write my book that never was, I took the story of the gates and added to it an entirely separate event. I had just learned that my father knew the whereabouts of an arms cache from the time of the Civil War.

One evening on Railway Road, I saw him walking just ahead of me. We were both on our way home: I from eight hours of daydreaming at the Land Commission where, over fourteen years, I was to set a kind of record as the world's longest-serving temporary clerical assistant; he from his work tending the gardens of a house that had once been called 'Enderley' and was now 'Santa Maria'. As I caught up with him, I saw that his face was dark. His gait was stiff-legged, as much from anger as rheumatics. I saw his clenched fists, the knuckles visible at the sleeve-ends of someone's hand-me-down overcoat that was too big for him. He was moving so fast that as I caught up I said: 'Run, why don't you?'

He said, without malice, 'Run me arse,' and walked faster.

His new employers were making the last of his working days a misery. From boyhood until old age he had worked in 'Enderley' for a Quaker family named Jacob, who manufactured biscuits. They were The Quality. Personal honour was to them not a luxury or even a virtue, but as innate a part of their lives as lavender in a pillow, or the genuflection of flowers as they passed. They took honesty and service for granted for no other reason than an inability to imagine their absence, and so they left the cook, the maidservants and two gardeners to go about their duties in peace and unmolested. When the Jacobs died and the house became 'Santa Maria', the new owners kept my father on. They were Catholics and self-made. Being themselves part of an evolution from peasantry to a new and native middle class, they, the grandchildren of servants, looked at my father and their housekeeper from Claregalway and saw a reflection of themselves. They interfered, they bullied; in their own eyes they were islands of probity in an ocean of petty theft and a day's work for a week's pay. The new owner, a schoolmaster who had married a successful *couturière*, would stand over my father and, with a smile as thin as a penny ruler, say: 'Mr Keyes, aren't you the great man for finding work to do that keeps you out of the sun?'

At home afterwards, he treated my mother and me and, incidentally, my mad aunt Mary, to a recital. 'The Master, God rest him, always called me "Keyes". But the whoor's ghost that's in it now has to stick a "Mister" in front of it. And do yous know why? I'll tell yous why. Because he knows he hasn't the shaggin' right to call me "Keyes" without the "Mister". And why hasn't he the shaggin' right? Because he hasn't the shaggin' breedin'!' He struck the table with his fist; a cup jumped and Mary said 'Jesus'.

When the Jacobs died they had taken not only their own world with them, but also his. Bog-trotters like the schoolmaster were the new Quality, and, as we walked towards home, I needed not ask him how the day had gone. Our way home brought us past Foley's pub at the corner of the Barrack Road, where several cornerboys – my mother's brother Sonny among them – habitually decorated the window sill. Sonny would give my father a distant, dark-eyed nod suggestive (quite falsely) of old injustices, while the others would defer to him with a respectful growl of 'Ha'sh oul' day' or 'That's not a bad one.' My father, holding a poor opinion of idlers, would reply, if he deigned to do so at all, with a grunted "Tis, so,' or "Tisn't.' Today, however, one of the group seemed to have drink taken, for he staggered both my father and myself by calling out: 'Eh, Keyes, where did you bury them guns?'

My father was wiry and had red hair that even in old age turned grey only at the edges. His temper, whenever he was called out of his name, would flare up like match and splutter out as quickly, but today it was the shattering of an oil lamp. The jeer had hardly been uttered when he was across the road and took the cornerboy (who was all of forty) by the throat. The others were too taken aback to move, except my uncle, Sonny, who had a nose for danger that was acknowledged to be second to none and went hopping off around the corner on his short leg.

A verbal barracking began, with my father shouting several times over, as if it were an incantation, 'Are you blackguardin' me, you whoor you?' This was accompanied by a shake which, if it did not snap the other's head off at the neck, threatened not only to put him through Foley's window but the Tullamore Dew looking-glass behind it. The cornerboy's comrades began to gather round, saying 'Aisy, aisy,' and 'Sure all the man said was'. They plucked at my father's sleeve, but not with such force as might impede what, given the passion he was in, bade fair to bring sunshine to the greyness of their day.

The man in my father's grip was one of the kind who loitered on the outside of a public house solely because indigence prevented them from doing so on its inside. I knew him to be a crony of my uncle Sonny's. He habitually wore an askew smile of disgust as if, no fool he, he had the world's measure. Like Sonny, he had put it to the test and it had failed. His face was usually suffused with a kind of porter flush, but now, with hands around his throat – calloused hands, with the clay of a day's planting still under the nails – it was turning purple, and his smile was far away.

My own role in all this was the passive one of standing across the road in the lee of the Bank of Ireland and saying 'Da . . . Da . . .' in a low voice audible, I hoped, to my father, but not to passers-by who might associate me, the wearer of a collar and tie, with a street brawl. Of a sudden, I saw him release his victim and heard him say: 'There's still a few of us left. From here on in, wherever you go to at night, keep lookin' behind you.'

He set off again, as fast as before, ignoring a frightened shout of 'You bloody oul' madman' from his rear. I was too shocked to follow him at once: not merely because of the attack on the cornerboy, although I had seen no reason for it other than the bad temper he was bringing home with him from 'Santa Maria'. I had often heard him make threats, usually incoherent and always empty; this time, he had used the language of a gunman.

He had been 'out' in the War of Independence and remained

'out' during the Civil War that followed. He was given a rifle, but never saw a bullet. He did arms drill at weekends, wearing an empty bandolier, but the nearest he came to engaging the enemy was on the day he saw a news picture in the *Irish Independent* purporting to show a squad of Black and Tans capturing armed I.R.A. men in County Kerry. The caption was 'Hands Up!'

A gateway in the background seemed oddly familiar, and it came to him that the photograph had been taken at the entrance of Killiney Hill, or Victoria Park, as the Protestants called it, up the road from Dalkey. It was a fake, a piece of trumped-up propaganda. Incensed, he took a tram into Dublin, laid siege to the public office of the *Independent* and demanded to see the 'man in charge'.

'Do you mean the editor?' he was asked.

My father had never heard of such a being as an editor and assumed that he was being fobbed off. He replied that he did not want to see any gobshite of an editor; he wanted the boss man. Matters deteriorated at this point, and he was asked bluntly to state his business. He flung his newspaper upon the counter with a flourish, then took two steps back and all but folded his arms like Tom Mix in the pictures. 'What kind of gobdaws are yous,' he said, 'to be made eejits of be the English? Do yous not know Killiney-shaggin'-Hill when it's there in black and white in front of yous? Are yous blind or what?'

He was shouting. The few people who were in the office put their own business aside and looked on. One of them was an R.I.C. man who, as yet unnoticed by my father, was there on duty in case the Republicans should attempt to gain control of Independent House. My father leaped forward and struck the newspaper a blow of his fist.

'Them and their "Captured in County Kerry",' he said. Then, his face livid, he emitted a roar of 'County Kerry me arse!'

A tremor ran through the R.I.C. man like a ripple over a lake. It may have been that he took exception to what in 1921 was strong language or, perhaps, like many of his kind, he happened to be a Kerryman.

'Oh, them's the Black and Tans for you,' my father said. 'The dirt and the leavin's of English gaols.' Then, moving off down one of his own favourite by-roads, he declared: 'Aren't they in me own town at this minute, shootin' innocent women and childer in their beds?' As he spoke, he knew that no Dalkey person of any sex or age had ever been shot in bed or out of it, but he had never been so disloyal as to remain silent and see his own town made little of by the failure of the English to put it to the sword. 'Aye,' he went on, 'an' they lifted babies in the air on their bayonets.'

'Is that a fact now?' a voice said into his ear.

'It is,' he said and saw that he was addressing the R.I.C. man.

He was led twice from the office and twice returned, each time to describe a new and more colourful atrocity. Finally, thrown out bodily into Middle Abbey Street, he informed the receding back of the R.I.C. man that it belonged to no true Irishman but a paid hireling of the Crown.

'The coward wouldn't stand his ground,' he said to my mother that evening. 'But he heard me right enough, bad scran to him,' 'Aye,' she said drily. 'And you got the worth of the half-day's pay you lost and the return tramfare to the Pillar.'

Where the growing of flowers was concerned, my father had genius, but as a gunman he could be relied upon always to grasp the wrong end of the revolver. Nor could he have won an argument, never mind a war, for, once vehemence took possession of his tongue, sense went from it, evicted like nestlings by a cuckoo. When I heard the chill in his voice as he warned the cornerboy to keep looking behind him, it was as if I were listening to a stranger.

When I caught up with him a minute later I asked: 'What was all that about?'

'Nothin'.'

'What ailed you? I thought you'd have to be dug out of him.'

Silence.

31

'Anyway, what was all that about burying guns?'

'Hold your tongue.' He fetched me a look. 'You have too much old talk out of you.'

At this point, the Dublin bus drew up, the driver's door opened and our dog, Blackie, alighted. Travelling by bus into town and out again was his hobby: he did it all day every day until tea time. He had begun three years before by accompanying a neighbour of ours, Mr Keogh, who was a tram-driver. The dog would sit happily on the front platform, his makeshift leash tied loosely to the driver's handle that was like an outsized coffee grinder. Last year, when the trams gave way to buses, he adapted more easily than most of the crews, including Mr Keogh, who opted for retirement. I never met the busman who was not glad of the black dog's company. More than once, the melancholy thought occurred to me that he was more widely travelled than I.

We walked home together, the three of us. As the garden gate screeched open, my father said: 'C'mere to me.' He looked towards the house. 'You're to say nothin' to herself, do you mind me?'

I nodded, then thought to put a price on my silence.

'What about burying guns?'

'Will you shut it!' For a moment it was as if he would make to throttle me as he had done the cornerboy. Beyond the front window I could make out the inquisitive silhouette of my mother; probably she was wondering why, instead of coming in for our tea like Christians, we were in the garden colloguing. My father said something indistinctly.

'What?'

Snapping. 'I said I hid things.'

'What things? Do you mean *guns*?'

'Uhh.'

'What's the big secret? Look, if every waster in the town knows about it, then —'

Fiercely, hating them: 'They know shag all!' He looked across the dark roofs of St Begnet's Villas towards the granite cliffs of Dalkey Hill, as if he were their equal for silence.

Wresting the truth from him – or, rather, his version of the truth – was as wearying as tweezing splinters from a finger, and so let me put in one sentence what took the beginnings of a hundred. When the Civil War was dribbling to a standstill, my father was summoned to a dawn meeting with his Commandant and informed that he had been chosen to hide a residue of arms, ammunition and explosives until the day came when, to use the phrase beloved of the diehards, 'We shall rise again!'

Once his story was at last out, a familiar sob arose in his throat and a dampness came into his eyes. 'An' I done it,' he said. 'I stripped the guns an' I iled them, and then I wrapped up the shaggin' lot, Mills bombs an' all, in ile-cloth. An' they'll be waitin', ready an' willin' when the call comes, even if I'm dead an' gone itself.'

It was past believing. For a trust as sacred as it was secretive, the Commandant had chosen a man who was reputedly the most garrulous in all of the Old Dublin Brigade. What was even more remarkable was that, against the odds, my father kept his mouth shut. All my wheedling could not draw from him the size and precise nature of the arms cache; and, as for its burial place, the first time I dared ask him was the last. Twenty years later, he died without letting go of his secret, possibly because there was by then no one left to whom he could usefully tell it.

It was only as I wrote the foregoing that it came to me with hilarious clarity where the arms were and still are to this day and why my father had been the ideal man to bury them. Without meaning to do so, he even gave me a clue that day at the front gate. My mother, who became a tigress whenever she got wind of a conversation that did not include her, flung open the front door and asked if we would prefer to be carried in to our tea, or have it carried out to us. As my father and I walked up the path there was time for a last question. 'Yes,' I said, 'but if there were guns to be buried —'

'Tell the shaggin' town, why don't you?'

'I mean, why did they pick on you?'

He smiled unexpectedly. 'God, but you're a comical boy. Sure what better man could they pick?'

In those days, I had no notion where the arms were, but I knew where I wanted them to be. My brain was seething with the great satirical novel. It would be a latterday *Valley of the Squinting Windows*, and its time was ripe. The year was 1949, and there were six thousand books on the banned list, with as many more yet to come. Mr de Valera, spurned at last, was sulking on the Opposition benches, but the country remained in thrall to his vision of comely maidens dancing at any given crossroads as a kind of cultural millennium. His ideal might never come to pass – the weather alone would see to that, never mind that the native diet of bread and potatoes would hardly produce a corps de ballet of comely maidens – but the dream was mandatory. It was a rejection of all that, by dint of being foreign, was corruptive. More importantly, it was asexual and, on that account, just possibly not immoral. If the Pope was Christ's vicar on earth, Mr de Valera was Archbishop McQuaid's in Ireland, in which capacity he saw to it that whenever his Grace sneezed the country's nose ran for a month.

When I thought of my book I modestly tried to keep the word 'Swiftian' at bay; still, and to face facts, greatness seemed to be unavoidable once I had complied with the small formality of writing it. It never occurred to me that, throughout the land, a legion of weedy youths were sitting hunched over kitchen tables or shivering in linoleum-paved bedrooms, each one fashioning the great satirical novel or play. Whichever it was, it would topple the idols and unwhiten the sepulchres. It would expose the venality of the gombeen men and the urbane tyranny of the priests. It would, for all time, put Ibsen in the ha'penny place.

My own novel was to be set in a small town artfully called Drane, but understandably pronounced 'Dreen'. It took for its departure point the story of Honor Prendergast, her twins and the saga – at least it would be a saga in *my* version – of the iron gates. To this, like a literary Escoffier, I stirred in another ingredient: a sub-plot which told of a veritable mountain of high explosives, buried since the Civil War and still volatile. And, in a master-stroke of narration, this gigantic bomb would exist at the exact point where the gates would be built. I had my *dramatis personae* in readiness, with the Canon at the centre of the web as a village Richelieu. And, rather than make a show of my father, I gave his role to a local character: a drunken, one-armed I.R.A. veteran named O'Connor, painting the lily by making him one-eyed and one-legged as well.

When it was time to start, I laid in a stack of pilfered minute paper from work. The irony of using civil service stationery to launch an attack upon the rotten shorings of society did not occur to me: I was simply trying to save a few pence which were better spent on Alan Ladd and Donna Reed in *Chicago Deadline* than on ruled notebooks. My writing table was a flat-topped trunk in my bedroom. Its disadvantage was that I could not get close enough without barking my knees against the front, so in the end I sat sideways. Banishing from my mind such Lorelei as the billiard hall, the Roman Café, and the sea-front girls with nuns' eyes forever downcast, I began.

I had written an entire chapter before the discovery came that I had not the faintest idea of how to write.

It was not a matter of skill or artifice, or even the Holy Ghost's failure to descend. To say pompously what was plain truth: I had not yet begun to live. I was waiting to become a person, just as my friends and I waited for jobs, or a new suit, or money from nowhere, or the end of a hated virginity. We looked about us for the future and saw no sign. We waited, dimly aware of an instinct that warned us to do no damage to the waiting room. A wanton act, born of despair that a door would ever open, might mean the forfeiture of one's passport, so that the waiting room would become forever after a living room.

Our needs were diverse. Jackie Whiston wanted a job that would take him away from the corner of Marine Road where he stood the year round: sometimes with his face upturned to the sun; at others, trying to blow winter from his fingers. Dan Cleary was wild with grief that, on his two pounds a week as apprentice to a watchmaker, he seemed never likely to marry Nora Kavanagh. When his parish priest warned him of the perils of long courtships and Dan protested that he had no money, the reply was a genial, 'Erra, boy, sure all you need is a bed and a frying pan!' Joe Byrne yearned to go to Birmingham, where his father worked in exile. Oliver Mongan's ambitions were not so earthbound: he wanted to be Tyrone Power and, failing that, to marry Joan Fontaine; there were moments, however, when he lowered his sights and confessed that, at a push, he would settle for any girl who had a nice chest and was sincere. As for me, I caught the 9.07 to Westland Row each morning to sit with thirty others in a room where I could feel my life withering. I lived for the day when I would be quit of the Land Commission and could think of no other way out than by writing. It came as an unpleasant shock to discover that words, simply because they were *my* words, did not come forth golden-born.

If *Sex on Thursdays* ever had a claim to exist, it was as a child of a time forever gone. Written today, even if written well, it would be a curiosity: an assembly of grotesques that once were real and seem funny only from the safeness of distance. If anything is worthy of recall, of the casting of a net into the past, it is perhaps that time of waiting and how we passed it.

As for my father's arms cache and why, of all people, it was entrusted to him, there can have been no better hiding place than beneath three acres and a half of lawns, an orchard, flower-beds and a meadow, where the gardener happened to be a stalwart of the I.R.A. rank and file. Like myself in the matter of the civil service writing paper, my father's Commandant would probably have seen no irony in burying the guns in the garden of 'Enderley', the home of members of the Society of Friends, even had he known that, with Catholic owners, it was later to become 'Santa Maria'. Perhaps it proves that even arms dumps may be ecumenical.

2

In our town, people die but are not permitted to grow old. Once, a few years ago when I was still a smoker, I became conscious of an old woman glaring at me in the local newsagents'. Addressing the morning air, she said: 'I know the root up the arse his mother would-a gev him, standin' there with a cigar stuck in his fat gob.' Then, as a kind of envoi, uttered with a hatred that was almost sensual, she added: 'An impudent pup the like of him.'

The pup was in his mid-fifties at the time and his mother was fifteen years dead, but that, as far as the old woman was concerned, was the splitting of hairs. I was one of a younger generation than hers and always would be, just as I would forever be my parents' son, or rather – and it made the debt greater and my treacheries more heinous – their adopted son. I might as well never have grown up, married, lived abroad, and written plays under a rashly taken pen name. Now I was home again, where I was Jack Keyes and the local cottage industry was the craft of shrinking distended heads. Here, the world's opinion counted for nought. Of those who foolishly thought themselves exempt from the judgment of the town, there were a hundred voices to say 'I know him' in tones as final as they were unforgiving.

Over the next year or so, I saw my elderly critic here and there in the town and usually in deep conversation with a crony. As our eyes locked, I would veer across the street like a fishing boat making for a lee of the jetty, but the abuse would follow me the length of the Bus Lawn or down Convent Road.

'There's the whelp now,' I and half the town heard her say.

'God, but isn't his poor mother better off where she is, lyin' in the wet clay of the Kill of the Grange, than to have that cur fornenst her.'

The day came when I saw and heard her no more, and all one knew for certain was that if she had died it was not – considering her vocal powers – from lung disease. I was given no respite from torment, for her duties were at once taken over by another old woman, rather in the manner in which the secret formula for a liqueur is passed on from a monk on his death-bed to his appointed heir. Her successor, plump and trim in a grey coat wisping with borders of pale fur, hailed me by name in Castle Street and said: 'I'm the daughter of "Oats" Nolan.'

I thought, for an insane moment, that she was announcing the title of a song which she proposed to sing to me there and then. Instead, she went on: 'You put my father into your play, *Da*.'

I said carefully: 'I mentioned his name in it, yes.'

She said: 'Nick Keyes, oul' eejit the like of him, took you in out of God knows where and put a roof over you when your own wouldn't have you. He brung you up, so he did, and gave you a name, and the way you paid him back was, you put him in a play. Your poor mother was disgusted be that play.'

I should have left her with the last word, knowing that she would take it in any case, but I could not resist delivering what I foolishly thought to be the perfect quelch. 'That's odd,' I said, 'seeing as how she was seven years dead when I wrote it.'

Her eyes were bright splinters of contempt. Her heel twitched, ready to be turned upon. 'Well then,' she snapped, 'she was disgusted by something else you wrote.'

Probably she was. Patrick Kavanagh once said that anyone who writes a poem that a policeman can understand deserves whatever he gets. As much may be said of a writer who chooses to live in the village where he grew up; and his worst crime lies not in the nature of the words he sets down, kindly or wounding, but that they were set down at all. To take a man's character over a game

39

of Twenty-Fives, or to sip slander from the lip of a pint glass, is no more than human nature, and in any case your victim is at that moment probably saying as bad or worse of you. It is between neighbours, if not friends. To parade him naked in a book or a play for the world to see is an indecency. And it is less than no excuse to protest that you did it out of affection and in praise: you will be leered at for cuteness and told: 'Oh, I'm sure it was. Jasus, do you see the green in me eye? It's blackguarding, what else?' And then the clincher: 'Sure why else would he write it?'

What is not so easily answered is why my grey-haired tormentors even now strike a faint chill of fear into the heart. Perhaps I suspect that they may be in the right of it and that, for all my worldliness, which in truth is not much, I am the 'whelp' they take me for. Or it may be a legacy of the days when, although my friends and I were in no sense delinquents, the elders of the town knew us to be what they called 'proper go-boys', bent on whatever sins best belonged in the dark. Of our enemies, the priests were the most easily fooled. They came towards us, enveloped in a priest-smell of incense and talc; we simpered, stood upright, saluted and said 'Good evening, Father,' and they smiled, saluted back and knew you to be good lads at heart.

Just as a cat will leap on the lap of the one person in the room who hates animals, I have always and disastrously been a magnet for my natural enemies. When I was fourteen, Father Creedon threw me out of the confessional for not knowing the *Confiteor*; later the same year, during a religious knowledge lesson at Harold Boys' School, he had almost suffered a stroke when, wholly in a spirit of theological enquiry, I asked: 'Please, Father, what's adultery?' The war with Credo, as we called him, had, however, begun even earlier.

To my grief and the grief of others, I have always been what Americans call a joiner. A psychiatrist would probably say that, having been rejected by my natural mother, I was attempting to find a place where I might 'belong'; whatever the cause, within ten years I was thrown out of the altar boys, the choir, the sea scouts, the Local Defence Force, at least one dramatic society, and Butlin's holiday camp.

It was actually my mother's idea that I should 'join the altar', and become – in her eyes at any rate – a kind of pygmy priest. Once a week after tea the church clerk, Dessie Swords, taught the new boys how to pronounce clumps of Latin responses, which we then learned by heart. No one told us what any of it meant: only that when it was all memorised we would be permitted to serve at Mass. Meanwhile, on special occasions and as a kind of show of strength, we would emerge, like formation dancers, from the sacristy, each boy a mother's dream-come-true in lace surplice and scarlet soutane, and sit out of harm's way in a pew off to one side of the high altar.

I remember, and with reason, a Sunday afternoon marked by a form of devotions known as the Golden Hour. This was rather like several of the once-monthly Holy Hours rolled into one. The altar was hardly visible behind banks of flowers, and there were so many candles that it took Dessie Swords ten minutes to light them. The church was crammed to the doors. Even my father, who bore us off to the Picture House every Sunday of the year, had been shanghaied, my mother saying that, if she could make a sacrifice for God, my father could make one for her. 'It's missing the serial I mind,' he confided to me. 'Now we won't be able to folley the shaggin' thing.' I could not have agreed more. No one had told me that becoming an altar boy meant having to renounce Flash Gordon. 'You begged to go on the altar,' my mother said, lying through her teeth. 'You tormented me, and sign's on it, the altar is where'll you go if I have to swing for you.'

And so, with seven others, I stood in the sacristy in the red soutane that was our equivalent of dress uniform. It was not unlike waiting in the wings of a theatre: from the body of the church and above the throb of the organ we could hear whoops, wheezes and coughs. Then Father Creedon, always vast and, today, dazzling in his vestments, came up behind us and we started off in double file: eight small ponies drawing a golden coach. Nothing quite prepared us for the blaze of candles, their smoke stinging the eyes, or the sickly scent of the flowers. Already the packed church was almost airless and, as we crossed to the pew, a familiar fear gnawed at me.

In those days I fainted a great deal. Or, rather, I would become weak in any confined place – although never, strangely enough, while at the pictures – and, as faces swam about me and the room stood on its head, would go staggering out, crashing bruisingly into door jambs and walls until, once in the open air and blind to all onlookers, I would assume a foetal position on the ground, grass or concrete, rained on or dry. Looking out now at the wall of faces, among which somewhere on the fourpenny benches were my parents, and feeling the wave of heat, I all but succumbed to an urge to lie down and curl up there and then. It seemed unlikely that I would survive the Golden Hour which, tossing its head at earthly time, usually lasted an hour and three-quarters.

Thirty minutes of this were occupied by Father Creedon's sermon. He was a portly, majestic man who seemed to overflow the pulpit. His pink hands conducted angelic choirs. His speech was orotund and slow: an ocean swell that rose and dipped. From somewhere in the congregation a snore rasped: a harsh, metallic snort that became a death rattle as the soloist was nudged awake. Wedged in the altar pew, I had begun to get over my initial panic and to feel that I might, after all, survive the afternoon. It depended upon whether there was a Benediction, for Father Creedon was famous for swinging the thurible like a fast bowler coming up to the crease, and even his own not insubstantial bulk had been known to shimmer and vanish in the haze of incense. My fear was that the overpowering odour might fatally tip the balance in my own case. As the sermon boomed on like distant guns, I whispered to Billy Costello sitting next to me: 'Will there be Benediction?'

From the pulpit Credo said: 'And then at that simple village wedding feast, Jesus turned to His beloved mother and said will the boy who is talking on the altar please leave.'

He had changed course from Cana to Dalkey without as much as a hiccup, and so it was only when his massive head swivelled towards the altar that what he had said sank in. Five hundred pairs of eyes, which a moment before had been glazed and cataleptic, now brightened and looked with interest at the altar boys. I felt my heart slow down and knew that the blood had drained from my face. Perhaps it had not happened: perhaps I had dozed off and dreamt it. And yet if so, why was Father Creedon silent? His hands grasped the velvet cushion at the pulpit's edge. He spoke again, loudly and with the deliberation of a hanging judge: 'I said, will the boy who is speaking on the altar *leave!*'

The last word was uttered with such a roar that when a tram rumbled past just then its noise seemed no more than an echo. A tremor, part unease, part delight, went through the congregation, and I bitterly regretted not having fainted earlier on. Ten thousand Father Creedons could not have made me rise and walk off the altar, disgraced before the town, and so I sat and tried to look not only innocent but unconcerned. This might have worked had not the other altar boys cunningly absolved themselves from suspicion by turning to stare point-blank at the pariah. I felt the blood rush back to my face in double measure as if to make up for its defection, and the bowel-loosening thought occurred that Credo might actually descend from the pulpit and expel me by force. Instead, having piled a second eternity of silence upon the first, he turned away, his face glowing like an angry moon on the parishioners, and said: 'And Jesus told his mother "Woman, you know that my time has not yet come."'

It was a reprieve, or rather a stay of execution. The looks I now received from the other altar boys told me that Credo would probably maim me for life once the Golden Hour was over. I began to feel ill. To alleviate the symptoms, I attempted to think, not of future terrors, but of happy moments in the past, but all I could remember was that I had disgraced myself in front of the town, my own parents included. I thought of taking a tram into Dublin after tea and starting life over again with a new identity.

After an eon or so, the water had been turned into wine at Cana, and Father Creedon squeezed his way out of the pulpit and returned to the altar, flicking in my direction as he passed a look that was like the kiss of a bullwhip. Dessie Swords came from the sacristy and assisted him into a vestment of some magnificence. Its silver threads threw back the candlelight, as did the Celtic cross, entwined with shamrocks, which was worked down the front and back in gold. It was a long garment and Dessie acted as train-bearer as Credo moved to the altar steps where, all in one superb movement, he knelt, disembarrassed Dessie of the train and flung it behind him, where it spread out fan-like on the steps without the minutest wrinkle or fold. It had been said in the town, and with pride, that there was not a priest, or a bishop either, who could come within an ass's roar of Father Creedon's expertise at manipulating a chasuble.

He began to pray. I was doing so myself, swearing to God that if He kept me from falling into a dead faint I would give up telling lies and kneeing my mad aunt Mary in the behind as she walked past. God, as ever, knew when He was being sold a pup and answered me with the sight of Dessie Swords producing a smoking thurible and handing it to Credo. I became even weaker. The shame of being frog-marched, unconscious, off the altar, thereby becoming the most notorious twelve-year-old in Dalkey twice in one afternoon, paled when set alongside my need to breathe the clean air of the chapel yard. I knew that I had turned deathly white; the saints in their niches shook their haloed heads at me, and Christ on His cross disengaged one perforated hand and pointed it towards the way out.

I have only the account of eye-witnesses for what happened. I got to my feet, staggered towards the sacristy door, and tripped over Father Creedon's train, draped as it was down the altar steps. Then, in an attempt to prevent myself from falling headlong, I caught hold of him by the shoulders. At this point, accounts differed. Some said that I mumbled 'Sorry, Father,' others that in my delirium I said 'Sorry, Credo.' All were agreed that he ceased praying and looked around, first at my feet, planted on his golden train, then at my face. He flinched, so I was told, with appalled recognition, as if he had been slapped on the back by the Angel of Death.

As I left the altar, the trial of Father Creedon's vestment wrapped itself like a squid around my foot. I kicked it free. Next thing, there was cold air and the comforting rasp of gravel against my face. Once the dizziness had gone, there was barely time for a foray back into the vestry, while Benediction was still on, to change out of the soutane and swap my altar slippers for shoes. I was at home, pretending to read the *Hotspur*, when my parents came in. My mother said nothing at first, but took the pins from her hat and bore it, held high in both hands like a monstrance, to the wardrobe. My father opened the *Sunday Dispatch*, then looked at me over the top. He said: 'Who was the pup that was talkin' on the altar?' Without a moment's pause, I told him: 'Billy Costello.'

'There, Mag,' he said. 'Didn't I tell you it wasn't Jack?'

My mother gave me a searching look. 'Are you all right?'

'Yeah.'

'You look pasty-faced. I dunno what curse-o'-God bee got inside you that the be-all and end-all of your life was to go on the altar.' (Her shamelessness really knew no bounds.) 'Y'ought to give it up if you're not able for it.'

I did not tell her that the altar had, in effect, given *me* up. At school, I came in for a barrage of jeering ('Hey, Credo's lookin' for you!') and there were mock swoons wherever I went. Morty Mooney came up and said, meaning it: 'Jasus, I thought he was going to hit you with the thurible.' And an unforeseen consequence

45

was that my father met our neighbour, Tweedie Costello, and said: 'Isn't your young lad a holy terror for talkin' on the altar.' Tweedie was so wisplike that a summer breeze would blow him over, but whenever one of the Costellos misbehaved and was found out, the screams went the length of our lane. At the news that his son had been read out from the pulpit, he rushed home, picked up the nearest object to hand, which was an iron wrench, and flung it, catching Billy in the small of the back.

All the Costello children were red-headed and took after their mother, who was built like a house, and probably the martyred Billy duly gave me the thumping my lie deserved. If so, the memory is effaced by what happened a few days later. I was coming out of Mammy Reilly's newspaper shop, when a man shoved me up against the wall with such force that my head banged. I knew him to see: he was one of the town's elders. He collected Christmas and Easter dues and was a prefect of the men's sodality. At Corpus Christi he was among those chosen to carry the canopy over the Eucharist. Once, when there was whispering at Mass, I had seen his head rise like that of a bird of prey disturbed over its kill, and flinched as his pale eyes went in search of the heathens. He wore gold-rimmed glasses and a dark suit with small badges in the lapel. As he shook me, spittle hit my face.

'Filth,' he said in a whisper that was worse than a shout. 'Young bowsie. Desecrating the house of God. But Father Creedon is a match for you. He'll fix you. *And* your like.'

Once the shock had passed and I realised that he was talking about what had happened at the Golden Hour, I no longer heard the words, only the hatred. A white foam began to appear at a corner of his mouth, then, as if finding himself in an unclean act, he thrust me from him and walked away with quick female steps. The nakedness of his loathing stayed with me. I saw him again years later in a train compartment; he was in conversation, defending Irish war-time neutrality. 'We don't want Americans here,' he was saying, 'debauching our women.'

If I had not at once recognised him by his appearance I could not have mistaken that voice, which still bore witness that its owner had been to, and perhaps still lived in, one of the bedsitters of hell. It was as if I had rounded a corner and suddenly come upon an accident victim, the innards exposed. By then, Dalkey was no more than my dormitory; I stayed out of it each day for as long as my pocket and my mother's patience would bear, and I was not to see him again, but thanks to him I have never without revulsion heard the term 'God-fearing' used as if it were a Christian virtue.

As for Credo, I was to fall foul of him in years to come, but at least one potential disaster was avoided. A short while after the humiliation of the Golden Hour, two older boys came up, one on each side of me in the school yard. Their age was fourteen, and so they were as near to being men of the world as made no difference. They talked to me as an equal, offered me a bag of sweets and told me to take two. I was flattered. The conversation turned to Father Creedon. One of them said that I made a bad enemy, that from now on he would have a down on me. The other agreed; he told fearful stories of Credo's appetite for revenge, saying that he had been transferred to Dalkey because in his previous parish a boy had hanged himself. I swallowed the story more easily, because my mouth had gone dry with fear, than I could swallow the sweets.

'If I were you,' one boy said, 'I'd get on his soft side.'

'But how?'

'Before he comes looking for you,' the other said.

Again, I was now becoming frantic: 'All right, but how?'

They walked with me for a time in silence, their brows furrowed with kindly concern. Then one said: 'I know. The next time you go to him in confession—'

'To Credo? No fear.'

'No, wait. What you do is, you go into the box, you say "Bless me, Father, for I have sinned", and then you tell him that you've committed self-abuse.'

'Pardon?'

My two new friends carefully explained to me what self-abuse was. If you slept on the linoleum instead of in bed, or gave up taking sugar in your tea, or washed in cold water for a week, and if you offered it up, that was pure proof that you had mended your ways and wanted God's forgiveness. It was like doing a school examination in Irish: you got five per cent extra marks straight off for good intentions. The name for this kind of mortification of the flesh was, logically enough, self-abuse.

And so for the next few days I washed in cold water, although to be truthful it was little more than a few dabs of a face cloth. Then, assuring God that this was only a part-payment, with more purgations to follow, I set off for confession. Father Creedon was not one of those clerics who believed in silent prayer, and as I entered the church I could hear him moaning out a penance: 'You are to say five decades of the grand and glorious family rosary. *Ego te absolvo* . . .' when he had given absolution, adding – unconvincingly, I thought – 'God bless you', a little woman, stooped from age and a lifetime of toil, came out of the confessional. As she hurried down the aisle to say her penance before the side altar, I felt my nerve break. There was the possibility, I thought, that Father Creedon, being a contrary kind of man, might find no great virtue in my several days of diligent self-abuse. In the end, I funked it and went to confess my sins to Father Clarke, who as usual refused to listen to them, saying instead and with the height of jollity: 'Are you sorry? To be sure you are. Three "Hail Marys" and one for meself. Bless you, me child, and off you pop.' Nonetheless, at the back of my mind I felt that my daily chastisements of the flesh should not go to waste.

My chance came some weeks later when the Redemptorists arrived for the yearly mission. From Monday until Friday they struck terror into every heart, with descriptions of the hellfire which the God of infinite mercy had prepared for us, and on Saturday evening the town went, shivering, to confession. When my turn came, the slide between priest and penitent was slid back with such violence that my heart leaped. I began to speak, but a mixture of shyness and fright overcame me. I faltered. 'C'mon, c'mon, c'mon,' the missioner said, not unkindly, but as a man whose supper time was getting no nearer. This had the opposite effect, and I began to babble, peppering him with sins.

'Whoa there, whoa! Slow down, Neddy,' he said with a chuckle. He was not nearly as frightening in the confession box as he was in the pulpit. 'You're not racing at Leopardstown.' I could hear a snigger from the crowded pews outside. 'Now tell me, how old are you?'

'Twelve, Father.'

'Twelve? Begob, that's a great age. You must be bursting with sins to tell me.'

I knew that he was playing, if not to the gallery, then certainly to the listening benches, and, as far as I was concerned, more power to him. If it meant staying on his soft side, I was more than happy to let him be the one who got the laughs. However, and like the showman he was, now that he had softened up his audience, he switched to an earnest note.

'You know that Penance is a sacrament, don't you?'

'Yes, Father.'

'To be sure you do. Good lad. Therefore we must treat it with respect and not go rushing at it like a bull at a gate. Have you me?'

'Yes, Father.'

'Grand, so. What's your name? The first name only, now.'

'Jack, Father.'

'Jack? Aren't you the great man. Right, Jack, trot them out. As calm as you like, now. What depredations have you been up to?'

My chest swelled like a pouter pigeon's. This missioner was as nice a priest as a fellow could hope to meet, and it was evident that I had a good leg of him. I rummaged in my mind for whatever would please him, and at once it came to me. I was not one to hide my one and only poor light under a bushel, and so I said it loud and clear, not only for his benefit but for that of the eavesdroppers outside.

'Please, Father, I did self-abuse.'

I know it sounds absurd to say so, but there are different kinds of silence. At one extreme there is the mellowness, not unlike that of a good claret, when old friends come together and savour the pleasure of there being no need to speak. At the other there is the silence which exists only because of the terribleness of what might otherwise be said. The latter was the kind that ensued in the confessional, although, ever the optimist, I put it down to the missioner being momentarily speechless from admiration.

After a time, he whispered: 'What did you say?'

'Self-abuse, Father.'

'*Yes.*' It came out angrily, as if he were reproaching himself for causing me to say twice what should not have been said at all. 'And you say that your age is—'

'Twelve, Father.'

It was dark in the confession box, but my impression, peering through the wire grille, was that he had buried his face in his hands. He groaned softly and said 'Oh my God', which I took as my cue and once launched into the mandatory act of contrition: 'Oh my God, I am heartily sorry—'

'Stop!' Then, more calmly. 'Wait. This . . . thing. You're certain? I mean, you know what it was you did?'

'Oh, yes, Father.'

'My poor child.' Then, clutching at the only straw in sight, he said: 'And you say you did this thing just the once?'

Of course I had said nothing of the sort and so I hastened to make his day, even at the risk of immodesty. 'No, Father. Two times every day for a week.'

A deep sigh went through the confessional. He said: 'My child, do you want to become a degenerate?'

'Yes, Father.' Good manners impelled me to add 'Please'.

Quite sincerely, I thought he was offering to make me a

member of an élitist society of Catholic children, much as, at school, one was put in charge of the ink-wells, and, as I have said, I was nothing if not a joiner. My reply caused him to sit upright and squint at me through the grille, all but putting his nose through the cruciform gap in the centre. In the voice of one who has suddenly espied, not a straw to grasp at, but an entire haystack, he said: 'Tell me about this self-abuse.'

I did so. He gave a sigh of a different sort and laughed out loud: a short bark of a laugh that was more relief than merriment. I could not see what was so funny and was, in fact, disappointed that he said no more about making me a degenerate. He did not even let me tell him my sins, but said: 'Will you clear off out of this and say one Hail Mary. You divil, you.'

When I came out of the box, every face was turned towards me. Not until then, I realised, had they suspected that a candidate for sainthood dwelt in their midst, and so I dropped my eyes modestly, put the palms of my hands together, the fingers pointing heavenwards, and walked down the aisle trying to look next door to canonised.

It was a full two years before I found out what self-abuse was, and another two years before I found that the name for it was 'self-abuse'.

By then we had begun to move out into what we saw as the wide world, partly because wings are for spreading, partly because of our need to escape. The priests, as I have said, were not a threat: they looked about them for angels, and we made sure that angels were what they saw. As for the police, we kept out of their way. They instilled fear into us, which was no doubt exactly what they intended. Even the one we called the 'Cat' McDonald, of whom we walked in terror, was the kindliest of men (so we found out years later) once his policeman's mask was off. Our crimes were few: robbing windfalls from an orchard, or bicycling along the footpath known as The Metals, were the worst of them. For myself, I had been law-abiding every since, aged eight and on my way home from school, I had run behind a milk cart, turned the brass tap and was at once engulfed in a Niagara of white. The milkman sprang into the roadway and was after me as I fled screaming. For perhaps a hundred yards the pursuit hung in the balance, then I began to draw ahead. Ignoring the invitations from the rear to 'C'mere 'til I burst you', I took the corner of Rockford Avenue at a tremendous lick and could not believe it when, dead ahead, I saw my mother at the end of our lane, waiting for me.

'It's not up to me to tell you how to rear him, ma'am,' the milkman said, all but flinging me at her, 'but the weight of a hard hand never spoilt any child's rearing.'

It was a theory with which my mother concurred. As she flailed at my legs with the cane handle of our feather duster, she said bitterly: 'And you're the one I thought was going to be a priest.' It was the first I had heard of it.

I think that what we most feared was not the priests or the police, but ourselves: that we might some day become like Mr Mundow, who took offerings at the fourpenny door and looked exactly like his name, or Mr Finnerty, who once upon a time put his hand up women's skirts and now ran the Christmas savings club that was nicknamed the Diddlum. The town was their world. They believed that outside it there were dragons, to be kept at bay until death enabled them to stand down and at last stop worrying. They cared only for old ways and old songs; if they praised a book it was probably Charles Kickham's *Knocknagow, or The Homes of Tipperary*, which they had read in the long ago when there was time for books, and they would one day read it again, please God. In those days and ever since, whenever they lay on top of their wives in a silence that denied they were next or near a bed, never mind actually in one, they did so unfailingly in the dark and, to make assurance double sure, with their faces pressed into the pillow. Now, one of their sons was in the bank, another in Toronto, and the eldest girl in the Benedictines. They found safety in old phrases. They said: 'Sure aren't we all in the hands of the Man Above?', and Mr Finnerty knew, but never spoke of it, that the brown paper gathering dust on top of the wardrobe contained his burial habit, bought by Mrs Finnerty from the Little Sisters and kept in readiness because – and that was another tried and true saying – the day never dawned but had someone's name on it. They were not philosophers, but, if put to it, would say that it was better to do nothing at all than to risk doing wrong. They measured out their lives in droplets, like three-times-a-day medicine.

At the other extreme, it was easy to become like my uncle Sonny and his comrades, who would forsake the lee of Foley's corner only for the shelter of Gilbey's when the wind was from the north. Now and again, when signing on at the labour exchange, they found to their dismay that the corporation needed labourers for the laying of a sewage pipe, or a nightwatchman to mount guard over the pipe itself. Otherwise, they stood at one corner or the other, musing upon the conundrum of life, wondering who had done them down and how, when by birthright and an innate superiority they should have been on the pig's back for life. They talked about horse- and dog-racing and the Wicklow Regatta. They never ran out of bones of contention, for when a topic was at last dead and buried, it was only so that it might one day be exhumed from the grave, refreshed and ready for another outing. Their eyes missed nothing, and few walked the gamut of Castle Street without incurring their judgement. Jer Rooney was a proper gauger, and Jack English was a hook and a chancer, as were the whole seed and breed of him, while for Mr Dignam, whose son Charlie won a scholarship, my uncle Sonny reserved the very nadir of his contempt. 'He'll get on,' he would say with a look that told you he had Mr Dignam's measure, 'he'll be kep'.'

Sonny was my mother's younger brother. In middle-age, he had married a laundress name Kate Fortune with whom, as my father liked to remind us, much to my mother's vexation, he had been keeping company since old God's time. Opposites, so they say, attract, which may been true of Sonny and Kate, for she was a tall hairpin of a woman, while he was short and stocky, even if one made allowances for the gammy leg. The theory of opposites was borne out in his case by an apparent infatuation with a woman named Maddie Devlin, who was even taller and more gaunt than Kate Fortune. Her face, racked by martyrdom, was cadaverous. She had a dark moustache and there was a hirsute mole on her cheek. When she was not working at the pork butcher's she was forever either going to or coming from a meeting of the Children of Mary. Her way homeward to Sorrento Road led her between the Scylla and Charybdis of Foley's and Gilbey's. As she passed, Sonny would not accost her or even speak; his feelings went too deep. At her approach, he would swing into her path on the good leg and give her an unwavering look of his dark eyes, which were the pilot lights of a passion that Maddie, if she but chose, could turn up like a gas mantle. For her part, she took a tighter grip on her prayer book, moved her lips in an unheard ejaculation which was probably designed for such occasions and went hurrying past, her eyes fixed on any object except Sonny.

I once called out 'Hello, Maddie,' and she went to Kalafat Lane to tell my mother that I was making a jeer of her; so, since she never took open exception to Sonny's silent courtship, it may be that in a remote and unvisited corner of her mind she enjoyed it. He and Kate are dead these many years, but I saw Maddie in the town yesterday, and she looked away, knowing that not only was I still a pup but now an apostate as well. She looked not a day older, except that the moustache had turned white.

My first small step away from the world of my parents, Uncle Sonny, Maddie Devlin, Mr Mundow and the rest of them came with an incident as small and as terrible as buying a ham sandwich in Da Lundy's cakeshop. I was fourteen and had just won a scholarship to the Presentation Brothers, which to Sonny was proof of what he had long suspected: that, like young Charlie Dignam before me, I was above myself and too good for decent poor skins like himself. He harboured the belief that an adopted child who knew neither where he was got nor how he was got ought to least have the manners to lie low, instead of calling attention to himself with scholarships and codology. To me, going to Prez, as I learned to call it, had one drawback. When I was at Harold Boys' national school in Dalkey, I would run to catch a tram every Monday and Friday afternoon at three, climb to the upper deck and, like a jockey on a horse, spur it onwards to Dun Laoghaire. There, ensconced in the Picture House, my mother was waiting with my lunch in a paper bag: sandwiches of white pudding, milk in a Baby Power bottle and Scots Clan caramels for afters. Lesser heavens have been lost than that one: sitting in the front row of the sixpennies, choking from trying to eat and at the same time laugh at the saints of our innocence: Edgar Kennedy and Hugh Herbert and the great Edward Everett Horton. At Prez, however, the school was not over until 4.15: too late for the afternoon show. My mother knew better than to decree that I simply give up going to the Picture House except on Sunday afternoon; pictures were too much a part of our existence. More than passion, they were a kind of surrogate life. And so, with tea eaten and more often wolfed down, I was permitted to go out in the evenings.

There was, of course, a proviso. Let the sky fall and the seas turn to beef tea, but I would come straight home the instant the pictures were over. 'Half-past ten sharp,' my mother said, 'or that front door will be bolted.'

'Grand,' I said, uppity from excitement. 'Then I can stay out all night.'

'Shut your mouth.' She skewered me with a look, the while mobilising her troops, who as usual were not long in arriving. 'Well, that's the price of me,' she said, 'oul' eejit that I am, for being soft with you —'

'Look, it was a joke . . .'

She was unstoppable. One might as well bid a bullet to return in mid-course. '. . . giving you your own way in everything. Spoiling you, denying you nothing. And for what thanks? Oh, they all told me, me good neighbours. "He'll turn on you," they said. "You'll rue the day."'

It was a familiar tune, played this time not in anger, but from worry that some danger might befall me on my journeyings after nightfall, and, instead of waiting until the recital had ended, my father was rash enough to make a contribution of his own. 'Sure of course he'll come straight home, Mag. Where else would he go?'

At once she swung her guns away from me and trained them on him. 'Well, trust you,' she said, picking up the teapot for no other reason than to slam it down again. 'Trust you.'

'Trust him,' my mad aunt Mary said, sensing that she was on a winner.

'Trust me to what?' my father said. 'What ails you?'

'While you're at it,' my mother told him, 'why don't you tell him *where* he can go instead of the pictures? Why don't you trot it out?'

My father was as bewildered as I was. 'For the love o' God,' he roared, 'trot shaggin' what out?' I knew that he was becoming flustered, for he at once rephrased this and said: 'Trot out shaggin' what?'

My mother gave him the scalding look of one who has been trapped into saying more than she intended. 'You couldn't keep your mouth shut if it paid you,' she said.

'Not if it paid him,' Mary said.

'You hold your tongue,' my mother said.

Plainly, there existed some orchard of forbidden fruit between Dun Laoghaire and Dalkey of which neither my father nor I was aware. Into my mind came a vision of the kind of western saloon one saw in the pictures, with unshaven ruffians playing cards, silent women tucking dollar bills under their garters, Brian Donlevy, slit-eyed in black suit and string tie, and Marlene Dietrich singing 'See what the boys in the back room will have'. It seemed unlikely that there would be a saloon in our neighbourhood, even after sunset, and in any case I would in all probability not have been admitted.

And so the matter was dropped. Later that evening, however, I heard my mother, still in a bad temper, muttering to herself as she cleared the tea things. She was saying: 'Time enough for him to go chasin' after trollops, takin' them up the back roads, doin' God knows what and destroyin' himself over them.'

I all but guffawed, and small wonder. What was tormenting her was the notion that I would fall into the clutches of some Delilah from Sallynoggin, perhaps, or Glasthule. It would have made a cat laugh. I had better uses for my time and few pence than to spend either on a shrill, complaining creature who would tell her mammy if you said 'Jasus' or 'feck', who wanted to walk on footpaths instead of the grass, and who hated cowboy pictures and thought that blooming old Barbara Stanwyck was great. Not only were girls God's worst mistake, but, into the bargain, they hated you. I wondered if my mother had a slate loose. Later, much later, I realised the truth: she had opened a door for me into the future, had herself looked through it and was jealous.

The new regime began. It took a while to get used to seeing films in the evening: the people around you seemed different and there was the uneasy sensation of night deepening outside. And so for a few weeks I gladly observed my curfew, hurrying home as through a hostile land. One evening, as I got off the tram in Castle Street, a fellow I knew asked where I was going.

'Home.'

'What for?'

While I was trying to think of an answer that made sense, he said: 'Have you got fourpence?' Next thing, I was led into Da Lundy's shop, where in the daytime you bought sweets, broken chocolate and rock cakes. At night, as I now saw, there were three small tables with gingham cloths. The fellow took my fourpence and added fourpence of his own to it. He said: 'Two ham sandwiches and two glasses of milk, please.'

I was appalled. You bought sweets and chocolates and perhaps a doughnut in Da Lundy's; what you did not buy was *food*. Food was provided by your parents; it was what they were there for: to see that you had clothes and school books and a boiled egg at tea time. Once, Johnny Quinn, who lived at Number 5 in our lane, had put a finger to his lips and led me to Mrs Threadgold's house. When she answered the door, he made the kind of mewling whisper you heard from a tinker woman with her hand out for a penny, and Mrs Threadgold brought us a slice each of bread and jam. The realisation came that, without meaning to, I had become a beggar. My mother prided herself most of all on being what she terms a great manager: others would tell you admiringly that she was the devil for style. The beating I received for turning the milkman's tap on would have been a caress compared with what she would have given on learning that I had shamed her and taken food from a neighbour. Now, if I were to tell her that I had actually bought a ham sandwich, she would have said 'Anyone would think I didn't feed you' and tend her hurt for a week.

As the milk and sandwich were brought and I sat at the table, with its rough wood showing through a tear in the gingham, the feeling of guilt gave place to one of being an unabashed sybarite. I had never in my life experienced such sophistication. It was the sweet life, easy street, clover, the pig's back.

Only adults, I was aware, paid for their food. The mistake I made in Da Lundy's was in thinking that paying for my food made me an adult.

3

I was a snob. Instead of accepting the decent anonymity of the Christian Brothers school in Dun Laoghaire, I had foolishly opted for the cachet of Presentation. Because it was smaller and closer to home, my new classmates soon knew that they had a cuckoo in their nest. The cuckoo's father was a gardener, and his home – if such birds had homes – was a two-roomed cottage in a back laneway. It was called Kalafat Lane or Anastasia Cottages, as one preferred, but whenever I was asked where I lived, I remembered the *Magnet* and the Fat Owl of the Remove, who promoted his home from Bunter Villa to Bunter Hall. Accordingly, I gave my address as the not so lowly and quite imaginary Anastasia Terrace. It fooled nobody.

There were other terrors. On my first day, the roll was called, and to my dismay I heard the name 'John Byrne' being read out. I sat, not answering, then and when it was twice repeated. Later, in the school yard, I was summoned indoors. The superior, Brother Berchmans, was poring over the roll book. He jabbed a finger at the hated surname, and his adenoidal voice made my adopted name, Keyes, sound like a soda-water syphon. 'Kizz, is this you?'

I nodded. I knew that to be what they called illegitimate was an occasion for deep shame. There had been a sin of some kind, and because of it you were not the same as children who had parents. I had heard neighbours and ladies in the town tell this to my mother (my mother in Kalafat, that is), not in so many words, but by some pitying murmurs such as 'Wisha, God love him' and

'Weren't you great to take him!', accompanied by the movement of a hand which made to touch my hair, but desisted just in time. My mother would not dare to defend bastardy; instead, she behaved like a woman whose child is known to have committed murder, but who against all reason declares him innocent. When the Costellos up the lane gave me a book for my eight birthday and wrote my name as John Keyes Byrne on the flyleaf, such was her fury that I thought she would get gaol for them. Now, Brother Berchmans looked at me with scorn – whether for my cowardice or my flawed pedigree, I did not know – and said: 'Very well, Kizz, we'll keep your dark secret.' Then, crossing out a name on the roll, he wrote another. For a moment, the skeleton was safely back in the closet, but all my stratagems could not hide Kalafat Lane and the two rooms. Had I strutted into the school yard and cocked a snook at what the others thought, they would probably have left me alone; but instead of strutting, I skulked, and they sensed my shame as a dog is said to smell fear. For a year, until the sport grew stale, they doled out my punishment, and, at the back of my mind, deserving it, I took it as my due.

At the end of my four years in Prez, Brother Berchmans sent word that I was to come to him. As usual, he looked at me in the manner of one in whose path a dustbin had overturned. Perhaps I do him an injustice, but the impression persists that he was of the opinion that, whereas to be a scholarship boy who lived in a condemned cottage in a back lane was a misfortune, to be illegitimate as well could be reasonably construed as carelessness. He had a flat, white coffin of a face, with a nose that resembled the gnomon of a sundial and had earned him the nickname of 'Schnozzle'. He took me for a half-trot walk around the school yard, his robes slapping in the breeze like a wet sail. Trying to keep up, I was enveloped in a smell of angry carbolic.

He began by saying: 'You are no doubt aware, Kizz, that as of this day your scholarship to Presentation College is at an end?'

I said 'Yes, Brother' and waited for him to embark on the kind of stern valedictory which, in a Warner Brothers picture, a prison warden addressed to a two-time loser whose latest stretch had been served, and to which the standard response, usually delivered by an uncontrite George Raft, was: 'So long, Warden, see you in choich.'

Instead, what Schnozzle said was: 'We of Presentation have friends in the Department of Education.'

It was as if he had spurned the role of prison warden for that of Conrad Veidt as a Nazi agent, silkily reminding a humble old watchmaker – usually Ludwig Stossel – that the latter still had relatives in Germany. In my case, however, the words were less a threat than the prelude to a reluctant accolade. 'Our friends tell us, Kizz,' Schnozzle went on, 'that you have attained third pless' (he meant 'place') 'in Ireland in the Intermediate Examination.'

The Inter Cert was, as the name implied, a scholastic half-way house. Two years further on, the Leaving Cert, once obtained, would open the door to university. It was a threshold I had no thought of crossing: for one thing, I loathed school; for another, it was time I gave up living off my parents; and, for a third, I could hardly afford to take a tram into Dublin, never mind the cost of transporting myself into Trinity. (The question of attending the younger, Catholic university, U.C.D., could never arise; I was, as I have said, a snob, and as such clung to the belief – and, to my continued happiness, still cling to it – that in life there exist two classes: first class and no class.)

Schnozzle looked at me with his customary distaste. 'However, Kizz, before you bask in the glow of your great accomplishment, let me express the humble opinion that you could and should have achieved no less.'

His opinion was not in the least humble, but it was well-held. I had sat for the Inter Cert on three occasions. On the first, I had failed; on the second, I had scraped through. I should then have moved up a rung into Fifth Year, but on the first day of the new term I wandered into my old classroom and sat at my accustomed desk. It was from timidity, a fear of seeming to thrust forward, only to be pushed back for the impertinence. I waited for one of the Brothers to say: 'What the hell are you doing in Fourth Year, you thick, you? Go next door.' Not one of them uttered a word: presumably because none of them noticed. I stayed rooted where I was for another year, until I could have passed the Inter Cert, with honours and in my sleep.

Schnozzle and I had completed a round of the school yard when he came to a sudden stop. I saw emotions, as contrary as hares and hounds, go chasing across his face. Then he said, getting it over with like a man spitting out gristle in one lump, and the devil take table manners: 'In view of what some may see as reflecting credit upon the school, even if there are those of us who will beg to differ, the Presentation Brothers are prepared to keep you on here free of charge for two extra years.

Boys yelped as they ran around the school field. Liberation was in the air. It was the last day of term, and in a matter of minutes Brother Joseph would appear on the school steps, blow his whistle and shout 'Will ye get off home, the lot of ye!' For myself, I was like a man who, after four years of imprisonment, was standing at the gaol gates, his belongings under his arm, only to receive a message asking if he would very much mind returning to his cell for another two years.

I became aware, through my dismay, that Schnozzle was still talking. Rather than look up at that white, slab-like face, I lowered my eyes and noticed for the first time that his feet were enormous. I heard him say that I was lazy, that I lacked application, that the world and his wife knew that my days were spent in picture houses. He spoke of this golden opportunity, of how by seizing it I could repay the sacrifices made by my parents, good people that they were. He even made mention of another scholarship, this time to university.

The thought of my penal servitude being extended, not by two years, but a possible six, was a pain so exquisite that I looked at last up into his face. For no reason I recalled how, during my first, far-off week at Prez, he had forbidden boys kneeling at prayer to rest their backsides against the benches behind them. The word he had used was 'posteriors', which I had not previously heard, and so I smiled in appreciation of what I took to be a piece of Micawber-like grandiloquence. 'You think it's funny, Kizz, do you?' he said, for the first time but not the last, liquefying my bowels with the inevitable prologue to a caning: 'Git ahtside the door, plizz. Ah'll be aht in a minnit.'

He had looked at me then with the distaste of an epicure confronted with scrag-end, and his expression was not much friendlier now. His voice, however, had acquired a small match-flame of warmth. My future, he said, hung in the balance; I would do well to think long and hard, to stop being a boy, to grow up. 'You are a schemer and a dodger, Kizz,' he said, 'because you think of myself and the other Brothers as adults who are therefore enemies, to be feared and outwitted. Hear this or you are lost: we do not live in separate worlds, do you understand me?'

I replied, without understanding him: 'Yes, Brother.'

He dismissed me on a practical note. 'If you decide to accept this most generous offer, your parents need bear no financial brunt. The college will accept the schoolbooks you already have in exchange of the new ones you will require.'

He went flapping away from me across the yard. Forever after, whenever I have heard or read Tennyson's line 'For the black bat Night has flown', the image in my mind is that of Brother Berchmans.

We broke up early, soon after lunch, and I cycled the hundred yards or so from Prez to the Astoria. There were only one or two others waiting for the curtains to squeak apart to the combined sound of a fanfare and the crowing of the Pathé News rooster, and I sat in the sevenpennies thinking of Schnozzle and his offer. It was true that my mother could not wait for me to find a job and supplement the four pounds ten shillings my father earned weekly tending Enderley's three and a half precipitous acres. And yet I knew that today's news would bear witness before the world that she had reared a genius. At the thought that the Presentation Brothers would further educate me, free of charge, towards a vague but indisputably golden future, she would first of all tell the ceiling that as sure as God my codology would land us all in the Union, adding that my uncle Sonny was right about me having a smell of myself: that Gentleman Jack had become too grand for the likes of my father and her. Then, having had her grumble, she would with the ferocity of a tigress set about making any and every sacrifice to ensure that I stayed on at school – and if it meant that my father, who was already past sixty, must go on working until he was a hundred, then so be it.

I have two selves. One, like a stranger, stands apart and watched the other, and now this second self saw that I was weakening. The miseries of the past had already begun to recede; I thought instead of my mother's pleasure and of hearing her say, just this once, that I was a credit to her. In a daydream, I even walked the cobbles of Front Square in Trinity. It was too much. I roused myself, and both selves combined to confront the less nebulous problem of new school books for old. My intention had been to sell the old books, and I had made particular plans for spending the proceeds. The money had, as the saying went, its hat and coat on. In fact, only an hour previously, I had cleared out my desk at Prez, and––

An iron fist clenched shut upon my heart. It had come to me where the precious books were – or should be – at this moment: crammed tight into the saddlebag of the bicycle that I had left leaning against the side wall of the Astoria. It took me a year-long fifteen seconds to be out of my seat, through the Astoria's tiny foyer and into the lane. Not only were my schoolbooks already gone, but the thief, whoever he was, had had the labour-saving notion of taking the saddlebag as well. I quite deliberately chose to regard the theft as a straw in the wind. At home that evening, I wrote a letter to Schnozzle thanking him for his generosity, but declining his offer on the grounds that my conscience had told me to put aside childish things and (brazenly perverting a line from Yeats) dance attendance on my parents' old age. He did not reply. Having spent his adult life dealing with boys, he could probably smell a hypocrite a mile off.

I began looking for work straight away. Rather, it was my mother who did the looking, and, seeing no difference between one job and the next, she made me answer every advertisement in sight, whether in the 'Help Wanted' column of the *Irish Press* or on a postcard in Mammy Reilly's shop window. Once, she sent me to Bray, where an electrician needed an apprentice. After five minutes, he assured me solemnly that, were he to take me on, I would electrocute myself within the week. I was desperate for work, not only for self-respect, but because a job meant money, and money meant girls.

I had developed a taste for women during the years at Prez. This was remarkable, considering that at the age of fourteen I had taken Mrs Hammond's daughter, Gloria, on an outing to Dublin: an experience which, but for my natural resilience, would have made me a lifelong celibate.

It was my mother who, in a fit of apparent insanity, arranged that I should take Gloria to the pictures. Given her jealousy of other women, I have no idea why she connived at such an event, unless it was done in the knowledge that Gloria and I loathed each other. She lived in the same lane as my grandmother, and I could not have been more than nine when she stuck her tongue out at me as I walked peacefully by, licking a ha'penny ice-cream cone from Toole's shop. In the craft of effectively sticking one's tongue out at another person, the first requirement is that a discreet distance should be kept between the sticker and the stickee, but Gloria, with a woman's contempt for rule books, came so close that I was able to take hold of the neck of her frock and drop not only my own ice-cream down its front but also the cornet I had been sent out to buy for my mad aunt Mary.

'Where's Mary's ice-cream?' my mother wanted to know when I arrived at my grandmother's a minute later.

'I dropped it,' I lied.

'Oh, the shaggin' cur, me lovely ice-cream,' Mary groaned and tried to run me down with the old pram in which she kept her collection of dolls.

Just then, there was a banshee's wail, and, dragged by her mother, Gloria came up the garden path with gobs of ice-cream trickling down her legs. Justice was rough and immediate, but I would gladly have done it again. Gloria was a termagant, a shrew and a fury – in short, a girl – and now, five years later, because of an unholy alliance between my mother and hers, I was to be shackled to her for an afternoon. I could have said, half-meaning it, that I would die first, but two bribes were tendered and accepted: money for the pictures, and my first trip to Dublin unaccompanied by an adult.

When I called for Gloria, she was scowling, and I remember that she wore white ankle socks, for her mother told her not to forget that they were 'fresh on' today. 'Now, you'll mind her?' Mrs Hammond implored, handing me a bag of mixed sweets. I said yes, aware that Gloria was the kind of strap who could look after herself in a pit of snakes. As we set out, I looked up Sorrento Road and saw my own mother at the end of Kalafat Lane, giving me the kind of heartbroken wave one keeps for the last glimpse of a loved one sailing for Australia.

We had the day's first falling out as we boarded the Number 8 tram with 'Nelson Pillar' on the destination board. Gloria wanted to sit downstairs, whereas I, a trail-blazer at heart, preferred the open space at either end of the upper deck. Neither would yield, so we went our separate ways, and, as the tram swooped and sang down Bulloch Hill, I felt the wind hard on my face and saw the overhead trolley spit flame against the wires. As I browsed through Mrs Hammond's mixed sweets in the consciousness that an imperfect world could not offer much more happiness than this, the conductor appeared from below. He did not say 'Fares, please,' but stood rocking on the balls of his feet and grinding his teeth. His troubles on such a cloudless day were no concern of mine, and so I merely asked for two return half-fares to Dublin. He took my shilling, gave me the tickets and twopence change and suddenly said: 'Are them the sweets you stole off that poor young one?' Before I could answer, he snatched the bag, called me a right little bollix and bore the sweets downstairs to Gloria.

I had my revenge on the trip when we reached Dublin. As we alighted in the shadow of the Pillar, the air strident with the groans and clangings of the trams and the cries of the old ones selling fruit and flowers, Gloria set an unmistakable course for the Savoy Cinema. I shouted after her: 'Where are you going?'

She turned and looked at me as if I were a skivvy from the country who had had the impertinence to ask her if she had washed herself. She threw me a crust of an answer. 'To see *Smilin' Through*.'

I remembered having sat through a previous version starring Norma Shearer donkey's years before, when I was six, squirming with embarrassment while my mother wept buckets. Now that I was fourteen and my own man, I would eat my grandmother's soapy potatoes before seeing it again, this time with Jeanette MacDonald ullagoning about the little brown road winding over the hill. I told her: '*I'm* going to the Theatre Royal.'

She said: 'What's on there?'

I told her: 'Humphrey Bogart in *The Return of Doctor X*.'

She stood between the fruit-stalls of the shawlies who were screeching 'T'ree ha'pence deh luvly apples, tuppence deh ri-ep pay-ars' and bawled at me in a voice as hoarse as theirs: 'Humphrey Bogart? That's an old gangster picture.'

'No, it isn't,' I told her in the informed voice of a regular *Picturegoer* reader. 'He takes the part of a vampire.'

She screamed as if she had just seen one. It was partly the scream of a thirteen-year-old girl to whom horror films gave nightmares, and partly the envenomed howl of a virago who had realised that I was holding the purse strings and could call the tune. She hurled threats at me all the way to O'Connell Bridge: she would tell her mammy and my oul' one, her daddy and my oul' fella; she even mentioned an uncle of hers who was a sailor and due home for Christmas. Once across the Liffey she began wheedling. She told me seductively that *Smilin' Through* was in what she called glorious Techni-color. She said that I could have some of the sweets – no, all of the sweets, and she would treat us to the kind of ice-cream high-up people ate out of tubs with wooden spoons. I wavered; then, knowing that she would not only welsh upon her promises, but do so with a witch's cackle of triumph, I marched up the three front steps of the Theatre Royal. Realising, at last, that the iron had entered my soul, she yelled 'I hate yeh!' and hit me with the white handbag she had received for her Confirmation.

A minute later, we were watching a kind of variety show called *Apple Sauce* that preceded the film. The Royalettes danced; a skyscraper of a man named Noel Purcell came on, first as a woman, and later in a black coat and glasses as Mr de Valera: a fat woman and a scrawny one did Fred Astaire and Ginger Rogers; then a painted volcano appeared and a woman named May Devitt sang 'One Fine Day' dressed in a kimono. There was a quiz called 'Double or Nothing' with Eddie Byrne; finally, an organ came up out of the ground, was played and went down again, and *The Return of Doctor X* began. Gloria had kept quiet during the show, but now, even before the first victim's blood was drained, she was half-way under her seat. The film, as it happened, was only middling, which made my victory a Pyrrhic one. She would blame her nightmares equally on me and Humphrey Bogart, and Mrs Hammond – a tall, bony woman with a sharp, stuttering tongue, a long reach and knuckles of iron – would either clout me or tell my mother. And yet I had won a prize of sorts: never again would anyone in his or her senses suggest that I go out with a female. A kind of peace flowed within me, and, in the spirit of one who might as well be hanged for twenty sheep as a single lamb, I took out a large packet of Craven A and lit one after the other, ignoring a voice from under the next seat that said: 'And I'm going to tell your oul' one you smoked as well.'

She did, later on. We queued, not speaking, in the rain for our tram home and arrived in Dalkey like a couple of drowned mice. Soaked as she was, Gloria did not turn into her laneway, but followed me up Sorrento Road to my front door. I slammed it on her, but she turned the handle and marched straight in, with a cry of 'Mrs Keyes, Mrs Keyes!' Carefully waiting to burst into tears until she was sure that my mother was at home, she launched into a seemingly endless recitative, in the course of which she never once paused for breath, but connected the details of my various crimes with a gasped '. . . an', an', an', an', an' then he . . .' When she mentioned, which was true, that I had gone on smoking Craven A until an usherette came and threatened to put me out into the street, my mother fetched me a dirty look. Meanwhile, my father, half-way through his tea, was looking at Gloria as if she had just come down the chimney.

My mother, at last forcing a way through the wailing wall, asked: 'Did he hit you?'

The question took Gloria so by surprise that she stopped in mid-cry. 'Wha'?'

'I'm asking, did Jack lay either hand or glove on you?'

'*Him*?' The she-devil all but burst out laughing. 'Him, hit me? God, I'd burst him.'

'In that case,' my mother said, 'how bad you are! So will go you off home like a good girl and dry yourself. Your mammy will be worrying.'

I had rarely known her to be capable of such calm good sense. She took a towel and dried Gloria's hair, then set her on the way home. When the door was closed the sniffling had died away, she turned to me and said: 'Was the picture any good itself?' Then, before I could answer, she snapped at my father: 'You drink your tea.' She seemed quite unperturbed by Gloria's tales of woe; probably, she was relieved that I was now certain to remain a bachelor for life. As for my cigarette smoking, next day she actually bought a packet of ten Gold Flake and planked them down in front of me with a virtuous: 'And them's the last you'll get from me!'

My aversion to women was destined to wear thin. At school, Dinkie Meldrum showed me a smuggled copy of the war-time *Men Only*. It contained a nude photograph, demure by today's standards, of a woman kneeling, her hands modestly in her lap, her hair covered by a kerchief. He breasts might have been carved in marble, but from the moment I caught sight of her my years as a misogynist were over. For three days, I would waylay Dinkie and say off-handedly by way of concealing the molten lava in my gut: 'Show us that old picture again.' He would do so, whereupon I would shake my head, hardly believing that poor immature devils existed who actually derived pleasure from looking at naked women. Then, chuckling sadly to myself at human folly, I would walk away, trying not to buckle at the knees.

I was, as I have said, a joiner. While still at Prez, I enlisted in the sea scouts and, later on, the Emergency Communications Corps and the Local Defence Force. From the first of these, I was expelled; in the case of the second, I was issued with a bicycle and resigned when I fell off it and bent the front wheel; as a raw recruit in the third, I ruined an all-night manoeuvre and was told afterwards to go home and wait until I was sent for: which I never was.

It was my scoutmaster who first took me to the theatre. He was a slim, bald man named Richardson. He had a quick, almost girlish walk, and I never saw him address his wife, a plain, timid, frizzy-haired creature – without snarling. He took me to see Joan Hammond in *The Magic Flute* at the Gaiety, but it was war-time, and she refused to sing because the German ambassador was in the audience. Instead we were given *Ernani*, and I was fascinated to see that the leading tenor was suffering from a nose-bleed and spent the entire performance with his head thrown back, his face buried in a bloody handkerchief as he sang 'Solingo, errante misero', not to the implacable Silva, but to the flies.

On another evening, the Skipper, as we called him, took me to see Myles na Gopaleen's comedy *Faustus Kelly*, at the Abbey. It was poor stuff, and I was not at all taken by F. J. McCormick in the title role. I thought him dry and pompous; it was only years later, when I saw him as Fluther Good in *The Plough and the Stars*, that I realised where his genius lay: he became whatever character he played so completely that there was danger of confusing the role and the man. On the tram homeward, the Skipper suggested that we have cocoa and discuss the play, but instead of taking me to his house on Albert Road he led the way to our scout hut near the Forty Foot. He put a billycan on the primus to boil. We sat.

'It's weakening, you know,' he said.

I thought at first that he meant cocoa. It took me a while to realise that, without prologue, he had launched into a lecture on the perils of masturbation.

'It isn't manly. A true Scout will despise it for what it is: a habit that saps the energy and rots the brain. Never mind about it being a sin: that's Canon McGough's department. No, what concerns me is that it turns fine lads into contemptible weaklings: cowardly go-by-the-walls. Not to mention that it's a waste of precious seed. We're each of us given only so much, you know.'

I silently implored the water to boil and willed him to change the subject to *Faustus Kelly*. Quite apart from wanting to know what he thought of F. J. McCormick, the steadiness with which he watched my face was unsettling. I tried not to flinch and felt a tic leap high in my cheek.

'Boys who masturbate think that nobody knows. They do it where no one can see, in locked rooms, in bed and in the dark. They think they do it in secret. Well, more fools they.' He gave a

71

small, shrill laugh that did not reach his eyes. 'Any doctor can tell in an instant. He can look at them and say straight out: "That boy degrades himself." Will I tell you how?'

I said miserably: 'Yes, Skipper.'

'I mean, do you want to know?'

Teachers' pets are to be pitied. Sooner or later, if they are not to fall from grace, there is a reckoning to be paid. I was the Skipper's favoured one, envied by the others and justly resented, for I had few of the conventional scouting skills. I was too weedy to handle a heavy oar in the racing skiff and so, by default, became the coxswain; I could not swim or climb a rope or put up a tent or build a camp fire, never mind cook on one. What I excelled at was word games and whatever else needed a quick mind, without physical strength or dexterity to go with it. It was a quality that appealed to the Skipper; I was a match for him. Now, on the edge of a dark *terra incognita*, I looked back at him dumbly.

'Well, do you want to know or don't you?'

I heard the faintness in my voice as I told him yes.

He said: 'Right, I'll show you. Open the front of your trousers.'

I stared at him.

'Well, come on. Did you say you wanted to know? Just take your thing out and I'll show you.'

A whisper. 'I don't want to.'

'You what?'

'I don't want to, Skipper.'

It was if his old dog, a spaniel, had snapped at him. His face was suddenly new to me: a stone mask of dislike. He said: 'The reason I like Micky Farrell' – our patrol leader – 'is because he's so open and above board and doesn't make strange.' He extinguished the primus. 'That water will take all night to boil. You're out late enough as it is.'

A few days later, our troop was in the hut waiting to come to order for one of our twice-weekly meetings. In passing behind me, another boy flicked his finger and knocked my cap off. When

I whirled around, he dodged backwards and fell over the Skipper's dog, which had just preceded its master into the hut. We were at once called to attention, and the Skipper, his face and bald head scarlet with rage and hatred, ordered me to step forward and delivered a shrieking, five-minute tongue-lashing, at the end of which I was expelled from the 3rd Port of Dublin sea scouts for hooliganism. I was framed.

4

My first job was as a clerk in the offices of Columbia Pictures in Middle Abbey Street. My four years at Prez had atrophied into a kind of limbo, and the prospect of working for Columbia evoked agreeable images of Frank Capra, *Mr Deeds* and *Lost Horizon* and, at a less rarified level, *Blondie*, Charles Starret as the Durango Kid and Warren William as the Lone Wolf. The actuality was a public office in Middle Abbey Street from the ceiling of which apathy drifted down in flakes. The manager was Mr Jay, a lank-haired autocrat who affected a Protestant accent and the languidness of a feudal warlord strolling among his vassals. Prominent on his office wall was a framed telegram from Wardour Street in London complimenting him on his efficiency. The message was perhaps the last of an endangered species, for while I was there he was bombarded almost daily by telegraphed threats, insults and goads from the same source. His secretary, Miss Grace, sucked up to him shamelessly and loathed the rest of us. For a time, her habit of leaving by one door and seeming to return by another an instant later and in a change of dress made me wonder if I was having blackouts; then a kindly soul explained that she had a twin sister who dropped in every day. The only other person I remember, and with good reason, was a shapeless girl called Dolores who sat opposite me. She favoured floppy twinsets and seemed herself to be floppy underneath them; one was conscious of heavy, untrammelled breasts. She and I took turns at operating the small switchboard, but otherwise hardly spoke.

My pay was thirty shillings a week, and every day at lunchtime

I would cross O'Connell Bridge to the Goodwill Restaurant opposite Trinity. It was a far cry from eating a ham sandwich at Da Lundy's. There, for one-and-sixpence, you were given chunks of bread with soup so thick that a spoon would not sink in it, followed by a stew that was a bubbling archipelago of mutton, carrots, swedes and spuds. For a penny extra, scalding tea was splashed from a great metal jug into both your cup and lap, favouring neither. You sat at a long, bare table, and the cutlery was all but flung at you, but you were nourished, and in the war years and after, there was more to eating than avoiding hunger. It was a time of plague. Old people called it consumption, the young, T.B., and everyone had friends or family who had died of it. With a hypochondria that has been a loving companion down the years, I could not catch a head cold or stand on a weighing machine or feel a twinge in my chest without seeing myself, gaunt and hectic, expiring in a sanatorium at Peamount or Blanchardstown, and so, rather than run the risk of falling into a decline, I wolfed down the Goodwill's stew, gristle and all.

For all its virtues, it was not the kind of eating house where one lingered over a *demi-tasse*, and there was always time to walk in the little back lanes between Dame Street and the river and go hunting in secondhand shops for a *Blighty* or a *Men Only* that had somehow escaped the censors. Usually as I walked, with the mutton like a stone in my craw, I would try to work out what had become of me.

I knew of only one person who was deluded enough to regard my thirty shillings a week life as enviable, and he was my friend, Oliver Mongan, who lived his own life, not in the real world, but in the Picture House, the Pavilion and the Astoria. When aged eleven, he had fallen through a kind of tear in the educational net and had not been to school since. Instead, each morning he would sit at an upstairs window, and use a pearl-handled revolver to shoot me dead on my way to Prez. He and I had not previously spoken, but one day and to be obliging I clutched at my abdomen and bit the mud of

Tubbermore Avenue, and it constituted a kind of introduction. We became best friends. I learned that his mother, who had gone astray in the head after winning £500 in a crossword competition, had taken him out of school, and he was now educating himself. He read *Teach Yourself Psychology* and the works of Emile Coué and Dale Carnegie. He had also joined the Rosicrucians and was learning how to harness and utilise the energy of the cosmos. He believed that, sooner or later, he would be able to bend others to his will by sheer force of personality, and I had his word for it that he would not put this power to evil ends, but use it for the good of mankind. Already, he had acquired a steely penetrating look which he employed sparingly, aware that overuse might blunt its efficacy. Meanwhile, he lived and breathed films even more than I did and had a trunkful of clippings from *Modern Screen* and *Picturegoer*. To him, working in a film renters' office was like dying and going to heaven. It was no use telling him that the place was mean, that its people were sullen and defeated; nothing would do him but to believe that it was a rung, if a lowly one, on the ladder to Hollywood and, in his own case, the long-planned marriage to Joan Fontaine.

Oliver had so unshakeable a sense of his own destiny that I regarded him as a superior being, and his envy afforded me a glow of pleasure. Even so, it hardly justified a lifetime spent with Columbia Pictures or 'The Marvel of the Industry', as it styled itself. The staff were treated as clock-watching malcontents and on that account became so, and the pay, even in the winter of 1945, was insulting. In the event, however, I had even less of a future there than I imagined.

One January day, a grey shawl of rain came down the Liffey from the west, and I thought to go back early to the office and peck out on one of the typewriters the beginning of a short story. (I started at least one story a week, confident each time that, if I could only finish it, Frank O'Connor and Sean O'Faoláin would fold their tents in despair.) As I entered the public office I heard a female voice coming from the alcove where we hung our coats.

Evidently, two girls were having a gossip, and it occurred to me to tiptoe over, and leap in front of them with a heart-stopping yell. And so I crept softly to the alcove and made my leap. As for the yell, it hung frozen and unuttered.

Columbia employed a number of 'reps', whose task it was to travel the country hymning the glories of, and taking orders for, Warner Baxter in *Crime Doctor's Strangest Case* and the Three Stooges in *Crash Goes the Hash*. We, the deskbound, envied them as free spirits, and one of them – their doyen, in fact – was at present in the alcove furiously coupling with my bespectacled *vis-à-vis*, the amorphous Dolores.

She was hiccuping as her back thudded against the door leading to the basement. When they saw me, they faltered in their exertions, then quite literally ground to a halt. I stood as if petrified, one forefinger uplifted and my lips still rounded for the 'Boo!' that never came. Probably, I looked like an idiot, but at least I had the consolation that they were not in a mood to say so. As the earth showed no inclination to open beneath my feet, I went to my desk, picked up a pencil and began to scribble on the bare wood without the formality of using a sheet of paper. I was eighteen and almost certainly felt more guilty than they did.

The 'rep' came over to me, and I saw that in adjusting his dress he had skipped a buttonhole so that his flies pointed outward in a false tumescence. He gave me a raffish Errol Flynn smile.

'Listen,' he said. 'Be a good man and say nothing. You don't want to get the girl into trouble.'

As green as I was, I could still recognise a remark that dictated its own riposte, but even if I had had the audacity to deliver it, there was no time, for he went skipping out into Middle Abbey Street, leaving me with Dolores. She came over, tugging at her skirt, and to my horror I caught a glimpse of old-fashioned pink knickers, mercifully elasticised just above the knees. She sat on her accustomed chair, looked demurely at me through her bottle lenses and said: 'Did you see that fella gone out?'

I nodded, dumbly.

She said: 'Nobody here likes him. He's always trying to talk to me.'

Next day, something worse happened: she began to twinkle at me. Every time I looked up, she was smiling, and once she actually cupped a hand around as much of her bosom as it could contain: It was for a time perplexing, for her wantonness deserved no less than that she have the decency to blush, or at the very least to look away. It was not until later, when I was having lunch at the Goodwill, that the fog lifted and I suddenly knew the reason for the smiles and what I had mistaken for an itchy chest. She had decided that the only way to ensure my silence was by seduction. Whether this was to be in the nature of a bribe or an entrapment was no matter: either carried with it the same terror. The main course that day was shepherd's pie, and I thrust it from me, for once uncaring as to whether I caught consumption or not. Back at Columbia Pictures, she was still smiling. Once, while passing by my chair, she ran her fingers lightly up my spine.

Three months previously, I had sat for a civil service examination and, by coincidence, the results arrived that same weekend. I had won a temporary clerkship. My mother was in a daze of excitement: to her it was the next best thing to my having discovered a vocation for the priesthood. The civil service was respectability incarnate, and anyone who worked in it was, *ipso facto*, a genius. My mother's sister, Chris, had married John Bennett, who was in the Land Commission. In time I was to find out that John's grade was that of Paper Keeper, which was looked upon as an even lower life-form than Clerical Officer, but Chris comported herself as if he were the Minister for Lands. It could justly be said that her marriage to John had marked the first non-Sunday appearance of a collar and tie in the Doyle family, and she never allowed my mother or Uncle Sonny to forget it. Now, a generation later, if one overlooked my uncertain pedigree, the torch had been entrusted to me.

'Of course,' Chris took care to remind my mother over Twenty-Fives on the Sunday evening, 'he'll only be temporary. Not like John.'

'What differ?' my mother said. 'Isn't he made for life?'

She would have disdained to recognise the word 'temporary', even if she had known what it meant. As far as she was concerned, once my foot was inside the door of the civil service I was predestined to end up running the country. She was unshakeable in this, just as she knew that, had I instead chosen the priesthood, I would have been the first Irish pope.

She gave me a look of maternal pride mixed with incredulity. 'Made for life he is,' she said again. 'Tell him, John.'

'Oh, just so,' my uncle said, his face shining.

Everything about him shone: his pink cheeks, his bald head that was pinker still, his gold-rimmed spectacles, his scrubbed fingernails, his shoes. Years before, when I was small, he had worn spats. His soft, courteous voice belied his youthful nickname of 'the Curser' Bennett. My aunt's unfeigned devotion did not prevent her from managing him with the ruthlessness of a Chinese warlord, coldly telling anyone pass-remarkable enough to put their spoke in that it was for his own good. He was too adoring to protest; in fact, he was the gentlest of men, and it pained me to announce in his presence, never mind in front of my mother, that I did not want to go into the civil service.

To an appalled silence, which I knew would not last long, I tried to explain that, while I could easily escape from Columbia Pictures, becoming a civil servant was like climbing into a coffin and pulling the lid shut after you. This observation provoked a modest spectrum of comment.

My father said that I was a comical boy.

My aunt emitted a tinkling laugh that sounded like an entire orchestra of celestes and made me want to pick up the flat-iron from the fender and hit her with it.

My uncle said with great politeness: 'Well now, do you tell me so?'

79

My mother said coldly: 'What codology is this?'

She said a great deal more than that, with my aunt contributing the occasional leitmotif. I was unnatural, my mother said, I did not know what I wanted, I would rue the day, this was the thanks she got, this was the price of her, Sonny was right, himself (my father) was not good enough for me, any more than she was. Ironically, my uncle John, in an attempt to restore calm while her rage was as yet merely at gale force, was the one who sealed my fate.

He said: 'Excuse me, Mag, excuse me for interrupting you. But we have only the one life to live, and one road to travel—'

'Now don't talk foolish, John,' my aunt murmured. Being herself a literal person, she believed that figures of speech were not good for him.

He leaned towards her. 'What I mean, Chrissie, is that maybe Jack has inclinations of his own. Something more to his liking.'

'He's been offered a bobby's job,' my mother snapped, 'and he's turning his nose up.'

'With the greatest respect, Mag' – no one had ever taken offence at my uncle John and ever would – 'why don't we let him tell us what it is he wants to do?'

'Do you mean let him pick and choose?' she said. 'Much pickin' and choosin' *we* were ever let do. *We* done what we were told.'

She gave me the old familiar look that had a knife in it, then, with her lips closed to the size of a full stop, waited for me to tell her what was a better job than the civil service. My uncle John, risking another reprimand from my aunt, again produced a small metaphor. 'To be sure,' he said, 'Jack's the one who'll follow his star.' He, too, waited.

What I wanted was to become a writer, but I dared not say so. My mother read racing novels by Nat Gould and maudlin romances that were chosen for her by the girl in the tuppence-a-book-a-week shop, but I knew that no tendril of her mind had ever strayed towards the concept that books had authors, never mind that the writing of a book might be a way of life. I had no faith in myself: only longings and the knowledge that if my fever – the desire to write – proved not to be accompanied by the disease itself, then there was no life for me. The hope was so threadlike that one splutter of derision could have snapped it, and so I did not speak up, only sat and looked sullenly at the playing cards spread on our kitchen table and for the moment forgotten.

My mother, sensing victory, punched the side of one small fist into an open hand. 'You'll take that job,' she said, knowing now that I would. 'Be me song, you will!'

Later I consoled myself, rightly or not, that there was more to it than weakness. Bernard Shaw, who had cabbage water for blood, crowed that the true artist, meaning himself, would let his mother drudge for a living sooner than work at anything but his art. I was a weedy adolescent, too myopic to look for horizons. I lacked not only ruthlessness, but also the kind of arrogance which, in the young Shaw's case, saw the world in terms of no one's needs but his own. Another factor was that I had been adopted. My name was Byrne; my foster parents' name was Keyes (it was to be another ten years before I would hopelessly confuse matters by taking a pen name as well); and I had grown up in Dalkey as Jack Keyes. For all my mother's carryings on, she and my father doted on me, and affection is the deadliest of nets. More to the point – and art and artists bedamned! – there was debt that hung over me like a raincloud. And so I gave in, but I found a scapegoat. With my liking for a well-rounded tale, I chose to pretend that of two evils the civil service was the lesser. Columbia Pictures, even at thirty shillings a week, was bearable, but not when one thought of one hundred and forty pounds of elasticised and determined feminine flesh. And so I exchanged Middle Abbey Street for Upper Merrion Street and, shifting the blame from my parents, my aunt and uncle and myself, dumped the lot on Dolores.

Within the week I was sitting at a desk – or a table, as I learned to call it – just up the street from my uncle John. There were perhaps thirty others in the room, which was painted orphanage-green. Its cheerlessness was too absolute to have been accidental; despair seemed to have been knowingly mixed in with the paint and ingrained in the dark wooden floor tiles. There was not even a wall calendar as a sign that humans had passed that way; the only small unruliness came from a torn screen on which were pinned a dozen holiday postcards. At the other side of the screen was a woman who, more than any other at that time, was to influence my life. Her name was Kay Kelly. She was our typist and, on my first day, caught sight of the misery on my face, mimicked it most cruelly and within ten minutes had become my friend of ten years. Being myself only eighteen, I took her to be all of forty (she was thirty-two). She was slim; her hair was brown and bobbed. The screen was her way of cutting herself off, not only from draughts, but from the sight of the Staff Officer, Mr Drumm. Once, when she came over to my table for a chat, he arose from his chair and said pointedly: 'Good morning, Miss Kelly.'

She gave him a summer meadow of a smile, 'Good morning, Mr Drumm.'

His nostrils flared, and what had been underlined was now italicised as well. 'I said *good morning*, Miss Kelly.'

It took her a moment to realise that she was being ordered back to her typewriter. She laughed aloud: an unforced bubble of amusement that caused his Adam's apple to jolt to attention. It was as if she had committed the unimaginable *lèse-majesté* of telling him that he was a caution and needed only a clown's red nose to bring the house down. She swished across the room, still laughing.

'What are you going to do with yourself?' she asked me on that first day, her eyes wide. 'And ah, God, no, don't say you're going to be like that crowd of jack-asses, stuck for life in a bog hole.'

She nodded towards the other clerks, most of them middle-aged, who, so as not to wear out their blue serge, had donned the jackets, now ragged and spilling their innards, that they had worn on their first day, perhaps before the 1916 Rising. I did not hesitate, but told her what no one save myself knew. She did not even blink.

'A writer?' she said in a whisper. 'Aren't you great?'

I felt wetness come into my eyes that someone had more faith in me than I myself had. Then she put the icing on my cake and the sun in my sky. 'Can I type your manuscripts?'

Every day, I would catch the 5.14 home from Westland Row and bolt my tea, which, in that last year of what we called the Emergency, was coarse war-time bread and a slice of over-the-ration boiled ham ruthlessly cadged by my mother from Mr Cussen's shop ('God, ma'am, do you want me to starve me own childer?') This was accompanied by the daily and unvarying ritual of intimate discourse with my parents.

My father: 'Well, son, an'thin' strange or startlin'?' (I never knew where he had picked this up.)

Myself: 'No.'

My father: 'So how's the job?'

Myself: 'All right.'

My father: 'Oh, the Land Commission's a great place. Sure you don't know yourself.'

Myself: 'Uhh.'

My mother (muttering): 'Hasn't a word to throw to a dog.'

Then, after a minute, or more probably not that long, at the cold-water tap in the scullery, I was out by the front door, ignoring both the bakelite holy-water font and the shout from my mother: 'Bless yourself before you leave the house!'

My friendship with Oliver was dying a natural death. He had begun what in those days was known as a steady line, and the girl, one Maureen O'Reilly, quickly and correctly recognised me as natural enemy and embarked on the time-honoured female strategy of divide and conquer. Also, I had recommended Oliver for my job at Columbia Pictures, but to no end. Perhaps, when interviewed by Mr Jay, he had rashly made known his intentions towards Joan Fontaine; at any rate he had been shown the door, and both he and his mother decided that I was to blame. 'You must have dirtied your bib in some way,' Mrs Morgan said balefully. 'Why else would anyone say no to Oliver?' It was a rhetorical question, and for once Oliver disagreed with his mother, never mind that, in the opinion of the town and as a result of her crossword win, she was as daft as a brush. A chill set in.

I found new, less exotic friends. 'The Lads', as they called themselves, went to the pictures or the snooker hall, or for walks when payday, although bidden, would not come. Adventure was not welcome in their lives. Every Sunday and on one weekday evening, each of them went out with his steady girl friend, who was warm, loyal and loved him to distraction, and would sever his head from his body if he dared place a hand above her knee or upon the cliff-edge of her bosom. One day they would marry. My own ambitions were less admirable. Courtship could wait; what I desperately craved was easement from a throbbing libido. The Lads and I talked about girls – not their 'steadies', God forbid, but the pert creatures who paraded in pairs and threes along the sea front – and about what we would do to and with them if only given the chance; what they did not suspect was that I alone meant every word.

Luckily, perhaps, for me and for my mother's fears, I met with little success, 'little' in this case being a euphemism for 'none'. Once, in George's Street in Dun Laoghaire, a girl gave me a sidelong look. As I followed her around a corner into Clarinda Park, I bounced into a navy-blue wall that turned out to be the unyielding front of a policeman. 'Are you following that young one?' he asked. I tried stepping to one side, and so, as if we were waltzing, did he. 'Well?' he said.

My civic spirit was outraged by the suggestion that chasing girls was in some way illegal. For one of the very few times in my life, I told a policeman the truth. 'Yes, I am.'

He clamped a hand on my shoulder. 'Well, get after her, boy, and the best of luck. The little bitch has been asking for it all day.'

Once I had got over the shock, I skipped past him, almost dancing. Naturally, given the kind of luck I was having with women, my prey was by now nowhere to be seen. Clarinda Park had opened and devoured her. I flew blindly in all directions, like a bird trapped in a chimney, then went home and day-dreamed about her for a month, imagining in the most sudorific detail the hours of animal passion that would have ensued had I caught up with her.

Dun Laoghaire policemen were, by the way, a libidinous lot. Once, I was passing the Garda station shortly after midnight, only to be laid hands on by two Guards who were leaning against the spiked railings outside. For a moment, I saw myself as an innocent victim of police brutality, then I realised that they were positioning me between them. 'Stand dere and feast oor eyes on dat,' one said in a ripe Cork accent. I looked and saw a woman taking her clothes off in a bedroom of the Avenue Hotel opposite.

Occasionally, I would stay in town after work and sit in the gods of the Gaiety where for sixpence one could see a double-bill, with Mícheál Mac Liammóir in *The Man of Destiny* and Hilton Edwards taking forever to expire in *Tsar Paul*. The Lads were not playgoers, but I persuaded them to accompany me to *John Bull's Other Island*, with Hilton as Broadbent and Mícheál as Larry Doyle. The show ran late, and, because there was a tram strike in progress, the others left to catch the last train while I sat to the end. Earlier that day, I had bought a secondhand copy of the play and on the ten-mile walk home kept stopping under street lamps to memorise bits of Larry Doyle's speech in Act One. By the time the lights went out a few minutes after midnight, I had it off by heart and chanted it to myself until, with the night sky already lightening, I fell in through our front door to a cry from upstairs of did I know what time it was.

One day at work a fellow named Moroney asked if I wanted to

join an office dramatic society to be called Lancos. In those days I was too cowardly ever to say no, and so I gave him sixpence every Friday and even went to see their first production, which was Patrick Hamilton's *Gaslight*. It is a thriller which I even then found to be not the least bit thrilling, but Kay Kelly, who took a freakishly un-Irish pleasure in the success of her friends, thought it marvellous.

'Buy me a coffee,' she said afterwards. 'Here's the money.' Before I could speak, she said: 'Wasn't it smashing?', and, before I could reply to *that*, she said: 'I think plays are great. Listen, will the pair of us join Lancos?' She answered herself in the same breath. 'Yes, we will.'

I told her: 'I'm already a member.'

She said: 'Well, you sneaky thing,' and led me to Cafolla's for our coffee.

A week or so later, she came up and said: 'It's all arranged.'

'What is?'

'Lancos. I joined. We're doing a programme of one-act plays and I'm producing a French yoke called *Villa for Sale*, and you're to play the part of the man.'

Of the various deaths I had died in the course of my nineteen years, that one was the deadest. She mistook my instant pallor. 'Don't worry about it,' she said. 'It's not actually *in* French.'

I closed my eyes and saw an audience on their feet, not applauding but throwing things. A feeling, not dissimilar from the nausea I had felt while trampling on Father Creedon's chasuble, came over me. Kay prodded me in the chest until I looked at her. 'Stop fretting. You need it. It'll be *good* for you.' I made no protest, no plea. For one thing, to her whatever I said would have been as insubstantial as fog; I knew that had she wanted to, she could have talked me into leaping out of our third-floor window to fly on carbon paper wings the length of Merrion Street. More disturbingly, I realised that my shyness had a devil inside it that wanted to show off. That evening, I read the 'French yoke'. In fact,

I read it twice in case there was a waiter or a comic gendarme whose fleeting appearance I had missed the first time. The one-acter had been written by and for Sacha Guitry so that he might tear up the scenery as a sophisticated *boulevardier* named Gaston. He shared the stage with no one except three awestruck females, and the play ended, as I recall, with:

WIFE (*a querulous creature*): Gaston, what have you done?

GASTON (*smirking airily*): I? Earned a hundred thousand francs and a Corot!

(*Curtain*)

Rehearsals began, and I came to know others in the group. There was Róisín, who had a magnificent lip-curling sneer and would one day play Hedda Gabler to my Tesman; Eva, who was small, demure and wicked and could act the rest of us into the wings; Jimmy Keogh, who ad-libbed and interspersed his lines with verbal sound effects such as 'boinng' and 'gedoink'; and Denis and Jeannie, who were courting, which was just as well, for his voice was contralto and hers, by way of compensation, was a pleasant baritone. We rehearsed twice weekly in a barren unheated room in Gardiner Row, just across from Findlater's Church. Kay's idea of being a producer (nowadays we would say 'director'), was simply to look on and not only gurgle with laughter at every line I stammered, but actually to hold her sides and groan, 'Stop, stop.' This would have helped my self-confidence immeasurably, except that nobody else laughed. One evening, she volunteered a stage direction: 'Take your time here before answering. I know! Why don't you stroke your beard?'

'Ah, Jasus. What beard?'

'Don't be bold. I mean, the beard you'll be wearing. How else will we disguise it that you're too young for the part?'

Her brazenness, considering that it was she who had shanghaied me into murdering Sacha Guitry in the first place, was almost worthy of my mother.

When the first night came, I was catatonic. Someone drew red tramlines on my forehead in a futile attempt to simulate middle-age, and Kay stuck clumps of hair on my chin and upper lip. As the moment came for my entrance, she pushed me towards the stage and said: 'Oh, yes, I meant to tell you. I've used a new chair.' Before I had time to ask her to render this into standard English, a French maid, barely identifiable as Bridie White of Forestry, flung open a door in the set, gave me a saucy curtsey and said: '*Bon jour, monsieur*. Please to come een.' It was at this point, somewhat late in the day, that Kay pressed the buzzer that was the doorbell, causing Bridie to hiss in an un-French accent: 'Ah, Christ, Kay.'

Theatres no longer have footlights. This one did, which meant, mercifully, that the glare kept me from seeing the audience. They were not, however, out of earshot, for I heard the giggle of recognition that greeted each of us as we entered. Someone hissed: 'It's John Keyes Byrne from Collection Branch.' Meanwhile, there was the sensation of having walked into a room which had a sun lamp for a ceiling and was missing a wall. Bridie informed me that Madame would be down presently, threw me another curtsey and was gone. Lifting a bemused eyebrow like Clifton Webb in *Laura*, I took off my homburg, slapped my gloves insouciantly into it and made to place my walking stick on the tallboy as instructed. It was then I realised that, since the dress rehearsal, Kay had turned the set into a nightmare of feminine decor. There was chintz all about; every surface, including that of the tallboy, was crammed with tiny ornaments: vases, a snuff box, a cup and saucer, a candle-snuffer, china kittens. I found myself stopping, holding my stick like a billiard cue and aiming through the clutter. Not one ornament rattled, and a voice from the audience called out: 'Well potted, sir!' A roar went up. Some applauded.

A moment later, Pat Cafferkey came on as the lady of the house and invited me to take a seat. It was then that I saw what Kay had meant about using a new chair, for what Pat was indicating, to her own dismay no less than mine, was a child's rocking chair placed squarely at stage centre. Perhaps Kay had known exactly what she was doing, for, as Pat and I looked at the thing, the audience began to hoot. As the laughter escalated, I rode it instinctively. With no expression on my face except Arctic coldness, I sat very slowly, very carefully, on the tiny rocking chair. Out front, female civil servants were having seizures.

One of the most quoted lines in the history of film comes in *Forty-Second Street*, when Warner Baxter tells Ruby Keeler: 'You're going out a youngster, but you've got to come back a star.' *I* had gone out a petrified adolescent and had come back a ham. The only flaw in the evening came after the performance. A man appeared backstage and Kay, having congratulated me once again, took his arm and went off with him. I was deeply hurt, not because I had a crush on her, but because with the selfishness of the young I thought I owned her. It had never occurred to me that she would be feckless enough to have a life of her own. She was the only one who with utter certitude believed that there was nothing I could not do. A dabbler herself, she opened the door of theatre for me, and if my soul was not destroyed by the years in Merrion Street, I had her to thank.

The opportunity never came. One morning, I entered the office to find Mr Drumm sitting on the edge of his table as he regarded a cluster of women clerks who were squeaking furiously. He was in ripe form. As I signed the attendance book, he said: 'Mr Keyes Byrne, we need not go far to divine the cause of the cluckings in the hen house. There is a note in that particular cacophony that unmistakably betokens the presence of an engagement ring. I should say that our Miss Kelly is leaving us.'

And so she was. A month or so later, she shook hands, told me to keep up with the writing and went off to an eve-of-wedding party for her women friends only. I never heard from her again, but after two years her best friend, Peggy Mulligan, came in, her eyes red from weeping, to say that a month after giving birth to her second child, Kay had died of cancer.

I have a sort of half-fancy of one day arriving at the heavenly gates to be met by her, saying: 'Come on in, hurry up. We're doing a play, and I talked God into being the Protestant minister.' She would, too.

5

Mick, who became my best friend in the Land Commission, worked in a small office in Hume Street which he shared with, among others, a woman so nervous that she jumped in the air whenever he slammed a ledger. At our first meeting, when I was there on official business, he asked, apropos of nothing: 'Did you ever hear tell of Pavlov's dogs?' I said: 'Yes, why?'; whereupon he opened a heavy record book and banged it shut, and I saw a red-faced, tweed-skirted woman levitate, screaming, from her chair. Mick's boss was a bald countryman named Walsh, who had arteriosclerosis and was determined, for the sake of his pension, to stay in the service up to and far beyond the end of whatever usefulness he had had to begin with. Brooding upon his own troubles, he had never connected the slamming of the ledger with the woman's sudden leap in the air. Now, I saw him throw a ruler at her with a shout of 'Are you at it again? Shut up, you banshee, you.' In the Land Commission, eccentrics were the rule rather than the exception; even so, the people in Mick's office seemed to me to have more than the ordinary madness. I learned, in time, that not only did Mick carry anarchy around with him like a germ, but also he infected others.

He had a round, babyish face that gave him a more than passing resemblance to the film actor, Eddie Bracken, who usually played fumbling milquetoasts. Mick, on the other hand, had a military bearing and was a lieutenant in the Local Defence Force, our equivalent of the British Home Guard. He came from the hamlet of Lissycasey near the village of Corofin in County Clare, and our friendship was a collision of opposites. I was a townie: he was country. I was timid; he was brash. As a born romantic, I hoped for the best; as a realist, he awaited the worst. I was a weed who slouched along and was so puny that, even now, whenever I attempt to wear a coat over my shoulders cloaklike, it slides off. He, on the other hand, did not so much walk down a street as lead a victory parade of one, chest out, chin in. He had a brazenness that mocked the taking of offence. Once, we went together to donate blood at Pelican House, and he dutifully answered the list of questions: had he ever had T.B.? whooping cough? Smallpox? When the catechism was done, he assumed the look of a village idiot and volunteered: 'I had syphilis twice . . . but I'm better now!' Everyone thought this a scream; had it been I who said it, the consequent silence would have been colder than the plasma on its shelves in the vault.

Even when hardly out of his teens Mick was an accomplished womaniser. I envied him his conquests and his way of sweeping girls along effortlessly, nodding his agreement as they declared – meaning every word of it – that they were going nowhere with him and besides what did he take them for? With hindsight I wonder if, like most Irishmen, he really liked women. Certainly, they adored him, but the act of sex itself may have been a way of showing them up for what he believed them to be. The easier they were, the deeper went his contempt, the more brutal was his rejection. One evening, he called to my house, leaning his bicycle against the front wall. He had been out to Bray where he had picked up a Scotswoman on holiday. Among the gorse bushes on Bray Head he had made to kiss her, whereupon she had said 'Och, for God's sake, kid's stuff!' and pulled him down to her. Afterwards, they had walked into the town and, on catching sight of the Roxy Cinema, she said coyly: 'A true gentleman would treat a lassie to the pictures.' 'Fair enoughski,' Mick said. 'I'll just go and park me bike.' He left her to wait for him by the box office, wheeled his bicycle around the corner, climbed on it and pedalled the six miles to Dalkey and me. I listened to the saga open-mouthed. He finished it by saying: 'I was this side of Killiney by the time I remembered I had these.' He reached into his pocket and produced a pair of woman's knickers.

I was at first shocked beyond measure; then we sniggered. Finally, laughter set in and the pair of us fell about my parents' front garden, guffawing like the young jackasses we were. If I did not see what he had done as brutish, it was perhaps because his exploit had come to me at a remove, and, to use the words of Synge's Pegeen Mike, there was 'a great gap between a gallous story and a dirty deed'. Also, to us, as to our contemporaries, sex education was a thousand dirty jokes, told on street corners and in queues for the pictures. Sex itself, we had been told from the pulpit, was too sinful ever to be romantic, which was probably why we saw females as rather frightening creatures who were not quite human and therefore needed not to be so treated. One windy Sunday afternoon on Dun Laoghaire pier, I saw a girl's skirt blow up, revealing an undergarment that had a large, unmatching patch on the seat. A fellow named Joey Fitpatrick caught sight of it, too, and, although he and I detested each other, he ran over to me, hand outstretched, to celebrate the momentous sighting.

As for Mick, he was the eldest of four brothers. They lived in a tall house in Rathgar with their father, a schoolmaster, and a diminutive aunt named Moll, who tried to impose orders on the bedlam. I can still hear the cry go up of 'Hey, Moll, throw us an oul' ciggie' and see her, complaining for the sake of appearances, as she fumbled for her packet of five Woodbines. Their mother had died when the youngest was born, and Moll had come up from Clare to keep house. Perhaps it is plucking what O'Casey called 'magnificent meanin's' out of nowhere to say so, but I wonder if the death of a mother is not often looked upon as a kind of desertion for which all women must thereafter be punished. If so, it may go part of the way to account for the callousness of Mick's philandering; equally, it could well be home-made

93

psychiatry at its most glib. No matter; what did concern me in those days and for two decades to come was that Mick and I, who were relatively harmless while apart, had the effect, when together, of a detonator upon a bomb.

We are walking by the canal late one evening when I became aware of a call of nature. 'Piss there,' Mick said, indicating the gable end of a cottage. I thought the place too public for safety and said so.

'Ah, for God's sake, who's going to see you at this hour?' He pointed to a dark stain on the wall. 'Anyway, somebody's been there before you. You have a slash. I'll keep nix,' he said magisterially.

He looked both ways, up and down the canal. I set about my business and was in full spate when I noticed that a policeman had come around the corner of the cottage behind Mick's back and, with massive calmness, was already leafing through his notebook.

'I have ye now, oo dirty bugger oo,' he said. 'Gross indacency in a public place.' He took a ballet step backwards. 'And don't go oorinating on my shoe or 'twill be assault as well.'

I would probably have been sent on my way with no more than a warning had Mick not put his spoke in. 'Hold on there, not so fast. What ever happened to fair play?'

It was as if two of the guard's birthdays had unexpectedly come at once. He smiled upon Mick. 'And who might oo be?'

'Never mind about me. What I'm saying is, you're not going to shanghai him on a trumped-up charge.'

'Mick, shut up.' (This from me.)

The guard waved me to silence. He might have been Toscanini quietening the woodwinds. He said to Mick: 'A trumped-up charge, is it? I suppose you'll tell me that 'twas liminade he was pouring agin the wall?'

I had seen Edward Arnold as Daniel Webster addressing a jury of the damned in a film called *All that Money Can Buy*. He was an earthquake incarnate, but Mick put him in the ha'penny place as he propelled an arm, a hand and a forefinger towards the stain on the wall. Ripples furrowed the black canal water as, in a voice of thunder, he clinched the case for the defence. 'That pee is . . . *not . . . all . . . his!*'

To my surprise, the guard actually seemed impressed. 'Do you tell me?' he said mildly. His brain seemed to be working slowly, but in the desired direction. 'Right, so,' he said, licking his pencil. 'Grand. So tell me, how much of it is his?'

The upshot was that I was marched by the scruff of the collar as far as Portobello Bridge, with Mick trailing behind, chanting over and over 'I'm his witness', but keeping at a safe distance, just in case it occurred to the guard to charge him with obstruction. As for me, I could already see a headline in my parents' *Irish Press*: DALKEY YOUTH FINED FOR INDECENCY. When we reached the bridge, I heard Mick call my name.

'Listen,' he said. 'I'm off home. But don't worry. I won't see you stuck. They don't know who they're messing with when they mess with us. We'll give them lackery.' He added 'See you' and walked away up Rathmines Road.

The guard was as surprised by the defection as I was. We watched Mick lope off under the street lights. 'That fellow's a sleeveen,' he said. It was a pejorative word meaning a little mountainy fellow, as treacherous as he was unpredictable. Of a sudden, Mick was the real villain, and so my role became that of victim, whose worst sin was consorting with bad company. The guard assumed a gruff voice, said, 'Listen here to me, boy, for Jazus' sake,' and lectured me for ten minutes on the fine art of relieving oneself in public without giving scandal. Then he asked where I worked and, when I mentioned the Land Commission, told me stories of his upbringing on a farm at Ballyagran near Kilmallock. By the time we parted company and he said 'Safe home, now,' I knew that I had missed my last tram. Resigned to walking the ten miles home, I had turned down Richmond Hill, when a voice said 'Howayah?' and Mick appeared from the shadow of a front garden.

Before I could scald him with a look and go swiftly past, he was by my side, keeping step. 'I knew that if I acted the mean louser and did a bunk he'd feel sorry for you. I bet he did, too. Sure he was an oul' softy.'

I looked at him angrily, about to roast him for a Judas. Then I saw that his face contained nothing but transparent honesty and that what I had taken for betrayal was simply one countryman outsmarting another or, more exactly, a Clareman besting a Limerick man. All I could say to him was: 'I've missed my tram.'

'Sure I'll lend you a bike,' Mike said.

I went home with him and pedalled off at high speed an hour later, a glow in my breast from tea and friendship. Mick trotted after me to the corner of Dartry Road and called out to me, five seconds or so too late, that the bicycle had no brakes.

Dr Johnson said that being hanged in a fortnight concentrates the mind wonderfully. The same may be held true of writing a memoir: faced with a blank page, one asks the whys and wherefores of what for years has gone unquestioned: why, for instance, two people as dissimilar as Mick and I should have come together. From the start, he played one role, I another: I knew, for example, that if we were in the same room and he happened to break wind, I was the person at whom people would sniff. It never for a moment occurred to me that I might more safely go through the world with a less volatile friend: one who was not flint to my gunpowder. The answer was that with him, I became airborne. Too timid to trust to my own wings, I used his. For his part, his wildness pushed him towards self-destruction and, being aware of it, he made of me the lifeline that connected him with earth. I gave him a mooring.

He, too, was a member of Lancos, but as an actor he had two defects. One was that he refused to look at you, in the eye or elsewhere. It was as if, with the best of intentions, his gaze had started out towards your forehead, but grew tired on the journey.

You looked at him and saw two unfocused buttons, which in moments of acute histrionic emotion, turned upwards like the eyes of a dying El Greco saint. His other handicap was that, on stage and off, he favoured brown army boots which were size 10½. Whenever the time came for his entrance in a play, he was invariably in the dressing room nursing a bottle of stout or shoving the leading lady amorously against a wall. A chorus of whispered cries would go up – 'Mick, you're on!' – and the entire audience would hear the thunder of his boots as he charged towards the stage. On one such occasion an actress froze as he crashed on, taking half the door with him. Her line was a vexatious 'Do you always come upon people by stealth?', and it stuck in her throat. Mick, thinking that she had forgotten her words, tried to be helpful by saying 'I'm sorry I snuck up on you by stealth,' and it brought the house down.

When I was twenty-two, he caused me to be thrown out of Butlin's holiday camp at Mosney in County Meath. I have never been the kind of person who bounds from his bed with a glad heart to the Tannoyed cry of 'Wakey, wakey!' or who, except under extreme duress, would wear a cardboard Edwardian moustache and sing 'Nelly Dean', but a rumour was sweeping Dublin to the effect that, where sex was concerned, Mosney made Messalina's Rome seem like a Carmelite convent.

It was common knowledge that Englishwomen, their morals in flitters from six years of war, were coming to Ireland to eat farm eggs and butter, unrationed steaks and any young Irishmen they might find. In going to Mosney, my intention, as one of the last-named, was to be as findable as I was edible. It was a coincidence that Mick was at the Gormanstown army base at this time, doing his annual reservist training, and that the two camps, holiday and military, adjoined each other.

I arrived on the Saturday afternoon with perhaps two hundred other holidaymakers and was no sooner off the train than I noticed public toilets labelled 'Lads' and 'Lassies'. As I walked towards the former a redcoat cried out 'He'll get lost!' This generated roars of mirth from the new arrivals, and I spent fifteen minutes in the toilet waiting for either the crowd or my blushes to go away. It was as inauspicious a beginning as I had feared, notwithstanding the assurances from my colleagues in the Land Commission that my luck was about to change for the better and that I could not fail to return from Mosney either with gonorrhoea or in a test tube.

My chalet mate proved to be a man from Coleraine who was on his second week at Mosney. We had not sooner shaken hands than he asked me if I liked women and, without waiting for an answer, informed that he had a midnight assignation with a Miss Morris and a Miss Watson, both from Manchester. They had gone, he said, to Dublin for the day, planning to return by the last bus, and had invited him to drop in later and bring a friend. Seeing as how (and I can still hear his Northern accent) both women were, true as God, as hot as mustard, would I oblige? My senses swam. I had hardly set foot in Mosney, and already my virginity was all over bar the panting.

After dinner, the minutes crawled as I waited for midnight when Miss Morris (or perhaps Miss Watson) would make me hers. At last, unable to contain myself for excitement, I thought to pass part of the time by walking the mile or so to the front gate of Gormanston camp to leave a note for Mick. Recovering from manoeuvres with the regular army, he would, I knew, be delighted to learn that my own fortress was at last about to fall. I went out by the front gate of Mosney, and it was as if I were quitting a kind of Shangri-La, for at once rain began to fall in swaying curtains that swept across the flat fields. At the camp gate, I gave a note to the sentry and squelched back to Butlin's, and it was not Shangri-La after all, for the rain kept falling. It made bulls' eyes on the swimming pool and sighed across the Kiddies' Korner and the putting green, then combed through the crab grass and the sand dunes, to become one with the sea. I was soaked through and went straight to the chalet to change my clothes. In the gloom, a naked figure was sitting on my bed.

Never reluctant to clutch at straws, I thought for an instant that the mountain had come to Mahomet and that Miss Morris (or Miss Watson) had returned early from Dublin and, try as she might, had been unable to bank the fires of her passion until midnight. Then I saw that my unclothed visitor was Mick.

'Howayah.'

'What are you doing here? And why are you in your pelt?'

Mick placed my bed pillow modestly upon his lap. 'I was wearing me civvies, ready to go for a jar with the lads. Then I got your note, so I took the short cut by the beach. I got pissed on.'

I switched on the light. Steam was rising from his clothes which he had carefully piled on the other bed. Already the bedspread was soaked. I asked again: 'But what brought you here?'

He said: 'I just thought it might be nice to see you.'

Of course he was lying fit to damn a saint. The person he thought it would be nice to see was not me, but Miss Morris (or Miss Watson). He wanted her for himself. I had been a fool to send the note, and twice the fool to put my chalet number on it. Now I thanked heaven for the rain, for without clothes to wear, he could not follow me to the Englishwomen's chalet, ply them with a fake broth-of-a-boy accent as thick as a doorstep of soda bread ('Now that's a *real* Irish brogue!' they would certainly exclaim, loving it), and steal what was mine, if not by right, then certainly by need. As I changed into my good suit he watched me as if there were only one bottle of stout left in the world and I were drinking it. He said: 'Have you e'er an oul' rag I could put on?'

Coldly: 'No.'

'Well, at least could you dry me suit so's I can go home?'

That seemed reasonable. Anxious to be rid of him, I gathered up his clothes and took them to a nearby building which from its hot breath as one went past I had guessed to be the laundry. On the way, I met a girl who had sat opposite me at dinner. She was dressed up for the evening dance and asked me where I was taking the pile of clothes. It was then that I made yet another mistake. I

99

told her, making a meal of it, about Mick crawling along Mosney beach in the rain and through the barbed wire. 'And if I don't bring his suit back,' I said, chuckling suavely, 'he'll never see Gormanstown again.' She gave me a razor blade of a smile and went on her way.

When I returned to the chalet, my new friend from Coleraine was there with Mick. He was in a foul temper, which had not been improved by the discovery that his bed was all but awash.

'You can sleep there tonight,' he told me, 'for I'm damned if I will.' He added, venomously: 'And you needn't think that either of us is sleeping any place else. We've been shat on from a height.'

He had just come from the chalet occupied by the Misses Morris and Watson. They had returned from their day in Dublin in a state of advanced drunkenness, and the latest bulletin was that Miss Morris (or Miss Watson, perhaps) had been sick into their washbasin, which had promptly clogged up, and that she was now insensible. The Northerner said in disgust: 'I'm going to the Pig and Whistle.' Seeing the dejection on my face, he told me: 'Cheer up, old son. Sure if we don't get them tomorrow night, we'll get their likes.'

For me, there was to be no tomorrow night. Mick went back to camp at two in the morning, shivering in a suit that was still damp; and at lunch time a redcoat came and asked if I would be so good as to call to the Commandant's office. As I left the table I heard the girl from the previous night say: 'That's fixed him.'

The Commandant was British, with flat Brylcreemed hair, and looked as though he should have been in charge of a destroyer in a war film. There was perhaps ten pounds in banknotes and silver on the desk in front of him. He pushed it towards me, then delivered himself icily, as if I were an Ordinary Seaman who had disgraced the ship.

'My information is that you have assisted an unauthorised person to infiltrate the camp. That cannot be permitted. The unused portion of the cost of your holiday is here refunded. The camp police will escort you to the Dublin train.'

I felt like Richard Attenborough in *In Which We Serve*, and even more so when he bade me a clipped, Noël Coward-ish 'Good day'. I was stunned. To my certain knowledge, nobody in all of history had ever been thrown out of a holiday camp; one would as soon be expelled from Mountjoy Prison for hooliganism. On my way to the chalet, I remembered what the Commandant had said about the camp police, and knew that I must at all costs avoid the crowning shame of being dragged bodily out of Mosney. I packed, ramming my clothes any-which-way into a suitcase, and was slamming the door behind me when two men dressed in blue tunics came around the corner. They were between me and the way to the front gate, so I ran towards the sea, past the paddling pool and the donkey rides. A few people looked around. Terror is the fastest of all runners, and the policeman fell back as I reached the beach and made for Gormanstown camp.

I cannot remember how I made contact with Mick, but I was smuggled into one of the huts and given a cot for the night. That evening there was an impromptu concert in my honour, the high point of which was a soldier, quite naked except for a tin helmet, dancing by candlelight and languidly making his bayonet serve as an ebony walking cane as he sang 'Me and My Shadow'.

Next morning, Mick advised me to go north to Belfast instead of Dublin and home. 'The Orangewomen,' he said, 'have their tongues hanging out for it. You can't miss. Only don't let them know you're a Catholic. If they ask you, say you're a Proddy-dog.' And so I hitchhiked to Drogheda and from there took a train across the border.

It was my first time out of the Republic – or the Free State, as the Northern Irish called it and still do. All was new to me: the Union Jack flew on Royal Avenue; the police wore bottle green and carried guns in tiny holsters. The accents were harsh, the words frugal and workaday, not Sunday morning words as in the South. Everywhere, there were men and women in service uniforms. Even in those days, long before the murderers and their bombs, Belfast was at small risk of being mistaken for a seaside resort, and so I exchanged its red brick for a pleasant guest house in Bangor, nine miles away. On my first morning there, I walked towards the sea front and, along a pleasant sunlit avenue, came across a girl being held at bay by a snarling dog.

She wore a dark uniform. Red hair flared out from under her peaked cap. She was green-eyed. I see her still: a creature out of the better kind of dream. I picked up a small stone and threw it at the dog. Considering my eagerness to play the role of a knight charging to the rescue, the animal was fortunate that I did not pull a garden gate off its hinges and throw that at it as well. At any rate, it fled. The girl gave me a long cool look and said: 'Thanks. Mind, you needn't have bothered.'

Not knowing what to say, I gave her a great tongue-tied shrug.

She said: 'I suppose now I've been picked up.'

I went red and shrugged again, this time almost dislocating my shoulders. We strolled together for the best part of an hour, and, once my accent told her that I had come from the 'Free State', she was friendly and inquisitive in the dry northern way that seems not to give a hang whether you answer or not. The moment came when she said: 'I have to go now.'

'Will I see you again?'

It was her turn to shrug. 'Try Castle Park tomorrow evening.'

Given my appalling luck, I was certain that she would not turn up, but she was there, trim in her uniform, strolling across the grass as if the park were somehow hers. 'It's yourself,' she said with a mocking but not unkindly smile 'the wee mon that saved me from the wolves.' At five feet, eleven inches, I was anything but a wee mon, but I let it pass. We sat beneath a tree and watched the sun go down. We seemed to be the only people in the park, and, after a time, she put her face up and said: 'You'd better get a move on. They close the gates at sunset.' I kissed her, and, what was even better, she kissed me back. Made reckless by success, I unbuttoned her tunic jacket, but when I attempted to do the same to her white blouse she took hold of my wrist and, without seeming to try very hard, held it in a grip that came close to snapping my hand off.

'None of that,' she said pleasantly.

Cunning young devil that I was, I thought to defuse the moment with idle chit-chat. 'By the way,' I said insouciantly. 'I meant to ask. Which of the services are you in?'

'I'm not in the services,' she said. 'I'm in the police.'

It is acknowledged among my friends that whenever I make a mistake I do so in style. I mean that in saying that she was 'in the police', she was too self-deprecating by half. I discovered this later when, on saying goodbye with what began life as a bold peck on the cheek and ended up with a poltroonish handshake, I asked if her parents approved of her choice of profession. She said: 'Well, my father does. But then he'd have to. He's the Chief Constable of Belfast.'

On the train back to Dublin, my virtue as intact as ever, I remembered her with affection and found it easy to forgive Mick for causing my expulsion from Mosney. If bitterness crept in at all, it did so only on one occasion each year for the next decade, when at Christmas I unfailingly received a card inviting me to return to Butlin's for more fun and sun.

Love came to Mick with the unexpectedness of summer hailstones. Her name was Angela; she was petite and dark. She told Mick that she was the illegitimate daughter of a well-known tenor, who conceived progeny among his female admirers as readily as he would launch into yet a fourth encore of 'My Mary of the Curling Hair'. On Dun Laoghaire pier one evening, Mick asked me if he should marry her. I was so taken aback that before I had time to segue into my impression of a tribal elder (I was, after all, a year his senior), he came to the nub of his problem.

'You see, what if Angela takes after her oul' one?'

'Pardon?'

'I mean her mother. She let some old ram go all the way with her. I mean, otherwise Angela wouldn't be here, would she? So supposing it was handed down from oul' one to daughter, like. The . . . ah . . .' He swallowed, and the word, when it came out, did so like a foreign body. '. . . the immorality.'

I looked at the harbour waves, as grey as the stone pillars of the two yacht clubs: the one at the pierhead for bank managers and chief clerks, the other for the kind of ascendant Catholics whose wives affected Protestant accents. Across from us, the mailboat's engines throbbed and the deck lights came on. Mick, it dimly seemed to me, was speaking out against wantonness in women.

'The evenings are drawing in,' I said, just in case I had misunderstood.

'Yeah.' Now that I had allowed him his second wind, he went on. 'I mean, what if it's in the blood and if Angela turns out to be . . .' – he took a breath, and his voice actually trembled – '. . . unfaithful to me?'

Time would teach me that it is commonplace for womanisers to insist upon chasteness in their intended life partners. Mick was, however, out of the ordinary run. It was not Angela's morals that were troubling him, for he and she were, after all, coupling happily whenever darkness or privacy, or both, permitted. She was sexually avid as he, and he would not have wished her otherwise. It was part and parcel of his contrariness that what ailed him was that, twenty years previously, his future mother-in-law had wanted for virtue.

He continued as if I were not there. 'Of course, for all we know, Angela's mother might have gone all the way only the once. The old get might have given her drink.'

'Why don't you ask her?' I said, trying to be funny.

'Too late. She snuffed it.' Love, blind as it is, does not often see a joke. 'And look at it the other way. A fellow might as easily marry a girl whose oul' one had been getting her oats morning, noon and night, tongue hanging out for it, the town bicycle, like, only she never got caught.' Mick was brightening by the moment. 'Do you know what I think? I think that a girl like Angela's ma was 'ud actually have to be a right innocent to be put up the pole. Would you not agree?'

I said yes, but a trifle absently. The theory that a promiscuous nature could be passed from mother to child had never before occurred to me. Now I began to wonder if my own irregular birth could be the reason for my permanent, if so far unsated, randiness. It was not a possibility that I was likely to discuss with Mick or anyone else, for I would have killed rather than let it be known that I was adopted; in my case, Mick, now that he had ensured Angela's lifelong fidelity by convincing himself that her mother had been more sinned against than sinning, was moving further along his marital agenda. Still using me as his sounding board, he discoursed on ways and means of renting a back basement in Belgrave Square on his clerical officer's pay, which was only a few shillings more than I earned as a temporary clerk. 'If I was to take a spare-time job,' he said, 'and if Angela could put up a few bob as well, then we would swing it in six months.'

He became the evening manager of a filling station. Each afternoon, he would leave his office in Hume Street a few minutes early, pedal like a maniac around St Stephen's Green and up Harcourt Street and arrive on the blow of five, to sit in a glass booth on the forecourt until one in the morning, taking money and giving change. Meanwhile, Angela found a job in Belfast demonstrating gas cookers.

Mick was in charge of three urchins who worked the petrol pumps in exchange for tips. They robbed him blind. He saw them doing so, thought of banging their heads together, but instead felt sorry for them and simply looked on. At the end of the week, he discovered that, as the person in charge, he was expected to make good any losses. Accordingly, his entire pay was forfeit, and, with a warning to pull his socks up, he was forgiven an additional five-and-ninepence. He tendered an Irishman's resignation: which is another way of saying that he did not bother to turn up on the

Monday. Meanwhile, Angela, to her delight, was earning twenty pounds each week. In those days, it was the kind of wealth one described more fortunate beings as 'rolling' in. A year of this, she wrote to Mick, and, never mind a back basement in Rathmines, they could put down the deposit on a house. He showed me her letter, keeping his hand over what he called the lovey-dovey bits. 'Tell the truth, is she the berries or is she not?' he asked, pink with pride. He went on about what a bloody great girl he was marrying, and how it was once in a blue moon that a bird was not only an oil painting but had brains as well, but even as he said it I noticed that something had gone wrong with his mouth. In a time long before the word came to be used in the sexual sense, Mick was a chauvinist. Love, admiration, carnal desire: all turned to ashes against the realisation that Angela was earning five times as much as he.

He knew he was a fool for minding; he knew, too, that the money was no more than a means to the glorious end of their soon being always together. He told himself for God's sake to have more sense. Then it came back to him how, after a week in the filling station, with his civil service collared-and-tied mates leering in at him through the window, he had ended up with that deficit of five and ninepence, and the humiliation came eating at him like a rodent. His common sense told him that the money was a blessing; his gut instincts spat at it for an insult. At first, his resentment was unfocussed; then it nagged at him that Angela, even without meaning to, had belittled him. 'Women!' he said, with a sideways grin that pretended to make light of it. 'I know what they're like. Sure Angela's no different. One day she'll use it for a stick to beat me with.'

When I argued with him, he packed me off to those far suburbs where I was no longer his confidant, at least where Angela was concerned, but I knew that he and she had begun to have fallings-out. He found pretexts for being short with her and, stiff-necked with pride, never as much as hinted that, by earning more than *he*,

106

she had impugned his manhood. I can see his face at this distance: the deceptively weak mouth set hard in the determination to be wrong at whatever cost. As for Angela, being female and in love, she flew, like a homing pigeon, to the conclusion least flattering to herself: that he had tired of her. She came down from Belfast at weekends and sobbed all the way home, late on Sunday.

Mick and I were in a Lancos play at the time. It was Joseph Tomelty's *Is the Priest at Home?*, and one day he rang up to ask if I would meet him for a drink before that evening's rehearsal. It was an unlikely request: we rarely drank, if only because we could not afford to, and when I arrived at whatever pub he had named, I saw that he was carrying a cardboard suitcase. He said: 'Have a jar. I'm off to Dun Laoghaire to catch the boat.'

'The boat? What boat?'

'What do you mean, what boat? The Holyhead boat. I'm getting out.'

He told me an unlikely tale of how, while on his way home the previous evening, he had been accosted by two gurriers, both the worse for drink. Words led to thumbings of the nose; then one of them attempted to kick Mick in the privates, whereupon he had picked up a half-brick – and here I knew it to be a cod of a yarn, for such missiles did not famously abound along Upper Rathmines Road – and flung it. According to his story, it missed its target and went through a chemist's window. Now, to avoid a court case, he was on the run. I asked him why. Had he been recognised? Did the police come? He became vague, ordered whiskies for us both and said that his crippled boss had, like a decent skin, lent him forty pounds, enough for a new start in London. Mick lacked the imagination to weave lies from whole cloth, so I knew that, sure enough, there had been some kind of jack-acting the previous night, but that he had seized upon it as an excuse to escape from the linoleum-runged treadmill of the Land Commission; from his home, which had lost its heart when the old aunt, Moll, had suddenly died a year before; and, most of all, from Angela, who had taken from him his God-ordained role as master of their lives. He ordered more drink. I was not used to spirits, and within an hour we were both legless. I remember telling him with ossified gravity: 'You're making a balls of it. Wrong end of the stick. Man who's . . . who's emigrating ought to be going *to*, not running *from*.' I then sang a spiteful chorus of 'Run, Rabbit, Run' to myself while he was in the lavatory. By the time I streeled after him to the bus stop I could hardly stand upright, but performed small figures of eight, using my hands to stroke the air, like a swimmer staying afloat. A conductor's bell rang twice, and, with a briskness that was the sting of an open hand across the face, he swung himself on board and called out: 'See you, so. I'll drop a line.' There was a cough and a consumptive shudder from the bus, and he was gone to Dun Laoghaire and the mailboat. To the end, I had not believed he would do it. I began to bawl.

It was a lamentable sight for those who chose not to look away: a young man, dead drunk in the middle of O'Connell Street, maudlin tears streaming down his face as, by trying not to weep out loud, he made noises that were immeasurably worse. I looked for my handkerchief, knowing that it was in Dalkey in my good suit. An old woman in a shawl came over to me. 'What's up, son? Are you in trouble?'

I told her with an enormous hiccup of grief: 'Me . . . me friend's gone to England on me.'

She gave a smile that embraced not only me but also the grief of the world. 'Ah, sure God and His Blessed Mother pity you this night.' Then, with an abyss between the saintliness of the tone and the venom of the words, she added: 'An' sure God is good, and the whoor's melt won't have a minute's luck.'

Within a year, Mick was married, but not to Angela. The same mulishness that brought him to Holyhead and beyond kept him from ever returning home, even for a holiday. 'When you leave a place forever,' he told me, insincerity shining from his brow, 'you can leave it only the once.' I saw him six times over the next thirty years, and each meeting was a disaster, usually because we could not let the occasion pass without celebration. I have often been the worse for drink, but only with Mick have I ever been an Irish drunk, with all that that implies: the rowdiness, the messing, the spilt drinks, the cold looks from strangers, the weaving from one pub to the next, the mawkishness that alternates with aggression, the moments of truth that are whole hours of barefaced lies. And, with the years, Mick never relinquished his role as my evil genius.

I met him for the last time in 1969. By then, I had for ten years been a full-time writer and was living in London. Mick telephoned me; he was in Clacton-on-Sea, training to become a teacher in, of all places, a reformatory. A recent television comedy series of mine had achieved a mild *succès de scandale*, and Mick said that if I would drive down and say 'a couple of words to a few of the lads' it would be a feather in his cap. To put it more brutally, for want of a real celebrity I would do to be going on with.

Whenever called upon to speak in public, I have always thoroughly rehearsed the most spontaneous of my remarks, but on this occasion I had a mental picture of myself sitting in a common room, toying with a glass of less than dry sherry and not so much lecturing four or five of Mick's colleagues as enjoying an informal discussion. One of them, tapping the dottle from his pipe, would courteously suggest that television was ('Let us be honest, sir . . .') sedation for the retarded; whereas I, just as Johnsonianly ('Come, sir, if you watch television you refute your own argument; if, on the other hand you do *not* watch it, then how can you possibly . . .'), would with a victor's quiet smile outflank him at every turn. At any rate, I thought it unnecessary to prepare notes or even to hit upon a theme.

I took a wrong turning in Clacton, and when I at last found the training college Mick was at the gate, hopping from one foot to the other. 'C'mon, c'mon,' he said by way of greeting, 'they're waiting for you.' I could not understand the fluster: I was there, after all, to chat with 'a few of the lads'. Mick rushed me up a path and through a concrete labyrinth, and I heard a sound as unmistakable as it was familiar. It was voices: several hundred of them chattering away fiercely as they waited for a performance to begin. I could even tell from the timbre that the show was late in starting and that the audience, captive to begin with, was in restive mood. I looked at Mick, not believing what he had done. One of his fellow trainees remarked afterwards that my face had gone chalk-white. All Mick said was: 'Sure you'll be great.'

He lied: I was not great. To begin with, the audience, wherever they had come from and however entrapped, was the kind that defies conquest: there were two hundred adults and as many schoolboys, so that to enlighten one half was to bore the other. In the event, and invidiously, I bored them all; at one nightmarish point it came to me that I was enmeshed in the coils of a Henry Jamesian sentence and had not the least idea of where or how it would finish. Afterwards, there were no questions from the floor and the audience filed out with the dispirited air of holiday-makers coming home from a fortnight of rain. I stayed for a single glass of sherry that was not so much less than dry as more than sweet. Mick was for once subdued and did not protest when I pleaded an evening engagement in London. I think he felt that I had let him down.

I did not hear from him again until nearly twenty years later, when a chatty letter arrived from New Zealand, looking for 'all the news' from Dublin, as well as the amateur rights to my play, Da. Mick was still acting and probably staring his co-stars un-flinchingly in the forehead. A fitful correspondence ensured, and I asked him if he would mind having his story told in a book – this one. His reply, as I expected, was: 'Fire away, only don't come the hound.' Later, we again lost touch. Today, while I was actually revising these pages, a letter arrived enclosing photographs of Mick and his lady friend, Helen. He is semi-retired and spends much of his time fishing for trout. Life is good. A separate letter was enclosed from Helen, saying that I would find my friend little changed. By way of demonstrating that the leopard's spots are where they have always been, she mentions that Mick recently had surgery for haemorrhoids and was afterwards grossly overcharged for a jar of laxative which was no more than bran with a sweetener. His response was to telephone an M.P. while the latter was making a radio broadcast and not only aired his grievance, but also acquainted all of the South Island with the more recondite details of what Helen refers to as his anal fissure. Eventually, a local hospital managed to silence him with a year's free supply of laxative.

Mick lives in a town not very far from Invercargill. I looked it up just now in a gazetteer and discovered that it is not only in the South Island but at the southernmost end as well. It is probably coincidence, but, barring Antarctica, it is as far from Ireland as one can get.

6

Amateur actors have one quality in common with professionals; they take superlatives as their due. I have never in my life praised one of them so lavishly that it for one moment crossed his or her mind that I might be overdoing it. Even so, our group – Lancos – was not bad. We attempted O'Casey, Ibsen, Arthur Miller, Eugene O'Neill and the brothers Quintero. Some of our members belonged, too, to the grandly named Dublin Repertory Company, which in fact had no repertoire at all, but favoured allusive plays from the French of Jean-Jacques Bernard, Jean Sarment and François Mauriac. Its presiding genius was a window dresser named Chris Clinton. He rubbed his nose furiously while directing; and his pet words were 'diffident' and 'crystallise'. Reticence was his high altar, and his most frequent instruction was 'Could we have less of the Sweeney Todd?' Plays such as *Le Printemps des autres* and *Le Feu qui reprend mal* were exquisitely boring and, on that account, much admired by the critics and that sizeable minority to whom merely being entertained was as vulgar as eating the heel of a loaf or potatoes with the skins on, and to my surprise I was asked to play Blaise Lebel, the sinister tutor, in Mauriac's *Asmodée*, translated as *The Intruder*. As a piece of miscasting, it bordered on the lunatic. If I had a talent, it was for playing comedy, and I was never funnier than when trying not to be; but, with an amateur's iron ego, I said yes at once, thereby not merely courting disaster, but putting an engagement ring on its finger and naming the day as well.

Asmodée is the story, if one can describe it so strongly, of a young Englishman who comes to spend a summer with a refined French lady and her daughter. The latter, in the manner of French *ingénues*, has been kept in tremulous ignorance of the world's baser ways, and it is in the nature of things that the young couple should fall in love. They do so; but the mother, a widow, finds that the boy has in all innocence caused passions, long dormant, to come awake in her own bosom. We infer this from her moments of a typical bad temper and a tendency, in the middle of a translation into English, to revert to her native French with small impatient *moues* and murmurs of '*Tiens!*' Not far away is the sinister tutor, who is loved unrequitedly ('Blaise, how can you treat me so?') by the governess, a querulous creature. His amorous sights are set, however hopelessly, upon his employer, the widowed chatelaine.

The young Englishman was played by Tadhg (pronounced 'Taig') Murray, whose acting skills were tempered by a reddish, bony nose, cavernous nostrils, a receding jaw which perpetually sagged in seeming stupefaction, and a swooping Cork accent which turned the simplest prose sentence into a Verdi aria. He lived and died a bachelor, not because he was a homosexual, either overt or latent, but because the landlady of his digs took better care of him, so he said, than a wife ever could. He was the inventor of SPRAWL (the Society for the Prevention and Repression of the American Way of Life) and would pretend that his holidays in the country were recruiting drives. Every summer, I would receive a telegram from West Cork or the Aran Islands saying: 'SPRAWLING ALL OVER THE PLACE.'

We ran for a week at the Peacock, a pocket-sized theatre one floor down from its mother-house, the Abbey, which leased it out to reputable amateurs who, as such, could be trusted not to besmirch the mantles of Synge, Yeats and Lady Gregory. (O'Casey did not as yet merit a mantle; for, by remaining alive, he had failed to comply with the first Irish criterion of greatness.) In the second act of *Asmodée*, the following interchange occurred:

113

GOVERNESS (*distraught*): Blaise, is this goodbye, then?

LEBEL (*in a manner that bodes ill*): On the contrary. You will see me again very soon. (*He goes.*)

My exit obliged me to traverse the width of the stage. As I did so, the image came into my head of Groucho Marx, leering, waggling his eyebrows, tapping his cigar ash and quitting Margaret's Dumont's presence at an obscene lope. I did none of those things, but the mental picture must in some way have communicated itself to the audience, for they fell about. In the wings, Chris Clinton stared at me. 'What did you do?'

'Nothing.'

We listened in bemusement to the audience, who continued to shriek in happy memory, but of what I had no idea. On my next appearance, I was greeted with the throb of pleasure which welcomes the return of a well-loved comic who brightens an otherwise cheerless play. Somebody applauded. A lady whispered 'He's come back,' and in that small auditorium her voice was a thunderclap. At once I heard the concerted groan, far worse than the unkindliest of laughter, of a hundred people trying *not* to laugh unkindly. I was supposed to stand at my employer's elbow while she wrote a note summoning her daughter. Peering over Kitty O'Brien's shoulder, I saw that she had written in block capitals: 'FOR GOD'S SAKE WILL YOU STOP IT!' She put the dot under the exclamation mark so savagely that the pen went through the paper. Aloud, she said 'Monsieur, have the kindness to give this to Mademoiselle Elise.' As I walked towards the door, someone whistled Laurel and Hardy's theme tune. Everyone was suddenly having a good time, with the exception of the critic of the *Irish Times*, who next morning said that a talented company's brave attempt at a piece of dramatic filigree had come to nought because of an inept performance in a key role. He named names.

By the time I read the review, I was on the 9.07 a.m. train to Westland Row and work, and it was too late to turn back. All that day, our office echoed to jovial cries of 'Has anybody seen my *Irish*

Times?' or 'What's on at the Peacock this week?' That evening at the theatre, everyone was so kind and pitying that I might have had a bereavement. Tadhg Murray consoled me musically: 'Deh *Times* has its hash and parsley, boy, don't mind it. Sure you were shovelling out caviare to deh shaggin' general.' The second-night audience was thin and dispirited, and my exit, which had previously brought the house down, now drew no more than a solitary snigger. The week dragged by, and on the Saturday, when I thought myself free of *Asmodée* for ever, Chris Clinton summoned the cast. Rubbing his nose as if it were Aladdin's lamp, he announced that, to recoup our losses, he had arranged for a Sunday night performance at the Little Flower Hall in Bray, twelve miles from town.

'It'll be a Sweeney Todd audience,' he said, 'so for once let us not be diffident.'

What he was saying was that Bray playgoers had forthright tastes, and, if they could not have the homespun comedies of Lennox Robinson, then they wanted drama that was full-blooded, such as Bryan McMahon's *The Bugle in the Blood* or George Shiels's *The Rugged Path*. The rarefied nature of *Asmodée*, with one Gallic nuance swooning upon another, was likely to cause murmurs, if not aggrieved cries, of 'Codology'. It was hardly, as Christ advised us, an occasion for 'diffidence'.

In the event, we did not commit the sin of over-acting; rather, we put into the play what Mauriac had been so foolish as to leave out. To the devil with pussyfooting: we gave them drama and knew we had a success on our hands when an excited whisper was heard from the audience of, 'God, the mother's in love with the young lad.' As for me, I had at last hit a kind of stride. In the play, my character was a spoiled priest, and on that account the audience, being Irish and mostly Catholic, took a proprietary interest in me. During Act Two, when I was giving what I knew in my bones was a three-dimensional portrayal of a man brought low by sins of the flesh, a child began to cry in the audience. Its mother and a few others hushed it, at which, delighted by what it took for encouragement, it turned up the volume. It and I competed for some few minutes; then the mother, at the end of her endurance, turned upon the infant with a howl of: 'Shut up! Shut up, or I'll get him down to you!' She was, of course, referring to me.

Unless he happens to be playing in Grand Guignol, it is never pleasurable for an actor to find himself brandished like a fist at delinquent children. It is even worse when he is giving a performance which, if there were justice in the world, would draw tears from a turnip. It is a knife-blade in the heart when, seemingly in response to its mother's threat, the infant becomes instantly docile – and that is what happened in the Little Flower Hall. The child's silence was an invitation to the audience to look upon me with new eyes. They happily did so, and my acting career went sharply downhill, reaching bottom with the climactic scene between the tutor and his employer.

'Madame' has discovered that the young Englishman is not for her; she must send the lovers away, pick up the shards of her own broken life and survive as best she can. Seizing his opportunity, the tutor tells her that all is not lost; happiness may still be hers if she will but choose a half-loaf over no bread. To this end, I had what an actor loves most in the world after money: a four-minute speech; and it ended with the words, tenderly spoken: 'Are you listening, Marcelle? Are you listening?'

As the script demanded, there was a suspenseful pause, and then Kitty O'Brien turned to me with ice-blue eyes and delivered the ultimate rebuff. 'I beg your pardon, Monsieur Lebel,' she said, 'but I thought I heard you call me by my first name.'

Humiliated, I was supposed to mumble abjectly and slink off, but before I could do so a female voice from the audience spoke out clearly. Evidently its owner was one of my few remaining admirers, for what she said was: 'Ah, the poor fucker, he's done for now.'

Twenty years later, I took a curtain-call from the stage of the Kurfurstendamm Theatre in Berlin. I had written a play which was not unanimously liked, and booing broke out from the rear of the stalls. I felt the smile on my face become a rictus, and, to survive the barrage, ransacked my mind for an even worse débâcle. Into my head came that Sunday evening in Bray. The audience on that occasion did not boo: they shrieked. They howled like ruptured sewage pipes; utter strangers fell sobbing into each other's laps; a man toppled off his chair.

My first instinct was to get off the stage and out of Bray; then I remembered that this evening marked my last every performance as Blaise Lebel. I saw myself months – perhaps years – in the future recalling the ignominy of this swan-song and going red with shame. A cold anger came over me. I was damned if I would allow the Philistines to win; just this once, I would have my way with them. I stood stockstill, now facing the audience, with Kitty O'Brien staring at me, wondering why I had not yet gone. Then, with a daring that was not in my nature, I raised a hand for silence. To my delirium, it worked: the laughter slackened and died away with a last gurgle like the farewell of water in a bath. With the audience back in the hollow of my hand, I turned to Kitty and ad libbed a line, delivering it with consummate dignity.

'Goodbye, madame. I think it unlikely that we shall meet again.'

It was my finest hour and, leaving the stage, I could feel an ovation welling up and about to erupt. Unfortunately, my way off was by way of a flight of stairs, which was no more than three wooden steps, the topmost vanishing behind a piece of scenery. Once an actor had attained this summit and was safely out of sight of the audience, he did a careful about-turn, knelt and just as gingerly lowered himself to stage level. Such was the panache of my exist, however, that I not only took the stairs at a run, but did so two steps at a time. There were, as I have said, three of them in all.

In mid-air, my hands, shooting out for a means of breaking my fall, found and seized upon a length of rope or thick cord hanging from above. I have no idea what it was attached to, but it held and I swung like Tarzan on a vine, not further into the wings, but back on to the stage, carrying a part of the château wall with me. The flat – a sheet of canvas stretched on a wooden frame – fell forwards and sent up a cloud of dust. It was not dense enough, however, to hide the sight of me coming in to land, or of Tadhg Murray, industriously buttoning his flies preparatory to his entrance.

Kitty O'Brien looked at me as if under the impression that I should by now be at the local S.N.C.F. station waiting for the Paris train. Her lips parted as if to speak, but the manner of my return, not to mention the dust storm, had routed all thought from her mind, and her mouth closed again like a steel trap. It would be nice to record that a *bon mot* tripped off my tongue, but all I managed to say was a whispered, 'Sorry Kitty I mean Madame.' It went unheard, but it was no matter. Laughter again billowed from out front and crashed like breakers on an alien shore. I heard a chair fall over. People were saying, 'Stop, stop.' You knew that months and perhaps years from now, old people would wake up in the small hours, think of this evening and choke to death, their elbows stabbing the air in anguished entreaty that a priest be sent for. As for me, there was nothing to do but attempt to leave the stage for a second time. Understandably, I was distraught; otherwise, I would not have gone up the steps again.

My course was set before I realised that the collapse of the flat had revealed the stairs in their pathetic entirety. I was at the top of the three steps in a trice, and stood there like a gold medallist in the Idiots' Olympics. It was an image that may have occurred to members of the audience, for applause broke out. As to the means of getting down, I was for a moment undecided, then leaped boldly towards the wings, hardly noticing Chris Clinton and Tadhg Murray, who, in full view of the audience, were struggling to hoist the flat back into place.

In the last scene of *Asmodée*, the young couple have gone away and the household has resumed its quiet tenor. Madame looks at the recalcitrant tutor, now and forever brought to heel, and says: 'You may read to me, Monsieur Lebel.' Whereupon, taking a volume from the bookcase, I would say 'Flaubert, Madame?' and bring the play to its end by adding somewhat coyly: 'Perhaps *L'Éducation Sentimentale?*' On this Sunday evening, the curtain fell when Kitty O'Brien went to the French windows, looked out into the gathering dusk and cooed: 'Monsieur Lebel, will you come and read to me?' She had little choice because by then, I was already past Shankhill, pedalling furiously towards home and still wearing my stage make-up: a patina of number 3½ Leichner grease paint, eye-shadow, a crow's nest or two, and a satanic white streak in my hair.

My intention was never to return to Bray, but a month or so later an amateur actor, in his *alter ego* of electrician, fell off the roof of the town hall, and at a weekend's notice I was asked to take over his part in Paul Vincent Carroll's *The Old Foolishness*. That was when I first encountered Father Maurice Browne. He was senior curate of Bray, a Tipperary man and greyhound fancier. He was tall, balding, suave and autocratically benign. His walk was patrician, his smile gracious. When you spoke to him, his ear swung towards you so that you could count its hairs, but his pale blue eyes twinkled at passersby, as if inviting them to witness his readiness to humour even the most lowly of God's beings. His condescension was natural and unforced; as a man of simple faith, he never wavered in the belief that he was doted upon by his parishioners. He had written a novel of country life entitled *The Big Sycamore* and was presently at work upon a play, *Prelude to Victory*, set in the days of the Black and Tans and rabidly anglophobic. He promised to write me what he called a plum role, and, when the time came, I was cast as 'Third Black and Tan', with one line: 'Which w'y did the bawstid double back?' – an enquiry which, when one thought about it, seemed to answer itself.

Like most of Paul Vincent Carroll's plays, *The Old Foolishness* has as one of its major characters a tyrannical canon, compared with whom Edward Moulton Barrett would have seemed not only of sunny temperament but positively waggish as well. In the Bray production, this cleric was played by a mild fellow named Peter Nolan, whom short-sightedness had endowed with a scowl of direst villainy; also, his rented suit, originally of clerical black, had turned green with age and gave him the appearance of a troll. Before the first act was over, a small queue had formed outside the presbytery to lodge a complaint with Father Browne in his capacity as priest, local censor and cultural guru. He came backstage after the performance and beamed upon us.

We were great, he said, Oh, topping; grand, A.1. And there was not an iota of harm in the play. Sure no one minded the man Carroll. What was he and writers the likes of him but poor blades of apostate chaff cut down by the winnowing wind of Heaven?

Possibly, I emitted a small snort of mirth at the alliteration, for his gaze fell on me, calm and smiling.

'Ah, he said, 'we have a newcomer among us. From the city, I have no doubt.'

'He's from Dalkey, Father,' the group's leading actress, Ronnie Byrne, volunteered, adding: 'He took over from Colbert Martin.'

'Do you tell me? And from Dalkey.' He kept me trapped in the kindly searchlights of his eyes. 'Ah, a grand little town, part of the borough of Dun Laoghaire, home of the West Britons, or do I mean the Little Englanders, what would we do without them? And you're a grand actor, yes, you are. All I was privileged to see of you was in Act Three, but I split my sides. However, the Bray people (sure God love them) are not as well up in the ways of the world as, dare I say it, the inhabitants of the Pale. Not as sophisticated as your excellent self, have you me?'

Artful devil that he was, he waited for an answer and got it: a cowed and barely audible 'Yes, Father.' It was Father Creedon over again, but this time the de luxe streamlined version.

Having settled my hash, he bathed the others in the soup-kitchen glow of his affection. Every one of them lived in the town and was known to him, and he addressed them as if he and they were fellow-conspirators. He told them that as good Catholics all – the three Protestants among them went red with shame and looked at the floor – the innocence of the devout, simple people of Bray was in their hands. Rather than become an occasion of scandal, let them not squander their time and talent on such unworthy babblings as *The Old Foolishness*.

One of the company piped up: 'Sure we weren't planning to do it again, Father . . .'

'Ah, grand.'

'. . . only at the Killarney drama festival next Sunday.'

Father Browne laughed with warm incredulity. 'Killarney? Do you mean it is your intention to perform this play, for want of a better name, in front of poor country people? And this is how the town of Bray is to be represented in the country of Kerry? No, you are making mock of me.'

We all gaped at him. The silence ended when he suddenly said 'God bless you all' and went quickly out of the hall, having first made the sign of the cross at us, concluding it with a lateral gesture that, had his fingers been a razor blade, would have slashed every throat in the place. He was gone before I realised that our play was banned.

He can't stop us from bringing it to Killarney,' I said, at once earning the snarled reply: 'You don't have to live here.'

Censorship carried the day, and the group replaced *The Old Foolishness* with *Frieda*, a tame melodrama from their previous season. It was the story of a German war-bride who arouses strong, if well-bred, emotions among her husband's Loamshire family, and once again I inherited a role originally played by Colbert Martin, he of the town-hall roof. It was the tiny role of the local vicar, and, being a quick study, I left the business of learning my few lines on the long finger: an hour's mugging up would suffice. I had never been to Killarney, however, and that glorious

121

summer day was spent lolling in a rowing boat on Lough Leane, one's senses blind drunk with the restless light that upon an instant created new mountains and as quickly exchanged them for old.

My words that evening were uncertain, but I wobbled through as far as my exit line: 'Remember what St Paul says: "Be not zealous over-much."' Instead, it came out as '". . . be not over-zealous muchly."' No one laughed; probably the audience assumed that 'muchly' was effetely upper-class English. In any case, the plays at Killarney were no more than an appetiser before the banquet itself: this being the appearance on-stage of the adjudicator, Micheál Mac Liammóir.

I had, of course, seen him countless times at the Gaiety and the Gate. His satins were Wilde and Beardsley. He wore stage make-up in public, varying it subtly with the seasons so that he was not tanned in winter or merely pink in summer, and sported an unlikely wig of jet black. His voice did not speak, but crooned; it told of an explosion in a caramel factory; it flowed over its listeners, drowning all in its path, rolling in languorous flood over the weirs of stops and commas, stopping to draw breath not even between words but within them. He could not or would not pronounce the sound 'ow'; from his lips, a particular sentence, a favourite of elocutionists, would have emerged as a ripe 'Ho no, brrone co'. He believed in the theatre as a temple of which, an unregenerate Edwardian, he was high priest. The jargon of theatre includes the term 'throwaway lines'; Mac Liammóir never threw away a word in his life.

In the town hall at Killarney, he came upon the stage as we the actors stood behind him. He bowed to us, turned to the audience, placed the back of one hand against his forehead as if to avert a swoon, then summarised *Frieda* in one great non-stop exhalation: 'Ladies and gentlemen this is the kind of play you know the kind of play it is Father's dead pass the marmalade.'

He went on to hold forth upon some of the performances,

weaving not so much a tapestry of words, as a verbal Book of Kells, illuminating his manuscript in mid-flight. Of our young leading lady, Annaliese Fuchs, he deduced, correctly, that she was not German but Austrian and, like Professor Higgins homing in on a Lisson Grove accent, actually named the Viennese suburb where she had grown up. He let us off lightly, but as soon as the curtain had fallen he enfolded a terrified Ronnie Byrne in a Don Juan embrace and said: 'Oh, my poor naughty darling, was I awfully cruel to you?' Catching sight of me as I looked on, he said: 'Ah the reverrrend gentleman. You were marvellous, did I mention you?' Before I could reply, he dragged me over to a leather-bound notebook that lay open on his lectern. 'There! That's what I said about you,' he exclaimed for all to hear and slammed the book shut before I could read a syllable.

Years later, while reviewing for *Plays and Players*, I was so intemperate as to speak ill of Mac Liammóir's Claudius, damning it as 'the same old glutinous marzipan'. Although we had not yet met, apart from that moment in Killarney town hall, he kept the clipping in his wallet and would read it aloud on public occasions – once at a luncheon where, mortified, I was present. It was years before he forgave me, if he ever did. Towards the end of his life, I wrote a piece describing him and his partner, Hilton Edwards, as a pair of 'incorrigible Renaissance men'. He wrote me a long, effusive letter quoting from *Twelfth Night*: 'I can no other answer make but thanks, and thanks and ever thanks'; and ended by advising me: 'Jack, never grow old.'

The last time I saw him was at a party. He was thin; his legs had become spindly and weak. He had given up wearing his wig, revealing, to everyone's amazement, a perfectly good head of hair underneath, and had recently undergone an operation for cataracts. A pair of horn-rimmed spectacles now hung around his neck, but he was too vain to wear them in public. When the time came to go downstairs for supper, I saw that he was unsteady on his feet and asked if I could take his arm.

He said, the voice still a word-caressing purr: 'No, darling Jack, but I'll tell you what we can do. As we go down, walk behind me with your good right hand on my left shoulder and your dear face not far from mine. In that way, you can guide me while we pretend to be having a *tête-à-tête*.'

When he died a few months later, he took the precious little that was glamorous about Irish theatre with him.

As for Father Browne, he was later promoted out of Bray and became parish priest of Ballymore Eustace in County Kildare, but still I had not seen the last of him. It was the policy of Lancos Productions to mount two plays each year: one, a glossy affair, done to show our colleagues at work that we were really too good for the likes of them; the second, a crowd-pleaser which toured to country villages, with the profits halved between the local priests and ourselves. Word came from Father Browne that we would not be unwelcome in Ballymore Eustace. A high tea would be provided.

We arrived by bus and went, as directed, to a café where a woman put a cup of tea and a small triangular ham sandwich in front of each of us. A heroic soul asked for another sandwich. 'Only the one has been paid for,' the woman told him and the rest of us, with a look that all but turned the milk in its jug. It needed only Wackford Squeers to explode upon the scene with a cry of 'Here's richness!'

Outside the parochial hall, Father Browne greeted us affably, his eyes fixed, as usual, on a point somewhere down the street. His genius as an impresario was shortly in evidence, to a degree where we had cause to reflect that Rome's gain was Broadway's and the West End's loss. It was a Sunday, and, as soon as the evening devotions were over, his curates and a small band of parish elders assumed the roles of German shepherd dogs, driving the worshippers from church to hall as if they were sheep on their way to be dipped. Only a handful of the poor devils struck out for open country and escaped. The hall filled up to the point where one could not have introduced a cat without the danger of mass suffocation. Those unable to find chairs sat on the bare floor, the window sills and the radiators; a few young gymnasts were actually astride the rafters high up under the roof.

I squinted out through the curtain and calculated that our share of the night's proceedings would go far towards fulfilling our dream of some day travelling to one of the British drama festivals. Father Browne was at my elbow. I said: 'What a crowd. I've never seen any thing like it.'

'Well you may say so,' he replied gravely. 'Oh, a washout.'

I searched his face for a sign that he was joking.

He sighed: 'Well, that's Ballymore Eustace for you. Ballymore Useless is more like. Oh, a hopeless people. They'll support nothing.'

He had had to raise his voice to be heard over the babel from the audience. As he walked away with a smile that King Lear would not have scorned to use, I took another look through the curtains just in case what I had seen the first time had been an hallucination brought on by hunger.

Our play was *Cartney and Keaveney*, a sour farce by George Shiels, a crippled writer who wrote crippled comedies in which cupidity always won and the devil had the best tunes. I played Cartney, a sponging ne'er-do-well who ends up coercing landlord and employer into supporting him rent-free and work-free for life. Rural audiences loved its rascality, and the packed house at Ballymore Eustace cheered us to the crowded rafters. Afterwards, Father Browne conducted the mandatory raffle for two hundred cigarettes.

'Let us not ask Cartney to draw the winning ticket,' he said, eyeing me and chuckling. 'Given the kind of scoundrel he is, he might draw out his own.' Adoring laughter broke out.

And so he himself conducted the draw, announced the winning number, only to see me, brandishing a raffle ticket, come forward to claim the prize. For once, his smile slipped as I accepted the ten packs of Capstan without having the decency to implore that they be raffled again. A few weeks later, he wrote to us, reiterating that the occasion had been a 'washout' and sprinkling vinegar on the wound by adding that our high tea had used up the few miserable shillings taken at the door. His letter was accompanied by a small box of chocolates for the ladies of our company. In a spirit of pure malice, I sent him an invoice for his half of the performance fee. He replied saying that the evening's proceeds, had there been any, would have gone towards the needs of the parish, therefore the question of paying royalties did not arise. The uncorrupted ways of the country, he reminded me, if he could make so bold, were not the ways of the city, where the pound note was God Almighty.

We steered clear of Father Browne after that, which in a way was a pity, for our production of *The Righteous are Bold* would have gone like a house on fire in Ballymore Eustace. It was a melodrama in which a girl returns home to County Mayo after working as a servant in London, where her employers obliged her to participate at a séance. She is hardly back under her parents' thatch than she has spat upon and decapitated a statuette of the Virgin (the play was an Abbey Theatre stalwart, and the programme invariably featured a note saying 'The holy statues broken in this production have not been blessed'). In Act Two, the wise old parish priest diagnoses the girl's problem: she is a victim of diabolic possession. The third act contains the exorcism and ends with the death of the priest, which, in accordance with spiritual swings-and-roundabouts, is deemed obligatory in such proceedings.

Our visit to Blessington on the edge of the Wicklow hills met with such acclaim that we were invited to give a return performance. There was a national petrol strike on at the time, and no buses were running on Sundays; undaunted, the local priests possessed what they called 'a great leg' of the local undertaker and had us conveyed the sixteen miles from town by hearse and two mourning coaches. The brace of curates were the jolliest of fellows and as plump as capons, and had so much enjoyed the play on its previous visit that, without a word to us, they had contrived to enliven the evening with a few special effects. The first of these occurred early in Act Two when I, as the old priest, was putting a flea in the ear of the local doctor, an agnostic. The latter role was played by a man whom I shall call Jim Beamish, a barrel-chested ex-army captain with a fiery military moustache, who happened to be a roaring alcoholic. He had only recently dried out from an eighteen-month rampage and, for a big man, looked as if a summer breeze could be the end of him. His face had a pink, damp look.

'Doctor,' I said to him suavely, 'have you ever heard of a person being possessed of the devil?'

On the instant, there came an apocalyptic clap of thunder and the stage was enveloped in light of a hellish green. The audience screamed in an ecstasy of terror. Cries were heard of 'Oh, Jesus, Mary and Joseph'. The lights flickered and reverted to normal, but Beamish's face remained as green as if it had been dyed. His forehead shone. In reply to my line, he was supposed to say: 'Possessed of the devil, Father? I thought that you of all clerics were immune from such superstitious mumbo-jumbo.' What he actually said was: 'Christ, I'm in the jigs.'

He was not heard out front; the audience was chattering like rooks at sunset, telling each other what an unmerciful fright they had had. I seized the opportunity to try and steer the play back on course and fed Beamish my next line, which was 'My dear doctor, it is a foolhardy man who denies the existence of Lucifer.' At this, the thunder crashed again and the stage was once more bathed in a corpselike green. Beamish began to tremble all over like a condemned tenement when a train goes past.

It was now clear that we had only to mention the devil, Lucifer or Beelzebub for one curate, standing in the wings, to rattle his home-made thunder-sheet, while the other had the time of his life switching on and off the green fairy lights he had so lovingly strung above the stage. Beamish gave every sign of dropping dead at the next thunderclap, and so, thinking frantically ahead, I managed to get to the end of our scene by cutting every further reference to the powers of darkness. In the context of the play, it was like performing *Othello* without the kerchief or *Antony and Cleopatra* minus the asp.

Worse was to follow during the exorcism scene in Act Three. Audiences never failed to thrill to the sight of our star actress, Róisín Ni Nualláin (an understandable alternative to Rosie Nolan), bound hand and foot, writhing on the floor at my feet and spitting out what came as near to obscenities as an Irish parish hall could contain in the year 1954. During the interval, the ladies of the company had with much kissing and cooing and fluttering of eyelids restrained Jim Beamish from fleeing to the nearby Downshire House for a ball of malt, so that he was back on-stage, even if now crushed in spirit and only there as so much human furniture.

We came to what Americans call the 'top of the show'. Róisín, who was a niece of the comedian and pantomime dame, Jimmy O'Dea, had eyes as expressive as his. Also, and as I have said, she could curl her lower lip into the most malignant of sneers, and during the exorcism it came close to resembling a Swiss roll. She snarled and spewed out execrations, her bound feet kicking at whoever came near, while the audience sat dumb and whey-faced with horror. I began the business of casting out the demons: '*Exorciso te, immundissime spirituus . . .*' Out of the corner of my eye, I saw what was unmistakably a double-barrel of a shotgun poking out from the wings.

As Róisín emitted an ear-piercing scream to signal that the devil was quitting her body, there was an explosion that Father Browne could have heard in Ballymore Eustace seven miles away. A ball of fire travelled across the stage, and Róisín, as if by way of suggesting that Lucifer was still within her, achieved spontaneous levitation from a supine position to a height of several inches.

All that remained to happen was for the old priest to expire, presumably from heart failure, and in my condition it required not much acting ability. Jim Beamish, perspiring again, but now to a degree where he was fast dehydrating, managed to pronounce me dead and closed my eyes, his hands shaking so badly that I was unable to read small print for a week. As we took our curtain call, the parish priest of Blessington came on the stage. Compared with his jovial curates, he was of the old school and had probably first been given nightmares by the Redemptorists when he was six or seven. Calling us Cosmos Productions, he offered his admiration for such a thought-provoking drama; then, without putting a tooth in it, he told the audience that what they had seen was the kind of thing that happened to Irish girls who went to work in England. There were no exceptions, he said grimly. He then conducted a raffle for a bottle of Paddy.

By then, Jim Beamish had left the hall, and although it was now after licensing hours, found a publican who assisted him to alight from the water-wagon, and down the years was never again seen on or in the vicinity of that vehicle. The audience, on emerging into the unlit street, found themselves confronted by the village hearse which, unknown to them, was waiting to take the actors back to town. When a group of us climbed into the rear, some of the onlookers were reassured, others not.

As we drove off, people hung around in small bunches, afraid to walk the country roads home. That was two or three years before the first coming of television, and soon thereafter ghosts and the devil lost their power to frighten. It is perhaps a pity that when ignorance is laid to rest it must often take simplicity with it.

7

Once, at a party, I overheard a woman guest speaking to my daughter, who was then sixteen. She was using the kind of orphans-picnic voice that carefully spoons out a word at a time and has been put by for encounters with small children, mental defectives and people who read lips. 'What,' the lady wanted to know, 'will you do when you leave school?'

'I want to get out of here,' my daughter said.

I had been standing just to one side, glass in hand, smiling a half-smile on which I could either freewheel into the conversation or pedal away from it, as I chose. Before the smile could lose its footing, I bore it and the hurt, cold in my stomach, to the front window of our living room. The immediate 'here' my daughter had mentioned was the house we had moved into on our return from an exile in London. It looked out towards Wales, and on one or two sharp days each winter one could see the white cap of Snowdon, a shard of broken delph trodden into the sea. Off to the south, the Wicklow Mountains, like Edwardians on Whitsun, walked primly along the curve of Shanganagh. As well as our house, we had two acres of grass to lie in, an old tree, soft rain from the south-west and sunlight that stung the eyes. There were worse places to live. In the wider sense, the 'here' she wanted to get out of might have been Ireland as a whole, which was understandable. If, as Napoleon said, *tout soldat français porte dans sa giberne le bâton de maréchal de France*, it is equally true that, pinned behind every Irish First Communicant's rosette, there is a one-way mailboat ticket to Holyhead.

Less easy to face was the thought that she might have wished to be quit of her mother and me. It was unthinkable, and yet, just as every actor will accept as his due his one hostile notice amid an avalanche of praise, I unhesitatingly ran to embrace the idea that my wife and I had somehow failed our darling. All her life, we had tried to walk the razor edge between sternness and over-indulgence; in her teens, we treated her not as the child-that-had-once-been, but as the adult-that-was-soon-to-be. As parents, and not at all by design, my wife and I complemented each other to perfection. She could endure a crippling bereavement dry-eyed, and yet would openly lavish affection upon our daughter, one or two friends and all animals, rodents excluded. I, on the other hand, would sob uncontrollably at *La Bohème* or even at such bathos as Merle Oberon dying in Olivier's arms in *Wuthering Heights*, and yet was so incapable of physically embracing those I loved that I would go to absurd lengths to make plain that my fondness for them was not absent, merely lurking. My wife provided her daughter with food, love and warm clothes, nursed her when she was ill, drove her to school and attended the parent-teacher meetings that I shirked. I saw to it that *my* daughter walked in St Mark's Square, ate sauerkraut in the Alsterpavilion in Hamburg, saw *Robert and Elizabeth* from the front row, and read Maugham when she was eleven and Wodehouse – who was the more serious writer – when she was twelve.

These days, what my wife and I have come to share is less a daughter than a best friend; but for perhaps a week after hearing her so casually say 'I want to get out of here', I caressed my pain as if it were a lover's gift. I have always soon grown tired of my toys, and, once I became bored with being hurt, I grew up another millionth of an inch – it happens even now – and accepted that she simply craved for her freedom. Nothing, as they say, personal. She wanted her four years at Trinity, a roof of her own, and a life and an identity that were hers and not ours. Her bags were already packed. At her age, I had been just as eager to be on my way, but there was a difference. She was impatient for what lay ahead; I was uncaring as to what the future held: I simply wanted to escape from my parents and our town.

One evening, when I was perhaps twenty, I accompanied my father to the parochial hall to play House, which elsewhere was known as housey-housey, but would attain its apotheosis as Bingo. I have no idea why I went with him: possibly there was nothing worth seeing at the Picture House, the Pavilion or the Astoria; or perhaps my conscience told me it was high time I kept him company for an hour. Rather, I think I was making a half-hearted attempt to be part of the town, to put on boots that for once were not too big for me. I was not locally regarded as special, still less as a prodigy, but I had won a scholarship to a school for the sons of bank managers and pork butchers and had made matters worse by soaring far above the Dalkey earthlings and into the civil service (no one realised or, if told, would believe the very real degradation of what my mother proudly described to our neighbours as a 'bobby's job'). Also, I kept my nose in a book as I walked along; I was never out of picture houses and had not a word to throw to a dog. The town's verdict was that if you were eejit enough to adopt a nurse-child, I, in the heel of the hunt, was what you were liable to end up with. The House players were exclusively male; married women were supposed to stay contentedly at home, while the unmarried kind were either out courting or indoors offering up their acne, gift wrapping it for God, with rosary beads as string. I caught sight of my father's friends, Oats Nolan and Gunger Hammond. He went over to talk to them, and I heard him fire off his opening round: an immutable 'Do yous know what I'm going to tell yous?' If any took leave to disagree with whatever it was he told them, he would round upon the heretic with a face like a clenched fist and shout: 'What are you talkin' about, or do you know what you're talkin' about?' De Valera was his God, and sooner or later I could see his cheek-bones turn to a red as dark as yesterday's blood, and, as his voice rose, Father Kearney would cross the floor with an urbane 'Now, men, no politics.' I never knew whether the 'men' was meant in a gruff, comradely sense or was a kind of village apartheid that sited my father and his cronies as being half-way between males and gentlemen. The conversation would at once become a debate on whether today's running at Leopardstown or Fairyhouse had been fast or soft.

Father Kearney, who was to act as caller, positioned himself at the top table, and Young Gunger Hammond, who had inherited his father's nickname, distributed small tablets of stained wood, each criss-crossed into squares and with numbers hand-painted in red. Somehow, I was overlooked and put my hand up. When I had caught Young Gunger's eye, I said: 'May I have a board, please?'

He gave me one without comment; then I heard him snigger: 'A board!'

What I should have asked for was a 'card', but I had known no better – it was, after all, a piece of wood. Young Gunger moved behind me out of sight, but my ears were like radar, and I heard him guffaw 'Jayzus, a board!' There were a few appreciative cackles from those who were in on the joke, and, whenever he was in my vicinity for the rest of the evening, he would repeat 'A board!' as if it were funnier than Jimmy O'Dea being Mother Goose in the Gaiety. My father, over whose head it was, took note of the eruptions of mirth and made matters worse by nudging me and saying: 'Oh, Young Gunger is a queer harp!'

It was the most trifling of incidents, but if I remember it forty years later it is because I can still feel my cold rage against the town and the sniggers. I was not, they were telling me, as godly a being as I thought myself. More importantly, I was not of their number and would never be. Years later, I was to write a play called *A Life*, with a central character based on my old civil service nemesis, Mr Drumm. As a young man, he speaks at a public debate and is heckled by a group for the town ne'er-do-wells out for an evening's sport. Forty years on, elderly and embittered, he recalls the experience:

'I understood. It was a punishment. I had broken the eleventh commandment. I had tried to be different, to be a clever boy, the born genius. Well, they were not impressed. I had discovered that cleverness was like having a deformed hand. It was tolerated as long as you kept a glove on it. I actually believed that if I spoke well and carried the argument they would admire me. I craved it. I wanted to be One of Our Own. Dear God, what a contemptible ambition: to please the implacable.'

Probably, while inventing a past for Desmond Drumm, I had revisited that evening when I and the town drew up our separate battle lines; then, having inflated what had been a small embarrassment into a major humiliation, I bestowed it on Drumm, using it to alter the course of his stage life for the worst. A writer can have it both ways: he can return to the past, take a small moment that led nowhere, a road down which he dared not travel, and ask himself 'What if . . .?'

What had happened at the parochial hall was an incident, a nothing, a moment of elephantine fun for Young Gunger, who – the only Gunger, now that his father is long dead – passes me daily in Castle Street without a nod, for I am still not One of Our Own. In those days, though, I had a low humiliation threshold. I recall that I once went for lunch to the cafeteria above Woolworth's in Henry Street. It may have been pay day, for I loaded my plate with soup, a roll and butter, grey roast beef, soapy potatoes, ball-bearing peas, and a liquescent trifle. I found a table and set the tray down, only to see it tip over the edge with a Bartok-like discord of plates and cutlery. I could not have believed that a one-and-ninepenny lunch, including a cup of mud-coloured coffee, could have serviced such an impressive area of tiled floor. All conversation died. A hundred tatters of beef hung motionless, like battle banners in a lull, from a hundred forks. The silence could be heard two streets off as I salvaged the bread roll, wiped it on my jacket and bore it away, past the tables, the cane-backed chairs and the gapers. As I reached the stairs, a young waitress followed me. She said 'Ahem' very loudly, possibly because I was not of an age to be called 'Mister'. When I did not pause in my flight, she cried out: 'Young lad, come back. I have your dinner for you.' I flung back at her that I was in a hurry and ran out into Henry Street, brought closer to tears by the kindness than the calamity that had provoked it.

Behind my fury at Young Gunger and the rest of them, there was a sly back lane of my mind where I was already turning my chastisement to good use. It eased my conscience to be the victim, to have it thrown at me – or so I chose to believe – that I was an outsider. Now it was not I but the town who was severing what I hated most: the strings that tied me to home. No one could accuse me of desertion when, in a hundred small ways, I was being set adrift. If I was to be flailed at with briars, I would take care to emerge smelling of roses.

Every Sunday from the pulpit, Father Kearney sang the virtues of simplicity. Faith was to be accepted, not debased by thought. Women were modest, men manly; misfortunes were not to be railed against, but offered up. Our parish priest would have walked barefoot on hot coals rather than contaminate himself by reading the anti-Christ, James Joyce, and yet could not have agreed more passionately with Gabriel Conroy in *The Dead* that ours was a sceptical and 'thought-tormented' age. We should not, he said, seek to ape the ways of film stars in divorce-racked Hollywood. He mentioned, as an example of modern decadence, a recent street brawl between the MGM star, Franchot Tone, and a monogram B-player, Tom Neal, for the hand and private parts of a blonde actress named Barbara Payton. It did not occur to him that Crutch Kelly from Sallynoggin and Bomber Young who lived on the Bus Lawn had beaten each other to bloody pulp outside Larkin's pub only the previous evening. Harry Young, who was dark of skin, had earned his nickname because of his likeness to the 'Brown Bomber', Joe Louis, but the resemblance stopped there, and Kelly, who had a withered leg, ended the fight by wrapping his crutch around Bomber's neck. To Father Kearney, everyday mayhem, as long as there was not a Barbara Payton to contaminate the proceedings, was not in the least pass-remarkable. Having disposed of Hollywood, he had even less good to speak of England, an abode of godlessness and free-thinkers.

Simplicity was all. It was the bedrock of the faith of our fathers, which, as the hymn attested, was living still in spite of dungeon, fire and sword. To him, yeoman and foeman were indistinguishable. He told us stories of a whole convent school of innocent girls, who were flung over a cliff by the soldiery, and the nuns after them, for refusing to speak well of the Protestant God to the detriment of His Catholic counterpart. Those girls – with, of course, the nuns in attendance – had gone straight to Heaven. The nuns, he assured us, just in case a title of doubt should exist, would have gone there even if not thrown over the cliff.

Once, during the annual Retreat, one of the missioners came to Harold Boys' School. He was a Capuchin, a bluff, jovial chap who, while our headmaster, Mr Mullen, looked on, treated the boys as men of the world. For a reason lost in time, Mr Mullen was nicknamed 'Tabac', the Irish for tobacco. He was bald and red-faced, and in moments of stress would dislodge his lower dentures and rotate them gently around the interior of his mouth, with a faint rattling noise as they now and then collided with the stationary top set. He put them in motion when, to his alarm, the missioner invited us to ask whatever questions we liked. 'Fire away, lads,' he said, 'the bolder the better!' To Tabac, it was as if a tightrope walker, bidding farewell to sanity, had set fire to his safety net.

The missioner was in good hands, however. We liked him. He was nice to us, and we were nice in return. We asked him about

Heaven.

Would we go there, Father?

To be sure we would. Sure 'twas well known the world over that the Irish had a great leg of God. Were we not His favourites?

And would it be nice there, Father?

Oh, 'twould be grand. Lovely. Sure could it be anything else when it was called Paradise? Now, come on, lads, ask me a hard one.

And, and, and, and, and, when we got to Heaven, Father, what would we do there?

Do there?

In Heaven, Father, all day long. What would we do?

We would have a great time.

But how, Father?

How? Now that was a good one. How? What would we do in Heaven? Ah. Yes, to be sure. We would give praise and adoration to God in His glory.

All day, Father?

Every minutes of every day, bedad, and *in saecula saeculorum*!

His smile was a proud beacon of promise, and in its silence we could hear the click of Tabac's dentures revving up. Until then, the missioner had been swathed in the cocoon of our affection; now, instantly, the temperature dropped. We each had our own idea of Heaven. Some saw it as Dalkey Hill, Sorrento Park and the White Rock beach, all rolled into one long swoon of summer days and red sunsets; to others, it was an everlasting picture show, with Buck Jones in one cowboy film and the Three Mesquiteers in the next, and free ice-cream cornets squirted with raspberry syrup handed out in between. Mine was a wild amalgam of south sea lagoons, western ranges and Jekyll and Hyde's London, with myself cast as both Dr and Mr; but even by those whose heavenly aspirations were modest, an eternity of praising God, even though there were few who deserved it more than He, seemed a barren source of entertainment.

Like all missioners, ours was a showman, and he knew that his audience had cooled. His notion of Heaven, our faces told him, was a cod of a yarn. When he saw my hand go up to ask a question, his eyes looked like those of a drowning man who had espied a floating plank. 'Yes, yes, good lad,' he said, urging me to the rescue. 'Fire away!'

It was no more than a year since, as a twelve-year-old, I had confessed to another missioner that I had committed self-abuse twice daily for a week, and I was chary of repeating the performance. But a certain aspect of Heaven had long perplexed me, and now was my chance to sort it out. 'Please, Father, when I go to Heaven will I meet my two granddas and grandmammies?'

Relief two-stepped on his brow. I had shown him a backstairs.

'You will, you will so,' he said eagerly. 'We will be reunited with our loved ones. God has given us His promise.'

His eyes raked the classroom for another question, but I was not done with him yet. 'And please, Father, in Heaven will my four granddas and grandmammies meet their own eight granddas and grandmammies?'

Tabac's early-warning system was a wonder then and is still marvelled at in the town today, forty years after he at last succumbed to stomach ulcers and boys; and my question caused his denture to stall half-way through one of its orbits. The missioner again smiled upon me. 'Oh begob they will.' He essayed a little joke. 'They'll be all together, like Brown's cows!'

'And, Father, will their eight granddas and grandmas meet their own sixteen granddas and grandmammies?'

At this, his smile became strained. 'To be sure,' he said and looked elsewhere.

I was now counting on my fingers. 'And, Father, will *their* sixteen granddas and grandmammies . . .?'

What I was relentlessly conjuring up was an image of a heaven throned with a billion relatives: a nudging, milling, grunting, jostling crowd of them, stretching to the Elysian horizon and going back to the Year Dot and beyond. Eternity would not be long enough for them to find each other, and even when they had done so, the introductions and sortings out would take another eternity on top of that one.

I was taken aback when the missioner, who suddenly bore not even a passing resemblance to a nice man, snarled at me: 'You're so smart you'll cut yourself.'

I looked to Tabac for comfort; he looked back at me, giving none. His teeth, once again on the move, were clattering around like a goods train on an iron bridge. The missioner screwed his skull-cap down on his head as if it were a lid on a jam jar, enquired of our statue of St Anthony holding the child Jesus why he (the missioner) was wasting his time, and allowed Tabac to see him to the front gate. I knew I had done nothing wrong, and yet a score of voices urged me to escape through the window, over the far wall and into White's Villas. Instead, with bowels melting, I sat awaiting the slam of a door, a Krakatoa of a belch, the crashing of bottles as Tabac searched for his milk of magnesia, and the snarl – my summons to the gibbet – of 'Get out here, ye whoor's melt!' The pity of it was that on the subject of Heaven I had had a second question for the missioner, and now it would never be answered, any more than the first had been.

Pope Pius XI had been ill recently, and his doctors were sparing no effort to save his life. Like most popes, he was never more eloquent than when assuring his flock that they were heirs to the kingdom of heaven and the everlasting bliss which awaited those who died in God's grace. I had wanted to ask why he himself, nonetheless, seemed perversely determined to keep out of the place for as long as he could. It was not, I thought, an unreasonable question; in fact, it might well have earned me a few pats on the head instead of the punches on it that I was in for from Tabac.

Unlike the missioner, Father Kearney never invited questions, nor did people such as my parents presume to ask them. They were amazed and grateful to come safely through the world, and they did so by placing themselves under the protection of powers that were both temporal and celestial. Apart from mass on Sundays, they made their Easter duties, and attended their sodalities – my father's, every second Friday, my mother's, every third. There were evening devotions, Holy Hours, Golden Hours, First Fridays and the yearly Retreat; in addition, my father was dispatched to early Mass every morning during Lent, and I was dragged, out of bed, blind with sleep and vicious with temper, to go with him. Whatever the occasion, the message never varied. All unhappiness, privations, and injustices, all hardships, suffering and reverses were to be welcomed as promissory notes drawn on the Bank of Heaven and encashable after death. One did not seek payment in this world. To do so, to resist misfortune, to demand that life should be better, was a slur upon the ultimate justice of God. It implied that the heavenly bank either did not exist or was insolvent.

If the sun shone, you saluted people on the street and said 'That's a grand day, thank God,' and they said 'Isn't it great, thank God' back to you. If it rained, however, no blame was attached to Him. A fine day simply meant that in His goodness He had spared us the downpour our sins deserved. Sunshine was a gratuity, not an entitlement. When I was in the civil service, a fellow clerk cajoled me into attending a one-day retreat run by the Franciscans on Merchants' Quay. There was a slap-up Sunday lunch of spring lamb; the mood was expansive, and afterwards, as a few of us strolled in the garden, an elderly priest brooded aloud on the growing tide of agnosticism and how it could be blamed squarely on pride of the intellect.

'Ah, me,' he said, 'the curse, the terrible curse of modern thought! Thought! That wayward lamb . . .' (given what we had just eaten, it was an uneasy metaphor) '. . . that flees the shepherd's fold, a poor foolish creature that will have no truck with what is tried and true, but instead rushes headlong to the precipice.'

Everyone nodded suavely. I stepped out of myself and to one side and beheld a group of young men in grave and yet heady discourse with a respected elder. We seemed to exist in a bubble world, idyllic and out of time. It occurred to me that Oxford was perhaps not unlike this, except that instead of dreaming spires what towered about us were Dublin tenements. Sunday noises came from the windows: a radio, with Billy Cotton shouting 'Wakey, wakey!', a child being called in from play, a man laughing. Across the Liffey by the Four Courts, a bus coughed its life out. It was not Oxford or anywhere near, and we were walking, not with a senior don, but an old Franciscan whose simplicity only a poltroon would have confounded with deadly argument.

Nonetheless, the temptation was not to be resisted, and so, without pausing to reflect that the same simple old Franciscan could have polished off a dozen of me before breakfast, I delivered my word-thrust to the heart.

'But, Father, what answer would you give to a misguided person who was to ask you: If thought is so evil, why then did God give us the power to think?'

Some of the others looked shocked that I should so brutally open fire upon a sitting target, but the old priest blessed me with the gentle, pitying smile of one who has yet again seen a donkey fall into the most venerable trap in Christendom.

'My son,' he said, 'I would tell the poor creature you mention that God in His goodness gave us brains so that we would have the wisdom to know when not to use them.'

It was worthy of Chesterton.

My parents, if they had had brains, would have buried them in the backyard sooner than tamper with them. If a priest smiled and shook hands with my mother, it was tuppence to talk to her for the rest of the day. If my father blindly obeyed his employers, Mr and Mrs Jacob, it was not simply because they paid his wages:

rather, it was because, being non-Catholics who addressed him as 'Keyes' without a 'Mister' attached, they were his betters: the Master and the Mistress, as he called them.

In writing a memoir, one is not only enabled to journey to the past, but must also pay the fare by at last looking in the face what it had once been politic to ignore. I knew that my foster-parents' marriage was not a love match; it had been arranged, and when my mother referred to my father as a 'good provider' I thought her both fair and comradely. Now I must admit that it was the only praise I heard her give him. She resented him as an interloper in her life and, because he was easygoing, thought him a fool. They were not even bound together by children, for those they had were stillborn. My mother saw her life as hard and with few rewards. Once, she entered into negotiations to buy my father a new Sunday suit, to be paid for at a half-crown per week, but the morning came when he, who had always had the constitution of a mule, got out of bed and at once fell back into it with threatened pneumonia. My mother threw holy water on him and sent for Dr Enright who, with his usual sigh of resignation, told her that, please God, the patient would recover. 'Maybe he will,' she said to me when the front door was closed behind him, 'but thank God and his Holy Mother I didn't sign for the suit.' Her affection for my father – or her want of it – was in this case not at issue; she was a realist, who, faced with the possibility of life without a breadwinner, was already counting the shillings.

Her life held several pleasures; one of them was complaining that it held none. Another was that on Mondays and Fridays, when she had done her shopping in Lipton's and the Home and Colonial Stores – her tongue declined to make more of the latter than the 'Home and Cologne' – and bought my father's two ounces of plug tobacco at Sir Thomas Browne's, she would make for the Picture House. It was a redbrick flea-pit where, having entered directly under the screen, you then walked backwards up the aisle to your seat, already goggling at the film. On the wall of the box office there were framed stills from the 1929 part-talking *Showboat*, starring Laura La Plante; they were still there when the Bug House, as we called it, closed its doors and became a branch of Burtons. She loved westerns, gangster films, epics of the North-West frontier, slapstick comedies and dramas of mother-love. She despised so-called sophistication: she would say that Greta Garbo gave her 'the sick', and the sight of a dinner jacket or a night-club interior was the signal for a growl of 'Oul' codology'. She despised love scenes, and her world was never the same again when, in a film called *Riding High*, Gene Autry actually kissed the heroine. 'Oh, the cur,' she said.

In spite of this, she was addicted to romantic novels, although what she enjoyed most were stories of the turf. She left it to the girl in the tuppence-a-book-a-week lending library to choose them for her, but would refuse to read anything written in the first person. 'I want none of your old "I . . . I" rubbidge,' she would say. Of an evening when the house was empty, or she thought it was, she would draw up a chair to the kitchen range, stir the coals into a blaze, hike her skirt up, light one of my father's old pipes, and become immersed in Ruby M. Ayres or Nat Gould. If I came in suddenly, she would thrust the pipe under the chair cushion and affect to read on unconcernedly, paying no attention to the plume of tobacco smoke that arose from beneath her.

I never knew my father to read a book. He went to whist drives and walked the dog across the hill and through the rabbit wood. Each day on his way back to Jacobs' after lunch – dinner, we called it – he would stop off at the bookie's and bet a shilling on an each-way treble for my mother and him. The sort she was, rather than have misfortune come upon her unawares, she would meet it on the doorstep, and my father was hardly around the corner of our lane, home for the day, than she would snap at him: 'I suppose me curse-o'-God horse is down the field again, bad scran to it?' On the occasions when his news was good, he would reply to this by removing his hat and flinging it ahead of him through the open door, whereupon she, knowing by heart what she must now endure, rolled her eyes in the manner of an El Greco saint and moaned that, like Greta Garbo, he would give a body the sick. 'Gimme your hand,' he would say, at which to spite him she would put both hands behind her back. Undaunted, he would reach with awful ceremony into his pocket and plank her winnings down on the kitchen table, one coin at a time and with a look implying that he himself had been not only the jockey, but the trainer, stable-boy and horse as well. And, even if he were to put a million pounds in front of her, she would say stonily, as she always did when the last coin was banged down: 'Is *that* all?'

Their daily newspaper was the *Irish Press* – 'Dev's paper', my father called it proudly; 'That rag!' my aunt Chris would gasp in fastidious disgust – and on Sundays they would take the *Dispatch*, the *Chronicle* and the *Pictorial* among others. Once, when I was nine or so, I was sent to Mammy Reilly's for these, and on my way back a man took me for a paper boy and bought the lot. I was too timid to tell him the truth and arrived home in tears with a fistful of coppers.

My head is like one of the tall milk jugs my mother kept on the dresser crammed with odds and ends: bits of wool, snapshots, racing dockets, a yellowed prayer cut from *Ireland's Own*, buttons, elastic bands, rosaries with beads missing. I have no idea why I should remember a 1940 issue of the *Sunday Pictorial* which, taking note of Hitler's fifty-first birthday, enjoined its war-time readers to partake of the crumb of comfort: 'Napoleon died at fifty-two!' Alongside this was a photograph of a girl almost wrapped in a silken shawl. Its edges did not quite meet, and from shoulder to ankle there was visible a narrow but unbroken strip of flesh, giving the impression that she was naked underneath. My mother glanced at the page without comment, probably because what she saw was the shawl, whereas what fascinated me was not merely the strip of skin, three inches by forty-eight, that I could see, but the vast, merely guessed-at, never-never land that I could not. The censors and I, aged twelve, had dirty minds in common, for the *Pictorial* was banned for salacity not long after.

People of my parents' class did not have friends. My mother had her neighbours and my father his old cronies with whom he would linger a while at the harbour wall, but they did not meet these by appointment, nor did anyone, relatives excepted, come to the house as invited guests. It was not the done thing. To be married meant that the time for foolishness was over with, and friendships, having played their part, were to be put aside. The rules laid down that a man and wife should be sufficient for each other. A bad husband went out to the pub; a dutiful one stayed at home, except perhaps for the occasional whist drive. My parents listened to the wireless, ticked off horses on the racing page, and went to bed at eleven.

One of the black days in my father's life was when my grandmother died and my mad aunt Mary, my mother's sister, came to stay. My aunt Chris who, married to a civil servant and living in a house with stairs in it, was the success of the family, had promised the old woman that when the time came she would take Mary. In the event she reneged. 'John refuses to have her,' she told mother, as if that cherub would for an instant have looked crosswise at her airiest wish. The truth was that her neighbours in Albert Park (she had once given me a fearsome wigging for accidentally addressing a Christmas card to 'Albert Place') and friends on Burdett and Ballygihen Avenues were married to bank clerks and haberdashers, well-thought-of-men who, like John, wore a collar and tie on weekdays, and the thought of them finding out that she had a mad sister was too appalling to contemplate. And Mary was not a modest, unobtrusive sort of looney: she made a meal of it: she rolled her eyes, let her tongue flop out like a red leather bookmark, scowled, cursed her enemies, who were legion, and trundled a pram filled with dolls. She used this like a small bulldozer, aiming it unerringly at shins and calves and inflicting such grievous mutilations that one expected to see knife-blades on the wheels. Even without it, she was dangerous. One of the sights of the town was Mary, using her handbag as a mace, the while galumphing along like a rhino vandalising the African undergrowth.

My mother was delighted to take her, pram, dolls and all. She enjoyed putting Chris at a moral disadvantage; now, she could say that, although poor and hard put to it to feed another mouth, she was more of a Christian than her well-off sister, so full of codology that she walked like there was a poker stuck up her. It is just possible that, as a family, the Doyles may have loved each other, but I never saw the faintest evidence of any liking. My father had no say in the matter of Mary living with us. When my mother adopted me, ten days old, she did not even consult him in advance, but simply arrived home by tram one day with a *fait accompli* wrapped in several blankets; so with that as a precedent, he had less than no chance of thwarting Mary's arrival.

Years before, when the last of several still-births had almost killed my mother, a doctor told her that another pregnancy would be fatal. The Church, knowing that celibacy was, in every sense of the word, child's play, gave her the easy choice of chastity or death, and so my father was exiled at night to the sofa in the front room of the cottage they then lived in. After her menopause, he was permitted to rejoin her in the double bed, but Paradise was not long regained. With Mary's coming, he was once again dispossessed and moved back to the sofa, this time lying head to toe with me and unable to sleep for the wall-shaking snores of the runner-in sharing the double-bed next door. It neither lessened nor deepened his dislike of her that she hated him. She hated most people, perhaps all. There were those who said 'Sure God love her' and assured you that the saints in Heaven were putting bunting up in anticipation of her arrival. With the instinct of a ham actor in the rural fit-ups, she played to the hilt the role of afflicted innocent, but to me her capacity for malevolence was baffling; it suggested that the natural state of man was wholly Mr Hyde, with not a trace of Dr Jekyll in sight. My father, who was one of nature's softies, had only to look at her to start grinding his false teeth in rage. He did not court destruction by declaring open war, but he made sure to collide with Mary in doorways or nudge her off the pavement on the way to Mass. Knowing it was deliberate, she would squawk: 'Mag, Mag, do you know what he's after doin'?', and my mother, who could be very grand when out in public and was mindful of the regard of others, would smile sweetly for the world to see, while snarling out of the side of her mouth: 'Shut up, you rip, or I'll swing for you.'

Life became not much easier when we moved to a two-storey corporation house in St Begnet's Villas. Mary now had a bed of her own, but it was in the same room as my parents, and the snoring raged on, unabated, a kind of sonar by which I would find my way upstairs in the pitch dark, home from the pictures or the sea front. In waking hours, she would sit, muttering and furiously jerking her pramload of dolls to and fro, like a miner grading ore, while my father, catching sight of her, would munch his tongue in requited hatred. If jealousy was part of his detestation of her, he was self-deluding; she did not usurp my mother's affection for him, for there was little of it worth stealing. Whatever else, it cannot have helped that her presence in his house was a reminder that he had never been master of it. She outlived my mother by some years and him as well, so maybe in the interval of waiting for her to get to Heaven he had peace there for a time.

My parents enjoyed their life within its limits, and as they and I grew older it was their docile acceptance of those limits that, with the intolerance of the young pup, I found hateful. To them, life was to be survived rather than lived, and they gratefully accepted the shelter of the church, the Jacobs, the town and 'Dev'. They surrendered free will, trading it for a whist drive, afternoons at the pictures, a shilling on the horses, the Wicklow Regatta and – as a sop at the year's end – the great toy of Christmas. Sometimes, when my mother was angry at, say, a rise in prices, she would threaten to vote against de Valera's party at the next election, but when the time came she supported Fianna Fail as always. It was not out of loyalty, but from a blind gut-fear of change.

Six years after my father's death, I wrote a play in which I attempted to sort out my feelings for him and lay my anger to rest. 'You were a sheep while you lived,' the self-righteous son says to the old man's ghost, 'you're a sheep now.' I was not so foolish as to expect that he would ever hit out at his life, but I thought he might just once have asked it an aggrieved 'Why?' Only now, remembering an incident that for forty years has lain buried, do I realise why he did not. I was nineteen, and it was the day before Christmas Eve.

My mother was allergic to drink, and the allergy was for some years accompanied by addiction. My father and I came to dread holidays – Christmas, in particular, when an old friend would waylay her in Dun Laoghaire and, taking no refusal, steer her into a snug for just a thimbleful of sherry, or a ball of malt to mark the season that was in it. One sip, and she was lost. So too, for us, was Christmas. She was a bad drunk, with a wasps' nest for a tongue. Once the drinking had begun, the misery would drag on through the holiday and beyond. There were weeks of rows and sulks, of cries for heaven to bear witness that she was persecuted by pimps and informers. The house, no matter that we lived in it, seemed empty and cheerless; along our road, window curtains twitched as my mother came slowly home, hat askew, from another outing. No matter how watchful my father and I were – and he, lacking a cunning to match hers, was useless – our next-door neighbour, Mrs Dunne, would smuggle in Baby Powers and, if I implored her not to, would snap at me that, to suit a pup the likes of me, she was not going to disoblige her good neighbour. After perhaps a month, mortally in debt to Gilbey's the spirit merchants, my mother would become ill and take to her bed for a week, and that was the end of it until next time.

It happened that I intended to spend my first Christmas away from home. The previous summer while on holiday in Limerick, I had at long last given my heart without having it flung back at me. It was first love with a vengeance, and I was in raptures when the girl, Teresa by name, invited me to spend the holiday in the flat she shared with her cousin in Shannon Street. As the time drew nearer, I kept a fearful eye on my mother, but days passed and it seemed as if this would be one of the good years. My life was on the edge of change; the waiting-room door was at last opening, and I took heart from knowing that God, of all people, would have a sense of occasion. On December 23rd, I came home early from the office to pack a bag, say my goodbyes and catch the evening train. As I walked in at the door, she was standing by the kitchen table, one hand resting upon it on thumb and plump fingertips, and as soon as I saw the calm clear-browed look of a woman who had nothing to hide, I felt the old sickness trickle through me like bleeding. I had been a fool to believe it would be otherwise; it was the price of me.

It was unthinkable that I should get on a train and leave my father to cope with her over Christmas, and so I went to the post office and sent off a telegram to Limerick, knowing that it was the end of my romance. By the time I returned to the house, my father was home from work, waiting for tea he would be lucky to get and doggedly refusing to accept that she had drink taken. I behaved disgracefully. If my future was in bits, I saw no reason why he should enjoy the comfort of self-delusion. I asked him if he was blind. Or stupid. Could he not see what had happened, what we were in for, how this Christmas was lost as well as the others? He smiled, waved a hand at me. Not at all. What was I talking about or did I know what I was talking about? I was a comical boy. Sure the woman was grand. Never better. Not a feather out of her. He turned, eliciting her support. She did not look at him, only at me, the Judas. Then she went on moving about the room as if we were not there, her face set. He picked up his *Evening Herald* and opened it, a hiding place. I tore it away from him. He would not escape. He might not share in my misery, but he would taste of it.

At last, he gave in. He hardly ever lost his temper, straight off, but would begin at first to grumble. He played his old familiar tunes: weren't we all grand and happy and comfortable, owing nothing to no one? Sure where was the sense in, in, in, in? Wasn't she the best in the world when she hadn't a sup taken? The grumbling became anger. Christ almighty, what ailed her that she couldn't let the one week in the year go by without putting shaggin' poison into her? Making a show of herself. Soon, he was ranting, and, as always when he lost his temper, he became incoherent. Would he never have a day's peace with her? He would set fire to every public house in the whoorin' town, aye, an', an', an' Gilbey's along with them. She looked at him with contempt, then went from the room and upstairs. It would be a bread and jam tea. The anger dribbled away and became despair. He said 'I dunno' several times. God in heaven he said at last, but weren't we a misfortune family?

I told him with savage calm: 'I don't know why you bother talking to God. There isn't one.'

For a moment, he was about to go rambling on down his own road, then he looked at me and said: 'There isn't a what?'

'A God,' I said.

He stared. To my horror, I heard him say, and it was a moan of terrible triumph: 'You're right. There isn't a God, there isn't a God.'

Once, on Rockfort Avenue, my bicycle had skidded and the brake lever pierced the back of my leg. As the blood began to well, I begged to be given back the past few seconds of time, reclaiming the moment when I had over-twisted the handlebars at the sharp turn into Coliemore Road. Ten measly seconds had seemed a reasonable request then, and it seemed so now. I wanted the words, my father's and mine, unsaid. It was as if he had down the years kept hidden an ultimate knowledge that contradicted all that the town and the world were built on, that went against the sodality and the processions, the altar and the pulpit. He had buried it out of shame, for, if others were wiser and more well-up than he was, then it must be as untrue as it was sinful. Now, of a sudden, it had been said, and he was no longer alone. I had put him in the right.

That time went past; we got through Christmas as we had always done, and what I had said was forgotten, or at least never again spoken of. The stone was put back into place. After a few more years, the drinking stopped. When she was dead and it was too late, I wondered what real harm it had ever done. It was my fault as much as hers: I failed to shake off a bugaboo of childhood: the waking nightmare of seeing a mother become a stranger behind the same face. Children should at least grow up. In my father's case, what I had done was true wickedness, and it was no thanks to me that a vicious word or two cannot as magically shatter lives as it does in a play or a film. By next day he had simply swept away what I had said. Crumbs from a table.

I at least know now and for all time why he, like so many others, did not ask questions of their lives. It was because the God neither of us believed in tempers the wind to the shorn lamb. Probably, it had been given to my father to know that, for a simple man, the answers are not to be lived with.

8

The apogee of my life as an actor came in 1950 when the newly formed Dun Laoghaire Academy of Dramatic Art – DADA, for short – actually billed me as a guest performer. Even so, I was small fry, for they had engaged a guest *star* as well: a professional actor of great bulk, baleful aspect and empurpled proboscis, who spoke like a distant fog-horn and was on that account known among his peers as Doctor Moo. The play was Paul Vincent Carroll's *Shadow and Substance*. Also in the cast was my friend from the Land Commission Players, Jimmy Keogh, who, even though he was playing a country curate, still believed that the line of dialogue did not exist which could not be enhanced with a 'boinnng' here and a 'gedoink' there. He and I had our sights – but alas, nothing else – on the *ingénue*, whom I shall call Sandra: a wet-lipped eighteen-year-old who habitually stood with legs apart and pelvis thrust forward like a proferred hand. Although with her sultry looks, she was my ideal of the archetypal wrecker of homes, she remained perversely disinclined to practise on mine. The idealistic young schoolmaster was played by Vincent Ellis, who was also a co-director of the academy. He was lanky and stooped, and had a jutting lower lip. Unusually for an actor, he also had a speech impediment. There were kindly souls who referred to it as hardly noticeable, but when he said 'Good evening', it was likely to come out as 'Nyugn eenygning.'

The director of the play was his partner: a small circular lady named Sarah O'Kelly, whose husband, Christy, was the brother of the then President of Ireland, Sean T. O'Kelly. She had a profusion – a veritable *embarras de richesses* – of chins. She walked

– I had heard the expression, but had rarely seen it done – trippingly. She held her hands with wrists inward and palms daintily facing the ground, the thumbs, index and little fingers raised, and others curled. She resembled a dropsical fairy permanently on her way to an enchanted glade. In the moments when she was not telling us that this was deportment, she would reminisce of how her eldest child had been born during the 1916 Easter Rising; the climax of the recital came with: 'And God pity me, there I was in the agonies of labour, with the guns getting nearer and Mrs de Valera wiping the sweat from me brow.'

A small string ensemble was to play at our gala first night, and in this connection a musicologist, Jewish by name and in appearance, came out from town. Mrs O'Kelly, awed that a man who did not write out prescriptions should be addressed as 'Doctor', enquired as to his nationality. He bowed and said: 'Madam, I am German.'

She was thrilled to bits. 'Ah, go to God,' she said. 'A Jerry? Aren't you great!' Then we saw her give him the leer of one conspirator to another. 'And, Doctor, listen here to me, don't fret yourself.' And her arm, stiff and straight, shot out from the shoulder. 'We shall rise again!'

She was, in short, an Irish Republican: a breed that may be defined as the sworn friend of anyone, genocides included, who is not the friend of England. She and I were natural enemies. Where it came to acting, I combined my own name with that of my foster parents, so that I was John Keyes Byrne. Mrs O'Kelly enraged me by addressing me during rehearsals as 'Keyes Byrne', without a prefix. I retaliated by endowing her with a nickname. She came to hear of it and, from curiosity rather than umbrage, asked Vincent Ellis: 'Why does Keyes Byrne call me Charlotte?'

He told her, truthfully 'I nging id's neh veemanane for Nygarl Nysawnygn.'

It took her a while to grasp, but with patience she did so, that he was saying: 'I think it's the female for Charles Laughton.'

Ours was not a happy production. Mrs O'Kelly's theatrical experience had been a few walk-on roles at the Abbey Theatre in the 1930s, and what she knew about directing a play was confined to saying 'Enunciate, Keyes Byrne, you must een-nun-see-ate!' and, with every untrammelled pound of flesh juddering, demonstrating how we should walk across the stage. 'Pippa passes,' Doctor Moo said under his breath. Our star, too, had his troubles. For one thing, try as he might, he could not master his lines; for another, the actress who was playing the saintly maidservant, Brigid, was not only too old for the role by a score of years, but she had also been a diva in the Dublin Grand Opera Society and so projected her every line towards the rear wall of the auditorium. At last, Doctor Moo, losing his patience said: 'Will you for Christ's sake at least look in my direction! You're not in fucking *Madame Butterfly* now.' Mrs O'Kelly crossed herself and actually went to stand in a corner where she could pray uninterrupted. Our Brigid burst into tears; Doctor Moo, his huge face a storm at sea that Turner could have painted, set off for the bar of the Royal Marine; and Jimmy Keogh and I stared dry-mouthed with lust at Sandra, who as usual was performing the considerable feat of standing, hands at ease on her hips, and pubes at attention.

The first night was, in effect, the launching of DADA, and, to do justice to the occasion, evening dress was obligatory in the first twelve rows of the town hall. The excitement caused Sandra, whose acting debut this was, to become mildly hysterical, and I could hear her voice as I was making up next door in what served as the men's dressing room. Mrs O'Kelly was clucking at her and saying 'Sure you'll be grand', when the door behind me burst open and Sandra came in. She was wearing a corselet and black stockings held up by suspenders. Before the eyeballs had time to melt in my head, she said: 'I'm going to die, I'm going to die. My heart is slowing down and it's going to stop. Feel it.' I was the nearest person to her, which is perhaps why mine was the hand she took hold of and shoved inside the brassière part of the corselet. Doctor Moo, dressed for his role as Canon Skerrit, stared open-mouthed, the great nose pulsating, his teeth resembling a neglected corner of a cemetery. Sandra's breast was actually heaving, and my hand was full of it. It had never been so full. A nipple poked through my fingers. 'Do you feel it?' she asked, her eyes searching my face.

I told her: yes, I could feel it.

Mrs O'Kelly had followed her in and began to quack: 'Keyes Byrne, get your hand out of there.'

She caught hold of Sandra by the shoulders and pulled her backwards, causing my hand to flop out into the world like a fish regurgitated by a gannet. It was a close run thing: where that hand was concerned, another five seconds and only major surgery would have removed it. In time, Sandra was quietened down and the play began, but for me all that followed was anti-climax. I had been to the mountain top; I had seen the promised land. To be truthful, it was not in any case much of an evening. Doctor Moo still did not know his lines, and soon there was a brown stain on the elbow of his soutane, caused by his leaning on the newly-painted mantelpiece, ostensibly in pained meditation, but actually to solicit a prompt through the fireplace. Sandra was supposed to play the Canon's hoydenish niece, Thomasina; what she gave the audience was Rita Hayworth as *Gilda*. Her stage-fright might never have been; pelvis leading the way, she sashayed on the stage, swung her hips, sat, crossed her legs and showed her black stocking tops. A groan went up from the unruly element at the rear, and lechery swept down the aisles like a sirocco. As for Vincent Ellis, it was unfortunate for him that Jimmy Keogh's mother was in the audience and had had a drink or two, just in case the hall should prove not to be heated. She knew Vincent, for he lodged with the Keoghs, and she applauded his every exit. His proudest moment came with the line: 'Goodbye, Canon, you will be remembered, if at all, not as a classicist, nor as a priest, but for your love for a poor little miserable child.' He made heavy weather of the sibilants, especially in 'classicists', but burst through into open country with 'ngno lubb foh a moor ngiddle mignable ngiln'. As he turned to go, Mrs Keogh applauded again and shouted, 'Good man, Vincent!' Not recognising the voice and assuming that he was being jeered at, Vincent stood his ground and said: 'Ngo, venny ngnine! Ngaviagn for ngeh negeneragn.' A friend of mine who had a sister with a cleft palate later told me that what he had said was: 'Oh, very nice! Caviare for the general.' The audience may well not have understood the words, never mind their meaning, but they sensed that Vincent was no longer their friend and humble servant. There was a mutinous rumble and cries from the rear of 'Feck off' and 'Bring back Thomasina.'

The play ends when the servant girl, Brigid, is felled by a half-brick intended for the schoolmaster. As she lies dying, the Canon and the teacher, mortal enemies, face each other over her body, and Doctor Moo heart-rendingly delivered his line: 'Will that doctor ever come? Could we do anything of ourselves? God would guide us surely.' A voice from the back told him loudly, clearly and succinctly what to do with regard to Brigid, adding '... while she's still warm.' The advice was loudly seconded, causing those wearing dinner jackets to leap to their feet and glare at the unfortunates who were not, and Brigid's dying speech was drowned by demands, garnished with bouquets of adjectives and adverbs, that those blocking their view should sit down.

DADA did not long survive its first outing. Its second and final production was of Emlyn Williams' *A Murder Has Been Arranged*, and Mrs O'Kelly engaged the services of a producer who had the cachet of working for Radio Eireann. At the first read-through, Sandra took him to one side and told him how ridiculous it was that he should have to travel all of seven miles home after rehearsals. There was a spare room at home, she said, where he could be happily accommodated, and, if this story is to be believed, he was. As for the play, it began inauspiciously with the entrance of Vincent Ellis wearing tights and attempting to enunciate: 'I am the ghost of Caesar Borgia, the world famous poisoner.' Then, in the third act, the set collapsed in a manner eerily reminiscent of *Asmodée* in the Little Flower Hall in Bray a year previously. This time I fell, not off a flight of steps, but from a platform in pitch darkness, and once again, to my joy and the grief of others, there was a dangling rope begging to be caught hold of. An inquest was duly held, with Mrs O'Kelly as the coroner. It took her not long to unmask the culprit, whereupon she pointed her chins to the right and a pudgy forefinger to the left, the while declaiming: 'There, Keyes Byrne, is the door.' As I stalked out, her co-director chimed in with 'Ngungh nygnent!', which I took to mean 'Good riddance!' Three or four others, disenchanted with DADA and glad of an excuse to defect, walked out with me. I later learned that Vincent Ellis, while under the impression that I had formed a murder gang and was waiting for him in the street, sent for the police and demanded to be escorted home. He was in no danger: by then the pariahs were in the Roman Café drinking lemon soda and sexually defaming the waitresses.

Within a year or two, Sandra went to England and all that was heard of her was the occasional lubricious rumour which was as outrageous as it was probably untrue; nonetheless, we chose to believe it, if only to day-dream that it was happening to us. Two or three years ago in a pub, a handsome middle-aged woman came up, asked if I remembered her and introduced me to her husband. 'Is that the famous Sandra?' my wife said when she had gone. 'I don't know what all the fuss was about.' Probably she did not, but *I* do.

The DADA business depressed me. While I was glad to be quit of Mrs O'Kelly and her like, the manner of my leaving seemed to prove yet again that, having been born an outsider, I was fated to remain one. It seemed that the hole did not exist that was square enough to contain me. Around this time, I had a friend who managed the Pavilion Soda Fountain on the sea front and was known as Abie from his initials, 'A.B.' He suggested that we cheer ourselves up with a weekend away from home. 'I know,' he said, 'great place.' He let me in on his secret.

I said, almost shrieking: 'Belfast? What do you want to go to Belfast for?'

He looked at me as if at a thick. 'To ride women, what do you think?'

Even as my libido responded like a faithful old dog, I knew it was a lost cause. Nonetheless we set off by train one wet Saturday morning in October, walked with heads bent against the rain that was driving down from Cave Hill, and I saw Abie dart into a chemist's shop. He came out grinning, tapped his breast pocket and showed me the corner of a packet of condoms. 'Now,' he said, 'all we need is the women.' It was as if, having acquired a puncture-repair kit, he assumed that getting a bicycle to go with it was a mere formality. Next, we went looking for a bookshop, for he had been told that a certain edition of the *Arabian Nights* was commendably filthy. We found a shop on Royal Avenue, and the manager enquired as to our needs. Abie told him and was asked what translation he had in mind. He had not come unprepared. He reached into his pocket for the slip of paper on which he had written the details. 'This,' he said, 'will tell you all you need to know.' With a smirk, he handed the manager the packet of French letters.

In the evening, we went to a dance hall. Abie had been a commis chef at the Metropole when he was fourteen and so had skipped adolescence and what went with it: the street corners, the girls on the pier, the fourpenny rush with Charles Starrett as the Durango Kid, the Sunday-night hop and the walk home – half of it in pitch darkness once the street lamps had gone out at ten past twelve. When it came to dancing he could not put a foot under him. I, who stomped about as if I were signalling to a tenant downstairs, was not much better, but to my surprise the first girl

I asked up – it was a foxtrot – did not seem to be in the least bothered by my feet of lead. From the moment we came together, she slammed her hips into mine and began rotating them as if she were grinding flour. The friction was such that I wondered how my pelvic area stayed on the cool side of spontaneous combustion. I hardly dared give house-room to the thought that my sexual ship might at last have come in sight of land, but at least I began not to dislike Belfast. My eyes met the girl's. She smiled and asked: 'Are you up from the Free State?'

I told her yes.

Still smiling, she remarked: 'You'd be a Catholic, then?'

I had not practised my religion ever since the day, ten years before, when Father Creedon threw me out of his confessional for not knowing the words of the *Confiteor*, but her question took me so unawares that I again answered yes.

Her smile did not diminish; rather it broadened. She said quietly: 'I'm a Protestant,' and walked quickly away, leaving me in the middle of the dance floor, vainly trying to conceal her gift to me – an erection. Once I had conveyed my tumescence to a quiet place and, by sitting down and crossing my legs, had tucked it out of harm's way, I found myself not in the least dismayed by the snub. For one thing, it smacked quite enjoyably of martyrdom. To be punished for my faith – which, for the occasion, it now suited me to bring back into play like a dribbling old fountain – made a nice change from being told that I could not dance for skins or was a rotten coort – which was how we pronounced 'court'. For another, bigotry was not new to me: I had, after all, lived for twenty years among Irish Catholics.

There was, for instance, a chap named Michael Keogh, who, since his parents had died, took his Sunday dinner at our house, and had recently wooed and won a girl who was Church of Ireland. The marriage ceremony was to be performed by a Protestant minister, and Michael's best friend, fearful of God's wrath, went to the parish priest of Dalkey and asked for permission to attend. After pained meditation, the ruling came forth: 'Yes, you may do so – but be cool with him.' My mother, to her credit and my own astonishment, asked us if we had ever heard such codology, put on her good hat, left my father and me to fend for ourselves and went off to the wedding and the breakfast afterwards.

Before the evening was over, Abie and I found two girls – both Catholics, since the Protestants would not have us. One was named Belle McLaverty, a big girl with black hair and a mocking Northern laugh; the other, who laid claim to Abie by taking his arm, is less vivid in my mind. Her name was Cara, which means 'friend'. Abie, with optimism as unquenchable as it was unfounded, confided to me with a leer that this was auspicious. He told them that he was the catering manager for Odeon (Ireland) Ltd., and that I was a final-year medical student. We saw the girls to a bus stop, received a scalding kiss apiece and were invited to meet them next day at three.

Our evening was not quite over. Abie and I were staying at the Central Hotel, and he urged me into the Residents' Lounge to drink to our good fortune. The girls, he assured me, were as hot as mustard. It was an expression I had heard to my grief in Butlin's the previous year, as applied to two other odds-on favourites: the Misses Morris and Watson. I signalled to Abie to lower his voice, for we were not alone in the lounge. There was a man drinking on his own. I took him for a commercial traveller, even though it was Saturday and he was unlikely to have been on the road on weekends. He nodded; we nodded back; then, quite out of the blue, he asked us if we had ever been driving at night when the car was suddenly filled with golden light and there was the sound of many voices, all clamorous. I told him that alas, I did not drive. I tried not to look at Abie, who, I sensed, was trying not to look at me. The man seemed not to believe that we had never had such a commonplace experience. He glowered, as if suspecting us of being unsociable. Then, as if by way of proffering the benefit of the doubt, he told us about a murderer he had known.

This murderer was actually as nice a fellow as you could meet in a day's walk, fond of his jar and the bit of crack with his chums. His misfortune was that he had a wife who was a proper bitch. For one thing, she refused to believe him when he told her how, whenever he was driving at night, the car had been filled with— He broke off and smiled archly as if he were too cute for us. He said 'No matter', and told us about how this man had killed his wife by stabbing her through the throat with a pair of scissors.

'He was a bit of a genius,' our new friend said, 'because he convinced the police that he was mad. Of course he was every bit as sane as you or me.'

'Where does the evening go?' I said, standing up.

Abie was on his feet too, but the man was between us and the door. 'Stay,' he said. 'Have a jar.' Softly: 'You will.'

I noticed that his right hand was out of sight in his jacket pocket. Perhaps I imagined it, but the impression that has stayed with me down the years is that I could hear a small metallic snipping noise. We sat again. He rang for the night porter, ordered three lagers and, without bringing his hand into view, told us lovingly how the murder was done. No detail was too insignificant, from the blood-flecked walls to the cat's red paw marks, the dying woman's last gurglings and the banshee wail of the police car drawing near.

He said: 'Guess how long he was in prison for.'

I said: 'Dunno.'

He said: 'You sound hoarse. Have you a cold?'

I coughed and shook my head.

He said: 'Y'ought to watch your throat.'

The drinks came, and he took his hand temporarily from his pocket to pay for them. He said 'Slainte!', took a sip of his lager and said: 'He was found guilty but insane and ordered to be detained at his Majesty's pleasure. Two years, and not a feather out of him. Sure he could have done another two, and a third

161

standing on his head, no bother. Two short years for killing the bitch. What do you say to that for a bargain? Cut price, what?'

Luckily, the pun was unintentional, for if he had laughed I think I would have fainted. Abie, who seemed to have caught my cold, cleared his throat. He knew he was clutching at a straw, but he asked all the same. 'And . . . ah, when is he due out?'

'Amn't I telling you? He *is* out. A week since.'

Abie rose. The man stood up. Abie sat.

'And now, this fella, this friend of mine, he has a score or two to settle.

It appeared that voices had spoken to the man in his cell in the criminal asylum and had told him who among his neighbours hated him and would do him down. Now he would deal with them, one by one. Some were tale-bearers and informers, others had turned his wife against him, for she had not been a bitch to begin with. All would pay. Listening to him, I began to wonder what colour my hair was.

He stared at us with sudden suspicion. 'Are ye sure certain that voices don't talk to youse in motor cars?'

Leaving Abie to look out for himself, I replied that I did not own a car. My tone implied that if ever I was so fortunate as to acquire a motor, it would certainly come with a whole choir of voices fitted as standard. He did not seem wholly convinced, but nonetheless guided us through a verbal dossier on the murderer's ill-disposed and, did they but know it, doomed neighbours. On his list were the wall-eyed woman next door, who pretended to cook colcannon but was actually manufacturing poison gas; the man who had trained his dog to defecate in his – the murderer's – front garden; and the local minister, whom he had caught sniggering at him from the pulpit. He broke off to ring for more drink for himself. This time, when the night porter came, he ordered a double brandy. Fear being sometimes the father of courage, I seized on the diversion, sprang up and made for the door with a shout of 'Got to go. 'Night, now.' Abie, seeing my break for freedom, took off like a rocket, and, for a heart-stopping moment, we actually collided in the doorway. Once outside the lounge, we went straight and swiftly to our room and, without saying a word and as if we had been doing it every night of our lives, picked up a chest of drawers and shoved it against the door. Only then did I speak.

'I want to go home.'

'What? It's the middle of the night.'

'Tomorrow morning, then.'

'What about the girls?'

'Hump the girls.'

'We will, we will.'

I knew that his optimism had at last cracked, for he added a fervent 'Please God.' In the end, he talked me round and we met Belle and Cara in the afternoon. On that Sunday in Belfast, the only thing that was open was the sky; rain poured down. I tell a lie: the city fathers, when closing the cinemas and the pubs, had carelessly forgotten to lock up the zoo as well. We wandered about on the muddy pathways, staring at the giraffes and zebras and being stared back at in mutual misery. Then Belle had the idea that we should take a bus to visit her grandmother, who lived in a cottage under Cave Hill. We did so. She was a nice, if shapeless, old woman, sitting in an armchair that occupied most of the kitchen. She wore a cardigan over a torn jumper over an old gansy and had a rug across her lap. She seemed to be a semi-invalid. There was a down-draught in the chimney and our eyes stung from the smoke. When we had had tea with soot in it, Belle asked me if I really was a medical student. I was about to own up and tell her that I was a clerk, perhaps omitting the lowly part of it, when Abie chimed in to assure her that I was another Louis Pasteur in the making.

'In that case,' Belle said to me, 'Granny has a dropped stomach, and would you like to look at it?'

I did not know what a dropped stomach was and I still do not.

It was irrelevant, for I would not have wanted to look at her stomach even if it had never dropped. I caught a nightmarish glimpse of the old lady happily throwing the rug aside and preparing to hike her skirt up there and then. A voice began to babble. It was mine.

'I'm not allowed to treat people until I qualify.'

Belle said: 'Sure just looking at her isn't treating her.'

'I can't. I'm not supposed to.'

'Sure who'd tell on you?' As she spoke, she saw the look of panic on my face and did not insist further, but I knew she thought me disobliging for drinking her grandmother's tea and yet begrudging even the most cursory glance at the woman's abdomen. She said, with heavy sarcasm: 'I'm sorry, Granny, he's not supposed to.' Abie had gone pale at the thought of seeing the stomach, but with the danger past his usual pastiness seeped back, and I silently swore to be revenged on him. As we left the cottage, Belle scalded me with her eyes and hissed: 'One wee look wouldn't have killed you.'

For all her roughness of tongue, she was quick to forgive and, on the bus back into town, asked me about Abie, who was sitting with Cara a few seats back. 'Is he all right?'

'How do you mean?'

'Ach, you know. I mean, is he rough with girls, like?'

'Rough, how?'

'For God's sake, I mean *rough*. How many kinds of bloody rough are there?' She lowered her voice. 'Cara's a bit . . . ye know, delicate.'

'Oh, no, Abie's not like—'

'Will ye let me finish!' She ransacked her mind for an easy way of saying it. 'She has this wee bit of botheration. It comes and goes, like. You'd know all about it.'

I was about to say 'Why me?'; then, remembering that I was a doctor or as good as, I spoke like one. 'What seems to be the trouble?'

She told me what Cara's trouble was, and said: 'Have a quiet word with your friend, won't you? Tell him what ails her . . . just in case it happens the while he's with her. So's he won't fly into a panic, like.'

I assured her that I would speak to him. 'On the q.t., mind,' she said. 'Don't let Cara hear. The poor creature gets embarrassed.'

We took another bus to where Belle lived on the Lower Malone Road and were shown into the parlour. She said to Cara: 'I suppose I'd better feed the brutes. You keep them company.'

She went out. From where we sat, we could hear her clattering about, and presently there came the sound and smell of food sizzling in a pan. It was unmistakably a fry-up of bacon and eggs; sausages, too, would be part of it, as sure as tomorrow's rain, and perhaps even crumbly rounds of black and white pudding, each as thick as a baby's wrist. An Ulster fry is to northerners as ambrosia to the gods, and the greedy thought leaped in my head of fried potato bread to crown the feast. The sizzling reached a crescendo, and I saw that Abie's mouth, like mine, was watering and out of control. When Belle returned, she was pushing a food trolley on which were four plates, each containing bread and butter, a slice of cold ham, a scallion, quarter of a tomato and a leaf of lettuce. We were too polite to ask about the fry-up. I have no idea what became of it; it is to this day part of my life's mythology: a mystery to outdo the enigmas of Kaspar Hauser, the Iron Mask and the Turin shroud.

I did not get a chance to tell Abie about Cara's 'botheration'. After tea we played cards, then it was time for him to see her home. He had small, even, yellow teeth, and I saw them bared in a rictus of lechery as Belle showed them out. She returned a moment later, closed the door, flung me matter-of-factly on the sofa and jumped on top. She weighed a ton. She took hold of my necktie and twisted it in her fist until an ocean began to roar in my ears; then she suddenly looked up like a lioness interrupted at her feeding and said: 'I'd better see how the daddo is.' She went out again and was soon back.

To me, Northern Ireland was a foreign country, and I wondered what a daddo was. Somewhat anticlimactically, it turned to out be her father, who was in bed across the hall. At first, I thought the mystery was solved and that his presence in the house accounted for the Ulster fry, but Belle told me that he was suffering from heart disease and ate next to nothing.

'I'll tell you what he does eat: forty Gallaghers a day. Talk about thin, you'd see more fat on a skeleton.' She was angry. 'We put him in the front room because he's not supposed to walk up stairs. Stairs me bum, he's not even let out of bed, but the bloody man would get up if it killed him – and it will! The carry-on of him, you'd think he was in the Olympics. Christ almighty, and him with a heart in him like an eggshell.' She kept from crying by grinning into my face. 'And you needn't worry. I'm not going to ask you to examine him. You're no more a bloody medical student than what I am.'

Hovering between embarrassment and relief, I asked if her mother was alive.

'Oh, aye. She's with me aunt for the one evening she can get out of this kip all week. The poor woman's down to a shadow from nursing him.' This time the tears had to be blinked back. She said 'Ach!' loudly, brushing away the world and its woes, rubbed a knuckle into each eye, said 'Here's something you won't get in the Free State,' and jumped on me as before. In the wrestling match that followed, she kept breaking off to listen. 'Was that him?' she would say, or 'Did you hear a noise?' It made it difficult for me to concentrate, but Belle seemed quite capable of doing the work of two. She was excitable; where other girls, if one was lucky, simmered, she seethed. In a nuclear age, one would think of a meltdown. Out of a blur of clothing and a tangle of limbs, she said: 'I'm all worked up. You'd better get going.' I thought she wanted me to go home, but in her lexicon 'get going' had a different connotation. It was hard to believe, but my faith in the inherent depravity of women was about to be vindicated. The lean years were done with. I was trying to get my trousers off when she froze.

'Christ, he's out of bed!'

It was true: I had heard a floorboard creak. Her bosom, most of it exposed and some of it in my eye, was heaving. She said: 'We can't stop now, it's too late.' She got off the sofa, went to the door and stood with her back tight against it to repel intruders. 'We'll have to do it this way.' She pulled at her skirt, wriggling her hips. I saw a pair of French knickers descending slowly.

Men have been driven wild by sights less heady, but another vision had taken squatters' rights inside my head. I saw her father pitting his poor strength against the door as I ravaged Belle up against it, and dropping dead from the effort. Worse still, I saw him succeed in getting his head into the room, only to succumb from the sight of his daughter and a total stranger bucking like two dinghies in a Force Nine.

I said: 'We can't.'

Actually, it was a question. I needed only to have my feebleness swept mockingly to one side, and the story would have been different. Instead, a light went out in her face. She said: 'No. No, you're right, it's too risky.'

No kettle had ever gone off the boil so quickly. It was as if she had been instantly and magically replaced by a well-behaved twin. I turned my back to allow her to put her clothing in order. She noticed and said: 'Ah, thanks; you're nice. Now you'd better go on home. I have to get him back into bed.'

I gave her my address, kissed her goodbye and walked the two miles or so to the hotel, racing past the Residents' Lounge in case the man from last night should emerge, scissors in hand. It was an hour before Abie came in. He was trembling. His face was white.

I will say for him that he was not one to preface his news with such coy invitations as 'You'll never guess what happened.' Disdaining all preamble, he came straight to the good stuff with 'I think I've killed her.'

'Killed who?'

Of course, it was Clara he meant. He had seen her home; they had sat at the foot of her stairs; he had kissed her. At this, she had gasped, had a violent spasm and threshed uncontrollably about, arching her body in a series of terrifying shudders. Abie, babbling 'Stop, I didn't mean it' – although what it was that he did not mean was unclear – tried in vain to hold her down. At last, when she seemed on the point of levitating, she had collapsed, a corpse, and he had fled. He said with the calmness of a man who saw the hangman's noose swaying gently, inches from his face: 'I'm surprised the police aren't here.' I took care to put the two twin beds between us before I told him that Clara was an epileptic.

A few days later, I received a letter from Belle saying how impolite Abie had been to leave her friend lying sound asleep at the foot of the stairs for her father to trip over in the morning. Later still, one Sunday evening while I was at the pictures, a policeman came to our door. He asked: 'Does Jack Keyes live here?' My father answered yes. The policeman said: 'Well, I have very bad news for him. His old fella is dead.'

He handed my father a telegram that, because the day was a Sunday, had come to the police station. It said: 'Father dead love Belle.' All my own father had to do was look in a mirror to know that he was alive and well, but he was not the better of the experience for a month.

My parents were growing old. For years, they had seemed ageless, then, almost overnight, I saw them as a stranger might. My father's legs had become stiff; he walked with a stick; his clothes were too big. My mother lost some of her old appetite for a grievance; she avoided the east wind. For the first time, I thought of them as mortal. One of my earliest memories is of seeing the funeral of Biddie Byrne, who lived at Number 5 in our lane, and saying as my mother tucked me into the vast summer meadow of a double bed I shared with her: 'Mammy, you and me will never die, sure we won't?' Naturally, and since I was spoiled rotten and denied nothing, she assured me that we would not. It took only a few years to realise that, if there were exceptions, we were not of their number; it was most of a lifetime before I knew with certainty that my mother had been right unbeknownst, that nothing dies.

One day in the future, I was to write a play about my father, who was a simple man. My mother's role in it was by comparison minor, partly because I knew that she was too prickly a person, forever conscious of the world's opinion, to take kindly to being put in a play, and also because I was more than a little in fear of her. She maddens me: whenever I try to write about her, a stranger spills on to the page: querulous, sharp-tongued, slow to praise, her antennae alert for an injustice or an imagined snub. As a boy, I would dread being with her in the presence of old ones, for it was then that she was sure to trot out her invariable and final judgment on ingrates: 'The more you do for them, the less thanks you get, and in the end of it they'd hang you.' It was a long time before I began to understand her, and knew that the hard words and harder looks were a preparation for the day when I would fly the nest. In her mind, the desertion had already begun. My every act of independence was part of it: a tram journey to Dublin on my own; a weekend eight short miles away in Powerscourt camping with the sea scouts (I can still remember the strawberry filling on the sandwich cake that was bought especially for my homecoming), a holiday abroad, a dress dance – all were small acts of defection.

Perhaps the least small was my marriage. One evening, on the prowl for girls, my friend Mick and I dropped into a social club named the France-Ireland. We had known happier hunting grounds; most of the female members were well-brought-up secretaries from various embassies, and the *directeur*, a Monsieur Boisseneau, did not permit close dancing. When Mick attempted vertical copulation after his first ten seconds on the dance floor,

Monsieur Boisseneau tapped him on the shoulder. ''Ere,' he said, 'we 'ave three rules. We do not discuss releegion, we do not discuss politeecs, and we do not show too much what ees in zee 'art.' 'A dead loss,' Mick said on our way home. As for me, I had met a Belgian girl and, four years later, set off for Liege to be married.

Quite apart from the cost of travel, there was no question of my parents going to the wedding. 'Ah, it's too foreign,' my mother said flatly, deciding for them both. In case foreignness were not reason enough, she blamed my father, saying that he would never get on an aeroplane with his rheumatics. 'What are you talkin' about,' he said, 'or do you know what you're talking about? Amn't I up ladders every day of the week?' to which she said: 'You'd be a nice article to take to a foreign country.'

On the night before I left for Belgium, I thought the least I could do was spend the evening at home, but she would have none of it. 'What do you want to be stuck in the house for? Sure you may as well go to the pictures.' She added with a sniff: 'You'll be gone tomorrow, anyway, and long gone.' And so off I went to the Pavilion to see *The Night My Number Came Up*. I had robbed her of a wedding, and she was too proud to accept crumbs.

I may not have understood such small torments, but there were areas to be instinctively avoided, like a piece of torn skin that is too raw to be touched. Many Irish mothers cherish the hope that their doted-on son will enter the priesthood, but they do so, I suspect, for reasons that have less to do with piety than that another woman may not get her talons into him. When eventually I acquired my Belgian girl friend, the problem arose of how to introduce her to my mother, and I hit upon a method as ingenious as it was craven.

Our drama group was performing Bryan McMahon's play *The Bugle in the Blood* at the Bernadette Hall in Rathmines, and I reserved front-row seats for my parents. I placed my girl friend, Paule, next to my mother, but without telling either who her neighbour was. Instead, I gave my mother a large bag of sweets before setting out for the hall. My entrance came half-way through Act One, and I fetched a glance at the front row. Three sets of jaws were working in unison.

There are worse forms of cowardice, and one of these is to look away when one sees old age and infirmity come upon the Titans of one's childhood. I was guilty of this, not in terms of material neglect, but I turned my back upon my parents' mortality. It was a form of emotional cut-off, a refusal to look at them, and, for close on a year after my mother died, it preyed upon my mind. What nagged at me was nothing as strong as remorse, but rather the feeling that a son could have done better.

One evening, when I was lying in bed between sleep and waking, an experience occurred that I would hesitate to recount if I had not seen it repeated in every detail in a recent BBC television documentary on near-death 'out of body' phenomena. It was not a dream, of that I am certain, but a signal received on a wavelength of the mind. I was in a garden that was a blaze of colour, looking outwards over a white picket fence. My mother appeared on the path outside walking past and stopped at the closed gate. She was wearing a brown jacket and skirt and a hat I had seen in a photograph taken in 1927. She stopped to talk to me. She looked well and was amiable: not so much affectionate as polite. She said I was foolish to worry about her, that it was a waste of time that could be more pleasantly spent. She continued on her way, and my impression was that she had better things to do than stand talking to the likes of me.

I like to think that it was true.

9

So many now-acclaimed geniuses would never have been heard of were it not for me. It was I who first told the world about Dickens, Tolstoy, Maugham and Frank O'Connor. I discovered – on my honour I did – Alfred Hitchcock, Ernst Lubitsch and Jean Renoir, not to mention Georges Feydeau, Sean O'Casey and Kaufman and Hart. Verdi and Puccini were nobodies until I spread their names. They and others were my personal and exclusive discoveries. I would open a book, walk into a picture house, switch on the wireless, and at once I was a missionary, bent on spreading the true Word to the heathen. I knew that no one had yet heard of these gods of mine; otherwise, why were no comets seen, no fires on the hilltops, no bonnets hurtling over windmills? There was a girl in my office named Margaret O'Sullivan; she was from the country, red-haired, ten years older than I and a great reader. One morning, during the tea break, I changed her entire life, as I thought, by telling her of my latest protégé, a French writer named Maupassant. I was babbling about him for a time before I noticed that she was looking at me if I had just announced my engagement to a Protestant.

'You don't read *him*?' she said.

I said: 'Yes, why not?'

She said, and her voice was as shrill as a playground: 'Don't you know what he died of?'

In Ireland, even today, you can get blind drunk and run down a hobble of old-age pensioners, and there are those who will sympathise and blame not you, but the drink itself: a good man's failing. Let you embezzle, and take the soda bread from the mouths of widows and their children, and, although fingers may wag, you will be privately admired for a 'a cute whoor'. If you break a shopkeeper's head and steal his takings, the law may deem it a crime, but only a killjoy will call it a sin. This is not amorality, but rather a matter of elbow room: the loathing of sexuality looms so large in Irish life that all other offences must be shouldered aside to leave space for it to flourish. The difference between Irish Catholics and Christians is that where sex is concerned the former are inclined to invert the precept of the latter: that one should detest the sin while loving the sinner. A few years ago at a press conference, I saw a trim blonde lady across the room and thought her gamesome of eye. I asked my host, a southerner and an industrialist, who she was.

'Oh, you know,' he said languidly. 'The kind of woman you want to hurt.'

'Pardon?'

He spelt it out for me. 'The kind you want to beat up.'

I said: 'But I don't beat up women. I don't even *want* to beat up women.'

He gave me the amused look of a man who knew all about my perversions in a sound-proofed basement room in Waterloo Road, accompanying it with a nudge that told me not to insult his intelligence. He said: 'Now come *on!*'

His glance alighted on his own wife standing near by. They smiled and airmailed each other a kiss.

If illicit sex were on occasion permitted a toehold – metaphorically speaking, that is – it was confined to the rarified world of the arts and, even there, the demarcation lines were unyielding. A British television director working in Ireland made off with a blonde singer, the wife of a professional man, and thereafter found that work in the Radio Telefis studios was, of a sudden, non-existent. When, rather than starve, the pariahs betook themselves to London, a certain impresario – the doyen of Irish theatre

– boasted of his role of getting rid of them. 'We don't want them and their sort here,' he told me, adding a derisive Dublin term I have never been able to track to its source: 'Dirty elders!'

Bemused, I reminded him that a prominent Irish play director and an actor's wife had for years been having an affair that was as stormy as it was public. I said: 'How is it that no one ever chased *them* out of the country?'

'Ah,' he said with a smile that forgave my failure to grasp the niceties of such matters, 'but they're our own!'

When Margaret O'Sullivan asked me if I was aware of what Maupassant had died of, it was because she knew, as did all clean-living people, that an immoral man – or woman – could not possibly write a moral book. As a theorem, it stood so transparently to reason that you half-expected to find it in Euclid. At a debate on censorship at the Mansion House, I heard Sean O'Faoláin speak of the shame he had felt before his family and friends when a book of his was banned, making him in the public sight a pornographer. By then, the government list of proscribed books – itself a volume as bulky as Apuleius' *The Golden Ass*, which, after seventeen centuries, had at last been deemed unfit for the Irish to read – was approaching its peak figure of 12,000 titles.

The censors were not, as one might suppose, prodigious readers. All that was necessary to have a book removed from the shops and the public libraries was to send a copy to the Censorship Board with the offending passage marked. This, taken out of context, as in the case of Kate O'Brien's mere reference to lesbianism in *The Land of Spices*, was quite enough. As adolescents, we cherished banned books for their rarity value as much as for their salacity, although I remember vainly ransacking smuggled copies of both Richard Llewellen's *How Green Was My Valley* and L.A.G. Strong's *The Bay* in search of the dirty bits. Strong had a particular influence on me, for in *The Garden* and *Sea Wall* he wrote about Dalkey, the sea front at Sandycove and the Victorian roads I walked every day. One of his characters, the lame and kindly Paddy Kennedy, nicknamed 'the

Wingman', was actually known to my father who described him to me as he described nearly everyone else, as a 'queer harp'. Seen through a stranger's eyes, the strand at the White Rock, the rock pools along the front at Scotsman's bay, the sweep of the hill down into Glasthule, and even a tram ride to the pictures ceased to be ordinary and took on a grandeur that was never lost. Upon reading his book of short stories, *Travellers*, I wrote to Strong, young pup that I was, pointing out that his initials – for 'Leonard Alfred George' – spelt *lag*, the Irish word for 'weak'. His response, signing himself 'Weak Strong', was to invite me to tea when he next came to Ireland. I sat facing him for an hour, tongue-tied, and he probably went away thinking that I had been unable to come and had, by default, sent my idiot brother.

I knew two writers by sight: the poet, Patrick Kavanagh, and his arch-enemy, Brendan Behan. Kavanagh haunted Parson's bookshop on Baggot Street Bridge and ceaselessly cleared his throat with the sound of a very old car trying to start and failing. One morning, I came tripping over my feet into the shop, and the doyenne, Miss O'Flaherty, begged me to make less noise. 'Mr Kavanagh,' she whispered, 'is having his breakfast.' I peered behind one of the shelves and was in time to see him draining a Baby Power as fast as it would empty. He put the bottle in his pocket, made a hawking noise that caused the pages of *Ireland's Own* to flutter on its rack, and took out a safety razor. Then, without soap or even water, and to the accompaniment of a rasping noise that made my skin crawl like a snake, he proceeded to rid himself of a two-day beard.

Years later, I sat beside him on a flight from Rome to London and, as the stewardess went past, he called to her: 'Miss, for the love o' Jasus give us a large Paddy.' She either ignored him or failed to hear. His voice rumbled like a bowling ball through the cabin: 'English bitch.' He added, just as loudly, and each syllable was caked with the cow dung of Mucker, County Monaghan: 'British whoo-err!'

In the case of Kavanagh, the man existed almost wholly in his poetry, the finest since Yeats's; his voice and appearance were merely the leftovers. He had the look of a pig-jobber: the arms forever folded high, as if in aloof disdain that he had been offered a runt; he wore thick farmyard boots and a sweat-stained felt hat and had an askew face that seemed to have been squeezed in a vice. For all his harrumph and bluster, he could be faced down and was terrified of Brendan Behan, who knew with a slum-dweller's instinct who would run from him and who would stand. On hard-up days, when our lunch was a three-ha'penny potato cake eaten out of the fist as we ambled down Dawson Street, Behan was a familiar sight. He was not yet famous as a writer, but had been a Republican and an inmate of both Borstal in England and Mountjoy in Dublin. Such credentials defined him as a 'character', which is usually a Dublinese synonym for a bowsie or gurrier. He was a house painter, and it was said of him that he was decorating a certain pub, working and sampling the stock every weekday during the Holy Hour, and that the task had so far taken him two years. A friend of mine worked in his spare time for the Catholic Truth Society and sold religious booklets from a barrow outside the Pro-Cathedral. Behan came up with the careful belly-forward, head-back walk that told you his feet were tiny.

He asked: '*Tuigin tu Gaelig?*' ('Do you understand Irish?')

My friend proudly answered: '*Tuigim.*' ('I understand.')

Whereupon Behan unleashed the deafening roar of '*Tuigim* me bollix!' and went on his way, a listing galleon in a following sea.

He was unshamable: a show-off with an insatiable hunger for attention. His eyes were everywhere at once: in search of an audience, finding it, gauging its mood, dancing to its tune. Around town, he was known to be a 'decent skin' and 'one of our own'. Either term defined anyone who pronounced 'Jesus' as 'Jayzus', never employed a noun without propping a 'fuckin' up against it like timbers shoring up a tenement, got drunk and broke windows, gave half-crowns to children in the street, called old ones 'missis' and told them that they were the 'heart of the rowl', and displayed just enough erudition to hint that it was but the tip of an iceberg which good taste decreed should not be shown in its awesome entirety. All of this may have been innate and genuine to begin with, but once Behan discovered that the quality a Dublinman is most praised for is the absence of affectation, he milked the image for all that it was worth, knowing that anyone who fetched him a bleak look or threw doubt on his rough-hewn goodness would be scorned as a begrudger.

He had a street wit that was deadly. One of the highlights of an annual onset of culture known as *An Tostal* and now happily defunct was an historical pageant held in Croke Park. The climax of this was provided by the actor, Anew McMaster, who, wearing a white beard and dressed as St Patrick, saved Ireland for Christianity by tearing about the field and overturning a number of pagan idols. Behan had managed to scale half-way up one of the pillars of the grandstand and endorsed the proceedings with repeated roars of 'Good oul' God!'

He could be genial, but no Dublin street was wide enough or long enough to be shared with another writer. The city itself was too small, and his fear, even of those who offered him no threat, was so naked as to be endearingly childlike. My own first play had hardly begun to limp through an inglorious three-week run at the Abbey when I ran foul of Behan, who by now was known as the author of *The Quare Fellow*. Every morning on my way to Merrion Street, I called into Parson's bookshop, which was a haunt of his as well as of other writers. As I waited to be served, he would shuffle over and glare murderously from a range of a few inches. It was an undeclared war of attrition, and I fought back by pretending to be unaware of the vast, stubbled face, the pale blue eyes ringed with blood, and the sour smell of last night's pints. I knew it enraged him to be ignored, and yet to address me directly would be to lose face. After a week or so, he took to haranguing the ceiling.

'Is *Esquire* banned in this country?'

No one answered.

More loudly: 'For the love an' honour, is there ne'er a one to answer a civil question?' The ladies who managed Parson's allowed for the waywardness of the artistic soul, but I noticed that Behan did not court banishment by using an obscenity. 'I asked is *Esquire* banned here?'

Miss O'Flaherty simpered: 'Sure, Mr Behan, don't you know it is.' (It is true, for it was in those days notorious for its photographs of women showing not only their legs but also as much as three inches of bare midriff.)

'Is that so?' Behan said, still to the ceiling. 'I hear tell I have a play in it this month. I was paid for it right enough.' He named what seemed to me an enormous sum. 'Yes, I got the readies, the few shekels, but when a man can't read his own bloomin' play it's a bit of a —'

By then I was clear of the shop and pushing my bicycle at a run over the hump of the canal bridge.

Over the next two or three weeks, buying my morning paper was purgatory. There were, of course, other newsagents along the way, but this was a duel between Behan and me, although whether the battle was territorial, or for a purely moral ascendancy, I had no idea, nor, I think, had he. One day, he would brag that *The Quare Fellow* was due to go on at a place called Stratford East, and where the hell was that? On another, he would ask if anyone had ever heard of a fillum producer named Metro or Mayer or something who was trying to take out an option on his play. Then, staring at a point just southwards of my ear, he would say: 'What's an option when it's at home?'

One day, he did not appear. I had a holiday from him for perhaps a week and was beginning to think I was rid of him for good when he came into the shop almost blind from the ravages of a hangover. He had not washed for days; his face was purple, the eyes sunk in his head. There was spittle on his chin. *In extremis*, he spoke to me for the first time. He said: 'Hey, for Christ's sake, what day is it?'

Perhaps I thought he was trying to be funny. Or I may have been dismayed at seeing him come back to torment me. Whatever the reason, I snarled 'Shag off!' and flung out of the shop.

Behan came after me. He stood on the summit of the bridge as I pedalled off, his face a muddy, blood-coloured sunset. He brought into sight a fist that was usually out of sight inside the sleeve of his black overcoat. 'That's lovely,' he bellowed. 'That's exquisite. That's gorgeous fuckin' language.'

The next and last time we spoke was in the Brazen Head eight years later. He had perhaps six months of life left. He was sober. He said: 'You writin' an'thin'?'

I told him what I was working on and asked the same question of him.

He said: 'No. The way it is, I'm off the hard stuff. Once I get off the beer as well, I'll start writin'.'

A few days later, he went to a luncheon where some joker poured a vodka into his tomato juice. It sent him on a tear that lasted six weeks and landed him in Baggot Street Hospital for a month. When he was discharged I saw him on television and had to look away, for by then death was already on his face.

I remember one other literary encounter in Parson's bookshop, and it happened the year I made a stage adaptation of Joyce's *A Portrait*. It caused something of a splash at the 1962 Dublin Theatre Festival, and Frank O'Connor went to see it as a guest critic for one of the Sunday papers. His review began: 'I am proud to say that I did not like *Stephen D.*'

The play was no more than a scissors-and-paste affair with nothing of myself in it, and so in spite of O'Connor's eminence his contempt was no worse than a gnat bite. What did annoy me was not that he disliked the play, but that he took pleasure in disliking it. He himself was a Titan. I revered his stories; I had weaned myself on them; but later, as in the case of Patrick Kavanagh, I learned that whenever a writer is renowned for the depth of compassion in his work, usually very little of the stuff remains in the man himself. It was said of O'Connor that he was tetchy, vain, choleric and, like every Irish writer born to woman, disappointed. Still, I had not thought him small.

A few days after the review appeared, I was in Parson's and saw that a new edition of his stories had come out. I was about to buy a copy when Miss O'Flaherty said: 'No, don't take that one. I have a few here that are signed by the author.'

I said, primly: 'No, thank you. I'd prefer an unsigned copy. I admire O'Connor's work, but I don't care much for O'Connor. If you'll permit me to say so, I think he's a miserable, unmannerly bogman.'

She said: 'Oh, Mr Leonard', and looked in dismay, not at me, but over my shoulder. I turned in time to see a bespectacled man with white hair, white moustache and black eyebrows marching out of the shop, his face tight with anger. She again said 'Oh, Mr Leonard', this time softly, as a mother might weep for an apostate son.

Fifteen years earlier, in the late 1940s, O'Connor was only one of the Irish writers whose work was, in part, proscribed. Joyce, O'Faoláin, O'Casey, Kavanagh (who said: 'It's the price of me for writing poetry that a policeman could understand'): these and others were conscripted into what was known as the Legion of the Banned. In 1946, an amateur production of O'Casey's *Juno and the Paycock* was banned by the clerics who ran the Father Mathew drama festival, not because of its politics or the depicted brutalities of slum life, but because Mary Boyle, who is unmarried, is seduced and becomes pregnant. Radio Eireann solved Mary's problem without going to the extreme of banning the play. In O'Casey's text, the following occurs when Juno Boyle must tell her wastrel husband that their daughter is expecting a baby.

MRS BOYLE: It's about Mary.

BOYLE: Well, what about Mary – there's nothing wrong with her, is there?

MRS BOYLE: I'm sorry to say there's a gradle wrong with her.

BOYLE: A gradle wrong with her! (*Peevishly*): First Johnny and now Mary. It's not consumption, is it?

MRS BOYLE: No, it's not consumption . . . it's worse.

In the radio production, transmitted to perhaps half a million homes all over Ireland, the last two lines were amended to go as follows:

BOYLE: . . . It's not consumption, is it?

MRS BOYLE: Yis.

We did not feel oppressed by the lunacy: it was a game: us outwitting them. Like scavenger birds on a rubbish tip, we rooted in street barrows for books that had slipped through the net. On principle, we took, when we could find them, ragged copies of *Liliput* and *Men Only* and even *Razzle*, *Blighty* and *Reveille*, often with their occasions of sin scissored out by the previous owner. Irish authors were not too difficult to locate; usually their books had had a short run for their money before coming under disfavour, and had thereafter gone into hiding, like Jews from the Nazis. More seriously, a wave of post-war fiction was on its way from America; and, as naturally as a sparrow is swooped on by a hawk, copies were stopped by the customs and held, unread and unaccused, until the censors found time to attend to them. In such cases, there were few of us who did not have a friend, smiled upon by the gods, who went on holiday into the great world beyond Dublin Bay and could be persuaded to bear home, trembling as if for his life, Mailer's *The Naked and the Dead*, Robert Penn Warren's *All the King's Men*, James Jones's *From Here to Eternity* and Salinger's *Catcher in the Rye*, which today is not only looked upon with the indulgence shown to a reformed criminal, but is also a prescribed text in secondary schools.

Once a book was found, the new problem arose of how to pay for it. If the worst happened, you could steal it. My belief is that, thanks to the censors, the Dublin of that time became the world's best-read city. Also, there can have been few better towns in which to be broke. I once mentioned to one of my superiors at work that, apart from having three-ha'pence for an evening paper, I had no money. Envy came into his eyes – or, rather, his eye, for the other one was glass.

He said: 'But you have money at home? Or in the bank or the post office?'

I told him: no, not a penny.

He said: 'What's it like? Remind me. I've forgotten.'

I had no answer. Poverty can be described, for it is a presence, open to the senses: it can be touched, seen, even tasted; whereas being broke is its opposite: an absence. The kind we were, we thought that pockets were for hands and hankies.

One Friday, the impossible happened. There was a pay rise, even for temporary clerks, and, because it was retroactive, seventeen pounds fell in one great lump into my fist. It was not simply a windfall, but wealth: blinding and unreal; and, on that pay-day, four of us did the unthinkable and went for dinner to a restaurant, a basement place named The Subway. The waiter asked if we wanted to see the wine list. We stared at each other, at once helpless, then I heard my own voice say: 'Yes, why not?' I chose a bottle of red; it was brought, and the waiter poured a little into my glass. I had never before ordered wine, but I knew what was required. Aware that here was a great 'first' in my life, I was determined to make of it a moment that could be framed. As my companions looked on in awe, I swirled the wine around the glass, pretended to sniff the bouquet (then, as now, I had hardly any sense of smell), and took a delicate sip. No oenophile ever rolled a Château-Lafite Rothschild around his tongue as jadedly as I did, nor with such world-weariness murmured that it would 'do'.

The waiter said: 'Jayzus, sure it won't p'ison yah, anyway.'

No matter; for an hour, we were children in the finery of grown-ups.

Once, outside the Savoy Cinema, I saw a man in top hat and tails stepping out of a taxi with a woman who wore a glittering black dress that was like a second skin, and to me they were not alive at all. When I was six or so and my parents took me to the Picture House on Sunday afternoons, I would look up and down George's Street in hopes that I might catch sight of the lorry arriving with the lions and crocodiles for the weekly serial, *Jan of the Jungle*; and, in the same way, the man and woman might have been film creatures on their way to the screen.

Jammet's restaurant was a door and two half-curtained windows in Nassau Street. During Horse Show week, you went past it, stepping off the kerb as a couple, bowed out by the doorman, moved into your way. They were gentry, up for the show from Kildare, perhaps, or Westmeath. The man, somehow without giving the least suggestion of loudness, wore a jacket you could play draughts on. His bearing told you that he was the kind of person who would say 'shall' instead of 'will' all the time, as we did. He waited while the woman stood drawing on thin, chamois gloves. She spoke to him in a clear voice that neither whispered nor shouted and, you knew, never would. They had not expected you to move out of their way, because they had not seen you. The ability to look without seeing was what made them the Quality, just as stepping out into the street proved that you were not. You never expected or wanted to eat at Jammet's or the Russell or the Red Bank, heaven forbid, but a sore that smarted in a small, back corner of your mind was that neither were you ever likely to be the friend of anyone who did.

There were legends that walked the streets of the same city as we did, but not the same world. A frequent sight was the playwright, Lennox Robinson. I would gape at him, hardly believing that he was the author of *Drama at Inish* and *The Far-off Hills* in the actual flesh – although there was pitifully little of it. He was beanpole thin, and seemed to be wilting. His head towered above any crowd, as if he were a lone Christian crossing the floor of a mosque at prayer-time. He was hectic of cheek, lugubrious of mien. Threading his way through town, he seemed fey and aloof from the vulgar throng, although his pub obituarists were to say that, as a member of the Abbey Theatre board of directors, he had a Florentine gift for intrigue. He went about with a white Cairn terrier named Sylvester. They were a bizarre couple: the dog at the end of its leash put one in mind of a coracle towing a schooner. And, to use 'schooner' in a different sense, Robinson was often the worse for sherry. Once, with Sylvester, he patiently queued for two hours for the Bing Crosby film *Going My Way*, at the Capital Cinema while under the impression that he was waiting for the Dalkey tram. On another occasion, he was adjudicating a drama festival somewhere down the country, and his own play, *The Whiteheaded Boy*, was one of the offerings. The actors expected praise; instead, when it was over, he came on the stage, looking like a pair of lazy tongs standing on end and about to collapse. In limp desolation, he wailed to the audience: 'Did you see what they did to my beautiful play?'

He was an unlikely chronicler of simple lives. The people of his plays lived in small country towns. In *The Far-off Hills*, everyone wants what he cannot have. The sixteen-year-old Pet looks in the mirror and groans: 'I wish to God I had a different class of a nose.' Harold Mahony, who has not smiled since his wife went mad on their honeymoon, thinks he wants to marry Marian; she, as self-deluding as he is, is set on entering a convent. Robinson, the dreamer, the cloud-dweller, fashioned his earthlings with wisdom and affection, as if he lived among them, upstairs from a shop or in a granite house half-way along Church Street, with a picture of Father Maguire on the parlour wall. There is such a picture called for in the setting of *The Whiteheaded Boy*, and the author in a stage direction confides to us that the priest is 'No relation, but a lovely man.' It might be said of Robinson that, like Thornton Wilder of *Our Town*, he attempted to 'find a value beyond price for the smallest events in daily life'. As I say, I gawked at him on the street. His fame was such that people could not refer by name to Longford Terrace in Monkstown without adding 'where Lennox Robinson lives'. At their best, his plays were flawlessly constructed and, thirty years ago, were performed by every amateur group in the land. Today, he is an antiquity. His name appears here and there in the biographies of others. There is a life-sized portrait of him in the Abbey bar. He sits, hands folded, six feet and some inches of misery. It is difficult to buy a drink without wanting to offer him a sherry.

The time came when I tried my own hand at writing a play. It was a one-act entitled *The Man on Platform Two*, based on the old legend that Parnell did not die in October, 1891, but was spirited out of reach of his enemies. My friend, Brendan Ryan, who managed a snack bar in Dun Laoghaire, played Parnell and we entered the play for a festival at my old stamping ground, the Little Flower Hall in Bray. Father Browne was as yet the incumbent, and afterwards I was rash enough to invite his opinion. He said 'God bless you' to a lady who was passing, then smiled at the church steeple and told it: 'I don't like political plays. I don't like plays with a spleen.' Before I could ask him what he meant, he said 'Ah, Mrs Kinsella, a word in your ear!' and went off to talk to a woman he had espied with an eye that was somewhere in the back of his head. It took a while before I realised that although sixty years had passed, the clergy had not forgiven the adulterer, Parnell.

Later, I attempted a full-length suburban farce called *Nightingale in the Branches*. Lancos performed it. My crony, Mick, played a character I had based on his own father; Róisín was the mother; and Jimmy Keogh ad-libbed and said 'boinng' and 'gedoink' to his heart's content. A few years later, under another title and with only two words ('Yes, Da') of the original dialogue retained, it became Barry Fitzgerald's last film. Meanwhile, our production came and went, and the audience from work laughed and said wasn't it great, considering. My name was on the showcards; I was at last an author. To my disgust, the world went on turning regardless, and I continued to be stuck tight in the Land Commission like a sheep in a bog hole.

Mr Drumm, who could no longer stand the sight of me, had ordained my banishment to the room behind his, where my immediate superior was a Mr Cramer, a burly man with a cultured accent, a moustache and an Eric Von Stroheim haircut. He could not sit still, but constantly tore around like a demented bull. If he thought he might miss the bus home to Ranelagh at lunchtime, he would bark like a distraught wolfhound, send his table crashing into mine, which in turn rammed me in the stomach, and go charging out, lost in a slipstream of whirling paper. To no one's great surprise but his own, he eventually dropped dead.

Although he did not seem to be well-read, he once told me that he had a library of two thousand books. It was a rare confidence, for in the most kindly way he was a snob. As a mere Staff Officer, Grade II, he had either come down in life or failed to rise in it; but his family were gentlefolk, and he had been brought up to believe that, while all mankind were his equals, he was not of necessity required to treat them as such. We liked him, and thought that his death would be a toss-up between a heart attack and being run over, for he could not see a priest without rushing across the street to pay his respects.

At work, it was understood that on arrival we had ten minutes' grace in which to peruse the morning paper. One day, when Mr Cramer caught me covertly reading it at five past ten, he made such a huffing and puffing about it that I sulked and deliberately did not remind him, as I usually did, when the time came for his lunchtime bus. Suddenly, he jumped up, bellowed 'Blazes Kate, I'm destroyed!' and went tearing out, doors banging into the distance like cannon fire. He missed the bus and returned after lunch, eating Rennies as if they were peanuts. Later, red in the face, he said that Mr Drumm wanted to see me.

'Mr Cramer believes that he has cause to complain of you,' Mr Drumm said, making a church roof of his fingers. 'He alleges that you are wanting in respect.'

I asked, coldly: 'On what grounds?'

His nostrils twitched as if at an offensive smell. He had not spoken to me in a year. I had disappointed him. Everyone did, sooner or later, but to me, encased with him each morning in the same train compartment, he had made himself vulnerable. He never spoke of his life, but of books, or a rare visit to the cinema, and his wit impaled those of his colleagues, and they were legion, whom he considered to be time-servers or hypocrites. In my case, what happened may have been that I started to avoid him rather than be looked down upon as his toady. At any rate, he decided that his confidences had been betrayed and his good nature – which was virtually non-existent – abused. For all his prickliness, I had been fond of him. Being myself a mumbler, I was besotted with his gift for a phrase and his preciseness of speech. Also, he had a barbed integrity which he kept alive at the cost of letting much else perish: his friendships, peace of mind and, in Merrion Street, cronyism and the rewards for holding one's tongue. His enmity hurt me; I felt ill-used. Now, behind the coldness of his regard, there was the hurt of a cast-off suitor. For a moment – and then it was gone – I felt an urge to throw my arms around the old fool.

He said, echoing me: 'You ask on what grounds?'

Unwisely, I attempted to play him at his own game and say something trenchant and well-formed to the effect that, in the matter of collecting arrears of rent from the tenant farmers of Cork and Galway, I was his and Mr Cramer's to command, but it was not my function to act as the latter's personal nurse and alarm clock. Instead, I made a hames of it, mislaying a verb, marooning a noun on a foreign shore, starting a jerry-built sentence that caved in half-way through when, without warning, nasal catarrh closed upon me like a sea fog. Cruelly, Mr Drumm let me finish or, rather, wind down like an old timepiece clogged with grease. I fell silent; he waited; I snuffled and bubbled, and he waited some more. Then he showed me how it should be done.

'My friend,' he said, making it sound as if he would as soon seek out the companionship of an asp, 'your want of breeding is beyond mortal remedy' – I flushed, taking this to be a jibe at my pedigree or, rather, my lack of one – 'but between us we may yet instil in you the rudiments of good manners.'

What was damnable was that while one part of me wanted to throttle him, another was admiring his knife-clean enunciation and his command of language.

'According to rumour,' he went on, 'you have written a play for the theatre. I am told, and I would imagine it to be true, that among the desirable attributes of a dramatist, indeed of a writer, are humility and compassion. You seem to possess neither.'

He glared at the five or six other occupants of the room, who were happily listening. Their heads ducked out of sight behind the arrears schedules that were propped in front of them on wooden frames. Having disposed of them, Drumm returned to his muttons. I half-expected him to offer me a cigarette and a blindfold.

'As long as Mr Cramer continues to be your superior officer, you will show him courtesy and respect, do you hear me? In particular, you will do or say nothing . . . nothing, do you understand?' – I tensed myself, for here it came – 'to undermine his harmless delusion that he is a gentleman.'

There was a gasp, ecstatic and concerted, from behind the arrears schedules. I was not, after all, Drumm's victim; Mr Cramer was. I had merely been used as a cat's-paw to make him seem a fool and an upstart. By going-home time, the story was all over Collection Branch. By lunch-time next day, it had penetrated to the uttermost parts of the congested Districts Board in Hume Street and Forestry in Merrion Square, and as Mr

Cramer, in a stampede of one, went pounding towards the Ranelagh bus and his home-cooked lunch, there were winks and sniggers of 'Jayzus, did you hear what your man Drumm said about Jacko Cramer?' On the instant, he had a nickname unto death: 'Jacko the Gent.' I wondered why Drumm had done it: perhaps because Mr Cramer was forever putting on airs; more likely for the simpler reason that the Land Commission begot its own kind of pygmy cruelty.

Nobody, the State least of all, cared about us, and so we came not to care about each other. Indifference bred a meanness of spirit, which, in turn, engendered the petty jealousies and feuds, the tale-bearing and begrudgery that in time dragged to earth even those who flew highest. There were some who thought the work all the more tolerable because it required no skill; they did it, skimping if they could, for eight hours a day, slept for another eight, and lived an eight-hour life. At the end of the road, they would tell you, you could not whack the old pension. I wanted more. In the vaguest of ways, I had thought that once I had written a play I would be magically transported to a new existence. Every half-year, I refused to sit for an examination in written and oral Irish which would have led to advancement: I was afraid that a rise in salary might sap my will when the time came to break loose. Now, as the seasons came around again, it seemed that I would end my days, not merely as a civil servant but, thanks to my lunatic optimism, as a rank-and-file clerical officer; the common fate of boozers and losers like Joe McAteer and the chronically unwashed, such as 'the Needler' Maguire.

I had failed, too, in my chosen extra-mural career as a philanderer. As if in obedience to a secret oath taken at the onset of puberty, the women in my life, no matter what their shape and age, perversely declined to bend to my will. Even certified nymphomaniacs would smile at me half-way through our first and, not to put a tooth in it, last evening together and thank me in advance for being the first man in years to have respected their frailty. There is a kind of time limit in such areas, and, having exceeded mine, I gave up and became engaged to marry. As the wedding day approached, I was presented with a travelling bag by my colleagues. Drumm boycotted the ceremony. Pointing his umbrella, as if aching to impale those arriving for the speeches, he disdainfully stalked off to catch the 5.14 to Dalkey. The speakers were Mr Kilfeather, the Assistant Principal of our branch, and Mr Cramer, who had been pressed into service as the reluctant understudy for Drumm.

Kilfeather arrived, limping; it was the souvenir of a mishap from the previous week. He was an obnoxious man with obnoxious habits, and one of these was to quit his room at 4.45 each day, walk through the adjoining office that contained perhaps thirty clerks, and immure himself in the men's lavatory on the far landing. At precisely 4.57, the chain was pulled, and he would emerge, ostensibly to return to his room, but actually to see if anyone in the large office had dared to put his street clothes on three minutes ahead of time. The ploy would have been less contemptible had it not been so transparent; but it happened that a clerk named Oliver Whelehan had a habit as obnoxious in its way as Kilfeather's. Whenever he used the lavatory, he would conclude his business by unravelling perhaps fifty feet of toilet roll and ramming it into the bowl, leaving the thing unflushable until plumbers came from the Board of Works. No one knew why; nor, perhaps, did Oliver.

One day, the week before my presentation, Oliver made his customary use of the lavatory, and, a few minutes after he had gone, Kilfeather arrived on his daily routine of espionage. He lowered his trousers and underpants, sat, filled his pipe, lit it and dropped the match down the front of the toilet bowl. A few moments later, a loud *whoof!* sound was heard, followed by a cry of anguish, and a few women clerks who had the great good fortune to be passing were treated to the sight of Kilfeather hopping out of the W.C. with his trousers around his ankles and his pubic hair smoking like a tramp steamer outward bound for Mombasa.

As well as his limp, he had the more permanent affliction of a speech impediment, which caused him to pause and say 'Ummm' after every four or five words. Today, the audience writhed as each 'ummm' became longer and more tortured than its predecessor. I stood, red in the face, aware that a clerk named Donal Coughlan was conducting a conversation of his own immediately to my rear. Coughlan was tiny, with ears like teacup handles. He resembled a gnome. Because of treatment with cortisone when the drug was still in its experimental stage, his hair had fallen out and he was almost stone deaf, and, like many deaf people, he did not so much speak as yell. Kilfeather battled on, wishing me ummm happiness and hoping that all my ummm troubles would be little ummm ones. At last, he hit an 'ummm' that seemed endless: the room shivered as if a power plant were operating on the floor below. He paused as if to make a run at whatever he had in mind to say, whereupon, Coughlan roared in his Cork accent: 'Errah, deh trout down dere are very sulky, very sulky altogedder!'

At this, Kilfeather gave up and passed the torch on to Mr Cramer who, quite simply, had nothing to say. He huffed and puffed for a minute, and then inspiration struck.

He said: 'I'm sure we all wish Mr Byrne the very best, and we hope now that he's getting married that he'll settle down to work like the great man he is and give up all this playwriting nonsense.'

A frisson of sheer joy went through the audience. Mr Cramer, unaware that he had said anything out of the way, gave me the travelling bag with the best wishes of my colleagues, said 'Blazes Kate, look at the time!' under his breath and went hurrying out, followed by Kilfeather. At once, there was laughter. Everyone knew where my ambitions lay, and that he had put his foot in it. 'How,' Arthur Nolan said, 'can a man be so bloody insensitive?' 'Old gobshite,' someone else said.

I smiled and affected to share in the joke. Privately, Mr

Cramer's gaffe had struck a chord. There was that wooden trunk in my bedroom at home; it was my writing table, and to use it as such I was obliged either to bark my knees or sit with my legs to one side, out of the way. The alternative was the kitchen table downstairs, with my mad aunt Mary maundering on, as if she somehow knew that it made me as crazed as she was. On summer evenings, my mother would tell me that the sun was still splitting the trees and here I was hunched indoors over an old copybook. In the winter, she nagged at me to go to the pictures or to see my friends instead of giving them the go-by. 'And sign's on it,' she would say, 'in the wind-up you'll have no one left who'll throw a word to you, no more than they would to a dog.' Worst of all was when she would tell my father and Mary to be quiet because 'Jack is at his writin'', and the noise of three people deliberately not making a sound was louder than any thunder. And so I worked upstairs in the front bedroom, and let a summer and an autumn slide by, fashioning that first play of mine, crying at times when words, knowing that I was not their master, jeered at me like cornerboys. When Lancos performed it, my mother was in the audience. Afterwards, I asked, trying not to sound too eager: 'What did you think?'

All she said was: 'Too much oul' talk.'

Somehow, in a way I never understood and never shall, it had angered her: not the play itself, as harmless as it was, but that I had written it. I never again invited her to see a play of mine, not out of pique or in revenge, but to avoid a second slap in the face, as light as the first had been. She, who could take mortal offence at an unintended slight, did not mind in the least. Probably she was relieved.

I had expected too much of that play, pinned too many hopes on it. Like an inmate of the Chateau d'If, his brain softened from the years of solitude, I had convinced myself that by burrowing through a single wall I would at once reach freedom and the outside world instead of, as happened, another part of the prison.

Now, while I laughed with the others at Mr Cramer's failure to recognise that he had a potential genius on his hands, a small chill voice whispered that perhaps he was right and it was time I gave up the 'playwriting nonsense'.

10

On the few occasions when I am caught off guard and land myself on a public platform, there is always a smiling lady who raises her hand and asks if I have any advice for young writers. I invariably reply 'No', and for two reasons: first, because the blunt negative always gets a laugh, and secondly because writing is neither profession nor vocation, but an incurable illness. Those who give up are not writers and never were; those who persevere do so not from pluck or determination, but because they cannot help it: they are sick, and advice is an impertinence. When the Abbey Theatre announced a competition for new Irish plays, I forgot all about Mr Cramer's finger-wagging and went to work. This, I knew in my bones, would be the Big One.

It was nothing of the sort. I called it *The Italian Road*. I had been to Italy on holiday and stayed at a resort named Varazze some miles from Genoa. It had the only sandy beach on the Ligurian Riviera, but I never saw it. There was a heat wave, with temperatures in the high nineties, and I spent my days under a sun umbrella trying to make a glass of beer last for an hour. Eventually, I fled northwards to Milan and attempted unsuccessfully to find the cathedral: not one of the streetcars announced *Cathedrale* as its destination; they were all bound for a place named *Duomo*, whatever that was when at home. So I went to a music hall instead and heard an old tenor named Gino Franz sing tearfully in front of a rippling backdrop of Naples and Vesuvius. The audience was rowdy; empty bottles clattered down the aisle. Two utterly inept acrobats came on and were hooted off; the

Neapolitan backdrop was again unfurled, hitting the stage with a thump, and Gino Franz reappeared by public demand, quite overcome – as he doubtlessly was at every performance – by the acclamation. The more humility he evinced, the louder were the cries of 'Bravo!', and when he wept the audience stood, cheering. I had the time of my life, applauding and shedding tears of maudlin delight, and from that evening on Italy became not a reality but a myth: a kingdom to be one day regained.

My play was a kind of homage to the ideal. A youth, whose father is for no explained reason a schoolmaster in Ravello – a place in which I had not set foot to this day – lives with his alcoholic mother in a seaside boarding-house outside Dublin. He dreams that his estranged parents will become reconciled and bear him off to Italy and the sun. The action required that the play be set during school holidays; Christmas was too festive, summer too cheerful for the requisite greyness, and so I settled for Easter. When amateurs later performed the play, an eminent critic wrote of its brilliant symbolism, pointing out that the first act took place on Spy Wednesday, the day of betrayal, the second on Good Friday, the time of sacrifice, and the third on Easter Sunday, the day of spiritual rebirth. No one has ever believed that a playwright simply sits down to write a play without a thought entering his head of symbols, metaphors or subtexts, and Irish drama critics were in those days, as they continue to be, a breed of quack psychoanalysts in unswerving pursuit of what O'Casey called 'magnificent meanin's'. Unfortunately for *The Italian Road*, there were no critics moonlighting as play readers for the Abbey, who turned it down flat.

The standard was so abysmal, a letter tactfully informed me, that no prize would be awarded. I was not so much dismayed as stunned, for I had recently been at the first night of the previous year's winner, a play called *John Courtney*, and it was so flat-footedly dull as to send me out of the theatre grinning from ear to ear in the certainty that I had the contest in my pocket. What I had not grasped was that the tastes of the Abbey did not run to a play set in a Dun Laoghaire boarding-house and more concerned with the fate of its characters than with the perennial theme of what was wrong with the country.

The archetypal Abbey play of the 1950s was dominated by the seemingly Promethean figure of the 'Warrior': a doughty one-time guerrilla leader who is now a powerful businessman and county councillor. His integrity has been sapped by avarice; those who oppose him are genially ridden down. He has a kept woman named Margot in the nearby metropolis of Mullingar; she brazenly accompanies him to the Curragh races and smokes in public. He, the playwright is saying, is the New Ireland. His wife is a wretched creature, ignored by all and with nothing to say. This is because she is being saved up for a three-minute speech cunningly positioned at the end of the play and on that account assured of a round of applause. There are two children of the marriage: a daughter who is in love with the local schoolmaster, a young radical; and a son whom the Warrior forces to enter a seminary because of the social cachet of a priest in the family. There is a Machiavellian clergyman: the canon, who, as the local powerbroker, is a crony of the Warrior. And the mandatory comic relief is provided by a peripatetic handyman who believes that a wooden leg is hereditary.

The action has to do with how, for dynastic reasons, the Warrior marries off his daughter to an egregious middle-aged politician. To this end, the canon falsely accuses the girls' lover of interfering with one of his pupils, and an enraged mob – their voices are heard, off – drive him from the town. As counterpoint to this, the son arrives home and tells his father that he has no vocation for the priesthood. The Warrior says 'To think that I, F.X. Mulmartin, have spawned not a son but a weak-kneed, whingeing girl,' and sends him back to the seminary. Before he leaves, the boy says: 'Mother, I can't face it. Speak to me.' This being still Act Two, she says nothing.

The last act is the strongest. The son is led in, now dribbling and hopelessly unhinged by the horrors of ordination, and the daughter, rather than yield her body to a satyr, hangs herself upstairs in her wedding dress. The mother makes her speech, telling the Warrior that she has only stayed with him for the sake of the children, adding pathetically, 'There was a day long gone, Frank, when I had the good thought for you', and leaves the house forever. This coincides with the arrival of a letter from the mistress in Mullingar saying that she is actually an apostate nun and has decided to return to the convent. The final scene has been foreshadowed for an act and a half by the Warrior absent-mindedly rubbing his chest, wincing and muttering: 'The devil take that feed of greasy bacon.' This is known in the world of drama as play construction, and it enables the Warrior to succumb convincingly to a heart attack. He dies alone as sunset turns the room to flame, and a single autumn leaf flutters down outside the window. Slow curtain.

The Italian Road boasted few of these marketable ingredients. Also, it was probably not a very good play, but it was the best I could do. When you are young and a work is rejected, it is as if you were a rider thrown by a horse, and the worst part of it is not simply the bruising, but the convalescence of the spirit before you again seize both courage and reins. I stared at the returned script and the covering letter, which was not even personally typed, but stencilled, and grinned stupidly at my wife in a frail attempt to conceal the shame. We had been married for not much more than a month: it was an indecently short time in which to be found out.

She said: 'Why don't you send the Abbey *Nightingale in the Branches*?'

This was the suburban comedy that had been done by Lancos. Reasoning that I had nothing to lose, I at once gave her cause to regret the suggestion by touching her for eight pounds to have the script retyped – thirty years on, the realisation comes that I never repaid it. When I was on the point of mailing the play, it occurred to me that its having been previously performed by amateurs was bound to lessen the chances – already, to my mind, microscopic – that the Abbey would accept it. I typed a new title page, renaming it *St Luke's Summer*, and then set about disguising myself with a pen name. I thought of *The Italian Road* and of its callow young hero pining for Geothe's *Land wo die Zitronen blühn*. His name was Hughie Leonard, and it seemed to be a kind of poetic justice that, if by some miracle the Abbey did accept the play, I would be forcing him down their throats in one way, if not another.

If I had paused to think, what I needed least in all the world was another name. Legally, I was John Joseph Byrne: at least on my birth certificate my mother's name was given not as Anne Byrne, but as Annie, and she – with, it seemed to me, an unbecoming want of invention in a playwright's one known parent – had not only visited upon me the leaden names of John and Joseph, but also gave me a legacy of twenty years of utter misery by putting the stroke of a pen across the box headed 'Name of Father'. (For a time, I toyed with the idea that my natural father was no less than the dramatist, Denis Johnston, not only out of my admiration for his kind of plays that, uniquely, gave off neither the stench of tenements nor the headier smell of farmyard manure, but also because he had the same contempt for Anglophobic nationalism as I did. When at last I met him, I thought of asking him straight out, but funked it, mainly because in my mind I could see him recoil in horror with a cry of 'Christ, no: anything but that!') My adoptive parents' name was Keyes, and in Dalkey I was known as Jack Keyes and still am. It is as good a name as any other, even if, as I said earlier, there are those who utilise it as a means of keeping me in wherever they like to think my place is. In the Land Commission, I used the name John Keyes Byrne to set it apart from the common or garden John Byrne, which is as indigenous to Counties Dublin and Wicklow as John Smith is to London or Jean Dubois to Paris. Now, to John Joseph Byrne, Jack Keyes and John Keyes Byrne, I was about to add a fourth name and – by way of making a proper olla podrida of the affair and, in more senses than one, a jackass of myself – a fifth. Not only was Hugh Leonard added to the pantheon – and no such person exists, save as a name on a theatre programme or a title page – but also there came into being a Jack Leonard, a kind of half-way house used by those in the writing trade who knew me too well for one name and not well enough for another. The quack psychoanalysts might suggest that I was in search of an identity. I prefer to think, and it may be the same thing, that I did not have a name I cared to lay claim to as my own.

When submitting the play, I gave a false address: that of friends of my wife's parents, a Belgian couple name Ronsquin. One day six weeks later, Mme Ronsquin tottered, gasping for breath, up to our front door waving a letter signed by the Abbey's managing director, the ogreish Ernest Blythe. A contract was enclosed. The Abbey, having turned down the better play, had snapped up the other: my suburban farce that was seven parts Lennox Robinson to three parts Kaufman and Hart. Not only was Mme Ronsquin delighted for me, but so was her husband, a sprightly Walloon who, to my mortification, kissed me on the cheek and, using the *morceau* of English at his command, informed me that 'My whiff and me are very glad.' For several days, such was my rapture that I was in danger of drifting away from earth and over the trees. I was an Abbey playwright, the heir of O'Casey and Synge. The reality, as I discovered when I met Ernest Blythe, was not so glamorous.

Mr Blythe – even years after his death, my awe of him persists to the degree where I must grit my teeth to divest him of the Mr – had at one time been Minister for Finance and caused a sensation by reducing the old-age pensions by a shilling. He made other concessions – free coal, for example – to atone for it, but it never crossed his puritan mind that the old people preferred to put up with chilblains and spend the money as they pleased. I can almost hear him say in his Lisburn accent: 'Ach, d'ye see, they'd only sqaunder it on drink.' It was his ruin as a politician, and, like a daughter who has gone to the bad, he was shown the door, told not to darken it again and sent out into the storm, fetching up on the Abbey board of directors. It was not long before he had become its virtual dictator and was treating the theatre with the same high-handedness he had shown to the old-age pensioners.

I first met him in his Dickensian office in the Queen's theatre, which until recently had been a vaudeville house featuring a group of low comedians who styled themselves The Happy Gang, and a troupe of dancers of uncertain age and forbidding aspect, known as the Queen's Moonbeams. I had, as an adolescent, been privileged to see one of the latter come on as a dancing fireman, drop her hatchet and split her tights as she bent to pick it up. Alas for culture, those delirious days were past; the Abbey had burned down, and the Queen's was the home of the company until a new theatre was built.

My Blythe was a bulky man, made bulkier by a black overcoat two sizes too big, which he wore in the office. He had the round, inscrutable face of a Buddha. As he spoke, his hands were constantly on the move, the stubby fingers combing the air as if, like Irving's Mathias in *The Bells*, he had just espied the wraith of a murdered Jew. The simile is misleading, for I have never met a man less likely to pass the time of night with any ghost. He had hardly invited me to take a chair when, for no apparent reason other than the making of small talk, he launched into a genial reminiscence of the Civil War and told me how six Die-hards had been captured and were held by the Free Staters as hostages.

'Mick Collins wanted us to shoot all six of them,' he said, 'but I told him no. I worked it out mathematically, d'ye see, that we'd achieve the desired effect if we plugged only four. So I had my way. We shot the four of 'em, and I was right.'

He beamed as if he had just finished telling me the story of Goldilocks and the Three Bears. I realised then where his strength lay: he did not give a damn for the opinion of any man on earth.

He ran the Abbey as if it were an almshouse and he were the Master. It was by his decree that only fluent Irish speakers could become members of the company. In consequence, perhaps a third of those engaged were accomplished bi-linguists who, as actors, had their work cut out merely to stroll on, enquiring: 'Hurling, anyone?' One of my own plays had a cast of seven characters, of whom six were Dubliners, all members of the same family, and the seventh a Londoner. In the Abbey production, the accents were recognisably; Dublin (two: one tenement, one Rathmines), Mullingar (one), Donegal (one), Waterford (one), and Cork (one). As for the Londoner, the actor could not rise to an accent other than his own, and so I had him say, quite *à propos de bottes*, that he had lived for twenty years in County Cavan. To Mr Blythe one Irish accent was as good as the next, and, in any case, he regarded the performing arts as so much bunkum. The main function of the Abbey, he believed, was to revive the Irish language. Although he did not say so, at least in my hearing, I think he looked upon plays such as mine that were *not* in Irish as necessary evils. Another of his edicts was that actors' names were to be printed in Irish in programmes. When a players' council was at last formed and it was timidly suggested that the choosing of one's own stage name might be construed as a basic human right, Mr Blythe gave an assurance that changes would come, adding under his breath: '. . . . as slowly as the sands of the sea.'

In spite of a natural compassion towards my fellow-humans, I have always managed to endure the sufferings of actors with fortitude. Where my own fortunes are concerned, the point at which I sit up and pay attention is when a theatrical producer tells me that any fool can write a play. Mr Blythe not only said this, but sportingly proceeded to edit mine without any reference to me. To my apologetic suggestion that I would be more than willing to make my own cuts, he said, chuckling at such unheard of impudence, 'Ach, will ye go 'way outa that!' and swept me through his office door and into Pearse Street. In the display cases in front of the theatre I saw showcards for the forthcoming production of Behan's *The Quare Fellow*. It was currently having a great success in London, and Mr Blythe had for once broken his own rule by, in this case, actually asking for the stage rights of a play instead of letting the author come to the Abbey, hat – and script – in hand. Only he, however, would and did dare to change the *Fellow* of the title to the more Dublinesque *Fella*.

He had, he told me with honest pleasure, a genius for play titles. He did not like *St Luke's Summer* at all, and I came to dread the almost daily envelopes bearing the Abbey emblem of Queen Maebh trying to hold back an apparently rampant wolfhound, for they were certain to contain Mr Blythe's latest proposals for a sure-fire title. I parried them on one pretext or another: *in extremis*, I would tell him that a particular suggestion was an unwitting quotation from Shakespeare, knowing that, out of an innate loathing for all that was literary and therefore high-falutin, he would at once disown it. At last, he tired me out. He gave me my pick of either *The Big Day* or *Happy Birthday*, and I plumped for a lack-lustre hybrid: *The Big Birthday*.

When he discovered, as he was bound to, that the play had already been performed by amateurs, there were ructions. I had, he said, exposed him to the sneers of journalistic cornerboys and yahoos. Then the master showman, as he knew himself to be, came to the fore: he issued a press release declaring that the play had been 'wrested from the heart of the amateur movement'. I was forgiven. He even told me that I could now revert to my own name instead of hiding behind an alias. For me, it was too late; the new name had brought me luck, and I was superstitious.

In time, I was introduced to Ria Mooney, who was to direct my play. Mr Blythe knew that plays directed themselves and that any theory to the contrary was 'cod', and so he had given Miss Mooney the sinecure of staging each and every Abbey play. She was a delightful lady, if understandably exhausted, and she was part of history, for in 1926 she had played the prostitute, Rosie

Redmond, in *The Plough and the Stars*. She told me of the Abbey riots and how Yeats, assuming to himself the stature of demi-God, had strode on to the stage to chastise the rabblement with 'You have disgraced yourselves again!' What she remembered most vividly, however, was a cadaverous young man who sat in the front row of the dress circle, his sunken eyes burning as he snarled at her: 'Get off! You're a disgrace to your sex.' A few months later, she found herself seated next to him at dinner and recognised him at once. He was Sean MacBride, the future Nobel Prize winner and the most shameless example of poacher-turned-gamekeeper since François-Eugène Vidocq.

When rehearsals started, I was introduced to the cast and thereafter stayed away until I could bear the suspense no longer. Finally, I took a day's leave from the office, cycled to the Queen's Theatre and was propping my bicycle against the kerb when I heard a furious thumping. I looked up and saw Mr Blythe banging on the widow of his office. He vanished and reappeared a moment later, flapping down the stairs, his hands outstretched as if uprooting clumps of air.

'Go home to hell outa that,' he shouted. 'They've only been at it a week.'

He all but flung me at my bicycle, which toppled into Pearse Street. By the time I looked around, he was gone back to his office, probably to mutilate and re-christen some other unfortunate's play. A few years later, I spoke to him for the last time. He wanted to explain why, as a County Antrim Calvinist with not a spark of fantasy in his make-up, he was less than enamoured of a new play of mine.

'I like what's real,' he said. 'I don't like plays with a ghost in 'em.'

I answered him sourly, for I had by then learned impudence: 'Well, that disposes of *Macbeth* and *Hamlet*.'

He smiled, not at the sarcasm, but at my having perpetrated what to his mind was a *non sequitur*. He said: 'Sure how do them two enter into it? The Abbey doesn't do foreign plays.'

As for the *The Big Birthday*, it was a shrug of a play: not a failure, not a success. It ran for three weeks; later in the year, it was revived and made into one of those films in which Irish talents cavorted to an Elstree jig, addressed their betters – and they were legion – as 'yer Honour', and were as quaint as thatch. It is amusing that film people who pay for a play will then pay all over again so that it may be turned into a thing that is not that play. No matter, I had what I wanted: I could at last put 'playwright' after my name.

Not long ago, I met a lady named Kitty Carlisle Hart in Providence, Rhode Island. I have always been hopelessly star-struck, and I remembered the Marx Brothers' film, *A Night at the Opera* as a soulful Allan Jones serenaded her with 'Alone (with a sky of romance above)'. Moreover, she had married one of my gods, the playwright, Moss Hart. I told her of my admiration for his autobiography, *Act One*, than which there is no riper or funnier theatrical memoir, and said what a pity it was that he had not lived to write *Act Two*.

She said: 'Oh, I don't know. It would only have been "And then I wrote, and then I wrote ..." '

I recognised the cliché. It was a staple of 1940s film biographies of popular composers. A midway point was invariably reached where the hero had won through to a plateau of success and there was no more to his story than a bout of marital influenza and its cure. To give the illusion of plot, his voice would be heard on the soundtrack saying 'And then I wrote ...', whereupon the audience was treated to Betty Grable dancing to 'Hello, Albuquerque, hello', or a glum, cleft-chinned John Payne declaring that 'The worst things in life are free.'

In setting down these words, I took as my brief the part of one's life that is a kind of waiting room. Now, if it is not already too late, let me pay heed to the warning implicit in 'And then I wrote ...' and go no further than recall the manner in which I at last saw the door of that room creak open. It happened not all at once, but so imperceptibly that it was not clear, even to myself, that I was free to leave.

I am thinking of a July evening. My wife had been in the Rotunda Maternity Hospital overnight, awaiting the birth of our first and, as it transpired, only child. By now, my superior in the Land Commission was a lanky, almost skeletal, Kerryman who invested his spare cash on life insurance and kept the policies in a drawer in his table. I asked him for the afternoon off so that I could go to the Rotunda. He raised a hand, bidding me not to interrupt him. He was staring into the open drawer, his lips moving as he counted the policies. He muttered 'Shag it' under his breath, then looked at me.

He said, singing it: 'Ye what? Ye want to go to deh Rotunda. Go, den. Get deh hell out.'

I had turned to leave when he called me back. 'I bought a new wireless. 'Tis superb.'

'Is it?'

''Tis. Do oo know, deh wife Jetta and me, we can hear deh trains on it. True as God. All deh way up Trimlestown Avenue, we can hear deh train leaving Booterstown station.'

As I stood, itching to be off, he gave an impression of a steam train getting under way as heard through his new radio set. There was a slow, rhythmic '*Choo*-choo-choo-choo . . . *choo*-choo-choo-choo' which took forever to pick up speed. When the throttle was at last open, the performance showed no sign of abating, and I listened helplessly as the train thundered through Merrion Gates and towards Sydney Parade. As I was wondering if he intended to go the full distance to Westland Row, a wag somewhere at my rear gave an uncannily good imitation of a locomotive whistle blowing eerily across a western prairie: '*Whoo-ee-whoo!*' It was so startling that the train faltered momentarily on its journey, allowing me time to flee.

At the Rotunda, the hall porter said there was no news and so I went to the pictures. When I emerged at four thirty, it was raining. Normally, Irish weather is like the Irish character: it is rich in variety, but it lacks stamina: it sticks to nothing for long. This rain was different; it was down for the night. It had come in from the Atlantic, sighing across the Midlands: a soft, seemingly inoffensive drizzle that soaks through clothes, flesh and soul until you know it is there for life. I tried to shelter in doorways; it followed me. I went into Mooney's and there discovered that I had exactly a shilling in my pocket, twopence of which was earmarked for my bus fare home. The cheapest drink to be had was a glass of plain porter for tenpence-ha'penny, and I, the by now twice-produced Abbey playwright, was that vital halfpenny short. I could have ordered a lemonade or tomato juice, but whereas one can nurse a glass of porter or stout indefinitely, a soft drink is, for no reason this side of the paranormal, unnurseable.

Whenever I see Dublin in my mind, the day is July 11th, 1957. The sky, implacable, walks on stilts of rain; no grey stone could be as cheerlessly grey as the blank Tuscan face of the Rotunda; the rain had turned the dirt of the streets to shining grease. A plan formed in my head, and I went to stand at the junction of Parnell Street and Gardiner Street. It was still the age of the bicycle, and the cyclists came in their hundreds, like Apaches in a western, only not with war whoops, but silently, except for the jangle of a bell and the hiss of tyres on the wet. They rode huddled in rainproof capes, great waves of civil servants from across the Liffey: Northsiders who seemed to be treading air on their way to a warm room and tea. I knew – at least, I hoped – that somewhere in their number would be my workmate and best friend, Gerry Colgan. After perhaps twenty minutes and against the odds, I spotted him and jumped out into the tangle, calling and waving before the lights could change. I begged him to lend me a shilling; even that wretched ha'penny would do. I still see the bicycles whirring past and the drop of rain that declined to part company with the end of his nose as he confessed that his earthly fortune was a shilling less than mine. He would, however, go home, borrow money from his mother and return within the hour.

In the event, it was two hours, and by then I had paid four fruitless visits to the front hall of the Rotunda. There are not many aspects of human misery that a hospital porter does not encounter in his lifetime, but I doubt if a more sodden and pitiable sight than I was ever trailed pools of rainwater on the marble floor. When Gerry at last turned up, he was clutching a half-crown which we bore like the Holy Grail into Mooney's. Augmented by my own pittance, it was enough to pay for two pints of 'plain' which by a miracle of husbandry we eked out for three hours. The vigil should, if life had had the good taste to imitate the movies, have ended touchingly with the cry of a newborn and a joyous dance in the rain. Instead, and still childless, I went splashing off towards the last No. 52 bus. My daughter arrived at 2.40 a.m. and made her parents the butt of derisive jokes by being born on July 12th, known as Orangeman's Day.

One of the more familiar scenes in popular fiction is when the hero gazes upon the pink, wrinkled face of his first-born, who is usually a son, and vows – let the mountains crumble and the seas run dry – to lay the world at his offspring's feet. Thus fired, he sweeps all before him and become either a great man (*My Son, My Son!*) or a ruthlessly corrupt one (*Edward, My Son*). I made no such fine promise; on the contrary, I ballsed up what could have been a poignant moment when I showed my new daughter to Gerry when, a day later, he came with flowers and grapes, and getting my statistics in reverse, said: 'Look at her! She's six hours old and weighs only thirty-six pounds.'

What finally pushed me through the door of my private waiting room was not fatherhood, joyful as it was, but those hours spent walking, aware that the rainwater had become warm in my shoes: the slow, soaked trudge around Parnell Square, or down O'Connell Street to the river and back; the vigil in a dripping doorway across from Parnell himself, bronze and unpitying under his awning of Galway granite. The image is perhaps romantic; the reality was defeat. I had stayed in the civil service to help support my parents – at least that was what I told myself – who, now that I was no longer at home, were getting on insultingly well without me. I had remained in it for another two years because – and again it was what I told myself – a married man had at least one other to provide for. At least in part, it had been cowardice, done to buy safety – 'Made for life!' my mother had vowed. Instead, and on the night my daughter was born, I had not in my pocket the price of a glass of porter. If there were such a thing as a diploma in failure, it was mine. I stood face to face with it as the Student of Prague faced his *alter ego*. In thirteen years, my pay in the Land Commission had risen to just over eight pounds a week. I could hardly have been worse off without it.

Not very long afterwards, Granada Television bought my play, *A Leap in the Dark*. For reasons that one could only describe kind-heartedly as eccentric, they arranged a repertory production in Oldham to ascertain that it was suitable for television, and I was invited to assist with the rehearsals. They would telephone later and let me know the dates. I looked at my annual leave docket; every day and half day had been used up. I found a minute sheet and wrote out my resignation. I was amazed at how simple it was. A child could have done it: there was no skill involved. I gave it to our typist, said 'Any old time will do', and saw her add it to her pile. About an hour later, I heard her scream. When she brought the typescript to me, her eyes were twin bird's eggs. I put the paper, unsigned, in a drawer of my desk and sat back. I had never felt so content. All afternoon, people went out of my way to walk past where I was sitting. They did not speak; I might as well have been the scene of a crime. A few days later, the expected telephone call came. Faces rose into the light; everyone knew it was for me, for the caller asked for Leonard, not Byrne. I said, just loud enough to be overheard: 'Yes, I'll fly to Manchester on Sunday', hung up and took the resignation from my desk. I signed it and my heart sang with every step as I bore it the length of the room to my superior, who was again counting his insurance policies. He had heard rumours; he said: 'Are oo off, den?' Three days later, an acknowledgment came from Establishment Branch. I have it still.

'... You will be paid to 23rd September inclusive, but as your leave allowance to 23rd instant is 10½ days and as you have taken 21 days' leave to date, a deduction in respect of 10½ days' excess annual leave will be made from the balance of salary due to you.'

It did not say goodbye.

This time there was no valedictory speech. Someone – Arthur Nolan, I think – came over on my last day and, almost apologetically, gave me a small leather cigarette box that could not have cost more than a pound. Only a few people shook hands; I did not think less of them, but I was surprised, for their silence revealed that I had not suspected: that they felt as trapped as I had done. At four thirty, I spared their blushes by walking out of the room, papers in my hand as if I were going to Records Branch or the strong room, but instead went home and stayed there for all time. It took perhaps three years before I could wake up of a morning without the beginnings of a cold sweat because the dream was over and today was the day I must go back.

Not long ago, I bumped into man, a civil servant nearing retirement, who sang the praises of a play I had written. In Dublin, one learns to winnow goodwill from the occasional gambit: the pawn given in return for an attack. When I thanked him, he segued into a bleak smile and said: 'And I liked that television thing you wrote. That was great.'

Another pawn gone. 'Thank you.'

His smile was now in need of a crutch. 'Oh, aye,' he said. 'You gave it to us hot and heavy. Yes, you made a good thing out of that.'

I could all but hear the jingling of the pieces of silver – all thirty of them – in my pocket. When I did not respond, but waited for more, he added: 'And out of us.' I nodded and made to go, leaving the field to him, but he caught at my arm.

'But you outsmarted yourself the day you quit the service. Yes, you did, and do you know why?' I waited, while he made a meal of it. 'I'll tell you why.' Then, triumphantly: 'Because you could have been an Assistant Principal by now!'

He hurried off in the best of good humour, leaving me bested, worsted and unpensionable.

On the Sunday after I left the Land Commission, I caught my flight for Manchester. I had flown only a few times before and hated it. The Fokker-Friendship aircraft looked frail enough to disintegrate in mid-flight; what was worse, I was seated next to an elderly Dublin woman, dressed entirely in black. Her lips moved as we taxied towards the runway, and rosary beads were entwined in her fingers. I wondered if she had had a premonition. We took off, and she prayed all the way over the Irish Sea to Anglesey, her eyes closed, the beads clicking through her fingers, milestones to heaven.

It was the calmest of evenings, with the sun smirking behind us, as if it shone only on Ireland. The Isle of Man was visible to the north. I drank a whisky, ordered another and began to think that today might not after all be my last. My life outside the waiting room – my real life that is – was starting. A fat grin had begun to spread when a slip of paper was passed back to me. In those pre-jet days, there was time for the captain to issue a flight report giving such details as air speed, altitude, time of arrival. I glanced through it; at the bottom, next to 'Weather at destination' was written 'Fair'. It suited me at that moment to enjoy a bit of symbolism, seeing as it was in my favour. The fatness of my grin had become almost obese as I gave the paper to the woman in black. She opened her eyes, blinked at me, blinked at the slip, and took a pair of spectacles, mended with string, from her handbag.

I went back to my daydream. After a moment, she put a hand on my sleeve. I looked and saw that it was raw and calloused; it had been a hard life; now she was on her way to stay with a son or daughter who had married and settled in Manchester or beyond: it was her first time in an aeroplane. In Dublin, you would call her an old one. She held the flight report in front of my face, then let go of my sleeve to point to the bottom line that said 'Weather at destination'. The entwined rosary beads dangled into my lap.

Symbolism can cut both ways. There was doom in her eyes as she said piteously: 'Oh, my Jayzus, only "fair".'

Also by Hugh Leonard
available from Methuen

Home Before Night

'Superb . . . moving and very funny' William Trevor

Hugh Leonard's delightful autobiographical evocation of his Dublin childhood in the thirties and forties is like an Irish *Cider With Rosie* – crammed with people and conversations, rich in poetry, full of love, laughter and rare pleasures.

'Entrancing . . . the playwright author's gift of language and apparently total recall makes his account of growing up in the thirties and forties absolutely irresistible' *Sunday Telegraph*

'He has the simplicity and genius of Dylan Thomas and Brendan Behan . . . If you want to look at the South Dublin working class of the thirties and forties, here it is – a childhood that anyone would envy' *The Times*

Priest ridden ILL
smeel land
shrand
do nothing

Also by Hugh Leonard
available from Methuen

A Wild People

'Unputdownable' Keith Waterhouse

At the centre of a busy Dublin social circle, T. J. Quill is a man of many entanglements – friends whose brains teem with crazy schemes, a dead film director, an enigmatic wife and a melo-dramatic mistress. As the tangled web grows thicker, Hugh Leonard's brilliantly funny novel reveals a powerful insight into the fallibility of the human heart.

'I enjoyed *A Wild People* very much. The writing exhibits a kind of autumnal, small-boy relish for turning over stones and looking at what's beneath' Vincent Banville, *Irish Times*

'A richly comic portrayal of professional and personal rivalries within Dublin society' John Crowley, *Irish Post*

'A tremendous new novel' Pat Kenny, *The Pat Kenny Show*

SELECTED FICTION AND BIOGRAPHY TITLES
AVAILABLE FROM METHUEN

	ISBN	TITLE	AUTHOR	PRICE
☐	0413 77182 2	Red Poppies	Alai	£15.99
☐	0413 76990 9	Beautiful Dreamer	Christopher Bigsby	£12.99
☐	0413 77139 3	Achilles	Elizabeth Cook	£6.99
☐	0413 77160 1	The Name of the World	Denis Johnson	£6.99
☐	0413 77168 7	Home Before Night	Hugh Leonard	£7.99
☐	0413 77148 2	Out After Dark	Hugh Leonard	£7.99
☐	0413 77162 8	Focus	Arthur Miller	£6.99
☐	0413 77010 9	The Red Devil	Katherine Russell Rich	£7.99
☐	0413 75480 4	The Doctor	Laura Spinney	£6.99
☐	0413 76290 4	Sweet Hearts	Melanie Rae Thon	£6.99
☐	0413 77118 0	Shifu, You'll Do Anything For a Laugh	Mo Yan	£14.99
☐	0413 77125 3	The Collected Stories of Richard Yates	Richard Yates	£17.99
☐	0413 75710 2	Revolutionary Road	Richard Yates	£6.99

---

* All Methuen books can be ordered online at www.methuen.co.uk. They are also available through mail order or from your local bookshop

Please send cheque/eurocheque/postal order (sterling only) Access, Visa, Mastercard, Diners Card, Switch or Amex.

Expiry Date: .... Signature: ....

UK customers please allow £1 for the first book and 50p thereafter up to a maximum of £3 for post and packing.

Overseas customers please allow £1.50 for the first book and 75p thereafter up to a maximum of £5 for post and packing.

ALL ORDERS TO:

Methuen Books, Books by Post, TBS Limited, The Book Service, Colchester Road, Frating Green, Colchester, Essex CO7 7DW.

NAME:..

ADDRESS: ....

....

....

Please allow 28 days for delivery. Please tick box if you do not wish to receive any additional information ☐

Prices and availability subject to change without notice.

For a complete list of Methuen titles visit our website at:

www.methuen.co.uk